PATRONAGE IN RENAISSANCE ITALY

Other books by the author

Architecture of the Twentieth Century
L'Arte nella Storia dell'Uomo

PATRONAGE IN RENAISSANCE ITALY

FROM 1400 TO THE EARLY SIXTEENTH CENTURY

Mary Hollingsworth

JOHN MURRAY

First published in 1994
by John Murray (Publishers) Ltd.,
50 Albemarle Street, London W1X 4BD

A catalogue record for this book is available from the British Library

Cased 0-7195-4926 4
Paper 0-7195-5378 4

Typeset in 10½ on 13 pt Palatino
by Colset Private Ltd, Singapore
Printed and bound in Great Britain
by Butler & Tanner Limited, Frome and London

Contents

Illustrations

The author and publishers would like to thank the following for permission to reproduce photographs: Istituto Centrale per il Catalogo e la Documentazione, Rome; Soprintendenza ai Beni Artistici e Storici, Venice; Soprintendenza ai Beni Artistici e Storici, Florence; and Soprintendenza ai Beni Ambientali e Architettonici, Florence.

Acknowledgements

Amongst the many scholars and friends who have inspired me through their publications, generously shared their ideas and offered me their support, I would like to thank Elisabeth de Bièvre, Howard Burns, Daniele Casalino, John Clark, Caroline Elam, Richard Goldthwaite, Sir Ernst Gombrich, Francis Haskell, Charles Hope, Bill Kent, Julian Kliemann, Nigel Llewellyn, Andrew Martindale, John Onians, Tim Porter, Nicholas Ross, Nicolai Rubinstein, Lorna Sage, Richard Schofield, John Shearman, Robert Tavernor, Thomas Tuohy and Joanna Woods-Marsden. I would also like to thank Walter Kaiser and the staff at I Tatti for their kind hospitality. Finally, I thank Caroline Davidson, my agent, and Caroline Knox and Grant McIntyre at John Murray for having faith in the book.

A Note on Money

The relationship between the various currencies in use in Renaissance Italy was enormously complex. Each of the peninsula's numerous states had its own system of coinage, weights and measures. Most states had their own gold-based coinage, which was internationally recognizable: the Florentine florin, first minted in 1252, was made of 3.53 grammes of gold, while the Venetian ducat, issued in 1284, weighed 3.55 grammes. These currencies fluctuated against each other in response to market forces and fortunes were made by cleverly predicting rises and falls in the exchange rates. To confuse the issue further, many states also had a silver-based coinage, usually known as the lira (1 lira = 20 soldi = 240 denari), which fluctuated against the local gold currency, offering further opportunities for profit and loss. Wealth was assessed in gold, the currency of international trade, while the silver coinage was used for everyday transactions, such as buying food and paying wages.

In this book I have used the gold-based currencies for expressing costs and, at a very basic level, it is possible to assume a broad similarity between the major gold-based currencies in use in fifteenth-century Italy, though it is important to recognize that they were far from interchangeable.

It would be misleading to suggest equivalents in modern money for fifteenth-century currencies, but typical earnings provide some guidance: a skilled worker would have earned about 100 ducats a year, a soldier 24, and a mathematics tutor 100.

For
William, Edward, Richard, Alastair and Gabriel

Introduction

The Renaissance is rich in myths. The fame of Florence rests on her claim to be the cradle of Renaissance art and humanism, while her most celebrated citizen, Lorenzo de' Medici, politician, poet and connoisseur, epitomizes the universal Renaissance man. Both city and man are closely identified with Renaissance culture and the myths, which were first created around them during the fifteenth century, have now all but hardened into historical fact.[1] But Florence was not the only centre of Renaissance culture: Rome, Venice, Milan, Naples, Urbino, Ferrara and Mantua all made significant contributions to the cultural development of fifteenth-century Italy. And the word 'Renaissance' itself embodies the most potent myth of all. It was coined to convey the idea of a rebirth of the arts after centuries of cultural darkness that separated the glorious achievements of classical antiquity from fifteenth-century Italy, itself glorified by the comparison. The reality was, inevitably, more prosaic. The Middle Ages saw major advances in philosophy, literature, science and the visual arts. Moreover, the culture of antiquity was far from dead in the Christian world of medieval Europe, which had its roots in ancient Rome.

One of the most forceful myths of the Renaissance is the idea that its artists freely explored their ideas and created their masterpieces for enlightened patrons eager to acquire these works of genius. The methodology of many art historians, who study Renaissance art via its artists, has reinforced this myth. Their approach disguises the fact that it was the patron who was the real initiator of the architecture, sculpture and painting of the period, and that he played a significant part in determining both form and content. Fifteenth-century patrons were not passive connoisseurs: they were active consumers. Their commissions were not works of art in the modern sense of the term. Indeed, attitudes to art have undergone a profound change since 1400 and it can be very misleading to apply our concept of artistic patronage to the Renaissance.[2] In the fifteenth century, it was the patron, and not the artist, who was seen by his contemporaries as the creator of his project and this gave him the strongest possible motive for controlling its final appearance. Above all, the traditional art historical approach disguises the function of art in the fifteenth century and the central role it played in the construction of images for wealthy, powerful and ambitious patrons in Renaissance Italy.

Behind the myths, the numerous states that made up fifteenth-century Italy witnessed major upheavals that had profound economic, political, and social effects. Above all, the century saw the decline of the international culture of medieval Europe and the emergence of literary and artistic forms of expression intended to assert the unique traditions of each centre, above all, their associations with the power and prestige of ancient Rome. Humanists, those who studied the literature of antiquity and wrote about it using classical Latin and Greek,[3] revived the rules of Ciceronian Latin to replace what they saw as the debased Latin of the Middle Ages. Gothic, the visual language of medieval Europe and the style of northern European courts, gave way to forms that derived from antiquity. The change was far from uniform, nor was it complete. The aristocratic resonances of Gothic continued to have a strong appeal at the Italian courts, though they were less attractive in the mercantile and republican atmosphere of early fifteenth-century Florence. Moreover, Gothic was a Christian style and its use conveyed a religious morality that was not necessarily visible in the grandiose architecture of ancient Rome.[4] The problem of adapting an essentially pagan language to the demands of a Christian society generated widely different responses. It was the patrons who were the central figures in this change and it is to them that we must look for some explanations.

This book examines the development of fifteenth-century art via its patrons. I have concentrated on four groups: the merchants of Florence, those of Venice, the rulers of five of Italy's numerous independent princely states, Milan, Naples, Urbino, Ferrara and Mantua, and the papal court in Rome. Sadly, I have had to ignore the contributions of many less known patrons, notably the bankers and merchants of Siena and Genoa and the rulers of smaller states, such as Sigismondo Malatesta of Rimini.

The ability to commission works of art was inevitably restricted to the rich and powerful, and patterns of patronage were closely linked to the economic and political structures of each centre. An absolute ruler dominated the cultural life of the city. His expenses were considerable. Besides paying salaries for his courtiers, secretaries and servants, he also spent lavishly on providing visual evidence of his wealth and status in the pageantry of court life, staging extravagant entertainments for visiting dignitaries or erecting temporary decorations for wedding celebrations. He built and decorated his castles, palaces and villas, and endowed local churches, hospitals, monasteries and chapels. He might initiate programmes of urban renewal, make improvements to roads and canals or build fortifications to defend his realm. His collections would include expensive tapestries, elaborately bound and decorated manuscripts, valuable relics, gold, jewels and other precious objects. All of these had the additional advantage of being portable, and they could also be used as collateral for a bank loan. The pattern in Florence was different. The city was governed by an élite of wealthy merchants and bankers, and it was these individuals who were responsible for commissioning the palaces, churches and chapels that transformed the appearance of Florence during the fifteenth century. As members of the trade guilds, they might be involved in one of their corporate projects, serving on the committees that supervized the construction of the cathedral or an altarpiece for the guild altar in one of the city's churches. As individual patrons, their expenditure was limited by budgets that were modest in comparison with that of a duke. The Florentine banker, Palla Strozzi, paid just over 2,000 florins in dowries for two sons-in-law,[5] while the marriage between Anna Sforza, daughter of the Duke of Milan, and Alfonso d'Este of Ferrara involved a dowry of over 100,000 ducats.[6] Besides running his household and paying his taxes, the Florentine merchant concentrated on building and decorating his family palace and a chapel in his local church. He might also commission a portrait, build a villa on his country estate or buy costly jewels and books, which were expensive before the advent of printing in the late fifteenth century. The Medici were exceptional. The family's position at the top of the political hierarchy in the city encouraged them to aspire to the status of absolute rulers and their enormous wealth allowed them to acquire some of the trappings of princely prestige.

The belief that conspicuous expenditure was the principal element in the display of status was firmly established in fifteenth-century Europe, and architecture, sculpture and painting were seen as potent tools in the fabrication of images of wealth and power.[7] Renaissance patrons knew the value of the arts as propaganda. The massive ruins of ancient Rome testified to the scale and grandeur of the once mighty Roman Empire. Alberti referred to the Greek historian, Thucydides, who praised the builders of ancient cities for using magnificent buildings to convey the impression of having far greater power than they really possessed.[8] Pope Nicholas V believed that grand buildings were necessary to impress the power of the Church on ordinary people.[9] The Venetian government started work on the clock tower at a time of financial insecurity to show that the state was not bankrupt.[10] Buildings and their decoration were visible and expensive, and they provided forceful publicity for the prestige of guilds and governments, kings and popes.

We can enter the house of new acquaintances and make quick assessments of their status, background, interests, income and personality by looking at their paintings, books, furniture, cars or kitchens. The same was true in the fifteenth century but the scale of values was not quite the same. At the beginning of the century at least, the creative genius of the artist had no recognizable financial value. The cost of a work of art was assessed in terms of materials and labour, and the artist was paid for his skill as a crafts- man. The King of Naples paid 500 ducats a year to his official historian,[11] 400 ducats to his defence expert,[12] 144 ducats to the architect of the main reception room in his castle[13] and 24 ducats to his chief cowman and foot soldiers.[14] We tend to rate painting more highly than sculpture or architec- ture, but this pattern was reversed in Renaissance Italy. Architecture was expensive, and the most effective way of conveying prestige. A wealthy Florentine merchant might pay as much as 40,000 florins for his family palace and the castle of an absolute ruler would cost much more. The King of Naples, whose annual income was estimated at 830,000 ducats, allowed 14,000 ducats a year for his household expenses and spent over 250,000 ducats reconstructing his principal residence, Castel Nuovo.[15] Conspi- cuously expensive materials and elaborate carving were statements of wealth. Wood, a cheap material, could be made more expensive by its use in complex intarsia inlays, much prized at the courts of fifteenth-century Italy. Bronze was costly and a life-size statue could cost 1,000 florins. A similar marble sculpture would be much cheaper, only around 200 florins, the same price as a panel painting in an elaborate carved and gilded frame (see Chapter 3). Fresco was extremely cheap and a large scene could cost as little as 25 florins. Patrons who could afford it decorated their walls with tapestries. Borso d'Este, Duke of Ferrara, spent 9,000 ducats on a set for one of his reception halls but only 800 ducats on the frescos that decorated the walls of the enormous Sala dei Mesi in the Palazzo Schifanoia.[16]

In the Christian culture of Renaissance Europe, art was commissioned overwhelmingly in the context of religious duty. The Bible was clear that the acquisition of wealth for its own sake was bad and mercantile profits were particularly reviled. St Matthew reported how Jesus exhorted the rich to give away their fortunes saying that it was easier for a camel to pass through the eye of a needle than for a rich man to enter into the kingdom of heaven (Matthew 19,24). Wealth was justifiable only if used for charitable purposes, and giving away a percentage of it in charity was recognized by the Church as a means of expiating sins. It could take many forms. The Dominican Fra Giovanni Dominici (c. 1356–1419) recom- mended liberating prisoners, clothing the poor or giving alms to beggars, as well as building and repairing churches, monasteries and hospitals. But he added two important provisos: firstly, that God would not be pleased if men concentrated on building in dead stone and ignored the living, and, secondly, that charity should be exercised incognito.[17] Charity was certainly an important motive behind expenditure on religious projects, but the proliferation of coats of arms in churches and monasteries throughout the peninsula shows that these projects also played a major role in fabricating images of power and prestige for their patrons.

To the modern art historian, concerned with tracing stylistic change in art and architecture, the prime importance of these works is aesthetic. But attitudes were different in the Renaissance. The chapels decorated by a Florentine merchant, a cardinal in Rome or the Duke of Milan were statements of their owner's religious beliefs, not of their artistic sensibilities. The chapels were often burial chapels, built around their patrons' tombs, and their function was to provide a setting for the prayers needed for his soul and those of his descendants. In Venice, the *scuole* took over patronage of chapels to offer prayers for their deceased members. Altarpieces were commissioned to provide the visual focus for these prayers, and chapels might also be ornamented with fresco cycles and sculptural decoration. But art was only a small element in the costs involved. Patrons endowed their chapels with funds to cover the costs of regular prayer. Silver chalices and other liturgical furnishings, rarely discussed by art historians, formed a significant part of a patron's outlay. Priests celebrating services in the chapels might wear special vestments, embroidered with coats of arms, which would also be prominently displayed around the chapel. In short, the chapel celebrated the patron's achievements, hopes and fears, not the creative talents of his artists.

The architecture, sculpture, altarpieces and frescos could elaborate aspects of a patron's piety, such as his attachment to his name saint or his devotion to a particular religious order. Francesco Sassetti's chapel in Santa Trinità, Florence, was decorated with scenes from the life of St Francis, while Cardinal Oliviero Carafa's chapel in Santa Maria sopra Minerva in Rome was frescoed with scenes from that of the Dominican theologian, St Thomas Aquinas. These commissions also carried other messages. Civic pride, which was such a potent factor in the development of Venetian and Florentine art, played little part in that of Rome. Central to the development of the arts in Renaissance Rome was the controversy over the absolute authority of the Pope as supreme head of the Church. But papal primacy was not an important issue at the courts of Mantua and Milan. The most popular image of popular piety, the Virgin, had a particular political resonance in Venice, where she was one of the principal symbols of the state. Many patrons responded to the growing calls for church reform and Cosimo de' Medici, Francesco Sforza and Federigo da Montefeltro were conspicuous in their patronage of the reformist branches of the religious orders.

Form, content and style were all directly related to attitudes of wealth, which were far from uniform. Borso d'Este, Duke of Ferrara, could display his secular power and status in costly jewels, expensive architecture and lavish gilded decoration but the belief that extravagant expenditure was the prime vehicle for the display of authority and prestige was also subject to moral restrictions. In Rome the Pope was the focus of a debate about the appropriate life style for the head of the Church, and reformers criticized him for adopting the trappings of secular power instead of setting an example as the heir to the simple poverty of Christ and his Apostles. The rich merchants of Venice and Florence lived in societies where ostentatious displays of personal wealth were discouraged on both religious and political grounds.

Given the importance of art in the creation of images for Renaissance patrons, it is not surprising to find that they kept careful control of the craftsmen who carried out their commissions. Some rulers employed court artists, paying them regular salaries and rewarding them with living accommodation and other extras such as oil, wine or firewood. But most fifteenth-century artists were self-employed, and their relationships with their patrons were formalized in legally binding contracts. These contracts, many of which have survived, make fascinating reading. Art historians are often disappointed by the lack of references in them to style or iconography.[18] Such omissions were not forgetfulness on the part of the patron but an indication of where his interests lay. One of the few patrons to give detailed specifications governing the composition of her paintings was Isabella d'Este. She commissioned a series of mythological scenes (drawn up by her literary adviser) whose obscurity necessitated the precise instructions. Most contracts stipulated only three things: what was to be represented or built, how the expensive materials were to be used and how much it would cost. Style was established by the choice of the artist, who was usually required to draw up a plan or model of the project before the contract was signed. Cosimo Tura's style seems to have been a problem for his patron, Borso d'Este, who sent the artist to see a painting by Gentile da Fabriano, done fifty years before, to ensure that Tura understood his wishes. Generally, we have no record of the conversations that took place between patron and artist during these negotiations, but it is clear that the patron played a central role.

The process of architectural design was significantly different from modern-day practice. We attribute the development of Renaissance architecture to architects such as Brunelleschi, Alberti and Filarete. But our concept of the architect as the person who designs a building hardly existed at the beginning of the fifteenth century.[19] The range of talents involved in Renaissance architecture was vast: stonemasons, carpenters, goldsmiths, painters, intellectuals and civil servants all made significant contributions to its stylistic development. Buildings were constructed by armies of skilled craftsmen and manual labourers under the supervision of a works foreman, who took charge of the technical aspects of construction. This was Brunelleschi's job on the cathedral in Florence and Filarete's on the Ospedale Maggiore in Milan. Alberti, on the other hand, was not trained in a craft, and his role as the designer of two churches for Ludovico Gonzaga was a landmark in the emergence of the modern 'architect'. But the person with the deepest concern for the final appearance of his buildings was the patron, and there were plenty of fifteenth-century patrons like Cosimo and Lorenzo de' Medici, Pius II or Ercole d'Este, who are known to have been actively involved in the design of their projects.

One of the great strengths of the classical tradition, and a reason for its enduring appeal, is its ability to provide models for the whole of the political spectrum. Hitler, Napoleon and the writers of the United States' Constitution were all inspired to adopt aspects of classical culture to provide them with precedents for their power. In fifteenth-century Italy, it provided flattering models for tyrants, enlightened rulers and republicans alike. Humanists and artists played key roles in the creation of images for their patrons, producing impressive propaganda designed to boost their patrons' prestige. Humanists used the language of classical rhetoric and oratory, its tradition of lavish praise and eulogistic metaphors, to promote their patrons' power and authority. Artists were commissioned to produce visual images that showed them as worthy successors to ancient traditions. The new ideas developed in tandem with the old. Poets and musicians continued the medieval traditions of romance and chivalry at the Italian courts, and patrons all over Italy continued to commission paintings that were, in style and subject matter, strongly reminiscent of aristocratic Gothic. The adaptation of the language of classical antiquity varied from centre to centre. The political ideals of Cicero had a strong appeal in republican Florence but they were of little use for the defence of the absolute power of dukes and popes, whose humanists and artists could promote their patrons as successors to imperial Rome. Venice's traditional links with the Byzantine Empire and Constantinople were quite different from the papal claim to descent from St Peter and the emperors of ancient Rome.

But the experience of classical literature had a profound effect on patronage, on art and on the relationship between a patron and his artists. New types of art developed during the fifteenth century in response to demands of patrons for *all'antica* images, such as portrait medals and busts or classical mythological themes for paintings and frescos. Inspired by the writings of Vitruvius, Alberti wrote a treatise to encourage patrons to adopt the architectural language of antiquity. And the literature of ancient Greece and Rome revealed entirely new attitudes to art and artists. Humanists must have been surprised and excited to learn that writers like Pliny and Cicero had appreciated a statue or a painting principally for its aesthetic qualities, that they considered artists creators not just craftsmen and that a patron of the arts should be able to recognize genius. By the end of the century these ideas had begun to spread. There was a marked difference between Cosimo de' Medici and Galeazzo Maria Sforza, who employed craftsmen to carry out their ideas, and patrons like Francesco Gonzaga, who was aware that his employment of Mantegna as his court painter added to his status, or Ludovico Sforza, who employed the painter Bramante to oversee both the design and construction of his projects. By the time Michelangelo started painting the Sistine Chapel ceiling in 1508, the status of artists and architects had radically changed. So had the language used to describe art. At the beginning of the century, what interested the viewer, like the patron, was subject matter and value, which could be read in the cost of materials.[20] By 1500, a good painter was not just skilled at his craft; he brought an additional creative and personal talent to his work. By reviving classical ideas about art and adapting them to their own circumstances, fifteenth-century humanists laid the ground work for the development of modern aesthetics.[21]

Part One
Florence

1

Florence: A New Century

Once people have actually seen Florence . . . her great mass of architecture and the grandeur of her buildings, her splendour and magnificence, the tall towers, the marble churches, the domes of the basilicas, the splendid palaces, the turretted walls and the numerous villas, her charm, beauty and decor . . . they are no longer amazed at her achievements.

Leonardo Bruni, *In Praise of the City of Florence*, 1403–4

L eonardo Bruni was writing at the beginning of a momentous century for Florence and one in which the appearance of the city was to become even more impressive. For Bruni, a lawyer by training and one of the leading intellectuals of his day, it was precisely the scale and grandeur of Florentine architecture that provided him with incontrovertible proof of the city's greatness.[1] His text radiates pride in the Florentine achievement: her economic success, her political institutions and her cultural heritage. This sense of national pride was shared by his contemporaries and, indeed, the Florentines had much to boast about.

The visitor to Bruni's Florence could not fail to be impressed by the appearance of the city. Although unfinished, her cathedral, the Duomo, promised to be one of the largest in Europe. The elegant, octagonal Baptistery with its elaborately inlaid marble façade and costly mosaic interior furnished solid evidence of her prosperity. Numerous buildings, above all the huge Franciscan convent of Santa Croce and its Dominican counterpart, Santa Maria Novella, testified to the religious fervour as well as the affluence of her population. The Palazzo della Signoria, a massive fortress crowned with an imposing bell-tower, housed her government and was the focus of a large square embellished with an ornate loggia that provided an ostentatious setting for civic ceremonies. The square itself was paved, a rarity and an extravagance in medieval Europe.

With a population of around 50,000, this bustling, commercial city was the fifth largest in Europe, surpassed only by Milan, Naples, Venice and Paris. A census of 1427 showed 324 lawyers, 224 woodworkers, 192 builders, 90 innkeepers and vintners, 261 shoemakers and 101 tailors active in the city.[2] Her narrow streets and broad squares were thronged with people: government committee members walking from their offices to the Palazzo della Signoria, wives of rich businessmen on their way to church, priests and doctors visiting the sick, stonemasons going to work on the cathedral or servants running errands. They met friends and stopped to talk about family matters or current affairs, bought their bread, meat and wine, listened to the persuasive sermons of fiery preachers, watched the elaborate festivities and ceremonial processions organized at Easter or on the feast day of Florence's patron saint, St John the Baptist, laughed and argued, christened their babies and worried about finding husbands for their daughters.

Florence's richest merchants were entrepreneurs operating throughout Europe and the Middle East. The Florentine gold florin, first minted in 1252, was internationally recognized. Flourishing woollen and cloth industries were the basis of the city's prosperity. Florentine firms had branches in London and bought prized English fleeces direct from the producers. The city was famous for fine cloths, velvets, damasks and brocades enriched with gold thread. Merchandise was generally transported by sea and the Florentine government owned galleys which they auctioned off to the highest bidder, who then financed the journey as an investment, underwrote the risks of storms and piracy and scooped the profit.[3] Her bankers dominated the European credit market. The city was a thriving centre of international trade and home to merchants who made their fortune trading in places as far afield as Valencia and Hamburg, London and Tunis. Her shops and markets displayed wines and other luxuries from France, carpets from Persia, spices from India, silks from China, furs from Russia and elegant tooled leather goods made from north African hides.

By European standards, the Florentines had an exceptionally high literacy rate. We should not be surprised. They placed a high value on commercial profit and schools in the city taught the skills necessary for business: reading, writing and arithmetic. Successful traders needed to be able to keep accurate accounts of income and expenditure and to assess different insurance quotations. In the international arena, they needed to work out complex rates of exchange, for each Italian city had its own currency and system of weights and measures, as did other states in Europe and the East. The practical schooling of the Florentine merchant had little in common with the chivalric education received at the courts of northern Europe and it gave him a markedly different outlook on life.

Bruni was especially proud of Florence's republican government, guardian of the political freedom enjoyed by her citizens. Florence was one of many Italian cities that had taken advantage of the power struggle between the Holy Roman Empire and the Papacy, to achieve independent status under aristocratic rule in 1183. But it was primarily her merchants who benefitted from the dramatic expansion in trade during the twelfth and thirteenth centuries, and they acquired a potent new weapon: money. Economic power soon challenged traditional feudal authority. The conflict that ensued brought civic unrest on an unprecedented scale and divided the city into two factions: the mainly aristocratic supporters of the Holy Roman Empire (Ghibellines) and the predominantly mercantile supporters of the Papacy (Guelfs). During the 1250s, the Guelfs expelled their aristocratic rulers and set up their own representative government. Mercantile wealth replaced inheritance as the basis of power and guild membership, which had long been obligatory for trade, now became a prerequisite for political office.

All guild members over 30 years old who were neither bankrupt nor in arrears with their taxes were eligible for election to the committees that formed the new government. Its prime organ of power, the Signoria, was a committee of eight priors, two from each quarter of the city, chaired by the Gonfalonier of Justice. Its authority was restricted by a series of checks and balances designed specifically to avoid domination by individuals. The nine members of the Signoria served two-month terms of office and were then barred for three years from re-election. All proposed legislation required the assent of two other committees, also regularly changed, the *Dodici Buonomini* (twelve good men) and the *Sedici Gonfalonieri* (sixteen standard-bearers), and had to be passed by a two-thirds majority in two large general councils with a total of 500 members. Other committees were elected to advise the Signoria on issues such as foreign affairs, taxation and public order, and more committees were set up in times of emergency. Behind this complex network of committees, a formidable civil service of notaries and other officials provided administrative support. The superiority of the system was one of Bruni's principal themes. Although it was not a democracy by modern standards, in the context of a Europe dominated by feudal rulers it was an important step to give 6,000 members of a population of 50,000 an active voice in the government of their city.

The establishment of a solid constitutional basis for representative government during the 1290s acted as the spur for an ambitious programme of state patronage. A set of stone walls enclosed Florence's growing population. New streets imposed order on the old city centre. Above all, the state embarked on two projects that gave visual expression to the authority and prestige of the new administration: the cathedral (begun 1294) and the Palazzo della Signoria (begun 1299). Deliberately pursuing a policy of organized town-planning, the state thus created two centres for the city, one religious and the other political. The enormous size of the cathedral, with its lavish inlaid marble decoration, proclaimed Florentine prosperity.

But it was the nature of the new political regime that was reflected in the use of local stone on the façade of the Palazzo della Signoria and, a calculated piece of propaganda, in the initial laying out of the piazza della Signoria on the site of the palaces of the city's old aristocratic rulers.

Fundamental to Bruni's frame of mind, when he put pen to paper in 1403, was the fact that Florence was one of the few Italian city states to survive the disasters of the fourteenth century with her economy, her representative government and her independence largely intact. Poor harvests in the early years of the century had precipitated an economic decline throughout Europe. Demand for luxury goods fell and trade stagnated. The collapse of the Bardi and Peruzzi banks, two of the leading Florentine houses, after Edward III of England (1327–77) defaulted on a debt of 1,500,000 florins, sparked off a financial crisis in 1342–3. The situation was exacerbated by the Black Death of 1348–9 which swept through Europe killing as much as a third of the population. Urban centres were particularly vulnerable. Repeated outbreaks of the plague reduced the population of Florence from around 100,000 in 1340 to 50,000 in 1400. Her rival, Siena, never recovered after two-thirds of her citizens died. The plague brought political chaos and social unrest to a continent already suffering from economic depression. Civic violence fostered a desire for strong personal leadership, and this led to the restoration of hereditary rule in many places. The Florentine government's inability to deal with economic chaos led to the short-lived reigns of Charles, Duke of Calabria (1325–8), and of Walter of Brienne, Duke of Athens (1342–3). But the city's mercantile élite soon reasserted its power. In 1378 the government came through the most serious test of its authority, the Ciompi Revolution, managing to control serious internal disorder when rioting wool workers, demanding a share in government, sacked and looted the city.

Above all, Florence had retained her freedom. For Bruni, this meant not just the political freedom enjoyed by the Florentine at home but also freedom from foreign rule.[4] It is no coincidence that he was writing in the aftermath of a fortuitous Florentine victory over one of Italy's most powerful states, Milan. By the end of the fourteenth century, Florence had taken advantage of the decline of her rivals, Pisa and Siena, to extend control over a large area of Tuscany. But the city's independence was threatened by the expansionist policies of Milan. During the 1390s, the Milanese armies had conquered many of the north-Italian city states and moved south to capture Bologna and Pisa. Their next target was Florence. Her narrow escape from almost certain defeat owed much to the timely death in 1402 of the Milanese leader, Giangaleazzo Visconti, but it had an enormous psychological impact and made the Florentines keenly aware of their city's unique traditions.[5]

Throughout the Middle Ages Florence had proudly claimed imperial Roman ancestry and foundation by Julius Caesar. The image of imperial Rome was a powerful one and had provided a persuasive model for ambitious rulers from Charlemagne onwards. But it was far from appropriate for a city that had rejected monarchic rule in favour of representative government and when Bruni presented factual proof that the city had actually been founded before Caesar, at a time when the liberty of republican Rome had been untainted by imperial ambition, he was making a significant change of emphasis.[6] Bruni's thesis illustrates the key role played by the culture of republican Rome in early fifteenth-century Florence. Above all, it provided a forceful precedent that gave legitimacy to the city's political regime.[7]

Under the intellectual leadership of Coluccio Salutati, head of the Florentine Chancery (1375–1406), the city became the prime centre of early Renaissance humanism. Bruni and his contemporaries eagerly studied the literature of antiquity and its celebration of the virtues of civic liberty, equal opportunity and freedom from oppression. Cicero, in particular, provided an ideal of civic duty, of a moral citizen actively participating in government, whose decisions were guided by loyalty to his country rather than by self-interest. Cicero's influence was given visual expression in one of the reception rooms in the Palazzo della Signoria, where his portrait appeared with those of other prominent republican heroes, poets and generals in a fresco cycle (1385) of famous men, each with classically-inspired epigrams by Salutati.[8] The studies of the early humanists stimulated a desire to replace what they saw as the debased forms of medieval Latin with the rules of the classical language and to learn Greek. Salutati was instrumental in the appointment of the Byzantine scholar, Manual Chrysoloras, to teach Greek in Florence and the city became an important centre of Greek studies. Classical rhetoric provided a powerful new language for propaganda in the struggle against the tyranny of Milan. Giangaleazzo Visconti is reported to have said that, in wartime, Salutati's letters were worth a cavalry division.[9]

The literature of classical antiquity provided Florentine humanists with a new approach to the world around them, one that was based on provable fact rather than received myth. It was historical facts that gave Bruni the evidence he required to disprove the old myth of Florence's imperial foundation. This new approach had a manifest appeal in the mercantile culture of Renaissance Florence. Lawyers, bankers, merchants and shopkeepers dealt in facts, in weights and measures and, primarily, in calculable profits. It was a Florentine, Paolo Toscanelli who, having read in Ptolemy's *Geographia* that the earth was a sphere, realized it was possible to sail west to the Indies and wrote the letter that Columbus took to the King of Portugal.

Above all, pride in the Florentine achievement permeated the culture of early fifteenth-century Florence. Patriotism was a prominent theme in classical literature and one that spoke to the hearts of Salutati, Bruni and their contemporaries. Bruni's boast that the scale of Florence's greatness was embodied in the grandeur of her architecture was part of a growing awareness of the city's unique traditions. Histories of Florence, treatises on her political institutions, on her Tuscan language and on her fourteenth-century literary heroes, Dante and Boccaccio, were all inspired by classical precedents. But their prime theme was civic pride and national identity. And these two potent forces were given visual expression in an ambitious programme of artistic patronage, designed to promote an image of wealth and power for the city. Above all, they stimulated the emergence of Florentine styles in architecture, sculpture and painting that mark the beginning of what we know as the Renaissance.

2

Civic Pride and Guild Prestige

The Florentines attached enormous value to the appearance of their city. The city's new representative government had taken the initiative during the 1290s to build the prime images of Florentine power: the Palazzo della Signoria and the cathedral (the Duomo). State patronage of these key monuments had established a pattern of civic control which was soon extended to include many of Florence's important churches, convents and hospitals, significantly eroding the traditional rights of the religious orders. Instead of taking direct responsibility for these projects collectively, the government transferred most of them to individual guilds, the institutions at the basis of the city's political system. This solution to the problem of exercising state authority was uniquely Florentine and contrasted with the solutions developed in Venice or the Italian courts (see below). It also established guild rivalry as a powerful competitive spur to public patronage in Florence, a motive that can be seen behind many of the works of the early Florentine Renaissance.

During the fourteenth century, the Duomo and the Baptistery were allocated respectively to the Wool Merchants and the Cloth Merchants, the guilds in charge of the city's two principal industries. The Wool Merchants were also given responsibility for the Piazza della Signoria and its loggia, although the state retained patronage of the Palazzo della Signoria. When the government undertook the rebuilding of Orsanmichele, the city's grain market, they appointed the Silk Merchants to take charge of the project. Unfinished churches under the patronage of the various religious orders were allotted state subsidies to accelerate their completion and this provided the excuse for government intervention. The Franciscan convent of Santa Croce and the Benedictine monastery of San Miniato were both assigned to the Cloth Merchants.[1] The Bankers, the Lawyers and the Silk Merchants were each allocated churches with hospitals attached.[2] Central to the political life of Florence, the guilds now became her leading patrons and were largely responsible for the city's magnificent monuments.

1. Ghiberti, East (Paradise) Doors, Baptistery, Florence, 1425–52

In the exhilarating atmosphere that followed the Florentine victory over powerful Milanese armies, the city generated a wave of verbal and visual propaganda designed to promote its prestige. Bruni's *In Praise of the City of Florence* was one of many literary works that extolled the virtues of the Florentines, their history, language, government and cultural traditions. The guilds lavished funds on Florence's major buildings and launched a campaign of patronage that marked the beginning of what we call the Renaissance. The Cloth Merchants commissioned two costly sets of bronze doors to embellish the Baptistery (fig. 1). Ten guilds filled the empty niches on Orsanmichele with bronze or marble statues of their patron saints (fig. 2). The Silk Merchants' Guild founded the Ospedale degli Innocenti, an orphanage, and chose a startlingly innovative design for its façade (fig. 3). But the crowning glory of the city's skyline was the dome of the new cathedral, commissioned by the Wool Merchants' Guild along with an elaborate programme of sculpture to decorate this prime image of Florentine power. This dome, which could then claim to be the largest in Christendom, still dominates Florence today (fig. 4).

Unlike modern trade unions, which were founded to protect workers from exploitation by employers, the guilds had evolved out of efforts to safeguard mercantile interests against interference from the ruling aristocracy and their members included both employers and employees.

2.   Orsanmichele, Florence, begun 1337 (*left*, Donatello, *St George*, *c*. 1415; *right*, Ghiberti, *St Matthew*, 1419)

Membership was a sign of high social status and economic success; but, above all, it conferred the right to participate in the political arena. Seven major guilds controlled the leading industries and professions of Florence and it was to these that her wool, cloth and silk merchants, furriers and spice dealers, bankers and lawyers, belonged. Allotted three-quarters of seats on all government committees, they effectively governed the city and formed the upper crust of Florentine society. Less prestigious but still part of the mercantile élite that dominated the economic and political life of Florence were the fourteen minor guilds that represented the city's shopkeepers and artisans: butchers, bakers, wine merchants, shoemakers, sculptors and other tradesmen.

As the lever that guaranteed upward mobility in Florentine society, guild membership was strictly controlled. The doctor wanting to practise as a member of the Guild of Apothecaries and Spice Merchants and the sculptor wishing to join the Guild of Stonemasons and Woodworkers were both required to prove their skills before a panel of experts. Membership of the Bankers' Guild was compulsory for partners in the city's merchant banks but moneylenders and pawnbrokers were barred. New members paid a matriculation fee that varied according to the status of the guild. Entry to the prestigious Wool Merchants' Guild cost 25 florins, worth 100 lire in 1410,[3] almost six months' wages for a skilled craftsman, while the

3. Brunelleschi, Ospedale degli Innocenti, Florence, begun 1419

Vintners' Guild only charged 5 lire.[4] There were also annual membership dues. Failure to pay could mean imprisonment, as it did for Brunelleschi while he was in charge of building the cathedral dome.[5] In return, members could expect a measure of protection for their businesses as well as financial aid in cases of hardship, and the guilds would also arbitrate in disputes, function as bailiffs and seize property in payment of bad debts, or act as executors of wills.

Membership also carried duties and obligations. At a social level, guild members were expected to take part in celebrations for the feast days of their patron saints, to attend guild funerals and to march behind the guild banner on important civic occasions. The statutes of the Wool Merchants' Guild required members to observe forty-three holy days apart from Sundays.[6] There were other, more practical duties. Members of the Vintners' Guild were expected to inform on wine merchants who had not joined the guild.[7] The guilds also appointed inspectors from their ranks to supervise production within their industry. For example, the Wool Merchants' Guild fined members who produced substandard cloth.[8] Brick moulds were checked annually by an official of the Guild of Stonemasons and Woodworkers, who also monitored the quantity of lime used in brick production.[9] Respected members might be elected to serve on committees that dealt with artistic patronage (see below). But the most prestigious appointment within each guild was election to the governing body of consuls, which met in guild meeting halls to settle disputes, formulate industrial policy and administer guild funds.

It was characteristic of medieval Christian culture that the guilds were expected to devote their funds to charity. They all had their own chapels in at least one of the city's churches, where they financed masses on a regular basis. The feast days of their patron saints were celebrated with elaborate processions and donations of alms to the poor. Patronage of the arts was limited by the funds at the disposal of each guild and these varied considerably. Matriculation fees and annual membership dues formed the bulk of the income of the minor guilds, giving them relatively little scope for patronage beyond the construction and decoration of their guild halls, the commissioning of altarpieces for their chapels or, for some, of a statue of their patron saint on Orsanmichele. But the major guilds had been assigned responsibility for important churches, civic monuments, hospitals and other institutions by the government. This task not only involved the administration of substantial financial assets (including testamentary bequests[10] which allowed them far greater scope for patronage) but also imposed further obligations, notably construction, embellishment and repair.

This charitable expenditure had another, more calculated, purpose. Just as large companies today advertise themselves through sponsorship of sporting or cultural events, so the guilds competed with each other through patronage of the arts. Architecture, sculpture and painting, reinforced by a conspicuous display of coats of arms, provided the guilds with potent propaganda to communicate their power and prestige. Lavish meeting halls in the expensive commercial centre of the city proclaimed their affluence, while the coats of arms of the seven major guilds on important public buildings were a reminder of their power.

Guild projects were supervised by an *opera*, a committee of members elected specially for the purpose. The guilds exercised far more control over their projects than modern patrons. Their initial task was the choice of a design. It was standard practice throughout medieval Europe to choose designs for prestigious public or corporate projects by competition. These competitions usually followed a standard format. The entries were assessed by a panel of experts, consisting mainly of sculptors, painters, goldsmiths and other craftsmen. But this panel was solely advisory and the final choice was always made by the patron.[11] For major decisions involving the expenditure of public funds, the *opera* might assemble a representative group of citizens to cast their votes as well. Smaller commissions were generally influenced by experience. Ghiberti, who had been employed by the Cloth Merchants on the doors of the Baptistery since 1403, was the obvious choice when the guild decided to commission a statue of their patron saint, John the Baptist, for Orsanmichele in 1407. Although official records are silent on the point, we can assume that extensive lobbying of the members of the *opera* played a key role, as it did in the wider political arena.

The responsibilities of the *opera* did not cease once the design had been chosen. The *opera* appointed by the Cloth Merchants to supervise Ghiberti's two sets of Baptistery doors organized contracts with the sculptor and his assistants, paid wages, bought materials and oversaw the installation of the finished doors.[12] The *opera* of the Duomo was responsible for its administration as well as its construction, decoration and repair. Account ledgers kept by the *opera* record payments for candle wax as well as marble and show that the *opera* appointed both the organist and the chief stonemason.[13] By far the largest building in Bruni's city, the Duomo was a massive undertaking and an important stimulus to the city's building industry. The *opera* was the major employer of construction workers in the city with up to a hundred stonecutters, carpenters, wallers and manual labourers working under the supervision of the chief stonemason. Independent craftsmen and suppliers also benefited. The *opera* bought bricks, ironware, rope and other materials from Florentine tradesmen and drew up contracts with quarriers for marble and other building stone. Carters were

4. Cupola of Duomo, Florence, designed 1367, construction begun 1420

employed to transport the stone to the site. Self-employed sculptors were commissioned to carve decorative details, ranging from capitals and cornice mouldings to the statues that embellished the façades.

Much of our knowledge of the building industry in the fifteenth century comes from the meticulous records kept by guild officials. Many of their huge leather-bound ledgers still survive today in the Florentine archives and they provide us with a wealth of detail on the day-to-day organization of a project, from the appointment of members of the *opera* and the minutes of their meetings to accounts of income and expenditure. Every item, however small, bought by the *opera* of the Duomo was faithfully documented in the neat italic script of its chief administrator. The reader can follow the careers of stonemasons as they rise through the ranks of the workforce and trace the network of customers supplied by individual ironmongers or marble quarriers, comparing prices and demand. Above all, the precise and detailed nature of the records provides us with tangible evidence of the business mentality of Renaissance Florence.

Florentine merchants knew the importance of drawing up contracts to regulate commercial transactions, and art was no exception. Complex legal documents stipulated the precise terms agreed by both parties. Artists and patrons were bound by clauses that covered size, format, subject matter, costs of materials and execution. There were also penalties for default by either party. The procedure varied, but generally the price of a statue was only fixed after it had been completed. Any advances paid while the work had been in progress were then deducted. When the *opera* of the Duomo commissioned Nanni di Banco, Donatello, Lamberti and Ciuffagni to make statues of the four Evangelists (1408–10) for the west front of the Duomo, it provided the sculptors with blocks of Carrara marble.[14] Donatello's statue of St John was still unfinished in April 1415 and the *opera* threatened him with a penalty of 25 florins, just over 15 per cent of its value, if he did not finish it before the end of May. But the threat was not carried out and the statue was finally assessed by a panel of experts at 160 florins.[15] Donatello's contract (1411) with the Linenworkers' Guild for a statue of St Mark to fill their niche on Orsanmichele was somewhat different.[16] His colleague, Lamberti, was commissioned to go to Carrara at his own expense and to find a suitable piece of marble, for which he was paid 28 florins. The finished statue was assessed by the *opera*, rather than by experts, and the 28 florins was deducted from the final figure along with the advances already paid.

Ghiberti's contract (1403) with the Cloth Merchants for his first set of bronze doors for the Baptistery had to take into account not only the high costs involved but also the time the project would take (the doors were installed in 1424).[17] The *opera* undertook to supply all the necessary materials and to pay Ghiberti 200 florins annually. Ghiberti agreed to finish three panels a year and pay the wages of any assistants. But he failed to adhere to the terms of the contract and the *opera* drew up another in 1407. Unusually strict, the new contract denied Ghiberti his self-employed status. In return for what was now an annual salary of 200 florins, he was expected to work on the doors every day and any lapses were to be recorded in a special ledger. He was also forbidden to take on any other work without the express permission of the *opera*.

Civic pride and guild prestige acted as powerful motives for guild patronage in early fifteenth-century Florence. Materials, scale and, above all, style provided the guilds with a variety of alternatives for the visual expression not only of the status and affluence of the individual guilds but also of their collective national identity, something that acted as a powerful incentive for the development of some uniquely Florentine solutions. These choices were to have a crucial impact on the history of western art and four projects stand out as fundamental to the emergence of the Renaissance.

Arguably the most prestigious building in Florence, the Baptistery was certainly the oldest of her major monuments, dating from the eleventh century. Decorated with elaborate inlaid marble outside and with costly mosaics inside, it had been assigned to the Cloth Merchants' Guild before 1300. One of the guild's first projects had been a set of bronze doors by Andrea Pisano illustrating the life of St John the Baptist in twenty quatrefoil panels (finished by 1336). It was no coincidence that the decision to commission a second set, in the same format, was taken in 1401 at a time when the Milanese armies were seriously threatening Florentine independence and the announcement of a prestigious competition provided propaganda for the Florentine cause.

We have two records of this competition. Ghiberti's memoirs describe how he won it, but not why.[18] More illuminating are the panels by Brunelleschi (fig. 5) and Ghiberti (fig. 6), depicting the *Sacrifice of Isaac*, the remaining two of the five commissioned by the *opera* from the shortlisted candidates. In appearance they were very different. Ghiberti's stylish and elegant interpretation was typical of the International Gothic. In marked contrast, Brunelleschi chose the dramatic moment when the angel wrenches the dagger from Abraham's hand as he is about to plunge it into his son's neck. His realism did not conform to current artistic taste but drew inspiration from earlier Florentine traditions, in particular the works of the city's most famous artist, Giotto (*c.* 1267–1337). The emergence of a distinctively Florentine style was to have important ramifications for the development of architecture, painting and sculpture in the city (see below and Chapter 3), but, in 1401, the prosperous Cloth Merchants' Guild was conservative. It is significant that it preferred Ghiberti's style which flattered the Florentines by using the elegant courtly language of northern Europe and created an immediately recognizable image of power and prosperity. It is also significant that Ghiberti's project would need one-quarter less bronze.[19] With fewer individual figures to solder onto the base, it was not only cheaper to make but it was also less risky to cast. Balancing minimum expenditure with maximum visual effect had an obvious appeal in the mercantile culture of Renaissance Florence.

Ghiberti's first set of doors, which depicted twenty New Testament scenes with the four Evangelists and four Doctors of the Church in similar panels below, were finally installed in 1424. The following year the *opera* decided to commission him to make another set, illustrating the Old Testament (fig. 1).[20] But this time the *opera* was more innovative. Tastes had begun to change. The quatrefoil panels of the earlier doors did not allow

5.   Brunelleschi, *Sacrifice of Isaac*. Florence, Museo dell'Opera del Duomo, 1401

for the exploitation of recent artistic developments and the *opera* rejected a programme, submitted by Leonardo Bruni, for twenty scenes and eight prophets in the same format as the earlier sets.[21] Instead, they opted for a design that incorporated a number of different events in each of the ten square panels. Heavily gilded and surrounded by elaborately carved naturalistic ornament, these doors were a decisive statement of the status and affluence of the Cloth Merchants. But promoting its image was expensive and the Guild overstretched itself. Its four major projects alone (the two sets of doors by Ghiberti of 1402–24 and 1425–52, his statue of St John the Baptist for the niche on Orsanmichele of 1413–17 and a new frame for

6. Ghiberti, *Sacrifice of Isaac*. Florence, Museo dell'Opera del Duomo, 1401

the Pisano doors in 1452–64) came to over 35,000 florins.[22] Heavy expenses forced them to apply to the government for financial assistance in 1428, but they were refused. The guild was obliged to take out a loan that stood at 1,800 florins in 1429.[23] In 1454 it stopped all payments except salaries.[24]

Originally built as a loggia for grain merchants in the 1280s, Orsanmichele had on one of its pillars a miracle-working image of the Madonna which became the focus of an important cult during the fourteenth century.[25] The present building (fig. 2) was begun in 1337 under the supervision of the Silk Merchants after the first loggia had been destroyed by fire. The new building was planned as an open loggia with one bay reserved for veneration of the image and two upper storeys for grain storage and offices. By 1390 the loggia had been closed in and the whole of the ground floor was reserved for the cult of the image.[26] Meanwhile, in 1339, the Silk Merchants had obtained permission from the Signoria to allocate the fourteen external piers of the loggia to individual guilds, who were each to decorate their pier with tabernacles holding an image of their patron saint.[27] These tabernacles were to become the focus for the guilds' religious and civic ceremonies. But by 1406 only six guilds had fulfilled their obligations. The importance that the government attached to the appearance of Florence was given the force of law when, in 1406, it threatened the confiscation and reallocation of niches not filled within the next ten years.[28] The guilds were spurred into action. By 1416, eight guilds had commissioned statues for the church and three more soon followed.

Orsanmichele offered a unique site for a direct comparison of the status, power and prestige of both major and minor guilds. The major guilds secured prime positions: the Cloth Merchants' niche was closest to the Piazza della Signoria and the Wool Merchants' niche was next to the main entrance to the church and opposite their palace. Cost was another clear statement of wealth. Art historians have tended to ignore the tabernacles themselves, concentrating instead on the stylistic aspects of the statues inside. But the carved canopied recesses formed a significant proportion of the total cost. Their inlaid marble decoration and elaborately carved detail was time-consuming and manifestly expensive. The Linenworkers' Guild spent 200 florins on their tabernacle, almost twice as much as on their marble statue of St Mark by Donatello.[29] Only the major guilds were rich enough to commission a bronze statue from Ghiberti, who, with the success of his first set of doors for the Baptistery, had become the leading sculptor in the city. Bronze was expensive and the risks involved in casting increased the statue's potential cost. The vast sum of 945 florins spent by the Bankers' Guild on a statue of St Matthew by Ghiberti (fig. 2) included additional expenditure required to cover the mistakes made in the first casting.[30] The guild was obliged to raise a levy of 200 florins from its members to finance these extra costs. By contrast, a marble statue of similar size cost from 100 to 150 florins.[31] Bronze was a real statement of prestige and this fact did not escape the attention of the Wool Merchants' Guild, one of the few to complete its niche before 1406. In 1425, the guild commissioned a new bronze statue of St Stephen from Ghiberti to replace their earlier marble figure. The document recording this decision is explicit: the old statue was inferior to Ghiberti's bronzes for the Cloth Merchants and the Bankers and, fully conscious of their status as one of the city's most prestigious guilds, they felt obliged to rectify the situation.[32]

The stylistic options open to both major and minor guilds were much the same as those that had faced the Cloth Merchants' Guild when it had had to choose between Ghiberti and Brunelleschi for the commission for the Baptistery doors in 1401. Once again, the Cloth Merchants opted for courtly elegance and a recognizable statement of prestige and so, significantly, did two other major guilds, the Bankers and the Wool Merchants. But many of the minor guilds, under less pressure to compete in an international arena, preferred images of real people, statues that emphasized Florentine achievement in a style that was strongly resonant of Giotto's frescos of a century earlier. The Armourers' statue of *St George* (Donatello) (fig. 7), the Linenworkers' *St Mark* (Donatello), the Stonemasons and Woodworkers *Four Crowned Martyrs* (Nanni di Banco) and the Smiths' *St Eligius* (Nanni di Banco) were not elegant or refined but solidly human figures, dressed in realistic clothes rather than the stylized drapery of Ghiberti's statues. In art historical terms, Donatello's and Nanni di Banco's statues represent a landmark in the evolution of a new style, revered by generations of art historians as that of the Renaissance. We tend to associate artistic genius with originality and for this reason often judge Ghiberti as the less creative artist. But this is not the way these two sculptors appeared then. It is inconceivable that the wealthy and important guilds would deliberately commission something they perceived as second-rate.

The major guilds were not always conservative. The Silk Merchants chose a significantly new style for the Ospedale degli Innocenti (fig. 3), a charitable orphanage under their patronage. National identity and civic pride had a powerful impact on their choice. Brunelleschi's design (1419) had little in common with the current taste for ornate Gothic pointed arches and elaborate decoration, seen, for example, on many of the guild tabernacles on Orsanmichele. It was a novel design but, like his competition panel for the Baptistery doors and Donatello's guild statues on Orsanmichele, it recalled older Florentine traditions. Brunelleschi's design for the Ospedale was immediately recognizable: its elegant round arches supported on Corinthian capitals and triangular pediments over rectangular windows could also be seen on two of the city's oldest buildings, the Baptistery and the church of San Miniato al Monte. What the Silk Merchants commissioned was a design that rejected an essentially foreign style, Gothic, in favour of an older, national style, Tuscan Romanesque, inaugurating the emergence of a consciously Florentine architecture.[33]

While the guilds were commissioning sculpture for Orsanmichele and the Baptistery, a more dramatic visual change was taking place in the city. Florence Cathedral, started at the end of the thirteenth century, was now nearing completion.[34] This prime image of Florentine prestige and power

7.   Donatello, *St George*. Florence, Museo Nazionale, *c.* 1415

had been allocated to the Wool Merchants' Guild in 1332, but the funds at its disposal were inadequate for such an enormous project. Accordingly, the government deducted 3 lire from every will to supplement the building fund and government appointees shared places with guild members on the *opera*.[35] But the issues that affected the appearance of this immensely important building required a broader consensus. Like most major architectural projects of the Middle Ages, the building was not designed all at once. The new cathedral had been begun by 1296, when Pope Boniface VIII gave 3,000 florins towards its construction.[36] But it was not until 1367, when the nave was nearly complete, that the *opera* finally decided on the form of the east end, choosing a design submitted by a group of painters and stonemasons.[37] Planned on a scale unparalleled since the fall of the Roman Empire, their ribbed octagonal dome (fig. 4) was not only ambitious but it bore only a distant resemblance to the cathedrals in other Italian cities. This unambiguous statement of the unique nature of Florentine power, chosen by the *opera*, was only accepted after a referendum of the Florentine electorate.[38] The dome could indeed claim to give visual expression to the power of the Florentine Republic. However, the fact that it was still unfinished in 1400 was undeniably damaging to civic prestige and its completion became an urgent priority.

The *opera* may have made an innovative choice but the desire to be different posed major problems for the craftsmen in charge of its construction and a competition was held in 1418 to find a solution. Architects, as we know them, did not exist in the Renaissance and projects were submitted by a wide variety of people, including Giovanni di Gherardo da Prato, who lectured on Dante and acted as chief administrator of the *opera*.[39] The project finally chosen was that of Brunelleschi, a sculptor and goldsmith by training. His intention, to construct a double-shelled dome with the ingenious use of herringbone brickwork and without the traditional use of a wooden support, caused so much controversy that he was appointed to supervise its execution. Appointing the designer to supervise the execution of his project might seem normal to us but it was unusual in the early fifteenth century.[40] Architectural design was open to a wide range of talent, but construction required technical knowledge and it was invariably supervised by the chief stonemason employed on the site. Brunelleschi's appointment was a major landmark in the emergence of the modern architect. We may rate the creative ideas of a designer more highly than the technical expertise of an engineer, but this aesthetic standard did not hold true in the Renaissance. Brunelleschi was showered with praise by his contemporaries more for his oustanding abilities as an engineer than for his style.[41] The *opera* of the Duomo, meeting to discuss his memorial, praised his inventions, which had saved them so much money.[42] Above all, his technical skills had enabled the Florentines to complete the principal land-mark of their city.

The *opera* of the Duomo was responsible not only for the construction of the Duomo, its upkeep and repair but also for its internal and external embellishment. The Duomo was easily the most extravagant building in Florence. Its inlaid cladding was colourfully made up of local red and green sandstones and white marble imported at considerable cost from Carrara. Although the *opera* had started a programme of sculptural decoration for the façade and the north door, the Porta della Mandorla, in the 1380s,[43] it had been interrupted by the war with Milan. During the relative peace that followed, the determination with which the *opera* had applied itself to finishing the construction of the Duomo also infected its desire to embellish the building. In 1408 the *opera* commissioned seven-feet high statues of the Evangelists for the façade of the Duomo from Nanni di Banco (*Luke*), Donatello (*John*) and Lamberti (*Mark*), with the intention of commission-ing the best of these to carve the statue of *Matthew*, although in the event it was given to Ciuffagni.[44] A relief of the *Assumption of the Virgin* was commissioned from Nanni di Banco for the Porta della Mandorla (1414–22).[45] Nanni di Banco and Donatello carved a series of prophets for the campanile.[46] The *opera* commissioned an enormous amount of stained glass for the windows of the Duomo, much of it designed by Ghiberti.[47] Two marble singing galleries by Luca della Robbia (*c.* 1432) and Donatello (1433) were installed in 1440.[48] Ghiberti and Brunelleschi both worked on the chapel of St Zenobius, started in 1432. Its centrepiece, an ornate shrine holding the head of the saint, was decorated with bronze reliefs by Ghiberti.[49]

Above all, the *opera* gave visual expression to strong feelings of civic pride. Religious imagery dominated the decorative schemes for the exterior of the building but Florence's national heroes were given pride of place inside. Her recent military successes were commemorated in equestrian portraits of two of the foreign leaders of her mercenary armies: Essex-born Sir John Hawkwood (Uccello; 1435) and the Italian Niccolò da Tolentino (Castagno; 1455). The leader of her cultural phalanx, Dante, was honoured with a frescoed portrait (repainted in 1464 by Domenico di Michelino). And after his death in 1446 Brunelleschi himself was given a memorial in the church complete with verses composed by the Chancellor, Carlo Marsuppini, that compared Brunelleschi's skills to those of Daedalus. The *opera* recorded that he had been assisted only by God and the Virgin.[50] It was an unprecedented honour for a craftsman and it reflected the enormous importance the Florentines placed on the visual arts to display their prestige and power.

3

Merchants and Morality

In the bustling commercial centre of Florence, merchants, shopkeepers, artisans and labourers practised their trades, making and losing the profits that were the prime sign of their success. Rich and poor lived as neighbours in the city's four administrative districts which centred on the churches of San Giovanni (the Baptistery), Santa Croce, Santa Maria Novella and Santo Spirito. People's lives were bound by a web of relationships created by family and neighbourhood loyalties that influenced whom they married, whom they selected as godparents for their children, which political faction they supported, whom they chose as business partners and which religious confraternity they joined. Their decisions created further obligations and this complex network was central to the economic, political and social life of fifteenth-century Florence.[1] At the top of this network was the ruling élite, her wealthiest citizens and members of families who could trace their involvement in politics back to the early days of republican government. They were responsible not only for her economic prosperity, her tax system and foreign policy but also for the very appearance of the city. As members of the seven major guilds, they were behind the spectacular programme of corporate patronage that was transforming Florence. As private individuals, they also made significant contributions to the development of western art.

Much of what we know about the private fortunes of Florentine merchants comes from the detailed records of taxes still preserved in the city's archives. It was characteristic of the commercial mentality of Florence that taxes should be assessed according to means rather than as the simple poll taxes levied in the rest of Europe. Forced loans, or *prestanze*, based on estimates of the resources of each household, were raised for specific purposes, for example to cover the expenses of the wars with Milan in 1403. The inefficiencies inherent in the arbitrary assessment of the *prestanze* led, in 1427, to the development of a new tax, the *catasto*, based on a more precise calculation of wealth. Invested capital, rents, sums owed by debtors and other sources of income were all listed as taxable assets from which sums owed to creditors were deducted along with a uniform amount of 200 florins for each dependent relative, leaving a net figure on which tax was payable. The state also required its citizens to finance the public debt with loans that were converted into interest-bearing shares in the state bank, the *Monte*.

According to the records of the 1427 *catasto*, there were 86 citizens with net assets of over 10,000 florins and a further 317 with over 2,500 florins.[2] These merchants were rich by Florentine standards. A skilled stonemason working on the Duomo earned about 60 florins a year.[3] Ghiberti, the city's leading goldsmith and a prosperous artisan, had assets of 999 florins (including land and *Monte* shares valued at 714 florins) but his obligations, his wife, two children and creditors, amounted to 1,074 florins, leaving him with a negative total.[4] Inevitably there were strong links between wealth and political power. By far the richest citizen was Palla Strozzi, an influential figure on the conservative side of Florentine politics (see below). His net resources came to 101,422 florins, with investments in land, *Monte* shares and a partnership in a banking firm.[5] The leader of the conservative faction was Niccolò da Uzzano, the wealthiest taxpayer in Santo Spirito and sixth in the city, with net capital of 46,402 florins. At the head of the opposition was Giovanni di Bicci de' Medici, whose net capital of 79,462 florins made him the second richest man in the city.

Money was a thorny issue in early fifteenth-century Florence. Many of the city's most powerful men were bankers who, by the nature of their trade, inevitably transgressed the ban on usury. The prosperous merchant was faced with a dilemma: the Bible made it clear that God disapproved of material wealth but profits were the prime sign of his success. More importantly, as Bruni recognized,[6] they were manifestly the basis of Florence's independence, her economic prosperity and her political achievement. Florentine humanists questioned whether wealth was so very bad. While the Church attempted to reconcile the Christian ideal of poverty with the realities of commercial exchange, Bruni and his contemporaries began to explore the works of Aristotle, Cicero and other classical authors to develop new moral codes that justified the acquisition of money and governed its expenditure.[7] Praise for the rejection of material possessions was replaced by an emphasis on the hard work that had gone into building up fortunes and the honourable use made of them. It was precisely this affluence that enabled the rich to fulfil the civic duties and religious obligations imposed on them by the culture of Christian and republican Florence.[8]

Civic duties and religious obligations played a central role in governing the expenditure of wealthy Florentines. Supporting the state through taxes and *Monte* shares was part of the financial burden imposed on the rich. Marriage, the prime means of extending family ties, was taken very seriously and a prosperous merchant could expect to have to find as much as 1,000 florins as a dowry for his daughter. As part of their duties as Christians, the rich were expected to give away part of their wealth in charity. Partnership agreements often stipulated that a proportion of the profits were to go to God.[9] Amongst the many charitable donations recorded in the account books of Francesco Datini (1335–1410), the famous merchant of Prato, were presents of oranges to a hospital and a pair of spectacles for a monk.[10] Ilarione de' Bardi, the general manager of the Medici bank, who showed net assets of 14,853 florins in the 1427 *catasto*, used his profits to finance dowries for poor girls.[11]

It was in the context of these civic duties and religious obligations that wealthy Florentines made their contribution to the appearance of their city. Participation in guild projects was one of the responsibilities of a guild member, more indicative of political prestige than artistic interest. Palla Strozzi and Niccolò da Uzzano, both members of the Cloth Merchants' Guild, were involved with the commissions for the Baptistery doors.[12] Niccolò's brother, Angelo, and Giovanni di Bicci de' Medici were among the members of the Bankers' Guild who donated funds for Ghiberti's *St Matthew*. The two highest contributors for this statue were Lorenzo di Palla Strozzi and Cosimo di Giovanni de' Medici, who each gave 26 florins.[13] The potent sense of civic pride that inspired these rich and powerful citizens as guild members also infected them as individuals. They played a prominent role in the embellishment of their own districts, building the huge palaces that identified them as members of the ruling élite and taking the lead in the construction and decoration of their parish churches.

The principal motive behind the proliferation of chapels and altars in Florence's churches was the compelling need to atone for sins especially for the acquisition of material wealth. Like charitable donations and taxation, patronage of the arts in early fifteenth-century Florence was primarily an obligation imposed on the rich. It was not the product of a well developed aesthetic urge. But private patronage was bound by a different set of moral codes to the corporate activities of the guilds. Institutional patronage did not carry the stigma of vainglory attached to private display. With a political system designed to avoid domination by individuals, republican Florence was wary of blatant exhibitions of personal affluence. Sumptuary laws attempted to control extravagance in dress and behaviour. The Church encouraged patronage in a religious context provided it remained anonymous. Fra Giovanni Dominici (*c.* 1356–1419), a prominent Dominican preacher, specifically condemned the use of coats of arms, arguing that God could see what was done from Heaven.[14] But, in a society where wealth was the principal measure of hard work and success, conspicuous expenditure was the obvious sign of achievement. A high *catasto* assessment, a large dowry or a generous charitable donation, all testified to a merchant's prosperity and prestige. Art and architecture were more permanent. In their palaces and chapels, their fresco cycles, altarpieces and tombs, these rich businessmen manifested a strong desire to proclaim their worldly success as well as the need to expiate their guilt for the world to come. How these merchants balanced the moral restraints imposed upon them against their desire to give visual expression to their wealth and status forms the principal theme of this chapter.

There was no prestigious residential area in fifteenth-century Florence. The site of a rich merchant's palace was determined by traditional family loyalties to a particular district. They were literally family palaces: ownership was often shared by numerous heirs and some were built to house more than one household, like the palace begun by Niccolò and Angelo da Uzzano (*c.* 1411).[15] These palaces were the prime statements of family status in Florentine society and it was a sign of the republican culture of the period that they were broadly uniform in both scale and style. They were massive structures, eight or nine bays long and three storeys high, with rusticated ground floors, string courses separating the upper storeys and ashlar framed windows. Fourteenth-century palaces had had huge arches on the ground floor that were rented out as shops but this practice died out after the introduction of the *catasto* (1427), which exempted palaces producing no income. Ilarione de' Bardi's palace (1420s) was designed with arches that were then bricked in; but the Uzzano palace next door reflected the new trend, with a solid rusticated ground floor pierced only by an impressive entrance.[16] Above all, these palaces bore a striking resemblance to the Palazzo della Signoria, the home of the city's republican government, a resemblance that gave visual expression to their owners' membership of the ruling élite.

Interiors were designed with practicality in mind. Courtyards with open loggias provided cool air during the swelteringly hot summers. Plumbing was surprisingly efficient and many of them had their own wells for fresh water, cesspools for waste and lavatories. The main reception rooms and bedrooms were on the first floor, the *piano nobile*, with further rooms for guests and children on the upper floor.[17] Servants slept in the attics. The huge rooms were sparsely furnished. Large chests were used for storing clothes, bed linen and books. More elaborate chests, painted with appropriate scenes, might be commissioned for a bride's trousseau. Large painted dishes were often given to celebrate a birth. Beds were sumptuous: Datini's was 12 feet wide and hung with canopies decorated with his coat of arms.[18] Important rooms were often frescoed with imitation tapestries or brocades, the real ones being hung only on special occasions. Most rooms also included painted panels of religious subjects. Giovanni di Bicci de' Medici and his two sons all had images of the Madonna in their bedrooms.[19] Datini had a fresco of St Christopher painted at the entrance to his palace, three religious pictures in his bedroom and another in his office.[20] Their function as objects of devotion far outweighed aesthetic considerations. The Virgin was venerated in the fifteenth century particularly in her role as intercessor with God. St Christopher, the patron saint of the traveller, had an obvious appeal in commercial Florence.

Amongst the treasured possessions of a merchant were his books. They were expensive and important status symbols. Before the invention of printing, they were hand-written and bound in elaborate leather bindings. Many humanists acquired notable collections of classical texts but they were rare in mercantile inventories of the early fifteenth century. More typical of the period was Francesco Datini, whose books, kept in a chest in his bedroom, included religious works, a prayer book, a fourteenth-century chronicle of Florence and Dante's *Divine Comedy*.[21]

All important families had chapels in their local churches. Most of them were simply altars attached to the rood screen or nave walls. Only the rich could afford a separate space, like Niccolò da Uzzano, the patron of the main chapel in Santa Lucia, or his neighbour, Ilarione de' Bardi, who had a chapel in the same church.[22] The early fifteenth century saw a dramatic increase in demand for family chapels, stimulating the rebuilding of many parish churches, all financed by the provision of extra chapel space within what was essentially a communal enterprise. But the enormous costs of building meant that only the wealthiest Florentines could afford to construct their own family chapels, like the sacristies commissioned by Palla Strozzi and Giovanni di Bicci de' Medici (see below).

The principal function of these chapels was religious, not aesthetic. Despite the importance given by modern art historians to their pictorial and sculptural decoration, this formed only a small part of the total outlay. Besides altarpieces, fresco cycles and tombs, patrons also commissioned chalices, reliquaries and vestments embroidered with their family coats of arms. Above all, they endowed their chapels with funds in perpetuity for regular prayers for their own and their descendants' souls. This could be expensive. After the death of Giovanni di Bicci de' Medici in 1429, his sons gave 900 florins to San Lorenzo to pay for a service every Monday for the soul of their father.[23] Francesco di Antonio Maringhi, the chaplain of Sant'Ambrogio and patron of its high altar, left 800 florins in *Monte* credits in his will (1436) to finance a prebendary at his altar and to cover the annual celebration of the feast of the beheading of St John the Baptist (29 August). These provisions were later extended to include a special mass served by twelve clerics and an organist, followed by a meal, on the feast day of his patron saint.[24] In contrast with the money he spent on endowment, Maringhi only paid 240 florins for what was an exceptionally expensive altarpiece by early fifteenth-century standards, the *Coronation of the Virgin* by Filippo Lippi.[25]

Decoration was the most conspicuous aspect of these chapel projects and it provided the patron with a focus for the display of his personal wealth. Fresco was the cheapest option; it was quick to paint and the material costs were low. Castagno's frescoed equestrian portrait of *Niccolò da Tolentino* in the Duomo cost 24 florins.[26] Masaccio's fresco of the *Trinity* (fig. 11), commissioned by a member of the Lenzi family for his altar in Santa Maria Novella, could not have cost much more. Panel paintings were more expensive; they took longer to complete and there were other factors that could add to the price, all of which, significantly, were easily visible. Many altarpieces were set in elaborately carved and gilded frames, which could form a considerable proportion of the total. The 190 florins paid for Fra Angelico's *Linaiuoli Madonna* (1433) included 70 florins for the frame.[27] Gold and ultramarine were conspicuously expensive materials and large numbers of figures took time to paint.[28] Maringhi's high outlay on Filippo Lippi's *Coronation of the Virgin* was immediately apparent in the inclusion of over fifty figures and an elaborate gilded frame. It is hard to imagine that these details went unnoticed in the commercial culture of fifteenth-century Florence.

It is essential to any understanding of Florentine Renaissance art to recognize that it was the patron and not the artist who was seen as the creator of his chapel. We might talk about Filippo Lippi's *Coronation of the Virgin*, but the picture itself tells another story. The praying figure, indicated by the angel holding a scroll that reads 'He carried out the work', is a portrait of Maringhi not Lippi.[29] Like the guilds, the private patron played a central role in the design and execution of a project. Painters were bound by contracts that stipulated what was to go into the work. The patron, with the approval of the authorities of the church involved, chose the subject and often specified both the quantity and the quality of gold and ultramarine to be used. This was not surprising. A family chapel celebrated the financial, political and social prestige of its patron, not the artistic talents of its craftsmen. It was the patron who asked for intercession. It was his tomb in the chapel, his portrait in a prominent position in the altarpiece and his coat of arms on display. Above all, his choice of artist determined the style of the decoration and the language that gave visual expression to his self-image. In a period of stylistic change, this choice took on an added significance. Three projects stand out from the many chapels built and decorated during the first decades of the century: Palla Strozzi's sacristy at

Santa Trinità, Giovanni di Bicci de' Medici's sacristy at San Lorenzo and Felice Brancacci's chapel in Santa Maria del Carmine.

Palla Strozzi was an imposing figure in the society of early fifteenth-century Florence, inheriting vast wealth from his father as well as the prestige of belonging to a powerful family that had been prominent in government throughout the fourteenth century. He was no businessman and took little part in the running of his bank, but pursued a distinguished career of public service, playing an important role as ambassador for his city.[30] A friend and sponsor of leading humanists, he made a major contribution to the development of humanist studies in Florence and acquired an outstanding collection of classical texts.[31] Such collections were rare in early fifteenth-century Florence, but their increasing appearance was an indication of the growing importance of classical culture in the society of the period. As the patron of his family chapel in Santa Trinità, Strozzi also made an important contribution to the development of Florentine art. But neither his wealth nor his prestige lasted. In 1422 he wrote that he had spent 30,000 florins on his father's funeral, the chapel, dowries and business losses.[32] He paid over 2,000 florins in dowries to two sons-in-law, Felice Brancacci (see below) and Giovanni Rucellai (see Chapter 5), and, according to Rucellai, paid 160,000 florins in taxes between 1422 and 1433.[33] Possibly his business losses were avoidable, but the expenses incurred in paying his taxes, his daughters' dowries and for his father's chapel were part of the obligations imposed on him as a wealthy Florentine citizen. His net capital fell from 101,422 florins in 1427 to 39,142 florins by 1433.[34] Worse was to come: in 1434 he was expelled from Florence for his opposition to Cosimo de' Medici and he died in exile.

As befitted the leading family in the parish, the Strozzi played a prominent role in the embellishment of their local church, Santa Trinità, the main Florentine house of the Vallombrosan Order. In 1383, the monks petitioned the *Signoria* for money to assist in rebuilding the church and a committee of local citizens was elected to oversee the expenditure of these public funds.[35] Largely complete by 1405, the church was an early example of what was to become the standard type, lined with chapels in both transepts and nave. Local families acquired rights over the new chapels.[36] Palla's father, Onofrio Strozzi, financed the rebuilding of its hospital and obtained patronage rights to the sacristy, which he planned as a funeral chapel for his branch of the family and dedicated to his patron saints, Onofrius and Nicholas. It was endowed with 2,000 florins worth of *Monte* credits to pay for daily masses and special services on the saints' feast days.[37]

After Onofrio died (1418), Palla took over responsibility for his father's projects. He donated funds and an altarpiece by Gentile da Fabriano to the hospital,[38] but his prime concern was the completion of the sacristy.

The project was ambitious. Pride of place went to Onofrio's tomb, an elaborate marble sarcophagus, now attributed to Ghiberti.[39] In addition to the building, Palla paid for expensive decoration and lavish furnishings, including choir stalls, carved wooden doors and an elegant marble portal, also attributed to Ghiberti, who was appointed in 1420 as a supervisor for the construction of the choir stalls and paid for unspecified designs.[40] Palla also commissioned Gentile da Fabriano's *Adoration of the Magi* (1423) (fig. 8) for the sacristy.[41] One of the few Biblical events celebrating wealth, the Adoration of the Magi was understandably a popular theme in

8.   Gentile da Fabriano, *Adoration of the Magi*. Florence, Uffizi, dated 1423

fifteenth-century Florence. Palla and his father were portrayed directly behind the youngest King, Onofrio holding a falcon to make a pun on his family name (a *strozziere* was a falcon trainer).[42] The altarpiece was expensive and its cost, 300 florins, was clearly visible in the elaborate gold frame, the number of figures and the large quantities of gold and ultramarine used for the clothes of the Virgin and the Kings.[43]

In his will of 1447, Palla was explicit about his own role: he described the sacristy as having been conceived, planned and begun by his father but executed and completed by himself.[44] He did not refer to Ghiberti or Gentile da Fabriano, but his choice of them was significant. Both artists were well established exponents of International Gothic, the elegant and stylized language of the courts of northern Europe. Palla was a member of the Cloth Merchants' Guild and involved in the decision to give the commission for the Baptistery doors to Ghiberti, rather than to Brunelleschi (see Chapter 2). And for his own project, Palla preferred this traditional and courtly language that would create an easily recognizable image to give visual expression to his family's wealth, its long-standing prestige in Florentine society and his own aristocratic aspirations.

Like Palla Strozzi, Giovanni di Bicci de' Medici was also a prominent member of the ruling élite, descended from a family of bankers that had been active in politics since the late thirteenth century but whose influence had declined.[45] A shrewd businessman, he engineered his success by securing the lucrative papal account in Rome and built up what was to become one of Europe's leading banks.[46] Giovanni di Bicci's growing affluence was reflected in his tax status. In the 1403 *prestanze* he was forty-ninth in the city and twenty-first in his quarter; by 1427 he ranked first in the quarter of San Giovanni and second in the city.[47] Wealth brought political ambition. Giovanni di Bicci's commercial prowess furnished the basis for the emergence of a new faction in Florentine politics and his family's dramatic rise to power. The Medici party (built up under his leadership and with the active participation of his nephew, Averardo, and his son, Cosimo) drew its support from other branches of the family, men related to the Medici by marriage, employees and partners of the Medici bank and residents of San Giovanni, in particular those from the district of the Lion d'Oro that centred on San Lorenzo.[48] By Giovanni di Bicci's death in 1429, the party had become an active force in Florentine government, challenging the traditional ruling group within the élite.[49] Under the leadership of Cosimo, it was to have a decisive effect on the political structure of the city (see Chapter 4).

Plans to rebuild the eleventh-century church of San Lorenzo took formal shape in 1418 when the residents of the Lion d'Oro and the Prior of San Lorenzo petitioned the *Signoria* for permission to clear an area by com-

9. Brunelleschi, Old Sacristy, San Lorenzo, Florence, begun 1421

pulsory purchase to enlarge the choir and transepts of the old church.[50]
Like Santa Trinità, this was a parish project and one in which the rich
families of the district played a key role. Giovanni di Bicci was one of the
wealthy residents elected to the *opera* in 1416 for a three-year term.[51]
While the Chapter was to finance the new main chapel and retain its
patronage rights, the transept chapels were to be acquired by local families,
many of whom were represented on the *opera* and almost all of whom
had strong links with the Medici party.[52] Giovanni di Bicci played the
most prominent role, taking responsibility not only for a chapel in the
new transept but also for the sacristy.[53] The motive stated in the petition,
for the glory of God and the beauty of the city, reflected the importance
that Florentines placed on the appearance of their city but the project
should also be seen as a statement of the growing power of the Medici
party.

Giovanni di Bicci's involvement with San Lorenzo bore strong superficial
resemblance to that of Strozzi at Santa Trinità. Both were the richest men
in their quarter and acquired patronage rights over the sacristies in their
local church, which they planned as family burial chapels. Both spent
conspicuously in building and decoration. But their stylistic choices were,
significantly, very different. While Palla Strozzi underlined his links
with European aristocracy, Giovanni di Bicci opted firmly for new struc-

tural forms and an assertion of local decorative tradition. His sacristy (fig. 9), attributed to Brunelleschi, introduced a series of new forms to the Florentine architectural vocabulary. Its hemispherical dome, pierced with windows at the base and supported by pendentives, had its sources in the pre-Gothic architecture of Europe and Byzantium.[54] A much larger melon dome could be seen in San Marco in Venice and the combination of dome and cubic space beneath was identical to the thirteenth-century Baptistery in Padua.[55] The structure of the building may have been unfamiliar but its articulation with fluted Corinthian pilasters and other details in *pietra serena* was strongly resonant of Tuscan buildings of three centuries earlier. Like the Silk Merchants in their choice of a design for the Ospedale degli Innocenti, Giovanni di Bicci rejected Gothic, the style of Europe's ruling élite, in favour of a more overtly Florentine architecture. Above all, his choice must be seen in the context of Palla Strozzi's far more traditional project. At a time when the Medici party was beginning to challenge the political structure of the city, it is not surprising that Giovanni di Bicci should give visual expression to his new wealth and power in the choice of a style that broke decisively with that of the establishment.

Although rich by Florentine standards, Felice Brancacci was not in the same league as Palla Strozzi or Giovanni di Bicci and his expenditure on frescos to decorate his family chapel in the Carmelite church of Santa Maria del Carmine was considerably more modest than their costly building projects. A moderately successful silk merchant, Brancacci declared net assets of 2,281 florins in the 1427 *catasto*, with investments in land and *Monte* credits as well as his business.[56] Public office took him to Cairo to negotiate on behalf of Florentine merchants and he also worked as a minor official for the government, where he was caught misappropriating funds.[57] But his family was good enough for him to marry Palla Strozzi's daughter in 1431 and, despite close links with the the Medici, he was exiled along with the rest of the Strozzi clan in 1434.

Brancacci's major claim to fame is the fresco cycle in his family chapel, universally recognized as a landmark in the development of Renaissance painting. It is frustrating that virtually no documentation has survived to illuminate the circumstances surrounding their commission bar the works themselves. Art historians debate their date and the contributions of the artists involved; but it is generally agreed that the project was started by Masaccio and Masolino (c. 1427–8), very shortly before Masaccio died in Rome, and was still unfinished when Brancacci was exiled. Neither artist is recorded working in the chapel, though Masolino is known to have painted stage props in the church for a mystery play.[58]

The cycle depicted the life of St Peter and its unusual inconography has been convincingly explained as a comment on three issues of current controversy: the antiquity of the Carmelite Order, clerical taxation and papal primacy.[59] The inclusion of Carmelite friars in *Peter in Cathedra* gave visual expression to their claim to be the oldest of the religious orders and the only one existing at the time of the Apostles. The exceptional prominence given to the *Tribute Money* (fig. 10) and to Christ's command 'Render therefore to Caesar the things which are Caesar's; and to God, the things that are God's' (Matthew 22: 21) highlighted the Biblical precedent for clerical taxation. This issue, controversial throughout Europe, had a particular relevance in Florence where the clergy had been much criticized for not paying their fair share of the heavy tax burdens imposed to cover the costs of war. Above all, the theme of St Peter was inevitably associated with the Papacy. Its choice, at a time when Europe was debating the Pope's claim to supremacy in the Church, took on a more central significance (see Chapter 15). The cycle promoted papal primacy and Brancacci had close links with this faction in the Church; two of its supporters amongst the Cardinals were his cousins and another, the Minister-General of the Dominicans, was a relative by marriage.

The way in which Brancacci's cycle promoted the supreme position of the Pope at the head of the Church was unconventional. Traditionally, both theological texts and pictorial representations dealing with the issue concentrated on two events: Christ giving the Keys to Peter (Matthew 16: 19) and Christ's charge to Peter, 'Feed my sheep' (John 21: 17).[60] Here, the former scene, the more important of the two, was omitted and the latter was relegated to one of the lunettes. At one level, this suggests that Brancacci, and presumably also the Carmelites, were anxious to avoid direct confrontation with the current controversy.[61] The cycle presented the issue by emphasizing Peter's claim to primacy amongst the Apostles through the events of his ministry, his special relationship with Christ, his ability to work miracles and his spiritual supremacy over secular authority. This choice of the evidence that verified the papal claim to supremacy in the Church, in preference to the actions of Christ that demanded unquestioning obedience, was also a reflection of that desire for provable facts, not received myth, which characterized the attitudes of early fifteenth-century Florentines to the world about them.

These attitudes were also given visual expression in a new pictorial style, one that was as overtly Florentine as the architectural and sculptural forms commissioned by the guilds (see Chapter 2) and Giovanni di Bicci de' Medici. Brancacci did not share Palla Strozzi's taste for gilded elegance and courtly imagery. Like Giovanni di Bicci, he preferred a modern language to give visual expression to his self-image, one that broke decisively with tradition and, above all, was distinctively Florentine. It was no accident that this new pictorial language emerged at a time

10. Masaccio, *Tribute Money*. Florence, Santa Maria del Carmine, *c.* 1427

when the Florentines were becoming aware of their city's unique traditions and their own national identity. The rejection of Gothic with its resonances of foreign and aristocratic power in favour of a more overtly Florentine style had a dramatic impact. Like the Ospedale degli Innocenti (see Chapter 2), the solid architectural forms providing the setting for Masaccio's *Trinity, (c.* 1427) (fig. 11) for the Lenzi altar in Santa Maria Novella were largely derived from the Tuscan Romanesque Baptistery.[62] They differed markedly from the intricate gilded Gothic detail on the frame of Gentile da Fabriano's *Adoration of the Magi* (1423).

Above all, the new style gave visual expression to the matter-of-fact world of the Florentine merchant. Like Brunelleschi's panel for the Baptistery doors and Donatello's statues on Orsanmichele, Masaccio's frescos for Brancacci aimed to convey the importance of the reality of Christian history not a remote, mystical world of heavenly beauty. This idea was not new. It had its roots in the sermons of Franciscan preachers, who emphasized the humanity, not the majesty, of Christ, and it had been given expression in Franciscan commissions in Florence painted by Giotto and his contemporaries. Masaccio's plain and solid figures had far more in common with Giotto's frescos in Santa Croce than the elegant draperies of Ghiberti or Gentile. The anguish on the faces of Adam and Eve in the

Expulsion was not a stylized formula but a representation of their genuine emotions. The buildings in the background of the *Raising of Tabitha* were recognizably Florentine. The people in the scenes looked real, many of the onlookers were probably portraits. And the exponents of the new style made their paintings and reliefs appear convincingly real by applying the mathematical and spatial skills that were an integral part of commercial exchange to develop the rules of perspective, which enabled them to create the illusion of a three-dimensional space on a two-dimensional surface.[63]

The new painting style was Florentine and mercantile, and it was also moral. Its development must be seen principally in the context of the early fifteenth-century search for new guidelines that not only justified the acquisition of material wealth but also governed its expenditure. The altarpieces and fresco cycles, commissioned by merchants to give expression to their financial, political and social achievements as well as to their religious beliefs, were an important and very visible aspect of that expenditure. While many humanists applied the moral values of republican Rome to the general issues involved, Alberti related them directly to the new style. Codifying current practice into his *de pictura* (1435), he laid heavy emphasis on the republican virtues of moderation, balance and harmony, criticizing the inclusion of unnecessary detail and the excessive use of gold or other costly materials.[64] The rejection of overt and extravagant displays of material wealth in favour of a plain and moral language, one that incorporated a subtle stress on the practical skills needed for commercial success, was an explicit statement of the republican culture of early fifteenth-century Florence.

11.   Masaccio, *Trinity*. Florence, Santa Maria Novella, *c.* 1427

4

Cosimo de' Medici

H eir to Giovanni di Bicci's fortune and leader of the Medici party, Cosimo de' Medici was ambitious for real power. Under his shrewd guidance, the party strengthened its political influence and soon threatened the established control of the conservative faction.[1] Friction broke out into open hostility and, in September 1433, a predominantly conservative *Signoria* exiled Cosimo together with other leading members of the family. But the party survived. Cosimo bided his time, keeping in close contact with his supporters. When the *Signoria* was elected in September 1434 and it was found to contain no prominent conservatives, the Medici party were jubilant. Cosimo came back to Florence in October and his return marked a radical change in the political structure of the city. The old conservative régime was effectively wiped out: around ninety citizens, including Palla Strozzi, were exiled and a further eighty were excluded from holding political office. The Medici party, with Cosimo at its head, had taken control. Power was still vested in the *Signoria* and the other elected bodies of the republican system. Guild membership was still a prerequisite for office. But the office holders were dominated by Medici supporters and the power of the guilds declined significantly.

At the core of Cosimo's spectacular rise to power was the success of the Medici bank. Giovanni di Bicci had passed overall management of this highly profitable enterprise to his son in 1420 and it continued to prosper. Aware of the possibility of a coup against him, Cosimo had avoided the financial penalties of exile by transferring capital out of Florence in early 1433.[2] Profits for the years 1420–35 totalled 186,382 florins and rose to 290,791 florins during the period 1435–50.[3] Between 1420 and 1450 the bank opened branches in Ancona, Pisa, Geneva, Lyons, Basle, Avignon, Bruges and London.[4] Its massive resources had proved a useful tool in building up the Medici party in Florence, providing tangible advantages like preferential loans for his supporters.[5] The economic and political power that Cosimo wielded at home gave him international influence. Pope Martin V granted him the right to have a chapel in his palace, an exceptional honour for a private citizen and indicative of his importance in Italian politics.[6] Cosimo used his wealth to intervene profitably in the affairs of the peninsula. His offer to finance the Council of Florence provided Pope Eugenius IV with much-needed support against the Council of Basle (see Chapter 18) and himself with a substantial profit. In 1450 he played a key financial role in the coup that toppled the Visconti, Florence's old enemy in Milan, bringing Francesco Sforza to power and allowing him to open a branch of the Medici bank in the city in 1452.[7]

Cosimo had changed the mould of Florentine politics. His vast fortune made him one of the richest private individuals in Europe and he used it to provide propaganda for his cause. Before his exile, his behaviour had differed little from that of his contemporaries. A member of the Bankers' Guild, he had served on the *opera* in charge of the commission for Ghiberti's statue of *St Matthew* for Orsanmichele and had been one of the highest contributors of funds for its completion.[8] He had also undertaken the rebuilding in the 1420s of San Francesco al Bosco, a Franciscan convent outside Florence.[9]

The change after 1434 was dramatic. Building a new palace and embellishing his family chapel in his local church of San Lorenzo were conventional enough but his further involvement at San Lorenzo and his active participation in projects to rebuild and decorate other churches and religious institutions in the city went far beyond the traditional extent of patronage. The scope of Cosimo's patronage was unprecedented for a private citizen. Its scale rivalled that of the richest guilds and gave visual expression not only to his enormous wealth but also to his prime position in the structure of Florentine politics. His major projects (San Lorenzo, San Marco and the Medici palace) will be discussed below. He built and repaired family villas at Careggi, Caffagiuolo and Fiesole. He also played a prominent role in the reconstruction of the convent of Santa Croce after it had been damaged by fire in 1423, paying for new dormitories and a chapel for the novitiate in the 1440s.[10] He rebuilt the Badia at Fiesole, equipping it with a new church, convent buildings and an impressive library (begun 1456).[11] Vespasiano da Bisticci, the bookseller who supplied the manuscripts for the Badia's library, claimed that Cosimo employed forty-five scribes to copy two hundred religious texts in twenty-two months.[12] He also contributed funds to other religious projects, including the rebuilding programmes at Santissima Annunziata, Florence,[13] and San Girolamo, Fiesole,[14] and he commissioned Ghiberti to make a costly reliquary for the relics of Saints Protus, Hyacinth and Nemesius for Santa Maria degli Angeli.[15] Outside Florence, he donated funds to churches in Assisi, Volterra and Venice, as well as to projects in Paris and Jerusalem.[16]

Cosimo's grandson, Lorenzo, recorded that the family had spent 663,755 florins on buildings, charities and taxes over the years 1434-71.[17] It is impossible to assess how much of this was spent by Cosimo, but architecture was expensive and the costs involved in constructing his projects formed a substantial proportion of the total expenditure on building. Lorenzo's letter also throws light on the reasons behind Cosimo's patronage. His motives were not aesthetic. Expenditure on religious institutions, charities and taxes were all aspects of the obligations imposed on the rich in Florentine society. Easily the wealthiest citizen in mid-fifteenth-century Florence, Cosimo fulfilled his Christian duties assiduously. His projects were largely religious. But the proliferation of shields bearing the Medici coat of arms in churches throughout Florence made it clear that he was also giving visual expression to his economic and political pre-eminence in the city. When Francesco Barbaro tried to persuade Cosimo to donate funds to a Venetian monastery, he based his argument on the publicity and immortality that Cosimo could obtain in Venice in addition to what he already had achieved in Florence.[18] The motives behind Cosimo's massive programme of patronage were mixed but one of the most prominent was self-promotion.

Immediately after their return to Florence, Cosimo and his brother, Lorenzo, concentrated their attention on the sacristy built by their father at San Lorenzo.[19] Giovanni di Bicci's sarcophagus was placed underneath a circular marble vestment table in the centre of the room. Elaborate intarsia cupboards and pews were commissioned for the walls. Donatello made painted stucco reliefs of scenes from the life of St John the Evangelist for the pendentives below the dome and two sets of bronze doors. The high costs of bronze casting had previously restricted the material to guild projects and its use here was a conspicuous statement of the family's enormous wealth. In the little dome above the altar, an astronomical fresco depicted the position of the sun, moon and stars for 6 July 1439, the official day of Union between the Eastern and Western Churches signed at the Council of Florence.[20] This was an occasion of theological importance and a triumph for Pope Eugenius IV but, more significantly, it was also a major political coup for Cosimo and a source of considerable profit for the Medici bank. His choice of such an explicitly modern theme to commemorate this event was significant. Ceilings painted blue and studded with gold stars to represent Heaven were common in medieval churches. But this scientifically accurate depiction of a particular day's sky was unfamiliar and probably inspired by descriptions of similar vaults in classical texts.[21] Cosimo's choice gave expression to the fifteenth-century Florentine desire for verifiable fact and the growing interest in the culture of antiquity.

Cosimo's involvement with San Lorenzo soon extended beyond the sacristy. The church was essentially a parish project. The rebuilding of the choir and transepts to provide chapels for wealthy local families had been begun, with much enthusiasm, in 1418 (see Chapter 3). In March 1434, while the Medici were in exile, the residents of the district had been granted permission to demolish houses in order to create a piazza around the church.[22] By June 1434, they had decided to rebuild the nave of the old church in response to increased demand for chapel space.[23] But lack of funds had halted progress. In 1440, the parishioners, the Prior and the Chapter met to discuss how they were going to finance the completion of these ambitious plans.[24] As the minutes of the meeting note, the situation was an embarrassment. While the Medici sacristy was conspicuously complete, most of the new transept chapels were only partly built. The Prior and Chapter blamed heavy taxation for their inability to complete their part of the project, the main chapel. To solve the problem, they offered to concede their rights over it to whoever was prepared to finance its completion. It cannot have been much of a surprise when Cosimo agreed in 1442 to take over responsibility.[25] He was unquestionably the wealthiest and most influential man in the parish and his acquisition of the patronage rights over the main chapel was an acknowledged statement of his prestige in the area.

Reports of the laxity of the Sylvestrines at San Marco had prompted Pope Martin V to recommend their replacement by a Dominican reform group from San Domenico at Fiesole in 1418, but the Sylvestrines proved stubborn and it was only after their case had failed at the Council of Basle that Pope Eugenius IV finally forced them to move out in 1436.[26] Two of the key pleaders at the Council on behalf of the Dominicans were Cosimo and Lorenzo de' Medici[27] and the two brothers now took over the patronage of the new convent. Like Francesco Sforza in Milan (see Chapter 12), Cosimo exploited the political advantages of association with the powerful movement for Church reform and took up the patronage of three Observant groups: the Franciscans at San Francesco al Bosco, the Augustinian Canons at the Badia in Fiesole and the Dominicans at San Marco.[28] The support he provided for San Marco was considerable. His contributions towards the living expenses of the friars totalled about 1 florin a day, and he used his political influence in Florence and Rome to obtain tax exemptions and other financial benefits.[29] Above all, he rebuilt the Dominicans' convent, paid for a new choir for their church, donated an impressive collection of books bought from the humanist, Niccolò Niccoli,[30] and commissioned lavish furnishings that included liturgical vestments and the convent's great bell.[31]

The new convent buildings, attributed to Michelozzo, were unadorned and austere, in keeping with the highly spiritual ideals of this group of

Dominicans and giving visible expression to Cosimo's support for Church reform. Ionic capitals, derived from Tuscan Romanesque sources, identified the cloisters and the library as important parts of the complex but they were noticeably plainer than the decorative Corinthian capitals in the church.[32] One of the convent's friars, Fra Angelico, painted frescos in the cells upstairs. The modern visitor is invariably struck by the beauty and simplicity of his work, but these frescos had a strictly functional role. Each cell was decorated with a scene from the life of Christ incorporating the figure of a Dominican saint and provided the friar with a visual *aide-mémoire* to assist him in his prayers and meditations.[33] The distinctive gestures of the Dominican saints indicated one of the nine states of mind that were the principal aim of St Dominic's 'Nine Ways of Prayer': arms outstretched signified Ecstasy, a low bow meant Humility and flagellation was Penitence.

In the public area of the main chapel, Cosimo was able to give more overt expression to his commercial prowess and political achievement. In 1438 he bought the patronage rights to the main chapel from the previous owner for 500 florins.[34] Work began immediately and in 1443 the church was consecrated to St Mark and to the two patron saints of the Medici family, Cosmas and Damian.[35] The Medici presence was indeed conspicuous. The family coat of arms was displayed on the walls and above the elaborate Corinthian capitals in the apse.[36] The altarpiece, commissioned from Fra Angelico (*c.* 1438), clearly related to its context. Three Dominicans, St Dominic, St Peter Martyr and St Thomas Aquinas, stood on the Virgin's left. St Mark, on her right, indicated the text in his Gospel that recorded Christ's command to preach, one of the principal roles of the Dominican Order.[37] But it was the Medici saints, Cosmas and Damian, kneeling before the Virgin, who occupied the most prominent position in the altarpiece and it was their lives that were recounted in the predella panels beneath. Above all, the pictorial language gave expression to Cosimo's self-image. The altarpiece included many of the features of the new Florentine style developed during the first decades of the century (see Chapters 2 and 3). A carefully constructed perspective framework focused the viewer's attention on the Virgin's face. The fluted Corinthian pilasters of her throne were Tuscan Romanesque not Gothic and the deliberate attempt to balance gestures and attitudes reflected one of the principal themes of Alberti's treatise on painting (1435). But there was little evidence that Cosimo shared Alberti's republican dislike of the overt display of material wealth. The altarpiece displayed Cosimo's immense fortune in the lavish use of gold, flaunting extravagance in gilded brocades and the expensive Persian carpet. By the time the church was consecrated in 1443, Cosimo had acquired the rights to the choir in San Lorenzo as well. Ownership of one main chapel was unexceptional but ownership of two was unprecedented and provided unmistakable evidence of his enormous power and prestige in Florentine society.

Cosimo's only conspicuous private project was his new family palace, built almost next door to his father's palace on the via Larga. On Giovanni di Bicci's death, the old Palazzo Medici had become the joint property of Cosimo and his brother, Lorenzo. Lorenzo died in 1440 and, after Cosimo had moved out, the old palazzo became the sole property of Lorenzo's son, Pierfrancesco.[38] These two imposing Medici palaces situated between San Lorenzo and San Marco made a forceful visual statement about the family's importance in both the district and the city as a whole.

The building, begun in 1445,[39] was designed to be impressive. Ten bays long (it was lengthened to seventeen in the seventeenth century), it was slightly larger than most contemporary palaces.[40] Cosimo covered the entire façade with dressed stone, a conspicuously expensive feature and one that it shared with the Palazzo della Signoria.[41] Like other palaces of the period, the Palazzo Medici proclaimed its owner's membership of the city's ruling élite by drawing on the style of the Palazzo della Signoria. But there were some significant differences. The Palazzo Medici was topped by a classical cornice not medieval battlements and its interior courtyard was enclosed by columns with elaborate Composite capitals instead of the plainer octagonal piers. There are good grounds for seeing the Palazzo Medici as a modern version of the Palazzo della Signoria,[42] suggesting the tempting parallel between old and new government. Above all, the Palazzo Medici proclaimed its ownership. The family coat of arms was an integral feature of the decoration, carved into roundels in the windows, in the court-yard and adorning the metal rings on the façade. (On the embellishment of the palace, see Chapter 5).

Cosimo's enormous expenditure was intended to be noticed and it was, attracting attention from his contemporaries on a scale unprecedented for the patronage of a private individual. His projects were seen as a measure of his immense wealth and power and earned him lavish praise in the poetry and prose that eulogized his achievements. This praise should be seen in a political, rather than an aesthetic, context; but the ways in which the buildings and their contents were described tell us much about attitudes to art and money in mid-fifteenth-century Italy. While on an official visit to Florence in 1459, the 15-year-old son of Francesco Sforza, Duke of Milan, Galeazzo Maria was impressed with the scale and luxury of the Palazzo Medici, mentioning specifically the size and number of rooms and the items which had obviously cost money, such as Cosimo's tapestries, his priceless silver and the workmanship of his wooden chests.[43] One of the Milanese courtiers present sent Francesco Sforza a more detailed account of the palace mentioning the imaginative and flattering arrangement of the Medici and Sforza coats of arms that had been planted in grass in the palace gardens to honour the occasion.[44]

It is a striking fact that contemporary descriptions of Cosimo's building projects make no reference to anyone we can readily identify as the designer. The tradition that Michelozzo was Cosimo's preferred architect and responsible for the Palazzo Medici, the villas at Careggi, Fiesole and Caffagiuolo, San Marco, San Francesco al Bosco and the novices' quarters at Santa Croce dates from the early sixteenth century and was popularized in Vasari's *Lives of the Artists*. Mid-fifteenth-century accounts of Cosimo's patronage rarely mention the name of any craftsman. One exception is that of Filarete, a Florentine sculptor working for the Sforzas in Milan: he added to his architectural treatise (c. 1464) a chapter devoted entirely to the projects of Cosimo and his son, Piero (see Chapter 12). Filarete referred to Donatello's bronze doors in the sacristy of San Lorenzo and described Brunelleschi as its architect;[45] but the only designer he mentioned in connection with Cosimo's building projects was Cosimo himself, attributing the design of the Badia at Fiesole to Cosimo and the Abbot, Timoteo Maffei.[46] In another contemporary description of the Badia, Alberto Avogadro was more specific, describing how Cosimo explained his ideas for the building to a master who then carried them out.[47] This account tallies with what we know about fifteenth-century architectural practice (see, for example, Chapter 5). Like the guilds, a private patron occupied a far more central position in the realization of his projects than his modern counterpart. And given the importance of his projects to the promotion of his own image, there is every likelihood that a patron like Cosimo was indeed one of the principal creative forces behind his projects.[48]

Above all, it was Cosimo's financial contribution that formed the focus of the praise by his contemporaries. Scale and quality were applauded. Expensive materials like gold, ultramarine, bronze and marble were listed comprehensively. Wood and brick were ignored. One anonymous author noted that Cosimo had spent 18,000 florins on the sacristy at San Lorenzo and 20,000 florins on the library at San Marco.[49] These figures bore little relationship to the facts; but exaggeration, an accepted device of classical rhetoric, was considered an appropriate way to praise excellence. Avogadro adopted the same device when he transformed the Badia at Fiesole into an architectural fantasy of alabaster, porphyry and serpentine.[50] Even Filarete's more prosaic account of Cosimo's patronage made expense the prime criterion for merit. In his description of San Marco, Filarete listed all that Cosimo built and, while he ignored the frescos and altarpieces commissioned for the convent, he did mention the elaborate intarsia wardrobes for the sacristy, rich hangings and chalices for the church and the priceless collection of books for the library.[51] At San Lorenzo he referred to columns cut from one piece of stone, to splendid vestments for the priests, to the marble tombs of Cosimo's family in the sacristy and to the bronze doors.[52] His prime concern was to outline the scale of Cosimo's patronage to show that the huge sums involved had been well spent.

But the response to Cosimo's patronage, like his political position, was by no means always so positive. Pope Pius II praised the quality of Cosimo's buildings but implied that they had generated envy.[53] Certainly, the scale of his patronage transgressed the republican dislike of excessive displays of personal wealth. The appearance of the Medici coat of arms in so many of Florence's religious buildings offended the Church. Archbishop Antoninus's attack on those who preferred to use their religious donations to pay for extravagant chapel decoration rather than to help the poor[54] may not have been directed at Cosimo, but the underlying accusation of spending to gain personal glory rather than spiritual favour undoubtedly applied to him.

It was in response to such critics that Timoteo Maffei, the Abbot of the Badia at Fiesole, wrote a defence of Cosimo's expenditure, citing the classical virtue of magnificence outlined in Aristotle's *Ethics* and given tacit Church approval by the thirteenth-century Dominican theologian, St Thomas Aquinas,[55] on the grounds that the rich should spend appropriately, according to their wealth and position. Presented in the classical format of a dialogue, Maffei's defence should be seen in the context of the early fifteenth-century humanist search for a moral framework outside the strict confines of the Christian tradition. Maffei justified the ubiquitous coats of arms on the grounds that their display would encourage others to emulate Cosimo. Now that Cosimo had effectively broken down the old religious and republican barriers against conspicuous expenditure, this is exactly what the next generation of Florentine patrons did.

5

For God, Their City and Themselves

Cosimo's return from exile in 1434 had established the Medici party as the ruling force in Florentine politics, a situation that was to last until 1494. Leadership of the party passed from father to son: Cosimo (d. 1464) was succeeded by Piero (d. 1469), Lorenzo (d. 1492) and Piero, who was expelled from Florence in 1494. From 1434 the city was governed by an élite of Medici supporters, members of the various branches of the family, men related to the family by marriage, partners in the Medici bank and families who owed their wealth and position to judicious support of the Medici during their rise to power. At the top of this network, Cosimo, Piero and Lorenzo were, in effect, successively heads of state. But they were keen to emphasize that this was not dynastic rule. Power remained vested in the *Signoria* and the other committees of the republican system, although the new Council of the Hundred set up in 1458 limited the power of the old regime.[1] Opposition to Medici control was marginalized and many dissenters were exiled. One particularly serious attack was made on Lorenzo and his brother during mass in the Duomo on Easter Sunday 1478 by members of the Pazzi family and their supporters, aided by the Papacy. Lorenzo escaped but Giuliano was killed. The ringleaders were executed and the event sparked off war with Rome (1478–80). Lorenzo now tightened his grip on government, founding the Council of Seventy (1480), whose members all belonged to the inner Medici circle. His own behaviour increasingly took on the appearance of a prince, the head of a new aristocracy, that dominated the economic, political and cultural life of the city.

Nowhere was the nature of the new regime better expressed than in the renovations carried out to the Palazzo della Signoria. These works, including the remodelling of the courtyard (1454) and redecoration of the two halls on the second floor (1482), were supervised by an annually elected *opera*. Its replacement in 1487 by a permanent committee, dominated by Lorenzo de' Medici and other members of the Council of Seventy, was evidence of the way in which power was increasingly concentrated in the hands of the Medici party.[2] The decision to remodel the courtyard was not very surprising, but the choice of design was significant. The *opera's* decision to hide the five storeys of the interior behind a new three-storey façade, embellished with roundels and evenly-spaced windows that had no relationship to the interior layout, created a courtyard that bore a striking resemblance to the palaces of private citizens, above all, to the Palazzo Medici.[3] The decorative scheme for the Sala dei Gigli, remodelled for the Council of Seventy, was even more telling. In good Florentine republican tradition, the fresco depicted the city's two main patron saints, St Zenobius and St John the Baptist, and six heroes of republican Rome. But the inscriptions beneath were carefully chosen not only to stress the virtues of a republic but also to encourage the patriotic acceptance of domination by an individual for the good of the country.[4]

It was the élite of Medici supporters that was principally responsible for the art and architecture commissioned in Florence during the second half of the fifteenth century. Changes in the political structure were reflected in new patterns of patronage. Corporate patronage began to decline as private citizens followed Cosimo de' Medici and gave expression to their own family status, commercial success and political prestige. The result was a spectacular building boom that had a major impact on the appearance of Florence. Streets of shops became lined with the houses of wealthy families and as many as a hundred palaces were built or remodelled.[5] Many churches were completely reconstructed and others were transformed by new chapels, cloisters, tabernacles, pulpits, altarpieces and fresco cycles, all proclaiming the identity of their patrons with coats of arms, portraits or inscriptions. Piero and Lorenzo de' Medici played central roles in this fever of activity, but there were many others involved and a large proportion of them had close ties with the Medici party.

Cosimo's example had broken down the moral restraints of the beginning of the century that inhibited personal ostentation and they faded into the background (cf. Venice, see Chapter 10). Wealth could now be proudly displayed. Alessandra Strozzi, describing the prosperity of her future son-in-law, boasted that her daughter would be wearing more than 400 florins when she went out.[6] Extravagance became the order of the day. In his biography of Cosimo, written in the 1480s, Vespasiano included a description of Cosimo complaining that his builders were not spending enough.[7] Whatever the truth of the story, Vespasiano manifestly believed that conspicuous expenditure was an essential component of prestige. Religious belief and civic pride remained central motives behind patronage but, in the more permissive atmosphere of the 1470s, the banker Giovanni Rucellai could write that his enormous outlay on architecture reflected not only his desire to honour God and his city but also to perpetuate the memory of himself.[8]

The literature of ancient Greece and Rome, which had inspired Bruni and his contemporaries with the republican ideals of civic duty and had provided a justification for Cosimo's expenditure, also contained other messages and ones that offered exciting new models for patrons who already saw themselves as the political heirs of republican Rome. These texts conjured up a vision of an élite of private citizens, wealthy, cultured and politically active, who lived in grand palaces in town and beautiful villas in the country, surrounded by their collections of paintings, sculpture and precious objects. Above all, the culture of antiquity provided the Florentines with a new language for the expression of their increasingly aristocratic aspirations and pride in their own and their city's achievements. Brunelleschi's contemporaries had praised him for his outstanding technical abilities, but Antonio Manetti writing in the 1480s claimed that Brunelleschi had revived classical architecture.[9] Taken at face value, this is misleading; Brunelleschi showed far more interest in Tuscan Romanesque than in antique prototypes. What Manetti's claim illustrates is the new and central importance of classical culture in late fifteenth-century Florence for the creation of an image of cultural superiority as propaganda for the city's power and prestige.[10]

The influential role played, directly and indirectly, by the Medici in the embellishment of their city, increasing preferences for elaboration and, above all, the adoption of classical style as the hallmark of the élite, form the key themes in the development of the arts in late fifteenth-century Florence.

The boom in palace building was financed mainly by members of families established in the political arena,[11] whose commercial success gave them the opportunity and desire to enhance their family status and personal prestige. Many were bankers, like Tommaso Spinelli, who had prospered through links with the papal court in Rome.[12] Two other bankers, Giovanni Rucellai and Filippo Strozzi, had both suffered through their association with Palla Strozzi (who had been exiled in 1434) and had unusually compelling motives for building palaces (see below). Members of new families also had a powerful incentive to proclaim their presence in the city, such as Bartolommeo della Scala, a miller's son who worked for Pierfrancesco de' Medici and was head of the Florentine Chancery from 1465 to 1497, Giovanni di Bono Boni, whose family had only recently acquired political acceptability, or Francesco Nori, an employee of the Medici bank who also owed his position to Medici favour.[13]

These palaces were built by men who had made fortunes in shrewd commercial dealing and cost a sizeable proportion of their patrons' capital. It is a striking fact that they were investments that brought no financial return and, moreover, that this boom coincided with a general lack of confidence in the economic fortunes of the city.[14] Resale and rental values bore little relationship to the cost of construction. Francesco Nori paid 2,600 florins for a substantial palace, built at the beginning of the century, which he then enlarged.[15] Building was expensive and a new palace would have cost him much more. The largest palace in fifteenth-century Florence cost its patron, Filippo Strozzi, nearly 40,000 florins, almost half his estimated income for twelve years from 1471 to 1483.[16] Rucellai spent over 1,500 florins just acquiring the site for his palace.[17] Many patrons were unable to complete their palaces and some, like Giovanni di Bono Boni, went bankrupt in the process.[18] However, these palaces were a very real investment in family honour, an issue of prime importance in fifteenth-century Florence.[19] Filippo Strozzi's plan to build a new palace in the heartland of traditional Strozzi property was greeted with considerable excitement by his relatives.[20] Giovanni Rucellai wrote that men do two important things in life: procreate and build.[21] The two acts are not unrelated; both confer a form of immortality. These Florentine palaces embodied not only the financial, political and social achievements of their founders but also their dynastic ambitions. Complex wills with elaborate arrangements for inheritance were designed to ensure that the palaces remained in the family[22] and all of them were embellished, wherever possible, with the family coat of arms.

With the notable exception of the Palazzo Rucellai (see below), the façades of these palaces differed little in style from those of the early part of the century. This was not surprising. Tradition was the key to respectability in Florentine society. Francesco Nori's extension to his palace continued the design of the earlier building and one of the most old-fashioned palaces of the period (begun 1464) was built with the new money of Giovanni Boni.[23] More common were façades that followed the style of the Palazzo Medici, traditional in format but embellished with the classical details that identified them as the homes of members of the ruling élite. Filippo Strozzi decorated his palace façade (fig. 12) with classically inspired iron torch-holders and a heavy cornice. When his brother-in-law, Marco Parenti, enlarged and renovated his old palace, he commissioned new all' antica doors and windows.[24] It was in interior courtyards that the new fashion for antiquity was most readily apparent. The sgraffito swags that ornamented the courtyard of the Palazzo Medici were copied by many patrons, including Tommaso Spinelli in the 1450s.[25] Classical columns and capitals were all the fashion, though the arches they supported reflected a reliance on Tuscan tradition. Few patrons went as far as Bartolommeo della Scala who built a barrel-vaulted loggia with arches supported by Doric piers and decorated with sculptural panels inspired by reliefs on Roman triumphal arches.[26]

12.   Palazzo Strozzi, Florence, begun 1489

Rucellai's palace (fig. 13) has caused much controversy amongst art historians.[27] The first and only fifteenth-century Florentine palace façade to adopt the classical orders, it has an important place in architectural history. And it incorporated other unusual classical details, notably the diamond patterning on the basement which derived from the *opus reticulatum* of Roman brick construction. It is this impressive use of classical details that lies behind the façade's traditional attribution to Alberti. Not surprisingly, this innovatory design had little impact on tradition-bound Florentines. The façade bears a striking resemblance to the Palazzo Piccolomini in Pienza, started in 1459 by Pope Pius II, and a distinctive masonry technique, exceptional in Florence, appears on both buildings.[28] Did the Pope copy Rucellai or was it Rucellai who copied the Pope? Unfortunately the evidence is inconclusive. The nature of the relationship between these palaces depends on dates and, despite the abundant information we have on the purchase of the properties that make up the palace, we can only guess when Rucellai's façade was begun.[29]

Much of what we know about the motives behind palace building and the process of design and construction in fifteenth-century Florence comes from the surviving personal records of Giovanni Rucellai and the account ledgers of Filippo Strozzi. These two patrons merit closer attention.

When Giovanni Rucellai looked back over his life up to 1473 he listed

13. Palazzo Rucellai, Florence, begun *c.* 1451

with pride first his health (he was 70 years old) and then his spectacular success as a banker and wool merchant.[30] As the prime indicators of the size of his fortune, he wrote that he had paid 60,000 florins in taxes, 10,000 florins in dowries and had spent considerable sums on building. The only non-architectural item he included was a gold brocade hanging for San

Pancrazio and he recorded its cost, more than 1,000 florins. He reflected that the making and spending of money were two of the greatest pleasures that man has in this world, but he could not decide which he preferred most!

Both Rucellai and Strozzi were immensely wealthy. In the *catasto* returns of 1457, Giovanni Rucellai's net assets of 19,406 florins made him the richest man in the quarter of Santa Maria Novella and third in the city after Cosimo de' Medici and the manager of the Medici bank.[31] Strozzi's income over the years 1471–83 has been estimated at 90,179 florins and his total estate was worth 116,000 florins at his death in 1491.[32] Both men came from well-established Florentine families, but, through their association with Palla Strozzi, both were also politically suspect. Rucellai, Palla Strozzi's son-in-law, avoided exile in 1434 but was excluded from government office. Filippo, a cousin of Palla, had been exiled (aged 6) along with many of his kinsmen. Both returned to favour through the influence of the Medici. Rucellai's fortune, his influential friends and relations and, above all, his determination to ally himself with the Medici party led to the betrothal in 1461 of his son to Piero de' Medici's daughter.[33] This link cemented his return to political respectability and he was elected to the *Signoria* in 1463.[34] Filippo, in exile in Naples, used his fortune and his friendship with King Ferrante to prove himself a useful intermediary between the King and Lorenzo de' Medici and he was granted an amnesty by Lorenzo in 1466.[35]

Rucellai and Strozzi were impressive patrons, embarking on major building programmes that were manifestly designed to give visual expression to their presence in the city. In addition to his palace, Rucellai built a family loggia opposite, the façade of Santa Maria Novella (see below), his burial chapel in San Pancrazio and villas at Quaracchi and Poggio a Caiano.[36] Strozzi's projects included his chapel in Santa Maria Novella (see below), villas on his properties at Santuccio, Capalle and Maglio and an oratory at Lecceto.[37] Both patrons chose distinctive, though very different, ways of making their palaces individual. Rucellai, significantly, began his building programme while he was still politically suspect and went further than any of his contemporaries in his conspicuous use of the classical language of architecture. Evidence for his motives is suggested by the fact that he made a point of recording Cicero's account of the political honour and general esteem that could accrue from a fine palace.[38] Strozzi, who remained outside the political arena and had a more compelling motive for restoring his family honour, built the largest palace in fifteenth-century Florence but also one of the most traditional.

Acquiring the site for a new palace in the built-up centre of Florence required both time and patience. Tommaso Spinelli had to petition the government and the Church to buy property for his palace[39] and

Francesco Nori benefited from the influential intervention of Lorenzo de' Medici.[40] Rucellai spent over thirty years buying up seven houses adjoining his old family property, beginning in 1428 when he acquired the first.[41] The new palace was begun by 1451 (when his tax returns list only one house) and comprised the five left-hand bays of the present façade. The interior loggia was complete by 1452 and in 1458 Rucellai acquired the property to the right side of his new palace. That he intended to buy the adjoining house and failed to do so is clear in the abrupt termination of the masonry work on the far right-hand edge of the façade.

The ledgers of the Strozzi palace (fig. 12) illuminate the central role played by the patron in the construction of his project.[42] Like the *opera* in charge of a public building site, Strozzi took all the major decisions on the form of his palace, hired his workforce and drew up contracts with suppliers of stone, wood, ironware and other materials. The ledgers also reveal the practical impact of Filippo's determination to complete the building as quickly as possible: the elaborate foundation ceremony held on 6 August 1489 (a date specially chosen by astrologers), the costs of transporting stone from quarries to the site, the wages paid to a workforce that, at its height, reached over one hundred, the amounts spent on each of the capitals in the courtyard, or on the elegant iron torch-holders and rings on the façade, emblazoned with the Strozzi crescent moons.

But perhaps the most significant fact to emerge from the Strozzi ledgers is that there is no mention of anybody identifiable as the architect. The rigid distinctions we apply to the roles of patron, designer and supervisor were not so precise in Renaissance Florence.[43] Payments were made to Giuliano da Sangallo for a wooden model (which still exists), but its lack of detail made it clearly inadequate as a blueprint for building and Sangallo had no further connection with the palace.[44] The supervisor of the project was Cronaca. Employed over six months after the building had been started, he oversaw the quarrying, transport and cutting of building stone as well as the design of details. He has been identified as the architect-in-charge but there is no evidence to suggest that he was the overall designer.[45] In the sixteenth century Vasari attributed the design to Benedetto da Maiano, but research in the archives has convincingly limited his role to the supply of two stone corbels and models for ironwork.[46] Rucellai's memoirs likewise offer little help to the art historian in search of his architect. It may come as a surprise to find that the patron of such an important project should fail to mention its innovatory design, or Alberti's role as architect, or even its links with the Palazzo Piccolomini. In fifteenth-century Florence it was the patron who was seen as the principal force behind his project. He was also the central figure in its realization. In the light of the evidence, it is difficult to deny either Strozzi or Rucellai significant roles in the design of their palaces.

The growing taste for extravagance was reflected in palace interiors. Inventories of the period show more luxurious furnishings and greater quantities of pictorial decoration than there had been in the first half of the century. The paintings, frescos and sculpture that decorated the palaces of wealthy Florentine merchants reflected not only their religious beliefs but also their secular interests in contemporary Florence and the culture of antiquity.

Giovanni Rucellai, like many other Florentines, was conscious that he was living at an exceptional time in the history of his city. Amongst Florence's claims to greatness, he boasted the quantity and quality of her artists and, more prosaically, the fact that her citizens had never before been so well dressed.[47] Of his own collection of paintings and sculpture, he wrote that he owned works by the best Florentine artists and listed them by name.[48] Pride in the city's cultural heritage had been central to patronage in the first decades of the fifteenth century but the literature of antiquity offered new models to promote the Florentine achievement.

Cicero's descriptions of his sculpture collection, the Elder Pliny's analysis of classical art in his *Natural History* and the Younger Pliny's account of his villa at Laurentium[49] portrayed a new type of collector, one for whom the possession of beautiful works of art gave aesthetic pleasure quite separate from any religious function or civic obligation. Implicit in their writings was the concept of a work of art as the creation of its artist and great art as the hallmark of a great civilization. The idea of artistic appreciation was largely alien to the Christian culture of fifteenth-century Europe; but it had a significant impact in Florence, where it stimulated the development of art criticism with a marked Florentine bias. The humanists Cristoforo Landino and Alamanno Rinuccini were inspired, above all by the Elder Pliny's analysis, to assess the artists of their own time in terms of the characteristics of individual styles.[50] Pliny was extolling the greatness of a past age, embodied in its art, as a contrast to the decadence of his own. Landino and Rinuccini adapted his method, using contemporary Florentine painting to provide evidence of the greatness of their own culture and to show that it equalled, even surpassed, the achievements of antiquity. The new status accorded to Florentine painters was plainly visible in the Duomo, where Lorenzo de' Medici organized monuments for Giotto and Filippo Lippi,[51] an honour previously reserved for military and literary excellence.

The paintings and sculpture commissioned by wealthy Florentine merchants for the decoration of their palaces remained overwhelmingly Christian in subject. In an inventory of 1499 of the old Palazzo Medici listing the possessions of Lorenzo and Giovanni, sons of Pierfrancesco de' Medici, well over half of the works of art were religious.[52] But new fashions stimulated the development of new types. The growing demand for portraiture reflected patrons' interest in themselves and their success. Immortality could be achieved through building and seen in paint or marble. Inspired by the example of the patricians of republican Rome, some patrons commissioned portrait busts of themselves for their palaces.[53] Antonio Rossellino made busts of Francesco Sassetti (1464), the general manager of the Medici bank, and of the humanist Matteo Palmieri (1468) (fig. 14). Benedetto da Maiano was commissioned to make portrait busts of the bankers Pietro Mellini (1474) and Filippo Strozzi (undated). Libraries of classical texts became far more common but portrait medals, with their overtly imperial overtones, were much less popular in Florence than at the courts of Mantua or Ferrara (see Chapters 15 and 16). The literature of ancient Greece and Rome provided new themes for art. Pierfrancesco de' Medici's sons owned paintings of the Three Graces and of Bacchus as well as two of the most famous images of the Renaissance, Botticelli's *Primavera* and *Minerva and the Centaur*.[54] There is some evidence that the sons also

14.   Antonio Rossellino, *Matteo Palmieri*. Florence, Museo Nazionale, dated 1468

15.   Botticelli, *Birth of Venus*. Florence, Uffizi, *c.* 1482

owned Botticelli's other great mythological scene, the *Birth of Venus* (fig. 15). These paintings have long baffled art historians and, although the precise sources for their complex imagery remain controversial, there is general agreement that the pictures reflect the ideas of the Neo-Platonic circle of humanists around Ficino.[55]

Unquestionably the most impressive palace in fifteenth-century Florence was the Palazzo Medici. Lack of documentation has made it difficult to be certain about who commissioned the many works of art that embellished the palace but there is a general consensus that Cosimo undertook the construction of the building and Piero was largely responsible for its decoration. Piero's tastes were for opulence. The fresco cycle in the palace chapel, Gozzoli's *Procession of the Magi* (1459) (fig. 16), showed little interest in the new pictorial language developed in the early years of the century (see Chapter 3). As Cosimo had discovered, a plain and moral style was an inadequate vehicle for displaying Medici prestige and Gozzoli's frescos were set in an idealized landscape and embellished with gilded detail. Significantly, the cycle bore a striking resemblance to Gentile da Fabriano's *Adoration of the Magi*, commissioned more than thirty years earlier

16.   Gozzoli, *Procession of the Magi* (detail). Florence, Palazzo Medici, 1459

(see Chapter 3) by Palla Strozzi, whose immense wealth and respected position in pre-Medici Florence made him the prime target of Cosimo's policy to exile all potential rivals on his return to the city in 1434. Piero's choice of theme and style can be seen as a comment on Strozzi's downfall and the rise of Medici power; but it also carried other political resonances. The Medici were prominent members of the prestigious Company of the Magi, whose charitable roles included a lavish re-enactment of the arrival of the Three Kings on the Feast of the Epiphany.[56] In the fresco cycle Piero and his father were portrayed in the retinue of the youngest King, whose harness was decorated with the Medici coat of arms. Above all, Piero's choice of this traditional and courtly image made clear his aspirations to princely prestige on a par with that of the rulers of the Italian courts and to recognition of his *de facto* position as head of state.

The main courtyard, the principal reception area of the palace, was an unmistakable statement of Medici wealth and status. The frieze was ornamented with the family coat of arms and stucco copies of valuable antique cameos in the Medici collection. Its centrepiece was a statue of *David* (fig. 17) commissioned by Cosimo from Donatello,[57] who also made a statue of *Judith and Holofernes* for the other courtyard. They were the first large bronze statues to be commissioned by a private individual in Florence. Bronze was expensive and its use by the major guilds for their

17.   Donatello, *David*. Florence, Museo Nazionale, *c*. 1430

statues on Orsanmichele had been deliberately designed to display their power. That the Medici could now afford bronze held a message that would not have been lost on the image-conscious Florentines. But the statues also carried other, more subtle messages. The *David* was the first male nude since antiquity and other classical associations included a triumphal chariot carved on Goliath's helmet, reflecting the growing importance of classical culture in fifteenth-century Florence. Above all, they had strong political overtones which were reinforced by inscriptions. Both David's victory over Goliath and Judith's over Holofernes carried a clear message of freedom from oppression. David, in particular, was a well-established and popular civic image of Florentine republicanism.[58] Another old symbol of the city's victory over tyranny was Hercules, the pagan embodiment of moral strength, and Piero chose to decorate the main reception room in the Palazzo Medici with canvases of the *Labours of Hercules (c.* 1460), commissioned from Antonio Pollaiuolo.[59] The choice of these two traditional images of Florentine liberty emphasized that the Medici were upholders of the republic; but the statues also suggest that the family was increasingly identifying itself with the state.

The inventory of the Medici palace, made in 1492 after the death of Lorenzo,[60] revealed an amazing collection of furniture, tapestries, sculpture and paintings, largely commissioned by Piero and Lorenzo, reflecting not only the current taste for antiquity but also their interest in the contemporary world. Their library of manuscripts of classical and Christian texts was outstanding. Piero's portrait bust (1453) by Mino da Fiesole (fig. 18) is the earliest dated fifteenth-century bust and Piero also owned a bronze statuette by Filarete of the Roman equestrian monument to Emperor Marcus Aurelius that was one of the first *all' antica* copies made in the Renaissance.[61] Amongst the paintings recorded in the inventory were Uccello's three scenes of the *Battle of San Romano (c.* 1455) (fig. 19), depicting a Florentine victory over the Sienese in 1432, as well as his *Judgement of Paris*, four representations of the Magi,[62] portraits of Federigo da Montefeltro, Duke of Urbino, and of Galeazzo Sforza, Duke of Milan, and three canvases of the *Labours of Hercules (c.* 1460) by Pollaiuolo. The Medici did not have the same status as their aristocratic contemporaries who ruled in Urbino or Milan; but they were rich enough to acquire the conspicuously expensive trappings of princely prestige, and the inventory recorded tapestries of hunts and tournaments imported from northern Europe, religious mosaics, antique sculpture and a gilded copper clock. Above all, the inventory listed the Medici collection of antique sculpture, cameos, cups and vases of semi-precious stones, gems, medals and coins.[63] One of the most precious items listed was the Tazza Farnese, a Hellenistic sardonyx cameo carved with an allegory of Cleopatra I valued at 10,000

18.   Mino da Fiesole, *Piero de' Medici*. Florence, Museo Nazionale, 1453

florins and acquired by Lorenzo from Pope Sixtus IV, when the latter sold off the possessions of his predecessor, Paul II. Piero and Lorenzo amassed one of the most impressive collections of the period and it provided very real evidence of their enormous wealth and prestige.

Rural property had long featured in the investment portfolios of wealthy Florentine merchants. A good way of balancing assets in more speculative commercial ventures, a farm also produced wine, oil, fruit and vegetables for private consumption in town. But the classical concept of the villa as a retreat from the demands of urban life, where one could appreciate the beauties of nature and indulge in leisurely intellectual and cultural pursuits, inspired these hard-headed businessmen with ideas of patrician grandeur. Alberti's treatise *de re aedificatoria* made a clear distinction between the practical requirements of a farmhouse and the more pleasurable function of a patrician's villa.[64] Lorenzo de' Medici's villa at Careggi became the meeting place for humanists who, in emulation of Plato's Academy in Athens, gathered to discuss philosophical issues arising out of their study of Plato, Neo-Platonic and other classical authors and Christian theology.[65] By the end of the fifteenth century, an elegant villa had become an essential feature of the property of a rich Florentine. Francesco Sassetti was immensely proud of his villa at Montughi, writing

19. Uccello, *Battle of San Romano*. Florence, Uffizi, *c.* 1455

that its beauty, and cost, had brought fame to himself and his family.[66] Like Pliny's villa at Laurentium, the garden of Giovanni Rucellai's villa at Quaracchi was ornamented with topiary hedges cut to resemble centaurs, philosophers and other appropriate subjects.[67] Above all, the classical language of architecture had a major impact on design.

Traditionally, country properties had been solid and heavily castellated, designed to withstand attack and to provide an image of physical strength. But this image was manifestly unsuitable for the patrician villa. The design chosen by Lorenzo de' Medici for his villa at Poggio a Caiano (fig. 20) was a reflection of the need to find a new language to express this change in function. Poggio a Caiano, once the property of Palla Strozzi, had been acquired by Giovanni Rucellai, but the collapse of his business empire had forced him to sell it in 1474 to Lorenzo.[68] Lorenzo's remodelling of the villa (c. 1485) was a major landmark in architectural history. Its new façade was open, with an arcade surrounding the base of the building and on the main floor an Ionic portico reached by two flights of (originally straight) steps. The pediment, decorated with an all' antica frieze, prominently displayed the Medici coat of arms. Lorenzo's interest in architecture is well-documented. He had Alberti's de re aedificatoria read to him[69] and he requested drawings of Federigo da Montefeltro's palace in Urbino and

20.   Villa Medici, Poggio a Caiano, mid-1480s

of San Sebastiano in Mantua.[70] The villa of Poggio a Caiano was built under the supervision of Giuliano da Sangallo and its design is generally attributed to him. But it is probable that Lorenzo, like his grandfather Cosimo (see Chapter 4), explained what he wanted to Sangallo, who then carried out the plan. The original idea of applying a temple front to the façade of the villa was far more likely to have been the product of Lorenzo's knowledge of classical and modern design and of his desire to construct a villa that gave unmistakable visual expression to his patrician status.

Despite the growing importance of patronage in the context of private palaces and villas, it was in the public domain of religious works that patrons most conspicuously flaunted their wealth and prestige. Coats of arms, portraits of donors and inscriptions proliferated. Freed from the moral curbs that had imposed some control on personal display in the early 1400s, patrons now proclaimed their status in family chapels and altars, cloisters and other buildings without restraint. And it was in the rebuilding and decoration of Florence's churches that Medici influence and involvement was most readily apparent.

The pictorial language developed in the early fifteenth century changed in response to new demands. In increasingly elaborate settings, the pagan culture of ancient Rome was adapted to the Christian context, providing models for architectural design, decorative details and figure styles. Some Florentines developed the taste for Flemish art (especially expensive tapestries) that was so popular at the Italian courts and provided evidence of their aristocratic aspirations. Tommaso Portinari, manager of the Bruges branch of the Medici bank, commissioned a Flemish artist, Hugo van der Goes, to paint the *Adoration of the Shepherds* for his family chapel in Sant' Egidio.[71] But art in late fifteenth-century Florence was overwhelmingly Florentine. Recognizably Florentine settings proclaimed civic pride and reinforced the reality of Christian legend. But the courtly elegance of Ghiberti and the solid austerity of Masaccio gave way to the materialistic, bourgeois world of the rich Florentine merchant as these patrons also sought to express their own commercial, political and social achievements. Ghirlandaio's *Confirmation of the Franciscan Rule*, commissioned by the manager of the Medici bank, Francesco Sassetti, as part of the fresco cycle for his chapel in Santa Trinità (fig. 21), was set in front of the Palazzo della Signoria and the scene included a portrait of Lorenzo de' Medici standing beside the donor. Tanai de' Nerli asserted his piety in portraits of himself and his wife as donors in the *Virgin and Child with Saints* (1494) that he commissioned from Filippino Lippi for the altar of his chapel in Santo Spirito; but he also recorded his pride in taking part in a mission to negotiate with Charles VIII of France by having himself portrayed in the background dressed in ambassadorial robes with his wife and child in front

21. Ghirlandaio, *Adoration of the Shepherds*. Florence, Santa Trinità, 1485

of the family palace near the Porta San Frediano.[72]

Cosimo de' Medici had played a leading role in rebuilding the convent of Santa Croce after a fire in 1423, financing quarters for the novices. But there were also other patrons involved. Like Cosimo, Andrea di Guglielmino Pazzi was not a resident in the quarter of Santa Croce. A staunch member of the Medici party, he commissioned a new chapter house in the cloisters, and now known as the Pazzi chapel (begun after 1442).[73] With its dome resting on pendentives decorated with roundels and walls articulated with fluted Corinthian pilasters, this chapel bore a striking resemblance to the Medici sacristy at San Lorenzo (see Chapter 3). Both buildings are traditionally attributed to Brunelleschi and Pazzi's choice of style underlined his association with the Medici party. There is some evidence to suggest that another non-resident, Castello Quaratesi, proposed a more conspicuous addition to the church when he offered to pay for a marble façade in the 1440s, but the project failed because he was refused permission to display his coat of arms.[74] Amongst the local residents building and decorating chapels in the church was Alamanno di Jacopo Salviati, a prominent member of the Medici party and brother-in-law of Pazzi.[75] Pietro Mellini, a wealthy banker, commissioned a marble pulpit (1472–6) from Benedetto da Maiano for the nave. Another banker, Tommaso Spinelli, whose fortune has been estimated at around 50,000 florins, left funds in his will for the construction of a hospital at Santa Croce. During his lifetime, he spent 6,921 florins at Santa Croce, 97 florins for his tomb by the family chapel inside the church and the rest on new cloisters for the convent, ornamented with his coat of arms, frescos of *Doubting Thomas* and *St Christopher* at the entrance to the convent and ornate intarsia wardrobes for the sacristy.[76]

After Cosimo's purchase of the rights to the main chapel in San Lorenzo, the ambitious programme to rebuild the church continued steadily. The unfinished transept chapels were completed and a new nave flanked by chapels was started in 1446.[77] Typical of the period, the piecemeal process of design and construction undermines the traditional attribution of the church to Brunelleschi, who was not mentioned in the building accounts and died in 1446, before the foundations had been dug.[78] As patrons of the sacristy, a transept chapel and the main chapel, the Medici were already prominent in their local church. Piero's pre-eminent position in the district and the city was emphasized when he was given unprecedented permission to distribute the chapels in the north nave to families of his choice.[79] Piero and Lorenzo visually reinforced the Medici presence by commissioning projects that included an elaborate lavabo for the sacristy, bronze pulpits for the nave, and elegant Ionic cloisters, all embellished with the ubiquitous Medici coat of arms.[80] Above all, they commissioned family tombs. Cosimo died in 1464 and Piero commissioned a simple inscribed plaque to mark the prestigious position of his father's tomb below the high altar in the crypt. Piero's tomb, commissioned from Verrocchio by Lorenzo, was markedly grander. Luxuriously carved in marble, porphyry, serpentine and bronze, the huge sarcophagus for the remains of Piero (d. 1469) and his brother, Giovanni (d. 1463), was placed in a prominent position, under an arch between the Medici sacristy and the Medici transept chapel. The visual evidence was clear: San Lorenzo was increasingly becoming the Medici church.

It was a demand for extra chapel space, again, that prompted the rebuilding of Santissima Annunziata, the Servite convent in the quarter of San Giovanni. The church was famous for its miraculous image of the Virgin, popularly believed to have been painted by St Luke, which attracted pilgrims from all over Europe.[81] The original plans of 1444–76 for the new church were ambitious. They involved replacing the main choir with a circular tribune and radiating chapels, transforming the side aisles into more chapels and adding an atrium to the front of the church.[82] The project was supervised by an annually-elected *opera* composed of local citizens who possessed chapels or tombs inside the church. Funds were provided not only by the sale of patronage rights but also by donations, including 200 ducats bequeathed by Gianfrancesco Gonzaga, Marquis of Mantua, and 1,050 lire (about 216 florins) from Cosimo de' Medici.[83] Cosimo was also instrumental in persuading the *Signoria* and Gianfrancesco's son, Ludovico Gonzaga, to add 2,000 florins of a debt of 5,000 florins owed by Florence to Ludovico for his services as captain-general of the city's army.[84] A number of prominent Miceans became chapel patrons. Orlando di Guccio de' Medici, a cousin of Cosimo and an employee in his bank, took over responsibility for a new sacristy.[85] The main chapel was acquired by Puccio di Antonio Pucci, who belonged to a family of wood and stone workers but his support of the Medici party in the 1430s allowed him and his family to move dramatically up the social scale; in 1434 Pucci dropped his artisan status and became a member of the Bankers' Guild.[86] Rights over the main chapel at Santissima Annunziata was a clear sign of his new prestige. In 1452 he gave these rights up in favour of a more conspicuous project, the construction of a family chapel attached to the church, an oratory dedicated to St Sebastian, for which his son, Antonio, commissioned Pollaiuolo's *Martyrdom of St Sebastian* (1475) for its altar.[87]

But it was Piero de' Medici who undertook the most conspicuous project inside the church, decorating three chapels and building a new tabernacle to house the miraculous image of the Virgin.[88] Classical in design and elaborately carved, the tabernacle was an unmistakable statement of Medici power. Its inscription proudly boasted that the cost of the marble alone was 4,000 florins.[89] And it was Piero's financial contribution that most impressed the Dominican Fra Domenico Corella, who praised both the quality of the materials and the skill by which the antique details were carved by modern craftsmen.[90]

If one church stands out in the context of late fifteenth-century Florentine patronage, it is the Dominican convent of Santa Maria Novella. Funds left by Turino Baldesi in his will of 1348 were used to pay for a cycle of frescos on the cloister walls of stories from Genesis, which included Uccello's striking experiments with perspective in the *Flood* (c. 1446).[91] The *Signoria* provided funds for the construction of a guest wing for important visitors to the city that was begun in 1418.[92] Private wealth was conspicuous inside the church. The Rucellai family paid for an elegant new pulpit (1443–8).[93] One of the small altars on the inside of the façade, decorated with Botticelli's *Adoration of the Magi* (fig. 22), belonged to Guasparre della Lama, a money dealer whose success enabled him to buy status in this

22. Botticelli, *Adoration of the Magi*. Florence, Uffizi, 1472–5

prestigious church before he was condemned for fraud in 1476.[94] Botticelli departed from the traditional representation of the Three Kings as a bearded old man, a dark bearded middle-aged man and a young beardless boy, and Lama's altarpiece has been convincingly shown to contain Medici portraits amongst the Kings and their retinues.[95] This piece of undisguised flattery reflected Lama's desire for social advancement. Amongst the residents of the quarter of Santa Maria Novella were three of the city's richest bankers, Giovanni Rucellai, Filippo Strozzi and Giovanni Tornabuoni, whose projects were flagrant displays of their wealth and status.

By far the most expensive contribution to the church was its new façade (1456–70) (fig. 23), donated by Giovanni Rucellai and paid for out of the income from his estate at Poggio a Caiano.[96] That the church possessed a finished façade at all was unusual; no other major church in Florence had one. The Duomo and Santa Croce acquired theirs in the nineteenth century and those of San Lorenzo and Santo Spirito are still unfinished. The new façade was costly and conspicuously so. The pattern of white Carrara marble and a local *pietra serena* made a direct reference to the Duomo, the most

23.   Santa Maria Novella, Florence, façade dated 1470

prestigious building in the city. The details of the façade, its columns and
capitals, the barrel-vaulted entrance, the classical lettering and the pediment all drew heavily on ancient Roman sources. Above all, the façade proclaimed Giovanni Rucellai as its maker in both the inscription and the
Rucellai sails of fortune inlaid in the frieze. In the 1440s Quaratesi had been
forbidden to display his coat of arms on Santa Croce (see above). Rucellai's
conspicuous exhibition of his private fortune is arguably the prime illustra-
tion of the change in attitudes that had taken place during the course of the
century.

   Prominent in politics throughout the fourteenth century, the Strozzi
family already owned the rights over two chapels in Santa Maria Novella

when Filippo Strozzi acquired his own chapel next to the choir from the bankrupt Boni family in 1486.[97] This was a conspicuous statement not only of the revival of his family's fortunes but also of his own personal achievement. Strozzi's tomb, by Benedetto da Maiano, was placed in the unprecedented position usually reserved for an altar. The chapel walls were frescoed by Filippino Lippi with scenes from the lives of St John the Evangelist and Filippo's name saint, Philip, that emphasized the theme of salvation.[98] The contract of 1487 drawn up by Filippo with Lippi throws an interesting light on Filippo's priorities.[99] No mention was made of the choice of scenes, which were to be specified later by Strozzi. Instead, the contract concentrated on the costs involved, detailing the surfaces that were to be painted, the incidental expenses such as scaffolding, Lippi's remuneration and, significantly, the quantities of gold and ultramarine that were to be used.

Giovanni Tornabuoni was a prominent Medicean. Brother-in-law to Piero de' Medici, he had been employed in the Medici bank since 1443 and was manager of the Rome branch from 1465 to 1494.[100] In 1486 he acquired the patronage rights to the main chapel in Santa Maria Novella, using his descent from Jacopo Tornaquinci, the owner of the first Dominican church on the site, to support his claim over bids from rival patrons, including Francesco Sassetti.[101] Tornabuoni's patronage of the chapel was conspicuous and expensive. To provide commemorative masses for his soul, he made over the income from a wool shop to the Confraternity of St Peter Martyr, a prestigious lay company associated with the church.[102] Above all, he completely refurbished the chapel, spending over 1,000 florins on costly intarsia choir stalls, stained glass windows, frescos for the walls and an altarpiece.[103] The theme of the frescos, the lives of the Virgin and of St John the Baptist, was identical to the original fourteenth-century cycle it replaced. But Tornabuoni's project, commissioned from Ghirlandaio in 1485, was modern. The *Birth of the Virgin* (fig. 24) was set in the interior of a wealthy merchant's palace, decorated with expensive inlaid wood panelling and *all' antica* details and a Roman triumphal arch formed the background to the *Massacre of the Innocents*. The contract with Ghirlandaio specified that the chapel was designed to honour Tornabuoni's family's prestige, something that was made evident in the *Annunciation to Zaccharias*, which included portraits of twenty-one members of the Tornaquinci-Tornabuoni family.[104] And in the same scene was an inscription by Poliziano that extolled the beauty of Florence, her buildings and treasures, proudly boasting that, in 1490, the city was prosperous, peaceful and healthy.[105] This complacency was about to be shattered (see Chapter 6).

The nature of Medici power had changed since the triumphant return of

24. Ghirlandaio, *Birth of the Virgin*. Florence, Santa Maria Novella, 1486–90

Cosimo to Florence in 1434. Piero had died of gout in 1469, two years after his father, leaving the 20-year-old Lorenzo at the head of the party. Educated by humanists and diplomats, he had been brought up as heir to his family's position at the top of the political and social hierarchy of the city. But his ambitions went beyond the role of first citizen of the republic. Contemporary sources described him as a statesman, poet and intellectual. He was certainly not a businessman, leaving control of the Medici bank to its director, Francesco Sassetti. A combination of inefficient management and a general slump in world trade caused the bank to decline and it crashed when the Medici were expelled in 1494.[106] Lorenzo was principally a politician, and he used his skills as a diplomat to play a leading role in maintaining a delicate balance of power in the peninsula. Perceived throughout Italy as head of state, he increasingly behaved like one.[107] He broke the long-standing Florentine tradition of choosing a wife locally and allied himself to one of Rome's leading families by marrying Clarice Orsini. He married his daughter, Maddalena, to Franceschetto Cibò, son of Pope Innocent VIII. And it was a sign of his princely stature that he managed to persuade Innocent VIII to make his son, Giovanni, a cardinal in 1489, thus ensuring the survival of the family's power in Florence into the sixteenth century.

Like his father and grandfather, Lorenzo was a prolific patron, though the nature of his involvement was different.[108] Lacking the financial security of his bank, he exploited his political position to financial advan-

tage, even borrowing from public funds.[109] Apart from his additions to the
Medici collections and his villa at Poggio a Caiano (see above), Lorenzo
also commissioned frescos for his villa Lo Spedaletto and in 1488 began to
rebuild the Observant Augustinian convent of Santa Maria a San Gallo
(which was destroyed in 1529).[110] He was also the principal force behind a
massive programme of urban renewal, the so-called via Laura project,
aided by legislation that offered attractive tax exemptions for those who
became involved.[111] There is evidence to suggest that the project was to
focus on an imposing new palace for himself, which, if built, would indeed
have made clear his princely aspirations.[112]

Lorenzo's exceptional interest in architecture has already been mentioned
(see above) and his pre-eminent position in Florence gave him ample scope
not only for indulging this interest but also, more importantly, for exercising his political power. By intervening in the bureaucratic machinery,
Lorenzo was able to help those trying to acquire land for their palaces, a
favour that had a clear political motive.[113] He was inevitably involved in
public patronage. He sat on the *opera* of the Palazzo della Signoria from
1487 to 1492 and was one of the citizens elected to judge the competition
for a new façade for the Duomo in 1491.[114] More surprising was his
appearance on the *opera* of Santo Spirito, the only non-resident to sit on
the committee.[115] On occasion, he deliberately exploited his position to
influence decisions. He was instrumental in replacing Giuliano da Maiano
by Giuliano da Sangallo as chief supervisor at Santa Maria delle Carceri in
Prato (1485)[116] and arranged Fancelli's appointment as chief supervisor on
the Duomo (1491).[117] And he used his reputation as a connoisseur to
political advantage outside Florence, recommending artists and architects
as diplomatic favours to the King of Naples, the Duke of Milan, the King
of Hungary and Cardinal Venier.[118] He arranged for Filippino Lippi to
stop work on the Strozzi chapel in Santa Maria Novella and go to Rome
to work for Cardinal Carafa (see Chapter 21). He sent Giuliano da Maiano
together with a design to Alfonso of Calabria for his villa of Poggioreale
outside Naples (see Chapter 13). There is also evidence of Lorenzo's more
active participation in architectural design, beyond the circumstantial suggestion of his involvement at Poggio a Caiano. He can be linked with the
design of Alfonso of Calabria's villa, Poggioreale (see Chapter 13). Giuliano
da Sangallo's appointment at Santa Maria delle Carceri was accompanied
by a change in design for the church that can be traced to Lorenzo[119] and
when the *opera* of Santo Spirito approved the model by Giuliano da
Sangallo for the sacristy of the church (1489), it was described as having
been commissioned by Lorenzo and following his ideas.[120]

Above all, Lorenzo was the central figure in the image of cultural
superiority promoted by fifteenth-century Florentines as propaganda

for their city's prestige.[121] Lorenzo's contemporaries sought appropriate precedents for him to surpass in the literature of antiquity, lavishing praise on his achievements as a politician and on his intellectual prowess. And part of the presentation of this image was Lorenzo's outstanding reputation as a patron of the arts. In this context, he was compared with Lucullus, a private citizen of the Roman Republic with a distinguished career of public service whose reputation as a patron of the arts was celebrated for its opulence and excess.[122] When the Medici returned to power in the sixteenth century, this reputation was expanded by Vasari and others into a compelling mythology that still threatens to obscure the real motives behind the development of the arts in late fifteenth-century Florence. Its original propagators would, with reason, be proud of the stunning success of their campaign.

6

Propaganda for the New Republic

T he year 1492 was a momentous one in European history. Columbus discovered America. Spain was victorious over the Moors in Granada and expelled Jews from the country to become a Christian kingdom, a major power on the European stage and one that was to play an increasingly important role in the politics of the Italian peninsula. In Florence, however, two other events had a more immediate and devastating effect. In April, Lorenzo de' Medici died and in August Rodrigo Borgia was elected Pope Alexander VI.

Opposition to the Medici family's domination of Florence had never been entirely stamped out. But while Lorenzo's political talents had been generally respected, the succession of his far less competent son provoked more widespread antagonism, even within the Medici party itself. Republican yearnings for the good old days before Cosimo's coup (1434) combined with increasing moral disgust at the blatant materialism of late fifteenth-century Florence provided the Dominican friar, Girolamo Savonarola, with a ready audience for his sermons. Preaching the prophecy of Revelations that God's wrath was about to descend on the city in preparation for a new Christian age (a message that took on added force as the half millenium drew near), this fiery and charismatic speaker urged his listeners to abandon their material values and repent before it was too late. His claim that Florence had no other King but Christ had a strong and deliberate appeal to republican as well as religious sentiment in the city and his prediction of approaching disaster was all too soon proved correct.

Piero had abandoned his father's diplomatic policy of maintaining a delicate balance of power between the major Italian states in favour of outright support for Naples against not only Milan but also Charles VIII of France (1483–98) who, as heir to the Angevin line, entered Italy in 1494 with his armies in pursuit of his claim to the Neapolitan throne. The French army attacked one of Florence's border fortresses and Piero, without waiting for authority from the *Signoria*, went to treat with Charles VIII, surrendering the ports of Pisa and Livorno to secure peace. The news reached Florence on 4 November and was received with horror and anger. Piero had behaved as if he, not the elected *Signoria*, were the head of the city's government. Events moved with startling speed. An emergency meeting of leading citizens was called and it became clear that Piero had lost the support of the Medici party. Ambassadors were sent to Charles VIII to persuade him that Florence was an ally and that the agreement with Piero was invalid. On 9 November Piero and his close family were expelled. By Christmas the city had a new constitution. And worse was to follow. Bad harvests and the escalating costs of war precipitated a serious economic crisis, made worse by the political turmoil that engulfed Italy in the wake of the invasions of Charles VIII and his successor, Louis XII (1498–1515). In 1501 Florence's independence was once again under threat, this time from Cesare Borgia who, with the help of his father, Pope Alexander VI, was carving out a state for himself in central Italy.

Savonarola's extraordinary talent as a preacher played a major part in the foundation of the new constitution.[1] At first, the old Medici party attempted to preserve its power by restoring the pre-1434 situation. But it soon became clear that more radical reform was needed and a faction of the party promoted the idea of setting up a new constitution based on the Venetian system without the figurehead of a doge. Popular assent was secured by using the charismatic Savonarola to act as their spokesman, who preached his famous sermon on 14 December. The laws establishing the new constitution were passed on 22 December. Like its Venetian model, the city's government was now based on a Great Council, open to all male Florentines over 29 years old whose forefathers had held political office. At its head was the *Gonfaloniere* who was regularly re-elected unlike the Venetian Doge who served for life. The Council of Eighty was set up as a smaller executive council similar to the Venetian Senate. But, despite the apparent changes, power was still firmly in the hands of the old ruling élite. Over three-quarters of those elected to the Council of Eighty in 1495 had served on the Medici councils or were members of families represented.[2]

In support of the new power structure, Savonarola preached forgiveness and only those very closely identified with the old régime were killed or exiled along with Piero.[3] Anger and resentment were directed at the Medici themselves and 9 November, the date of Piero's flight, was declared a national holiday.[4] The family were widely promoted as tyrants. The prominent republican, Alamanno Rinuccini, praised Lorenzo's talents as a politician but criticized his ambition, drawing a parallel with Julius Caesar.[5] Above all, the visual manifestations of Medici power were destroyed. The contents of the Medici palace, wall-hangings, sculpture and paintings, were auctioned off at Orsanmichele in 1495.[6] The following year the Medici gardens were bought by Savonarola's convent, San Marco,[7] and Cosimo's burial plaque was removed from the floor by the high altar in San Lorenzo by order of the *Signoria*.[8]

The new republican government concentrated on embellishing the symbol of its renewed power, the Palazzo della Signoria. In what was the most strikingly visible evidence of political change, many of the most famous pieces from the Palazzo Medici were sequestrated by the government for its decoration.[9] Donatello's bronze statue of *David*, once in the principal courtyard of the Palazzo Medici, now stood in the courtyard of the Palazzo della Signoria. Donatello's *Judith and Holofernes* was placed on the façade of the palace. Marble and bronze heads from the Palazzo Medici were consigned to the *opera* for the decoration of the new Council Hall (see below). The furnishings from the Medici chapels in their palace and San Lorenzo were appropriated for the decoration of the chapel in the Palazzo della Signoria. Orders were issued giving eight days' grace for the return of all bronze, marble and other items looted during the riots that followed Piero's expulsion. The state also commissioned new works, including sculpture, intarsia, paintings and a new clock for the palace, in a determined effort to demonstrate its authority and prestige.[10]

Above all, the new constitution was proclaimed in the construction of a large hall for meetings of the Great Council in the Palazzo della Signoria.[11] The decision to build the hall was taken in December 1494 at the same time as the constitutional changes were ratified, but the project did not get underway until the following May. On 11 May 1495 Savonarola preached a sermon on the importance of the Great Council to the Florentine government and the need to provide manifest evidence of its existence in a new structure.[12] Built above the customs house behind the old palace, the Council Hall was clearly visible from the piazza della Signoria. An *opera* was elected to take charge of the project and work started in July with the appointment of a stonemason, Cronaca, and a carpenter, Monciatto, to supervise construction. The same month, Savonarola advocated that work should stop on the Duomo, to release more men and materials for the new hall.[13] Speed was of the essence and the project proceeded rapidly. By December 1495 the walls were finished and the roof started. In February 1496 the *opera* commissioned ten master carpenters to start work on an elaborate coffered ceiling. By April 1496 the hall was in use, although its decoration took longer to complete. Its principal ornament was an elaborately carved wooden altar, commissioned in May 1498 from Antonio da Sangallo and Baccio d'Agnolo, two of the carpenters involved on the new ceiling, and finally completed in 1502.[14] Its altarpiece, commissioned from Filippino Lippi, was completed by Fra Bartolomeo in 1510 (see below).

In this period of major political upheaval and economic crisis, the new republic had compelling reasons to spend so visibly on the prime image of its prestige and authority. But private patronage virtually ceased. In dramatic contrast to the preceeding twenty years, the period from 1494 to 1503 saw few major new commissions. Financial hardship not only discouraged would-be patrons but also affected projects already underway. The Palazzo Strozzi, begun in 1489 (see Chapter 5), continued under Cronaca's supervision, but working conditions changed for the worse. Wage rates paid to masons employed on the palace were cut by up to 25 per cent in 1495.[15] The account books of the Palazzo della Signoria reveal a drop of 10–15 per cent in wages paid to its workforce in 1497.[16] These falls were higher in real terms as the cost of living increased dramatically.[17] But there were moral as well as financial constraints imposing limits on individual expenditure. In the new Christian atmosphere of republican Florence, there was a sharp reaction to the blatant materialism of the Medici years, encouraged above all by Savonarola.

Savonarola (1452–98), the son of a Ferrarese doctor, became a Dominican late in life (1475), developing a reputation as a learned theologian and a charismatic preacher. His fame spread. He was transferred to the Dominican convent of San Marco in Florence where he stayed from 1482 to 1485. Lorenzo de' Medici arranged for his return in 1490 and he was appointed prior in 1491. His success was immediate. He restored the strict rule of poverty in the convent which, under his leadership, saw a dramatic increase in friars, from 25 in 1474 to 120 in the late 1490s.[18] One of his converts was the son of the wealthy banker and prominent patron, Giovanni Rucellai (see Chapter 5), who became Fra Santi Rucellai and wrote a treatise outlining moral Christian banking practice. Savonarola was also influential in humanist circles.[19] Trained in the Aristotelian Dominican tradition, he debated spiritual issues with the city's leading humanists in an effort to promote Christian renewal. But it was in his sermons that he had the greatest impact on Florentine culture. He was charismatic, his message of repentance was unambiguous and he appealed directly to the emotions of his audience. His domineering style and puritanical ideals divided the Florentines.[20] In an attempt to persuade the city to abandon her pro-French policy, Pope Alexander VI excommunicated Savonarola, the leader of this faction. Savonarola's supporters rallied to his defence and he was accused of organizing a political party. Such activity was banned under the new constitution, and the accusation was convincing enough to condemn him.[21] He was executed in the piazza della Signoria in 1498.

Savonarola's impact on Florentine art around 1500 was considerable. On 2 November 1494 he had directed a stinging attack on rich patrons, their love of luxury and their desire for self-glorification.[22] He censured particularly those who had commissioned tombs beneath altars, arguing that only the saints had a right to such veneration. His censure was not aimed at patronage itself, but at love of material splendour. His sermons frequently referred to Florentine art.[23] Stressing the poverty and spirituality of the saints, he scorned the widely-held belief that conspicuous expenditure in a religious context would help a patron to Heaven. He criticized patrons who happily spent 100 florins on their own chapel but refused to donate 10 florins to the poor.[24] He disapproved of the proliferation of their coats of arms in the city's churches, in chapels and on priests' vestments. He put a powerful case for a return to Christian roots and his attitudes had a profound effect in the city. Art for Savonarola was visual scripture not a statement of the power and prestige of its patron. He attacked painters who portrayed the Virgin as a Florentine girl in all her finery, arguing that she should be dressed plainly. He objected strongly to immoral images, and organized bonfires to burn un-Christian books, paintings and other vanities. Above all, he pleaded for simple altarpieces, which would inspire devotion, with none of the irrelevant details that only distracted from prayer. And, significantly, his attacks were aimed mainly at patrons. It was these wealthy Florentines whom he considered responsible for the appearance of the city's churches and chapels.

Two altarpieces painted by Botticelli for unidentified patrons illustrate the new climate of republican Florence and the impact of Savonarola's preaching. One of the leading painters popular with the Medici circle before 1494, Botticelli had a brother who was an active supporter of Savonarola, though there is no evidence to suggest that Botticelli was as well. However, there is no doubt that the character of his works changed. His patrons no longer commissioned tranquil Virgins and Adorations of the Magi filled with Florentine pageantry, but preferred a more spiritual style and very different themes. Botticelli's *Mystic Nativity* was crowned with an inscription stating that he painted it in 1500 and drawing a parallel between his own age and the Apocalypse as outlined in the Book of Revelation.[25] In his *Crucifixion*, the background was divided by the figure of Christ on the Cross into two quite separate scenes. On Christ's left was a dark storm of raining weapons, while on his right daylight shone on a city saved by divine intervention. This city with its distinctive cathedral dome and campanile was recognizably Florence.

The altarpiece (1510) finally commissioned for the new Council Hall in the Palazzo della Signoria also displayed associations with Savonarola's ideas. Its painter, Fra Bartolomeo, had become a Dominican friar at San Marco in 1500. The painting showed the Virgin and Child with Saints, with the Virgin's mother, Anna, behind her looking up to Heaven. St Anna had been an image of republican freedom in the city since the end of the short-lived tyranny of the Duke of Athens, who had been expelled on her feast-day, 23 July, in 1343.[26] Above was a three-faced head illustrating Savonarola's description of the Trinity as light with three faces.[27]

Two close supporters of Savonarola commissioned altarpieces that clearly expressed their patrons' religious and political associations. In 1494, shortly before the expulsion of the Medici, Jacopo Bongianni, a prosperous wool merchant and close friend of Fra Santi Rucellai, had undertaken to finish the church of Santa Chiara and endow its main chapel.[28] For its altar he commissioned from Lorenzo de' Credi a painting of the Nativity (usually known as the *Adoration of the Shepherds*), which conformed to Savonarola's plea to avoid unnnecessary detail. Moreover, the figures grouped round the Child in the centre were clearly separated into two groups, heavenly and worldly, with Mary, Joseph and four angels on one side of the painting and two shepherds behind the kneeling figure of Bongianni on the other. Francesco Valori, Savonarola's leading political supporter, commissioned Filippino Lippi's *Crucifixion* in the late 1490s for the altar of his chapel in San Procolo.[29] The painting was explicitly an image for devotion. Christ, with angels catching the Blood from his wounds, was shown as the focus of the prayers of the Virgin and St Francis, both simply dressed. Skulls and bones below provided a lucid reminder of the frailty of human life.

In a telling example of the central role played by the patron in determining not only the iconography but also the style of a commission, Filippino Lippi's frescos for the Strozzi chapel in Santa Maria Novella, painted at the same time, were very different.[30] Commissioned in 1487 by Filippo Strozzi (d. 1491), this cycle was unfinished when Lippi went off to Rome to paint the Carafa chapel in 1488 and was only completed in 1502, by which date Strozzi was dead and the project in the hands of his heirs (see Chapters 5 and 21). Lippi's energetic and aggressively realistic scenes from the lives of St Philip and St John the Evangelist were filled with anecdotal detail and a striking contrast to the spiritual serenity of his *Crucifixion* for Valori. The fact that one was a narrative cycle and the other an image of devotion can only partly explain the disparity. The Strozzi family were prominent anti-Savonarolans and it is tempting to see Lippi's two distinct styles as visual evidence of this.

By 1503 Florence had begun to recover. Cesare Borgia's threat to her independence evaporated after the death of Pope Alexander VI in 1503. Political stability in the city was boosted by the election in 1502 of Pietro Soderini as *Gonfaloniere* to serve for life. The city's economy began to revive and, above all, the puritanical climate of the past decade started to lift.

In 1502 the *opera* of the Palazzo della Signoria began an ambitious programme of decoration for the Council Hall. Like the Venetians in their Council Hall, the Florentines chose images that combined religious and patriotic themes to display the prestige of their city and the nature of their government. The similarities were striking (see Chapter 8). The *opera* commissioned Andrea Sansovino to carve a statue of *Christ the Saviour* (1502) to go above the seat of the *gonfaloniere*.[31] Christ the Saviour was an obvious choice to commemorate the survival of the city through the trauma of the past decade, but the image had other levels of meaning in Florence. Savonarola had stated that the city had no other King but Christ. And the Feast of Christ the Saviour was celebrated on 9 November, the date of Piero de' Medici's expulsion. For the walls, the *opera* commissioned Leonardo and Michelangelo to paint scenes of famous Florentine victories, over Pisa at Cascina (1364) and over Milan at Anghiari (1440). Leonardo had been employed at the Sforza court (see Chapter 12), returning home after the expulsion of Ludovico Sforza in 1499. He started work on his fresco, the *Battle of Anghiari*, in 1503.[32] Michelangelo, who had just completed his statue of *David* (see below), joined the project the following year. To the modern art historian, the prospect of these two giants of Renaissance art working together is fascinating. Sadly, the paintings were never finished nor was Sansovino's *Saviour*. Leonardo started his frescos in 1505 but his work, like that in Milan, immediately started to deteriorate. Michelangelo went to Rome to work for Julius II in 1505 (see Chapter 22) and the project was abandoned.

Michelangelo's *David* is one of the best-known images of Renaissance art (fig. 25). The statue had a long history.[33] The *opera* of the Duomo had commissioned Agostino di Duccio to carve a gigantic prophet of Carrara marble for the cathedral in 1464. There were endless problems and Agostino did not abide by the terms of the contract, using only one block rather than the four prescribed in the contract. Finally, the *opera* bought the statue back after paying Agostino his expenses, and in 1476 Antonio Rossellino was commissioned to finish the statue. Nothing came of this attempt either. Then, in 1501, at the time of the greatest threat from the Borgia armies,[34] the *opera* revived the project, commissioning the young Michelangelo to complete it. The contract specified that the marble had been badly blocked out and made the first reference to the statue as a figure of David. Michelangelo was offered a salary of 6 florins a month for the two years the work was expected to last and the statue was eventually finished, six months late, early in 1504.

By the end of 1503 it was clear that the statue was exceptional and in January 1504 the *opera* called a meeting to decide where it should be placed.[35] The advisory committee of twenty-nine men consisted of the state herald, his assistant and a wide range of painters, sculptors, carpenters, goldsmiths and other craftsmen. They recommended four sites: the Duomo, the courtyard of the Palazzo della Signoria, its façade and the adjoining loggia. Only three, including Botticelli, gave the Duomo as their first choice. The majority opted for Botticelli's alternative, the loggia beside the palace, many of them stressing the need to shelter the statue from the weather. The assistant herald, concerned with the ceremonial aspects of the problem, suggested that its position in the loggia should be out of the way of state processions, a recommendation seconded by Leonardo. The other herald recommended that Michelangelo's statue should replace Donatello's bronze *David* in the courtyard of the palace, because the latter was not very good. Three members suggested that Michelangelo should be asked his preferences. The report of the meeting recorded what must have been a lively discussion of aesthetic, practical and, above all, political considerations. Despite their advice, the decision was taken to erect the statue outside the main door of the Palazzo della Signoria. Landucci's diary described in vivid detail how this 17-feet-high giant was carefully fixed in a wooden frame which was rolled on logs down the main street of the city to its new position in May 1504.[36]

In the more stable and prosperous climate of the early sixteenth century, private patronage revived. Wealthy Florentines could afford once again to commission artists to build and decorate their chapels and palaces. They were able to do so without censure as Savonarola's moral codes relaxed their grip on the city. Expensive new chapels were commissioned by the Pandolfini family in the Badia Fiorentina (1503–10) and the heirs of Giuliano Gondi in Santa Maria Novella (after 1503).[37] Pietro Soderini commissioned his tomb (*c.* 1508) for Santa Maria del Carmine, one of the only tombs put up inside a church since Savonarola had attacked the practice.[38] But the pictorial decoration commissioned for chapels and altars showed a marked change in theme. Many patrons preferred subjects that stressed suffering as a major element of spirituality. Others made oblique reference to the troubles of the past decade. Andrea del Sarto's frescos in the cloister of the Servite convent of Santissima Annunziata depicted the *Miracles of St Philip Benizzi*, a Florentine Servite (canonized in 1671) who had played a major role in pacifying the warring Guelf and Ghibelline factions in thirteenth-century Florence. Particularly popular was the theme of *Noli Me Tangere*, when Christ ordered the repentant Mary Magdalen to tell his disciples that he had risen.

A number of patrons commissioned private devotional altarpieces of the Virgin and Child from the Urbino painter, Raphael, who arrived in Florence in 1504 and stayed until 1508 when he went to Rome to work for Pope Julius II (see Chapter 22).[39] These lovely paintings emphasized the piety rather than the wealth of their patrons. Simply dressed, Raphael's Virgins had an

25.   Michelangelo, *David*. Florence, Accademia, 1501–4

ethereal beauty. The *Madonna del Cardellino* (fig. 26), painted for Lorenzo Nasi, showed two children with a goldfinch, a symbol of the Crucifixion and Christ's sacrifice for mankind. Many depicted Mary with Christ and St John the Baptist as toddlers rather than babies, emphasizing the maternal aspect of her role to provide an image with which family members could identify. The humanity of the scene was reinforced by the realistic depiction of the different textures of flesh, hair and material rather than of incidental detail. In contrast to earlier fifteenth-century images of the Virgin and Child, they were not set in elaborate, often architectural, settings but in evocative rural landscapes.

Portraiture revived after a decade of stagnation and one of the first portraits of the period was Leonardo's famous *Mona Lisa*, traditionally dated 1503. Commissioned by Francesco di Giocondo to paint a portrait of his wife, Leonardo exploited the effects of his *sfumato* technique to create an image which had little in common with the Florentine taste for linear precision. The wealthy wool dealer, Agnolo Doni, preferred Raphael's style, commissioning him to paint portraits (1506) of himself and his plump young wife, Maddalena Strozzi. Raphael minutely detailed their clothes and jewellery, carefully positioning their hands to display their expensive rings.

The Florentine republic was short-lived. Lorenzo de' Medici's determination to get his son made a cardinal had provided the family with powerful allies. With the formation of the Holy League (1511), an alliance between the Papacy, the Holy Roman Empire, Spain, England and Venice against France, the need to persuade Florence to abandon her traditional pro-French position became paramount. Cardinal Giovanni de' Medici was instrumental in persuading the Holy League that the best way to achieve their aims was to restore the Medici to power in the city. In 1512, the Holy League troops compelled Soderini to resign and the Medici returned in triumph. The carnival festivities in February 1513 focused on a magnificent pageant celebrating the Golden Age that Florence had enjoyed under the leadership of their illustrious ancestor, Lorenzo de' Medici, an age which had at last returned.[40]

26. Raphael, *Madonna del Cardellino*. Florence, Uffizi, 1505–6

Part Two
Venice

7

Venice: Heir of Byzantium

The motor launch that speeds the modern tourist from the airport across the lagoon to Venice may lack romance but the way in which the elegant pinnacles of the Doge's Palace and the shining domes of San Marco emerge from the hazy line between sky and water is as exciting now as it must have been to the traveller arriving by sea in 1400. Glittering and exotic, Venice was unlike any other European city and she zealously guarded this image.

In 1400 Venice was one of the most powerful states in Italy, the heart of a trading empire that stretched down the Dalmatian coast into the Aegean. She was one of Europe's principal commercial ports and, with a population of over 100,000, one of its largest cities. Built on a cluster of islands in a lagoon at the top of the Adriatic, she was protected from the sea by sandbars and from the mainland by water. The Grand Canal, a broad waterway lined with the palaces of rich merchants, snaked through the city, dividing it in two. Her maze of canals, streets, passages and bridges was crowded with people. Venice was a cosmopolitan centre and home to colonies of Germans, Greeks, Slavs, Jews, Turks and Armenians as well as native citizens. Traders from all over Europe and the Middle East did deals in the business quarter by the Rialto bridge, the only crossing over the Grand Canal. A great piazza in front of the city's main church, San Marco, and her government offices, the Doge's Palace, was the focus of Venice's political life and provided the setting for elaborate processions in celebration of state and religious festivals.

This rich and powerful state had developed from inauspicious beginnings. Small settlements of fishermen ekeing out a living in the marshes of the lagoon had been havens for refugees fleeing from the chaos of the barbarian invasions that hastened the collapse of the Roman Empire in the West during the sixth century. The city grew slowly. Charlemagne's treaty of 814 with the Byzantine rulers of the Old Roman Empire in the East left Venice under the nominal authority of Constantinople. But effective leadership was in the hands of the Doge (Venetian dialect for duke). By 1000,

Byzantine influence in Italy had faded and Venice was independent. Small and inaccessible but increasingly prosperous, she maintained her distance from the conflicts that ravaged twelfth-century mainland Italy. The fishermen had turned traders, and, exploiting their links with Byzantium, looked down the Adriatic at the lucrative opportunities on offer in the markets of the Near East.

Venice's wealth was built on international trade, a highly organized state enterprise.[1] Galleys were constructed in her huge shipbuilding yard, the Arsenale, and auctioned off each trip to private investors. Cargoes and routes were strictly controlled to avoid theft or smuggling. The galleys sailed under the charge of a captain, who represented the investors, and a state-employed crew of sailors, oarsmen, carpenters and caulkers as well as a navigator, book-keeper, priest and doctor. The galleys often carried passengers: diplomats travelling to the court at Constantinople, officials going to take up posts in Venetian colonies or pilgrims to the Holy Land. Their cargoes might include Florentine cloth, German copper and silver or glass and soap made in Venice. They returned from their Mediterranean voyages with salt fish and furs from the Black Sea, luxury goods from Constantinople, sugar, cotton and grain from Cyprus, silks and spices from the Levant, wheat and slaves from North Africa or wool and cloth from England and Flanders. The taxes charged on all goods entering the city formed nearly one quarter of the state's revenues.

Ruthless self-interest and devious diplomacy during the Fourth Crusade of 1202–4 gave Venice the opportunity to establish herself as a major power in the eastern Mediterranean. Having agreed to supply ships for transporting the Crusaders as well as fully armed galleys, Venice also made an alliance with the son of the deposed Byzantine emperor, who promised rich rewards to the Venetians and the Crusaders in return for their help in restoring him to the throne in Constantinople. The city was taken in 1203 but the promised payments never materialized. The following year the angry and dissatisfied armies, egged on by Doge Enrico Dandolo, decided to attack the city, divide its spoils and install their own Emperor. Venice's part of the bargain included an equal share of the loot and advantageous trading privileges with the new Latin Empire. More importantly, it gave them control of part of the old empire, including islands in the Aegean and towns on the Adriatic coast.

Latin rule in Constantinople was short-lived and the old dynasty was reinstated in 1261 with the help of the Genoese, Venice's arch rivals in the Mediterranean. For the next century, Venice and Genoa battled for supremacy in the Adriatic and the Aegean. When the Genoese won a resounding victory at Zara in 1379, in their enemy's territory of the northern Adriatic, it looked as if the Venetians might be beaten. But the following year Venice won the decisive victory of Chioggia on the edge of her lagoon. By 1400 she had revived her trading links and expanded her empire to become the major maritime power in the eastern Mediterranean.

Venice's independence from mainland Italy and her economic and cultural ties with the Byzantine East had been given powerful expression in her churches and palaces. Venetians followed the Greek Orthodox practice of dedicating some of their churches to Old Testament prophets, such as Job (San Giobbe), Samuel (San Samuele) or Moses (San Moisè). Many of them were built on the centralized Greek cross plan with arms of equal length. Tall Byzantine stilted arches supported on columns ornamented the façades of patrician palaces on the Grand Canal. But the clearest statement of Venice's eastern associations could be seen in the design and decoration of the basilica of San Marco, the prime symbol of her power. It had been begun in 829 and rebuilt c. 1050 on a Greek cross plan, crowned with five huge hemispherical domes resting on pendentives, deliberately designed to recall Emperor Constantine's church of the Apostles in Constantinople as rebuilt by Justinian (c. 550).

Significantly, San Marco was not the city's cathedral. The patriarchate of Venice was only created in 1451, by amalgamating two older sees, Grado and Castello. Unlike other Italian cities, but very much in the imperial tradition of the Byzantine East, Venice chose to maintain her distance from Rome and to forge close links between religious and political power. San Marco, unquestionably the grandest church in the city, was the private chapel of the Doge and attached to his palace (fig. 27). The basilica was decorated with imagery that testified not only to her triumph in the eastern Mediterranean but also to her immense wealth. The interior was embellished with gilded mosaics that, both in style and iconography, were closer to Eastern traditions. On the south side of the basilica, facing visitors arriving in Venice, stood two treasures looted during the Sack of Constantinople in 1204: a red porphyry statue (c. A.D. 300) of the four rulers of the Roman Empire and a pair of carved columns taken from the church of St Polyeuktos (fig. 28).[2]

Booty from Constantinople was proudly on display throughout the church. Carved reliefs, capitals and marble columns decorated the façade and, above the main doors, stood the famous four bronze horses that had once graced the Hippodrome in the old capital of the Eastern Empire. Inside, one of the basilica's most treasured possessions was an icon believed to have been painted by St Luke, the *Theotokos Nikopeia*, which had been stolen from the imperial palace. On the high altar sat the *Pala d'Oro*, an elaborate gold and jewelled altarpiece enriched with enamelled panels taken from Constantinople's churches. Composed of over eighty tiny religious scenes and portraits of prophets, Evangelists and saints, the *Pala d'Oro* was encrusted with pearls, sapphires, emeralds, rubies and other precious stones.

Above all, the church possessed the body of St Mark, reputed to have been stolen from its tomb in Alexandria by Venetian merchants in 828 and smuggled out of the city past Muslim customs officials hidden in a basket of pork. Its arrival in Venice provided the impetus for the construction of the first church and was the subject of some of the earliest mosaics in the new church after its eleventh-century rebuilding. Twelfth-century mosaics in the chapels flanking the main apse depicted not only the life of St Mark but also the story of the removal of his body from Alexandria. And it was this Venetian achievement, not the life of the saint, that was celebrated in mosaics (1260–70) in the lunettes above the main doors on the façade. The only original scene remaining shows the relic's reception by the Doge, patricians and prelates in front of San Marco, easily identifiable from the four horses depicted on its façade.

The myths that the Venetians developed to explain the origins of their city and to justify her power, prosperity and status in world affairs deliberately reinforced the links between religion and political power. Venice had no pagan past. She was a Christian city and the feasts of the Christian Church were celebrated in a uniquely Venetian context. On the last day of Carnival, the Doge and his councillors watched the formal trial and execution of a bull and twelve pigs in commemoration of the defeat of a twelfth-century Patriarch of Aquileia and his Friulian allies, followed by a ritual smashing of wooden models of Friulian castles in the courtyard of the Doge's Palace.[3] The Feast of the Annunciation, 25 March, was also the anniversary of the legendary date of the city's foundation in A.D. 421. The cult of the Virgin was particularly strong in Venice and the image of the Virgin crowned as Queen of Heaven was often used as an allegory for the city herself.[4] The Feast of St Mark, 25 April, had obvious civic associations. Ascension Day was not only the day on which Christ went up to Heaven; it was also the anniversary of a famous naval victory fought in 1177 on behalf of the Papacy against the fleet of the Holy Roman Emperor. The Pope had rewarded Doge Sebastiano Ziani with a ring to symbolize the city's marriage to, and dominion over, the sea. Each year the Doge's successor re-enacted the ceremony by sailing in his official barge out through the mouth of the lagoon and casting a golden ring to his bride, the sea.

Processions and festivities played a major role in the public ritual of Venetian society and the city's medieval town planners had constructed an impressive setting in the piazza in front of San Marco. In marked contrast to the maze of narrow streets and passageways of the city, this piazza was vast. Laid out by Doge Sebastiano Ziani in the twelfth century, it was lined with Byzantine round-arched arcades and had the basilica as its dramatic backdrop.[5] Religious feasts, visits of foreign dignitaries and major civic events were celebrated with huge processions in the piazza. Formally arranged with careful attention to precedence and spectacle, the Doge in his state robes paraded with members of the government in the distinctive uniforms of their office, with church dignitaries, members of the city's confraternities grouped behind their standards, and with musicians and torch bearers. These processions were deliberately designed to reinforce the myth of order and stability that stood at the heart of Venetian culture.[6]

Venetian society was highly stratified. At its top were the patricians, around 4 per cent of the population, all members of families who, between 1297 and 1323, had established control over the government by restricting eligibility for political office to themselves and their descendants. Thirty more families had been rewarded with patrician status for their services during the War of Chioggia (1378–81); no more were added until the seventeenth century.[7] They were traders, not aristocrats, and they dominated the political and cultural life of the city. Their right to rule was supported by a potent state ideology that emphasized their devotion to public duty and the perfection of Venice's unique political system, extolling its benefits of stability, social order and justice. This image, which was highly idealized, justified their position at the top of a clearly defined social structure that they had enshrined in law. And it proved remarkably resilient, remaining unchanged until the fall of the Venetian Republic in 1797.

Below the patricians, but clearly distinguished from the mass of the working population, were the citizens, or *cittadini*, who formed around 11 per cent of the population. Their status relied on proving long-term residence and at least two generations of non-manual trade. Foreigners could acquire *cittadini* status after twenty-five years' residence. Excluded by birth from political office, the *cittadini* participated peripherally in government by manning the civil service. Others were merchants, doctors, lawyers or manufacturers and this class included the city's leading painters and sculptors. Many were successful businessmen. A census of 1379 listing households owning property valued at over 300 ducats assessed 2,128 families of whom 57 per cent were patricians and 43 per cent *cittadini*.[8]

Venice's head of state was the Doge, a patrician elected for life by a special government committee. Venetians regarded the office of the Doge as the heir to Constantine's imperial position, uniting temporal and spiritual leadership. But a clear distinction was made between the office and its holder. The Doge was not a prince. In the coronation ceremonies in

San Marco, he was presented with the banner of his office; but he was crowned in the Doge's Palace by his peers, not by priests.[9] He was usually an old man; the average age of the doges between 1400 and 1572 was 72.[10] Six of the thirteen elected between 1400 and 1521 served terms of less than five years. Only four served more than ten years: Michele Steno (1400–13), Francesco Foscari (1423–57), Agostino Barbarigo (1486–1501) and Leonardo Loredan (1501–21). Short terms limited the influence of the Doge and old age encouraged a tendency towards conservative decisions. The Doge's authority was ambiguous: he was expected to provide leadership but his personal power was strictly curbed by the system of committee government.

The base of patrician government was the Great Council, open to all male patricians over 25 years old. It met every Sunday to vote through legislation and to elect the members of the various committees and magistracies that administered the city and its empire. With around 2,000 members during the fifteenth century, it was too cumbersome for effective decision-making and real power was vested in the smaller committees chaired by the Doge: the Senate, the College and, above all, the Council of Ten, in charge of state security. Patricians were firmly in control of their state. Ambassadors and the Captain-Generals of the city's navy were invariably patricians as were the holders of all important administrative positions in her colonies. They also ran the numerous magistracies that regulated and controlled every aspect of Venetian life: the city's grain supply, the sale of salt, the upkeep of lighthouses and breakwaters protecting the lagoon from the sea, street cleaning, rubbish collection, burials and patrolling the city's maze of streets, passages, canals and narrow bridges to curb the violence that was endemic in every major fifteenth-century European city.

Reinforcing the close ties between Church and State, ecclesiastical power was in the hands of the patricians, who ensured that the city's spiritual life remained firmly under their control.[11] The enormous wealth of San Marco was administered by prominent patrician laymen, the Procurators of St Mark. The Patriarch of Grado (of Venice after 1451), the city's leading churchman, was a patrician appointed by the Senate whose name was submitted for papal approval. Fifteenth-century Venetian cardinals were all patricians (three became Popes), as were the heads of the city's major convents and monasteries. Venetian patrician clerics played a leading role in the introduction of reformist branches of various orders, making the city an important centre of fifteenth-century church reform. All parish priests were under the direct authority of the Patriarch, who was also in control of the city's secular clergy. Only the other old-established male religious orders, such as the Franciscans at the Frari, were responsible to their superiors outside Venice.

The seat of patrician government was the Doge's Palace, housing not only the private apartments of the Doge but also the government offices, law courts and prisons. Situated beside San Marco, the palace formed one side of the small piazzetta, at right angles to the grand piazza San Marco, that led down to the waterfront and the official reception area for visitors. The first palace on the site, built in the ninth century, had been enlarged and transformed by Doge Sebastiano Ziani in the twelfth century. Built round a courtyard, the façades facing the piazzetta and the lagoon were decorated with Veneto-Byzantine porticoes, like those around Ziani's piazza of San Marco.[12]

In 1340, shortly after the patriciate had established its control over the city's government, the Great Council had voted to build a new hall for its meetings that would give visual expression to its new power. This project, which also involved remodelling both the façade facing the lagoon and the first six bays of the piazzetta façade, was a massive transformation.[13] In striking contrast to the round-arched porticoes of the old palace, the Great Council chose an exciting new design. An arcade of pointed arches carried on massive circular piers supported a more elegant colonnade of narrower pointed arches, interspersed with distinctive quatrefoil roundels. Above was a solid wall covered with tiles of red and white marble, pierced with Gothic windows embellished with elaborate tracery and surmounted by a distinctive row of white marble crenellations that were more eastern than European. But the combination of these various elements was distinctively Venetian.

In striking contrast to the rest of Italy, humanism played a relatively small role in the development of fifteenth-century Venice.[14] Unlike their counterparts in Milan, Florence or Rome, *cittadini* bureaucrats were not humanists. Their education in Latin and Greek was specifically designed to train them for careers in the civil service and their schools attracted few humanist teachers. Venetian patricians, who, as a wealthy élite in charge of administering their overseas empire, had an unrivalled claim to be seen as the heirs of ancient Rome, showed remarkably little interest in promoting themselves as such.[15] Venice had no classical past. While Bruni applied the tools of historical analysis to prove Florence's republican background, Venetian humanists found their city's Christian traditions and Byzantine links far more enduring. These associations became increasingly important as Venice changed direction.

The fifteenth century was momentous in the city's history. With the Genoese decisively defeated at Chioggia, Venice set about repairing the damage to her economy and prestige caused by the war. Her expansion in the eastern Mediterranean was dramatic. By 1400, she controlled ports along the Dalmatian and Albanian coasts, Corfu, parts of the Peloponnese and islands in the Aegean. She even ruled Athens for a short time (1394–1402). To protect her trade routes with northern Europe, she took advantage of the weakness of Milan following the death of Giangaleazzo Visconti in 1402 and conquered three nearby cities on the mainland, Padua, Vicenza and Verona (1402–5). This tentative move into Italian politics soon became deliberate policy, reinforced by the growing power of the Ottoman Turks in the Aegean and their conquest of Constantinople in 1453. By the end of the century, Venice's Italian territory stretched far into the Po valley and her expansion was seen as a threat to the balance of power in the peninsula.

Like the Florentines, the Venetians attached enormous importance to the appearance of their city. With a long tradition of exploiting the value of art and architecture as a vehicle of propaganda, they recognized its vital role in the promotion of an image of power, wealth and prestige. Visitors to Venice were understandably impressed. In their churches, palaces, guild halls and confraternity meeting houses, the Venetians had developed their own unique styles that gave visual expression to their distinctive culture, their religious beliefs, their individual status and, above all, their civic pride. Patricians, who dominated every aspect of Venetian society, were also prominent in the development of the arts in Venice. The committees responsible for state patronage were manned exclusively by patricians who were closely involved in the building, repair and decoration of the city's numerous churches. As individuals, they commissioned family chapels and palaces, altarpieces and tombs. Government control enabled them to influence and direct the activities of the *scuole*, the city's guilds and confraternities. Directly or indirectly, this ruling caste ensured that it played a leading role in the embellishment of its city.

8

The Image of the State

I t is difficult to overemphasize the importance of art as state propaganda in Venice. The complex created around San Marco (fig. 27), its huge piazza, the Doge's Palace and the piazzetta leading down to the lagoon, provided an impressive focus for the display of Venetian prestige and one that had been carefully designed for maximum impact on visitors and Venetians alike. Expensive architectural and sculptural projects testified to the city's continuing power and prosperity. In 1496 Domenico Malipiero reported in his diaries that, despite a serious financial crisis, work had started on the great clock tower in the piazza to demonstrate that the country was not absolutely bankrupt.[1] State-commissioned narrative cycles in San Marco and the Doge's Palace provided illustrations of the events and legends that had shaped the city's history. Above all, the choices of style and subject made by the state were uniquely Venetian, designed deliberately to promote an image of power and affluence abroad and to reinforce the myth of stability and perfect government at home. The fifteenth century was a period of major political change in Venice and the artistic developments sanctioned in state projects reflected the impact of this change as the city turned away from its traditional links with the East towards mainland Italy.

Not surprisingly, it was the city's ruling patrician élite that was responsible for the appearance of the images of state power. Concentrating on the buildings around San Marco, the patricians also took charge of other public structures, such as the Arsenale, Venice's shipbuilding yard, and the warehouses and market buildings in the commercial centre at the Rialto. Decisions concerning the construction or decoration of these projects were political and were decided in exactly the same way as other political issues. The initial impetus emerged in the discussions of the small and powerful committees, such as the Senate or the Council of Ten, and was then ratified by the Great Council. Supervision was delegated to a magistracy, usually the one involved in financing the project.

San Marco was the responsibility of the Procurators of St Mark. Elected

27. Doge's Palace and piazzetta, Venice

for life and with an automatic seat in the Senate, these nine patricians were, after the doge, the most prestigious men in Venice. Their prime responsibility was the administration of the substantial endowments of San Marco: hospitals, old people's homes and other charitable foundations, estates in the colonies and property throughout the city, including the porticoes lining the piazza San Marco and the buildings above, which they rented out as shops, stalls, inns and apartments. Their income also financed repairs and embellishments to the fabric of the church itself. Most other state projects were financed by the Salt Office. Unlike the Procurators of

St Mark, the *Provveditori al Sal*, or magistrates in charge of the Salt Office, were not elected for life and the committee changed regularly. Their principal responsibility was the control of the manufacture, purchase and sale of salt, a major source of state revenue. It was these funds that the state used for the upkeep of public buildings at the Rialto, the Arsenale, the lighthouses and breakwaters of the lagoon and, above all, for the construction, repair and decoration of the Doge's Palace.

Like the *opere* in Florence, these committees handled all aspects of their projects, choosing a design, employing craftsmen, paying for supplies and labour and keeping account of expenditure. Designs for major projects required assent from higher authorities. The plans for the east wing of the Doge's Palace were debated and approved by the Senate before being delegated to the *Provveditori al Sal*.[2] Formal competitions were less common in Venice and the artists who took charge of state commissions were usually well-known and with established reputations. Foreign artists were only employed on special occasions. The statutes controlling the craft guilds were strictly chauvinist, making it difficult for foreigners to operate in the city.[3] Special laws had to be passed to enable Lombard masons to work on the east wing of the Doge's Palace, a huge undertaking that required more skilled workmen than Venice could provide.[4] Large-scale projects were supervised by a chief craftsman, known in Venice as the *proto* (Greek: first). According to Benedetto Ferrini, a Florentine master working for Francesco Sforza in Milan, wages in Venice were double those in Milan.[5] But the state was not a generous employer. The Procurators of St Mark paid consistently lower rates to its craftsmen than were available elsewhere, attracting them presumably with the promise of regular work and the prestige of a state project.[6]

The Venetians showed a preference for piecework, separate contracts for each stage of the project enabling the committees to keep close control over progress. Like their Florentine contemporaries, Venetian patrons knew the value of legally-binding arrangements. Contracts for painting and sculpture normally involved a fixed price for labour and materials. Clauses bound the artist to an agreed design, the use of specified materials and a finishing date, with penalties for infringement. In 1400 the Procurators of St Mark offered Pierpaulo dalle Masegne 1,900 ducats to construct a balcony on the Doge's Palace (see below), giving him a year to complete it under penalty of 200 ducats.[7] The contract, which included the cost of materials, stipulated the use of Carrara marble for some parts, local Istrian stone for others. In 1438 the *Provveditori al Sal* commissioned Giovanni Bon and his son, Bartolomeo, to build the Porta della Carta for 1,700 ducats (see below), promising to supply much of the stone but specifying that the Bons carved the two principal statues, a figure of Justice and the Lion of

St Mark, from their own supplies (fig. 28).[8] The work had been agreed in a design drawn up by the Bons and given to the *Provveditori al Sal* presumably to ensure that the stonemasons adhered to it. One of the disadvantages to the patron of the piecework system was that it encouraged craftsmen to take on a project while busy with another. Bartolomeo Bon clearly infuriated the state in 1463 by accepting an advance for further work on the Doge's Palace and failing to start. He was obliged to adhere to a new starting date or have 200 ducats worth of his possessions seized. The *Provveditori al Sal* were forbidden under a penalty of 200 ducats to employ him again.[9]

Shortly after the end of the War of Chioggia (1378–81), the Procurators of St Mark had begun a massive programme of sculptural decoration in San Marco. By 1400 it was nearing completion. Inside the basilica was a new *iconostasis*, a chancel screen common in Byzantine churches, extravagantly decorated with statues of saints. The Procurators also commissioned a series of ornate tabernacles for relics in the main chapels flanking the apse. But the most visible changes occurred on the exterior. The solid austere outline of the basilica was disguised behind a wealth of highly decorative Gothic detail. Elegant new tracery contrasted with the massive old columns. Fancy cusped ogee arches cloaked the semi-circular lunettes on the upper level of the façade. Between them, Gothic canopies sheltered statues of saints, prophets and Evangelists, their gilded pinnacles transforming the skyline of the church.

In the new climate of expansion, the state also set about completing the new hall for meetings of the Great Council. Begun in 1340, the building had been completed by 1365 and a start had been made on its decoration. But work on this potent image of Venetian prestige had largely stopped during the war. Now, an ornate balcony was commissioned for the waterfront façade from Pierpaolo dalle Masegne, who had been responsible for much of the recent work in San Marco.[10] Like the basilica, the new balcony was richly decorated with Gothic detail. Its principal ornament was a statue of the Lion of St Mark. Elegant tracery filled the windows of the hall. An elaborate wooden ceiling was in place by 1419, built in the shape of an inverted ship's keel, a style popular in the town halls and churches of northern Italy.[11] By 1409, a fresco cycle had been begun to decorate the walls of the hall.[12] Unfortunately, these frescos no longer exist. They deteriorated rapidly and were replaced by canvases later in the fifteenth century (see below), which were destroyed by fire in 1577. But we do know the identity of two non-Venetian painters commissioned to paint some of the fresco scenes. Gentile da Fabriano and Pisanello were both leading exponents of International Gothic, the elegant and courtly style favoured by the courts of Italy and northern Europe. In their choice of artists and styles, the Venetian patricians opted for a language that was Italian and modern. But that was not true of their choice of theme.

The decoration of the hall had been started (c. 1365) with a series of portraits of Doges and, on the wall above the place where the Doge and his advisers sat during meetings of the Great Council, a huge fresco of Paradise by a Paduan artist, Guariento. Underlining the importance of the Virgin as one of the prime images of the Venetian state, the focus of the scene was her Coronation. The frescos on the other walls, begun by 1409, continued the Venetian theme. The Great Council chose to celebrate the city's power and status in a narrative cycle that recounted the events of 1177, when Doge Sebastiano Ziani played a major role in settling the quarrel between Pope Alexander III and Emperor Frederick II, Barbarossa.[13] Threatened by Barbarossa's armies, so the story runs, the Pope had fled incognito to Venice, where he was recognized and honoured by the Doge. Venetian ambassadors failed to negotiate peace with Barbarossa who launched an attack on the Venetian navy. Against overwhelming odds, the Venetians were victorious and the Emperor was forced to sue for peace. As a reward, the Pope gave Ziani a number of gifts that acquired ritual significance and accompanied the Doge on state occasions. They included a candle and a ceremonial umbrella, as well as the ring given after the naval battle to symbolize Venice's dominion over the seas. It was this event that the Doges reenacted annually on Ascension Day.

The core of the story may have been fact but its elaboration was uniquely Venetian, officially formulated by a government notary around 1320. A pictorial version of the story soon appeared in the church of San Nicolò in the Doge's Palace.[14] By the fifteenth century the story had become a vital part of the city's mythology. In 1425, when the frescos had begun to fade, the long explanatory inscriptions accompanying each scene were recorded by state order. This choice of theme for the decoration of the hall was conspicuously patriotic and in striking contrast to the portraits of republican heroes of antiquity that gave expression to Florentine political ideals or to the Arthurian legends and chivalric imagery that were designed to associate the courts of Italy with aristocratic rule. Above all, commissioned at a time when Venice's dominion was unchallenged in the Aegean and the Adriatic, this cycle was an unambiguous statement of Venetian power and status in world affairs.

The idea of extending Venetian control on the Italian mainland beyond the towns of Padua, Vicenza and Verona, in order to counter the threat of Milanese expansion, was debated hotly amongst the patriciate in the early 1420s. Doge Tommaso Mocenigo (1414–23) was emphatically against the policy. In a speech given to the Great Council shortly before he died, he warned of the huge financial and political costs of war in Italy and recommended exploiting Lombardy and the Po valley for economic rather than territorial gain. He strongly advised against the election of Francesco Foscari, a leading member of the opposition. But Mocenigo's warnings went unheeded. Foscari's thirty-four years as Doge (1423–1457) marked a major turning point in Venetian history. The success of his policy of expansion on the mainland committed the city irrevocably to the treacherous pit of Italian politics and decisively reversed her long tradition of isolation. As Mocenigo had warned, Venice was now caught up in a long and costly war. During the 1420s she took Brescia and Bergamo. Other towns in Lombardy followed. With the fall of the Visconti in Milan in 1447, Venice supported the new republic against Francesco Sforza who, with the help of Florence, united against Venetian expansionism. War continued intermittently until the Peace of Lodi was signed in 1454.

Expansion on the mainland was given powerful visual expression in the Doge's Palace with the decision to demolish the surviving part of the old Veneto-Byzantine structure still visible on the piazzetta. In its place, the elegant Gothic façade of the Great Council Chamber that looked out over the waterfront and continued round for six bays onto the piazzetta (see Chapter 7) was extended right across to San Marco (fig. 28). Uniformity and continuity were significant choices in this period of major political change. In 1422, six months before Mocenigo's death, at a time when the debate over expansion was becoming increasingly heated, the Salt Office was ordered to allocate funds for the project.[15] Initially, it had been put in the hands of the Procurators of St Mark, but there were problems with this arrangement and the *Provveditori al Sal* soon took over.[16] Demolition of the old façade began in 1424, almost a year after Foscari's election and the new building was largely complete by 1435. In 1438 the contract was drawn up between the *Provveditori al Sal* and Giovanni Bon with his son, Bartolomeo, for the construction of the Porta della Carta, a new ceremonial entrance to the palace beside San Marco (fig. 28). The doorway was set beneath an elaborate traceried window, surrounded by ornate carved details and flanked by statues in canopied niches topped by pinnacles. Gothic decoration now stretched across San Marco and both the piazzetta and the waterfront façades of the Doge's Palace. Rich and conspicuously extravagant, this was the language of European power and it was designed to provide a readily recognizable image of authority and prosperity for the Venetian state.

The statues commissioned for the new façade and the Porta della Carta expressed the nature of Venetian power. Its Christian context was prominent. Just as the Archangels Raphael and Michael had protected the corners of the fourteenth-century section of the palace towards the lagoon, so Gabriel was placed on the corner of the new extension by San Marco.

28. Giovanni and Bartolomeo Bon, Porta della Carta, Doge's Palace, Venice,
begun 1438

Beneath the Archangel Gabriel was a sculptured group of the *Judgement of Solomon* (c. 1430) (fig. 29), one of the best-known Biblical images of Justice and a choice that manifestly promoted the patrician myth of perfect government. And crowning the Porta della Carta was the allegorical figure of Justice with her scales and sword (fig. 28). The contract for the Porta della Carta made specific mention of this statue and also of a second, the Lion of St Mark or, as the contract put it, St Mark in the form of a lion.

The winged lion of St Mark is the best-known symbol of Venice. Conspicuous on government buildings throughout the city, it can also still be seen on gateways and town halls across northern Italy. But at the beginning of the fifteenth century, it was relatively new, having first appeared on coins and banners in the fourteenth century.[17] Its distinctive form derived from an Assyrian bronze chimera, possibly part of the loot from Constantinople, that stood on one of the columns in the piazzetta (fig. 27). By 1400 it had become one of the prime visual images of the state and was prominently displayed on both the balcony of the Great Council Chamber and the Porta della Carta (the statue of Doge Foscari was added in the 1480s; see below). This religious symbol of political power emphasized the close ties between Church and State in Venice but it also symbolized divine protection and approval for her rule.

By 1450 Venice was a major power in Italy but she was losing control of her maritime empire. Too preoccupied with carving out an Italian dominion, she had ignored the growing threat of the Ottoman Turks, who took Constantinople in 1453. From 1463 to 1479 Venice fought almost continual war with the Turks, losing one after another of her possessions and her trading links with the East. The peace treaty negotiated in 1479 was presented to the Venetians as a resounding victory but the reality was the forfeit of her major territories in the Aegean.[18] The city had changed direction. Her authority in the eastern Mediterranean was now seriously under attack from the superior Turkish navies. As Venice became increasingly dependent on her Italian possessions, so she turned back to her Byzantine roots to assert her identity on the mainland. In 1450 the Senate revived the cult of St Theodore: a major saint in the Orthodox church but of less importance in the West, he had been one of the city's earliest patron saints, but his role had diminished under the imposing presence of St Mark.[19] Venice had long promoted herself as the successor of Constantine's Christian Empire and the Doge as his heir to the imperial tradition in the Church. With the fall of Constantinople this image gained greater force.

At this time of major political upheaval, Venetian patricians developed a radically new style for the display of state power and prestige. This is what art historians call the Venetian Renaissance, but it took a very different form from that event elsewhere in Italy. Foscari's policy of expansion

29. *Judgement of Solomon*, Doge's Palace, Venice, c. 1430

30.   Attrib. Antonio Gambello, Arsenale, Venice, dated 1460

on land had brought the city into direct contact with Italian culture and, above all, with humanism. Venetian humanists, who were mainly patricians, were not concerned with the revival of the pagan culture of ancient Rome. On the contrary, they used the modern language of humanism in support of their city's established culture and her links with the Byzantine East.[20] These new attitudes had a profound effect on the appearance of the city. Venice followed the example of her Italian neighbours and rejected Gothic, the elaborate and conspicuously expensive style of European rulers. But, unlike them, she did not adopt the visual language of ancient Rome. Instead, she chose to assert a distinctive identity on the mainland and looked back to her traditional links with Constantinople to develop a language that provided an unambiguous statement of her unique Byzantine and Christian heritage. About 1430 the Procurators of St Mark had commissioned a mosaic cycle of the life of the Virgin from a Venetian International Gothic artist, Michele Giambono for a chapel (now the Mascoli chapel) in San Marco. The earlier scenes were set in ornate and complex Gothic structures, but the later scenes (c. 1450) had far more solid architectural backgrounds.[21] Delicate pointed Gothic arches had given way to round arches carried not on clustered and carved colonettes but on heavy piers decorated with figured marble panels. While the flanking fluted Corinthian pilasters suggest a Florentine influence (and there is indeed much evidence that Florentine masters worked on the mosaic),[22] the other elements of the settings could all be seen inside San Marco. The later drawings of the 1460s in the sketchbooks of Jacopo Bellini, a Venetian painter often associated with the Mascoli mosaics, reveal a similar revolution.

The new language was given public showing in a formal entrance portal for the Arsenale (1460) (fig. 30). This imposing structure flanked by paired columns may have been modelled on a Roman triumphal arch in the Venetian town of Pola in Dalmatia, but the columns carried Byzantine filigree capitals quite unlike Roman prototypes.[23] The style appeared in a more coherent form on the Arco Foscari in the courtyard of the Doge's Palace (fig. 31). Initially planned by Doge Francesco Foscari as a simple entrance to bring visitors into the courtyard from the Porta della Carta, the Arco Foscari was raised to a second storey by Doge Cristoforo Moro (1462–71) and embellished with sculptural detail by Doge Giovanni Mocenigo (1478–85).[24] Its combination of Veneto-Byzantine column types and capitals, continuous balustrade, Gothic pinnacles and decorative statuary came straight from San Marco.[25]

It was also during the battle with the Turks for supremacy in the eastern Mediterranean that the government decided to embark on another expensive and conspicuous project, the renewal of the twenty-two frescos in the Great Council Chamber. In September 1474 the Senate voted overwhelmingly (126 out of 134) to commission Gentile Bellini to take charge of a series

31.   Courtyard, Doge's Palace, Venice with Arco Foscari (begun c. 1450; enlarged 1460s), Staircase (begun c. 1486) and East Wing (begun 1484)

of canvases to replace the deteriorating scenes of Pope Alexander III, Doge Ziani and Emperor Barbarossa, painted less than a century before.[26] The official record of the commission specified the need to renew the cycle for the honour of the state and referred to the room as one of the principal ornaments of the city. There was no question of changing the theme. The project occupied the *Provveditori al Sal* and the city's artists for the next ninety years and was not finally completed until 1565.

Gentile Bellini, son of Jacopo, was Venice's leading painter. In 1479, after the peace treaty was signed, the Great Council voted to send him to Constantinople in response to a request from Sultan Mehmed II for an artist.[27] During his absence (1479–1480), his place was taken by his brother, Giovanni. By 1495 there were nine painters at work in the hall, their wages ranging from 60 ducats a year for Giovanni Bellini and Alvise Vivarini down to 6 ducats for the two apprentices.[28] Perugino, the only foreign artist commissioned, was offered a contract (1494) of 400 ducats for labour and materials with the proviso that the *Provveditori al Sal* must approve his design (he did not take it up).[29] One of the most surprising features of the project was the proposal made to Gentile Bellini when he was first appointed in 1474. The *Provveditori al Sal* undertook, unusually, to pay for materials and colours. In lieu of payment, Gentile was offered the next vacant *sansaria*, a sinecure giving its holder an income from one of the state-owned brokerages for life.[30] It seems to have been worth having: Titian's income from his *sansaria* in 1537 was assessed at 118–120 ducats.[31] When Gentile went to Constantinople in 1479, the same offer was made to Giovanni who, in 1495, was presumably waiting for his *sansaria* to come up.[32] This exceptional privilege suggested recognition of the key role of the artist in the creation of this prime image of state power. But it also had the more prosaic advantage of lessening the financial burden of the Salt Office, which was at the same time financing another major project, the rebuilding of the east wing of the Doge's Palace (see below).

The Great Council canvases were prime examples of what one art historian has aptly called the 'eye-witness' style.[33] The idea of ornamenting the bare bones of a story, in words or pictures, with anecdotal detail in order to make it seem real was common enough in the fifteenth century. But in Venice, the painted image had long been seen not just as a substitute for verbal description but also as visual proof of the event itself.[34] The 'eye-witness' style developed in response to this old tradition and it was uniquely Venetian. It had its sources in the processions and pageantry that characterized International Gothic painting but the 'eye-witness' painters did not depict the elegant and idealized world of courtly chivalry. The laws of perspective enabled them to construct convincing settings and their canvases showed a 'real' world, one that could be recognized by their Venetian contemporaries. Well-known landmarks and imaginary structures decorated with familiar details provided the backdrop while a few portraits stood out amongst the crowds of identifiable types, some witnessing the event, others occupied with ordinary activities of their own lives. Above all, the scenes celebrated everyday life. The anecdotal detail was not just local colour but a principal element in the visual authentication of the story. Tragically, the canvases in the Great Council Chamber cycle were destroyed by fire in 1577. But their impact on late fifteenth-century patrons was considerable and they provided the model, both in style and format, for the narrative cycles that were commissioned to decorate the meeting halls of the Venetian *scuole*, many of which still survive (figs. 32, 35 and 36).

As the century progressed, subtle changes occurred in the nature of the patrician power. As their maritime empire shrank under the Turkish onslaught, patricians were forced to turn to Italy for their livelihood. Merchants and traders were becoming aristocrats and they strengthened their superior status by requiring the registration of patrician births in a list, the Book of Gold, that defined the limits of the ruling élite.[35] The Doge increasingly took on the trappings of a prince as the tradition of honouring the office not the holder was reversed. Cristoforo Moro (1462–71) and Nicolò Tron (1471–3) both issued coins that rejected the convention of showing the Doge receiving his banner of office from St Mark in favour of their profile heads, an image of absolute rule popular at Italian courts.[36] In an unprecedented celebration of individual prestige, statues of Moro and Giovanni Mocenigo (1478–85) appeared beside the two Lions of St Mark on the Arco Foscari to mark their involvement in its embellishment and one of Doge Foscari was added to the Lion of St Mark on the Porta della Carta in the 1480s.[37] After the death of Mocenigo, it was decided to move the coronation ceremony of his successor, Marco Barbarigo (1485–6), from its previous privacy inside the palace to the more public setting of the court-yard.[38] Barbarigo was succeeded by his brother, Agostino (1486–1501), who increased the ceremonial due to his position, insisting that visitors knelt in his presence.[39] And to express the changing nature of ducal power he constructed a staircase in the courtyard to provide an elaborate setting for future coronations and for the reception of foreign dignitaries.[40]

This move towards a more princely figurehead for the state was not universally popular amongst the patriciate. Efforts were made to curb the power of Agostino Barbarigo's successor, Leonardo Loredan (1501–21).[41] The issue was also prominent in the discussions concerning the rebuilding of the east wing of the Doge's Palace after it had been badly damaged by fire in 1483. The debate was recorded in the diaries of the patrician

Domenico Malipiero.[42] Some patricians, he reported, were in favour of building a completely separate palace for the Doge further down the waterfront, linking it by a bridge to the old building, which would be reserved for government offices and the prison. The new palace would indeed have been an unmistakable statement of the increasing power of the Doge. But moderation and financial caution prevailed. The Great Council opted simply to rebuild the east wing, the solution which, significantly, kept the Doge firmly within the structure of patrician government.

The new wing (fig. 31), assigned to the *Provveditori al Sal*, was a massive undertaking. Antonio Rizzo was appointed *proto* in 1484 and the following year the government allocated 500 ducats a month from Salt Office funds normally scheduled for the repair of the lagoon defences.[43] Financial problems dominated the building from the start.[44] The *Provveditori al Sal* clearly found it difficult to cope with the organization of such an ambitious project. Soon after starting work, Rizzo complained that his salary of 100 ducats a year was inadequate; so the Senate voted him a state-owned brokerage and raised his salary to 125 ducats. Plans to appoint a full-time overseer at a salary of 300 ducats a year to keep a closer eye on how money was being spent were vetoed and the *Provveditori* were ordered to take turns themselves. By 1487 expenditure had got out of hand and they decided in the future to pay only those amounts due on agreements signed by both themselves and the *proto*. In 1491, Rizzo complained that the demands made on his time had forced him to close his shop and the *Provveditori al Sal* voted to increase his salary to 200 ducats. In 1493 work was temporarily suspended because they had run out of funds. By now the authorities were becoming suspicious. In 1496 the account books were confiscated and two senators elected to check them. Rizzo was accused of embezzling 10,000 ducats. He was sacked in 1498 and left Venice. A new *proto*, Pietro Lombardo, was appointed. He had established a reputation for honesty and hard work supervising the construction of Santa Maria dei Miracoli (see Chapter 10).[45] The new wing was finally completed during the sixteenth century.

The stylistic complexity of the courtyard façade of the new east wing poses many problems for art historians. With round arches supported by octagonal piers on the ground floor, pointed Gothic arches supported by clusters of columns on the main floor above and two further storeys heavily decorated with reliefs, the building does not conform to modern notions of Renaissance stylistic uniformity. But there can be little doubt that the complexity was deliberate. The Gothic pointed arches on the main floor relate directly to the main style of the building and the clusters of columns which support them are quotations from San Marco. But the dominating feature seen by a visitor on entering by the Porta della Carta was Agostino

Barbarigo's staircase, prominently displaying the Barbarigo coat of arms and those of enemy cities conquered during his reign. A relief of Agostino as the leader of a New Rome demonstrated the Venetian belief that their city, as heir to Constantine's Christian empire, had replaced the degenerate empire of pagan ancient Rome.[46]

Venetian expansion on the mainland provoked strong reactions from European rulers, who saw it as a threat to the balance of power precariously maintained between the peninsula's four other main states, Milan, Naples, Rome and Florence. In the political turmoil of the late fifteenth century, Venice used devious diplomacy to enlarge her dominion. Tacit support of Louis XII's conquest of Milan was rewarded with the prosperous Lombard town of Cremona. By avoiding involvement in Cesare Borgia's campaign to carve a state for himself in the Romagna, Venice was able to take advantage of the inevitable power vacuum when Cesare's father, Pope Alexander VI, died and was succeeded by the vehemently anti-Borgia, Julius II (see Chapter 22). By 1508 Venice's strength had become a serious threat and Europe joined against her in the Treaty of Cambrai (1508). The following year, the combined armies of France, Spain, the Holy Roman Empire, the Papacy, Mantua and Ferrara, launched an attack on the Venetian forces at Agnadello and routed them. Venice only survived by exploiting the political differences between her enemies. By 1511 she was one of Julius II's principal allies against Louis XII of France and she soon recovered most of her mainland possessions. But the wars had sparked off a serious economic crisis. Desperately short of funds, the government dramatically increased taxes and decided on the unprecedented move of selling non-voting seats in the Senate for 2,000 ducats each.[47] Work on all but essential projects ceased. It was only after the revival of the city's fortunes in the late 1520s that Venice was once again in a position to play a major role in the development of European art.

9

The *Scuole*

The *scuole* were a uniquely Venetian institution.[1] Like the confraternities and guilds in other Italian cities, their prime function was to provide their members with a focus for carrying out the charitable duties that were essential to their behaviour as good Christians. They gave housing and alms to members in need, looked after the sick, helped to finance dowries and executed wills. They cared for members after death, accompanying their funeral processions, attending their burials and, most importantly, saying the prayers necessary for saving their souls. The distinctive feature of Venetian *scuole* was that they also had an important civic role and functioned as agents of social cohesion by providing vital links between the divisive strata of Venetian society. They played a prominent part in the processions and ritual that accompanied the great state ceremonies in the piazza San Marco. Above all, they provided non-patricians with a sense of corporate identity in the highly structured framework of Venetian society and gave them an opportunity to give expression to their Christian beliefs and civic pride.

While their counterparts in other Italian cities were often regarded with suspicion by the authorities, the Venetian *scuole* were actively encouraged, and controlled, by the state. Although patricians were admitted as members, they were barred from the annually elected committees that administered the *scuole*. But they imposed their authority over the *scuole* through the Council of Ten, the powerful magistracy in charge of state security, whose permission was mandatory for the foundation of a *scuola* and whose approval was needed for the statutes that strictly governed its operations. These statutes covered all aspects of the behaviour of a *scuola* member and laid heavy stress on the moral and pious nature of the institution, with clauses banning such un-Christian behaviour as blasphemy, adultery and gambling. Government control ensured that the *scuole* supported the interests of the state and allowed it to monitor and direct the religious and civic duties of ordinary Venetian citizens. In a period when the call for Church reform could be heard all over Europe, the fifteenth century saw a marked increase in the foundation of new *scuole* in Venice.

The *scuole* were major patrons of art. Indeed, it is not generally realized how many of the famous paintings by Gentile and Giovanni Bellini, Carpaccio and other Venetian Renaissance artists were ordered by the corporate *scuole* and not by individual Venetians. Expenditure by the *scuole* was principally charitable. This was not just alms for the poor or help for the dying. As altars were the focus for their prayers for the souls of their dead brothers, the *scuole* acquired patronage rights to altars in the city's churches, paying rent for them and supplying the necessary liturgical vestments and fittings for the celebration of mass, including an altarpiece. The wealthier *scuole* leased plots of land from the churches for their own meeting houses, building and decorating a large chapter hall for general assemblies and a smaller room (or *albergo*) for committee meetings. And it was in these projects that *scuole* members expressed their religious beliefs and charitable obligations, their corporate identity and civic pride. Like the Florentine guilds, the *scuole* exploited the arts as an arena for the competitive display of their power and prestige in Venetian society. Above all, corporate action avoided the charge of self-glorification, a potent motive in the moral Christian culture of fifteenth-century Venice.

There were around 200 *scuole* in the city, each of them dedicated to a patron saint who provided a focus for collective prayers.[2] Membership united Venetian society at many different levels. Basic to their Christian statutes was the belief in equality before God. Patricians, *cittadini* and the working classes, men and women alike, all belonged to a *scuola*; only prostitutes and social outcasts were excluded. Most Venetian *scuole* were known as the *scuole piccole* to distinguish them from the *scuole grandi* (see below). They varied in type, size and membership. Trade guilds, or *scuole dell'arte*, covered the wide range of occupations in the city, such as boatmen, fishermen, carpenters, painters, cobblers, bakers and wine merchants. The large and prosperous Scuola dei Mercanti, whose patron saint was St Christopher, was dominated by wealthy traders. The sand merchants' *scuola*, dedicated to St Andrew, had only twenty members.[3] Some *scuole* provided a focus for the many foreign groups living in Venice. The Milanese dedicated their *scuola* to their city's patron saint, St Ambrose, the Slavs chose St George and the Florentines St John the Baptist. Other *scuole* drew their membership from a particular parish and focused on the local church. Many of the *scuole* founded in the fifteenth century were dedicated to locally popular saints, like those founded after the canonization of St Bernardino in 1450 and St Catherine in 1461.

At the top of the *scuole* hierarchy were five prestigious *scuole grandi* which drew their membership principally from the bureaucrats and rich merchants of the *cittadini* class: the Scuola della Carità and the Scuola di San Marco (both founded in 1260), the Scuola di San Giovanni Evangelista (founded in 1261), the Scuola della Misericordia (founded in 1308) and the Scuola di San Rocco (founded in 1478).[4] The *scuole grandi* were distinguished from the *scuole piccole* in a number of ways. They had all developed out of medieval flagellant confraternities; they were all-male and, with their membership limit set between 500 and 600, they were much larger and richer. There were also more subtle differences. Eligibility for election to the sixteen places on the administrative committee, the *banca*, chaired by the *Guardian Grande*, was limited to *cittadini*. This arrangement was deliberate state policy. It defined a role for the *cittadini* in the structure of Venetian society, thus avoiding the potential animosity of this powerful group excluded by birth from political office. During the fifteenth century the concept of Christian equality was adapted in the *scuole grandi* to allow their richer and more prominent members to leave the more unpleasant duties, notably flagellation, to the poorer brethren.[5] These changes, sanctioned by the Council of Ten, enhanced the power of the prosperous *cittadini* and allied them with the interests of the state. Like the patriciate, their survival depended now not only on Venice's economic success but also on the continuation of her established social and political order.

As with all important decisions taken by the *scuole*, the decision to build a meeting hall, to commission an altarpiece or narrative cycle was taken in a general meeting of members. Details were finalized by the *banca*, who drew up contracts with craftsmen and organized the finance. Supervision of larger projects was put in the hands of a smaller committee of three to five members.[6] The projects were financed from *scuole* funds, sometimes raised for the occasion. The caulkers' guild levied a tax on all its members to pay for the furnishing and decoration of their chapel in Santo Stefano.[7] The Scuola di Sant'Ursula financed a narrative cycle of their patron saint with funds provided by members of its *banca*.[8] Besides levies imposed on their members, the *scuole grandi* also obtained considerable state help to finance their ambitious schemes of building and decoration.

Many of the *scuole* were wealthy institutions. Their basic income derived from entrance fees and annual subscriptions, augmented by donations and legacies from members. The trade guilds attracted less pious offerings than the devotional *scuole*. Those dedicated to saints specifically invoked against the plague, such as St Sebastian, St Roch (Italian: Rocco), St Christopher and St Vincent Ferrer, attracted huge sums in offerings, bequests and new entrance fees during outbreaks of this deadly and much feared scourge of medieval Europe.[9] Some *scuole* possessed relics which provided a focus for pious donations. The Scuola di San Giovanni Evangelista had a particularly venerated piece of the True Cross which was carried in procession on feast days and was discovered to perform miracles (see below). The Scuola di San Giorgio degli Schiavoni, founded by Slav immigrants from Dalmatia, acquired a relic of their patron saint[10] and the Scuola di San Rocco went to considerable lengths to purchase the body of St Roch, paying 600 ducats for his head, hands and feet.[11]

Fourteenth- and early fifteenth-century altarpieces and decorative reliefs commissioned by the *scuole* to demonstrate the devotion of their members typically depicted a group of brethren before either the Virgin or their patron saint. The wealthy Scuola of San Giovanni Evangelista commissioned a relief (1349) depicting a group of anonymous brothers kneeling before their patron saint and an altarpiece (1380s) with equally anonymous members grouped around their Cross beneath the Virgin and Child flanked by St John the Evangelist, St John the Baptist, St Peter and St Paul. Uncomplicated statements of devotion, these images also stressed the brothers' equality before God.

The proliferation of new *scuole* during the fifteenth century and the changing concept of 'equality', especially in the *scuole grandi*, had a significant impact on the iconography of their altarpieces and reliefs. The *scuole* stopped commissioning groups of anonymous members in favour of the saints that expressed the individual identity of the *scuola*. Numerous altarpieces made specific references to the plague. The *scuole* dedicated to the plague saints had obvious reasons for including them, but they also appeared in subsidiary roles in altarpieces for other *scuole*.[12] The Virgin remained prominent as the central feature of devotion. And in Venice she carried a secondary meaning as one of the most popular metaphors for the city itself. The tiny *scuola* of sand merchants, dedicated to St Andrew, commissioned an altarpiece from Bartolomeo Vivarini for their altar in San Giovanni in Bragora showing the Virgin and Child with St Andrew and St John the Baptist (1478).[13] The cobblers' guild combined guild and state iconography in the lunette of the entrance portal to their *scuola* by depicting the cobbler Ananias being healed by St Mark (1478).[14] The Scuola di Sant'Antonio da Padova (which had been given exclusive rights to the devotion to this particularly popular local Franciscan saint by the Council of Ten and thus to the potential income his cult would produce) commissioned an exceptionally unusual statement of their identity. Bastiani's altarpiece (*c.* 1475–82) depicted the patron saint with two of his Franciscan companions, Bonaventure and Blessed Luca Belludi, neither of whom had been canonized.[15]

The urge to display was potent and competition was rife amongst the *scuole*. The acquisition of a carved stone altar (*c.* 1470) by the Scuola di Santa Caterina for their altar in Santi Giovanni e Paolo prompted the Scuola di San Pietro Martire in 1477 to replace their wooden altar nearby with a new stone structure.[16] Rich *scuole* could afford to commission more than the furnishings and altarpieces of their altars. The wealthy merchants of the Scuola dei Mercanti paid 250 ducats for an elaborate portal by Bartolomeo Bon decorated with statues of the Virgin and their patron saint, St Christopher, at the entrance to the church of Madonna dell'Orto that housed their altar.[17] When recording their decision to construct a new meeting house with a hospice, the Albanians of the Scuola di Santa Maria degli Albanesi specified that the new building would be for the glory of God, the Virgin, their patron saint, St Gall, and also for the Albanians themselves who would now have a hospice like the Armenians.[18]

Two foreign groups preferred to commission their own native artists rather than a Venetian to make an image which would not only convey the identity of their *scuole* but would declare their nationality in a distinctive style. The Scuola di San Giovanni Battista, which drew its membership from Florentines living in Venice, commissioned Donatello to carve a wooden statue of their patron saint (1438) for their chapel in the Frari. The Scuola del Rosario, founded by the large German community in the city, commissioned the Nüremberg artist, Albrecht Dürer, to paint his *Madonna of the Rosary* (1506) for their altar in San Bartolomeo in Rialto. Usually incorrectly known as the *Madonna of the Rose Garlands*, this altarpiece celebrated the devotion of the Scuola to the Rosary and their loyalty to the German Emperor Maximilian I, who was portrayed at the Virgin's feet.[19]

Most of the paintings and reliefs commissioned by the *scuole* conformed to Venetian taste and reflected the stylistic changes taking place in state projects. Antonio Vivarini's altarpiece (1446) for the prestigious Scuola Grande della Carità showed the Virgin and Child and the four Doctors of the Church in a crenellated and elaborately decorated Gothic courtyard strongly reminiscent of the Doge's Palace. The altarpiece (*c.* 1480) commissioned from Giovanni Bellini by the Scuola di San Giobbe for its altar in the Franciscan church of the same name depicted the Virgin and Child with Saints Francis, John the Baptist, Job, Dominic, Sebastian and Louis of Toulouse set in a barrel-vaulted space that was closed by an apse decorated with fictive mosaics and figured marble, clearly designed to recall the Veneto-Byzantine style of San Marco.[20] And in both these works, the figures were set together in a single unified space instead of in the earlier fashion of separate compartments for each saint. This new form, known as the *sacra conversazione*, created a greater emphasis on the 'reality' of the scene.

This same sense of 'reality' was also prominent in the narrative cycles that the *scuole* commissioned to decorate their meeting halls. These large rooms lined with canvases bore a striking and deliberate resemblance to one of the

32. Carpaccio, *St Augustine*. Venice, Scuola di San Giorgio degli Schiavoni, 1502–7

prime images of state power, the hall of the Great Council in the Doge's Palace. And, with the destruction of the canvases in the Doge's Palace by fire in 1577, the *scuole* cycles are the principal surviving examples of the 'eye-witness' style. In giving visual expression to their own prestige in paintings, the *scuole* made a conscious decision in their choice both of style and format to identify themselves with the state.

While the *scuole grandi* of San Marco and San Giovanni Evangelista (see below) had the means to commission the city's two leading painters, Gentile and Giovanni Bellini (who both worked in the Great Council hall), many of the *scuole piccole* commissioned a less well known painter, Carpaccio. Carpaccio made his reputation in these *scuole* cycles.[21] The Scuola di Sant'Ursula commissioned nine scenes from the life of St Ursula (1490–1500); the Scuola di Santa Maria degli Albanesi commissioned six scenes from the life of the Virgin (*c.* 1502); the Scuola di San Giorgio degli Schiavoni commissioned nine scenes of Christ, St Jerome, St Augustine, St George and St Tryphon (1502–7) and the Scuola di Santo Stefano commissioned five scenes from the life of their patron saint (*c.* 1511–20). Carpaccio also participated in the cycle for the Scuola di San Giovanni Evangelista (see below).

Carpaccio's scenes were filled with the incidental detail that was such a feature of the 'eye-witness' style, the pictorial version of the chronicler's anecdotal descriptions.[22] His *St Augustine in his Study* (fig. 32) was more a portrait of the study than the saint, with its meticulously painted furniture, books and ornaments, the armillary sphere on the saint's desk and his little white dog, surely one of the most endearing details in Renaissance art. Carpaccio's scenes from the life of St George, set according to legend in Libya, were crowded with turbanned Arabs and took place amongst the ancient Roman remains and Muslim minarets that made the scene convincingly eastern.[23] In *St George fighting the Dragon*, he painted a gateway, which has been identified as the Bab al-Futuh in Cairo and would have been known to Carpaccio through engravings. *St Ursula's Arrival in Rome* was set against the backdrop of a recognizable Castel Sant'Angelo. But the Venetian context of many of the scenes was unmistakable and deliberate.[24] Recognizable details authenticated the event. St Ursula's dream took place in Cologne, but Carpaccio's picture was set plainly in the bedroom of a Venetian palace. The backgrounds of the scenes were peopled with Venetians of all types, some chatting in groups, some viewing the scene in front of them, others walking alone or exercising their dogs. Though none of the buildings can be identified, nor was it intended that they should be, they all display recognizably Venetian forms, materials and motifs.

These cycles were not cheap. A canvas by Gentile Bellini for the Scuola di San Marco, measuring 347 × 770 cm., was valued at 200–250 ducats.[25] The most ambitious of Carpaccio's cycles, that for the Scuola di Sant'Ursula, involved eight canvases around 280 cm. high and ranging from 253 cm. to 611 cm. in breadth plus a ninth, 481 × 336 cm., for the altar.[26] The cycle probably cost as much as 1,000 ducats. In 1488 a general meeting voted to levy a tax on members of the *banca* to pay for it.[27] But it seems probable that further funds were contributed by the patrician Loredan family who were members of the Scuola and whose coat of arms was added to two of the canvases.[28] The Slavs of the Scuola of San Giorgio degli Schiavoni financed their cycle with funds attracted by papal indulgences granted for their support of the crusades against the Turks, whose expanding power in the Adriatic was threatening their homeland.[29] The gift of an important relic of St George from the commander of the Venetian fortresses on the Peloponnese, after they had fallen to the Turks in 1499, encouraged more pious donations and perhaps occasioned the commission.[30]

The major patrons amongst the *scuole* were the two wealthiest and most important, the Scuola Grande di San Marco and the Scuola Grande di San Giovanni Evangelista. Both moved into their own meeting houses early in the fifteenth century. The Scuola di San Giovanni Evangelista converted an old hospice by the church of San Giovanni Evangelista (1414–21).[31] The Scuola di San Marco built a new hall on land leased from the Dominicans of Santi Giovanni e Paolo next door to their convent.[32] The rivalry that developed between these two *scuole* during the second half of the fifteenth century resulted in some of the most impressive works of architecture, sculpture and painting in Renaissance Venice. Competition encouraged patterns of increasing extravagance. The Christian ideals of pious devotion and equality were less apparent in the new themes and styles that displayed the power and status of these *scuole* in Venetian society. The motives behind their commissions, the choices open to them, how they made their decisions and how they controlled the final apearance of their projects, all deserve closer attention.

Both founded in the mid-thirteenth century as flagellant confraternities, the Scuola di San Marco and the Scuola di San Giovanni Evangelista were amongst the oldest and most prestigious of the Venetian *scuole*. With the same patron saint as the city, the Scuola di San Marco had obvious attractions. The Scuola di San Giovanni Evangelista's main claim to fame was the possession of a relic of the True Cross, which had recently started to work miracles. Both *scuole* attracted a prestigious membership from the upper ranks of the *cittadini*, especially top civil servants and wealthy merchants. And, in the process of building and decorating their meeting houses, both *scuole* were major patrons of fifteenth-century architecture, sculpture and painting.

In the mid-1430s, the *Guardian Grande* of the Scuola di San Giovanni Evangelista was worried.[33] The other *scuole grandi* were embarking on ambitious programmes of artistic patronage. He mentioned the Scuola della Misericordia, the Scuola della Carità and the Scuola di San Marco by name and referred specifically to the wonderful and costly ceiling just finished by the latter. He urged his members to follow suit, in praise of God and for the glory of the Evangelist but also for the honour of their Scuola, and, one suspects that this was the important point, for its growth, which was now under threat. A prestigious and powerful *scuola*, like the state, had to demonstrate that it was influential and worth joining.

For reasons which will become clear, little remains of the decoration commissioned by the two *scuole* for their meeting halls in the early part of the century. But we know that the remarks of the *Guardian Grande* of the Scuola di San Giovanni Evangelista about the ceiling of the Scuola di San Marco bore fruit because his members voted to commission one as well, which was installed in 1441.[34] The Scuola had in fact decided in 1421 to decorate their Chapter Hall with scenes from the Old and New Testaments.[35] The following year it had enrolled Michele Giambono as a member, a benefit often given to a painter starting a major commission, but nothing is known of his work.[36] In 1437 the Scuola enrolled Jacopo Bellini, presumably to continue the project, but the cycle was replaced in the sixteenth century and the paintings have been lost.[37]

33.   Attrib. Pietro Lombardo, Entry Court, Scuola di San Giovanni Evangelista,
Venice, 1478–81

Not to be outdone, the Scuola di San Marco decided to decorate its
rooms. In 1444, the members decided unanimously to commission a cycle
for the *albergo* and the project (whose subject is unknown) was given to
Jacopo Bellini.[38] The following year the vote was much closer, 20–19 in
favour of a new altarpiece of St Mark for the Chapter Hall, a project also
given to Jacopo.[39] By 1463 they had decided to commission a cycle of Old

and New Testament scenes for the Chapter Hall and once again Jacopo was involved, this time with other painters including his son, Gentile, Andrea da Murano and Bartolomeo Vivarini.[40]

In the late 1470s the Scuola di San Giovanni Evangelista decided to embellish the exterior of their rather unprepossessing entrance court with an elaborate marble screen (fig. 33). With its square portal crowned by a semi-circular lunette emblazoned with the eagle of St John the Evangelist, its fluted Corinthian pilasters and elegant decorated frieze, the screen followed the lead set in state projects a decade earlier and, for a *scuola*, it was conspicuously modern. When the cobblers' guild commissioned an entrance portal for their meeting house (completed in 1478), they preferred an old-fashioned ogee-arched portal.

At this point fate intervened. A disastrous fire on 31 March 1485 destroyed the meeting house of the Scuola di San Marco, including the recently-finished paintings in the Chapter Hall. A disaster for art historians but a wonderful opportunity for the Scuola, which immediately set about rebuilding on a sumptuous scale. The extent of the disaster and the importance of the Scuola in Venetian society was reflected in government aid. The Senate assigned 4,400 ducats of state funds to the project. The Council of Ten allowed the Scuola to exceed its normal membership limit and exempted it from some of its charitable obligations.[41] Soon afterwards, a committee of four members was elected to supervise the construction of the new building for which the Scuola planned an ornate sculptural façade and, a notable innovation, a magnificent double-branched interior staircase.[42]

The plans for rebuilding were approved by the Scuola's landlords, the friars of Santi Giovanni e Paolo, and a lavatory for the use of the convent and the Scuola was placed under the landing of the staircase, its sewer emptying into the canal.[43] The contract for the Istrian stone façade (fig. 34), based on a design which had been agreed by the Scuola, was drawn up with Pietro Lombardo and his partner Giovanni Buora in 1489 at a price of 1,100 ducats, although the work seems to have been started earlier.[44] A well-established and successful stonemason, Pietro Lombardo had built the tomb of Doge Pietro Mocenigo and the church of Santa Maria dei Miracoli (see Chapter 10). The following year, Mauro Codussi was engaged as *proto*, presumably to complete the façade but principally to construct the Scuola's ambitious plans for a double staircase.[45] Codussi was also well-established and had been employed as *proto* on a number of the city's churches (see Chapter 10). By 1495 the rebuilding was largely complete and the Scuola broke.[46]

The new building was indeed magnificent. The elaborate façade was decorated with four huge carved perspective reliefs. Flanking the main

34. Pietro Lombardo and Giovanni Buora, façade, Scuola di San Marco, Venice, begun 1489

door were two panels with the Lion of St Mark standing in a coffered barrel-vaulted space, a clear statement of the ownership of the building which also carried strong overtones of the power of the Venetian state. On either side of the second door were panels depicting two miracles of St Mark, the Healing and the Baptism of Ananias. The prominence given to the Lion of St Mark shows that the Scuola was less concerned with the spiritual importance of its patron saint. Like the entrance court at the Scuola di San Giovanni Evangelista, the façade of the Scuola di San Marco adopted the new state style. But, with its semi-circular lunettes, coloured marble inlaid roundels and other details overtly borrowed from San Marco, it outshone its rival in complexity, extravagance and scale.

Meanwhile, the members of the Scuola di San Giovanni Evangelista had not been idle.[47] In 1491 they had successfully petitioned the Council of Ten to allow them to take on twenty-five extra members to finance improvements. In 1492 they were granted exemption from some of their charitable obligations and allowed to use the funds saved for their building. In 1493 they were given permission to take in another fifty members to finance a new ceiling for their chapter hall. In their petition, the Scuola pointed out that, apart from the devotion due to their relic, their building was a major ornament of the city and they referred specifically to the important foreigners who came to see their relic.

Two years later, in August 1495, as the grand staircase at the Scuola di San Marco was nearing completion, the Scuola di San Giovanni Evangelista petitioned the Council of Ten yet again for extra members to finance a new stone staircase of their own.[48] Negotiations for the land needed went slowly and it was only acquired in 1498. The *banca* was quite clear about what sort of staircase it wanted and immediately appointed Codussi as *proto* to supervise the construction of one similar to that which he had built at the Scuola di San Marco.[49] The funds from the new members, requested in 1493, had been spent on a cycle of paintings (see below) and the Council of Ten authorized the addition of yet another fifty members to finance the project. Having cleverly, and presumably with foresight, raised the ceiling of their chapter hall in 1493, they were able to construct a far more impressive staircase than their rival.[50]

In 1495, while the negotiations for the purchase of land for the staircase were under way, the Scuola decided to commission a cycle of paintings for their chapter hall and obtained permission from the Council of Ten to finance the cycle with the funds originally raised for the staircase.[51] Their petition declared that the paintings would do honour to both their relic and the state. The cycle they commissioned did indeed do honour to both, as well as to the Scuola.

The subject chosen by the Scuola was the eight miracles performed by their relic of the True Cross since it had been donated in 1369 by the chancellor of Cyprus, Philippe de Mézières, to the then *Guardian Grande*, Andrea Vendramin.[52] The canvases provide a fascinating insight not only into the visual preferences of the Scuola in the late fifteenth century but also into the appearance of the city and its inhabitants at the time. The miracles themselves had an overwhelmingly Venetian context, having all occurred in the city. The relic was remarkably partisan. Of the eight miracles depicted, six directly involved members of the Scuola.[53] Andrea Vendramin appeared in two of them, first as saviour of the relic after it had fallen into a canal and hovered above the water avoiding all other attempts to rescue it (fig. 35). In the other, the relic saved his ships from disaster, thus making him his fortune. Andrea Vendramin's family had been made patricians after the War of Chioggia and one of his descendants, another Andrea, had served as Doge from 1476 to 1478. This association between the Scuola and a leading patrician family was a clear statement of the Scuola's prestige.

The project involved the work of seven painters and was finally completed around 1510. Strong similarities between them in both interpretation and style suggests the close involvement of the patron. One of the prime

35.   Gentile Bellini, *Miracle of the Bridge of San Lorenzo*. Venice, Accademia, 1500

examples of the 'eye-witness' style, it was commissioned deliberately in emulation of the Great Council Chamber canvases. The Scuola had influence. It commissioned three scenes from Venice's leading painter, Gentile Bellini, who, significantly, had originally been put in charge of the renewal of the cycle in the Doge's palace (see Chapter 9). There is also evidence that Perugino, the one foreigner invited to work in the Great Council Chamber, was also the only non-Venetian artist commissioned to paint a scene in the miracle cycle, *The Deliverance of Andrea Vendramin's Ships*, now lost.[54]

It was usual in the depiction of miracles to celebrate the supernatural event. But this cycle did not. The scenes emphasized the public and ceremonial importance of the relic. They established the authenticity of the miracles by their recognizable settings and witnesses to verify the event.[55] They emphasized the prestigious position of the Scuola in Venetian society and, above all, they celebrated Venice herself. The miracles were submerged in the depiction of everyday life in the city, crowded with people who were totally uninvolved in what was happening. The *Healing of the Possessed Man by the Patriarch of Grado* by Carpaccio (fig. 36) showed the miracle taking place on the far left-hand side of the canvas. The scene's principal theme was the busy commercial area by the Rialto. Carpaccio recorded members of the Scuola crossing the old wooden Rialto bridge (replaced by the present stone structure in the sixteenth century), gondoliers paddling their craft on the Grand Canal and patrician palaces with their distinctive chimneys lining the canal. It is easy to see recognizable portraits in the government officials, rich patrician and *cittadini* merchants, Greeks in their distinctive broad-brimmed black hats, turbanned Muslim traders, messengers and servants, that crowded the pavements to create a scene which would have been familiar to any contemporary viewer.

Equally Venetian was the *Healing of the Son of Jacopo de' Salis* by Gentile Bellini, more commonly known as the *Procession in the piazza San Marco*. Jacopo de' Salis, a Brescian merchant in Venice on business, had heard that his small son had fractured his skull and, when he was in the piazza San Marco the next day to see the annual celebrations for the Feast of St Mark, saw the relic being carried by the members of the Scuola of San Giovanni Evangelista in procession. De' Salis knelt down and prayed. He returned home to find that his son had been cured without a blemish the day after the procession. Bellini's canvas depicted the procession in the piazza in minute detail, the kneeling de' Salis visible through a gap in the line of Scuola brothers parading across the foreground of the picture carrying aloft their relic. On the left, the neat ranks of the other *scuole grandi* lined up with their banners. On the right, government officials, musicians and the Doge himself streamed out of the Porta della Carta. The setting was

36.   Carpaccio, *Healing of the Possessed Man by the Patriarch of Grado*.
Venice, Accademia, 1494

unmistakably the piazza San Marco flanked on either side by the twelfth-
century Veneto-Byzantine porticoes, which were rebuilt in the sixteenth
century. In the background was the corner of the Doge's Palace with
senators and other officials standing under the arched loggia on the *piano
nobile*. But the centre of the picture was the basilica of San Marco complete
with its four bronze horses and mosaics celebrating the arrival of St Mark's
body in the city.

Perhaps the single detail in the cycle that gives best expression to the
changes that had occurred in the attitudes of the *scuole* during the fifteenth
century was the inclusion of five kneeling figures on the right of the *Miracle
of the Bridge of San Lorenzo* by Gentile Bellini (fig. 35). Clearly individual
portraits, these five figures were quite different from the groups of anonymous members equal in the eyes of God that were so common earlier in the
century, and they have been convincingly identified as the four leading

members of the *banca* together with Gentile Bellini.[56]

Gentile Bellini and his brother Giovanni owed their real loyalties to the Scuola di San Marco of which they were members. In 1492 they had offered to paint the new *albergo* in honour of their father, Jacopo, whose paintings had been destroyed in the fire of 1485.[57] The contract, unusually, specified that the Scuola was not to offer the commission to anyone else, thus ensuring that the brothers kept their options on this prestigious project.[58] This curious clause reflected Gentile's influence in the Scuola. He was in fact at the time serving on the *banca*, blurring the distinction between patron and artist that was normally clear in the fifteenth century.[59] And he was on the *banca* again in 1504 when it voted 8–3 to proceed with a cycle of paintings of the life of St Mark for the decoration of the *albergo*.[60] Gentile's contract for the first scene, *St Mark Preaching*, was unusual in that he was offered an annual salary of 25 ducats and a valuation when the painting was complete instead of the more common straight fee. Gentile was also expected to donate 50 ducats of the final price back to the Scuola! Most unconventional was Gentile's promise to make it better than the *Procession in the piazza San Marco* he had just completed for the Scuola San Giovanni Evangelista. Given the terms of his contract, it is interesting that Gentile's *St Mark Preaching* bore a striking resemblance to his *Procession in the piazza San Marco*. In a setting that was intended to suggest pagan Alexandria, Gentile made the focus of the scene a version of the basilica of San Marco, shorn of its glittering mosaics, Gothic details and statuary. To the left, stood an obelisk with hieroglyphics that prophesied the coming of Christianity.[61] The importance of the role of art as propaganda for the power of the Church and, above all, for Venice herself, could not have been more convincingly stated.

As with many other *scuole* projects, progress on the narrative cycle of St Mark was interrupted by the League of Cambrai (1509) and the ensuing economic slump. The *scuole* were expected to contribute their spare funds to the war effort and commissions fell. But the guilds had made their mark. Unlike the confraternities in other Italian cities, they had made a major contribution to the appearance of their city. Only the Florentine guilds, who took responsibility for the city's state projects, were patrons on a comparable scale.

10

Piety and Patriotism

Foreign visitors often commented on the uniformity of Venetian every-day dress. There was a general preference for simple black clothes with only the holders of important government posts distinguished by the scarlet, crimson or blue robes that were the uniform of their office. In this moral and Christian society, dominated by the ruling patrician élite, individual displays of affluence and achievement were discouraged. Wealth, while an essential prerequisite for patronage, was not the prime indicator of standing or success in the city. There were rich *cittadini* as well as poor patricians. Birth was a far more potent sign of prestige. Appointment to high government office carried more status than making a huge fortune. In contrast to Florence, it is striking how few private patrons stand out. In their palaces, chapels, tombs and altarpieces, patricians and *cittadini* alike showed a conspicuous lack of interest in self-glorification. Far more compelling was the desire to give visual expression to their religious piety, their patriotic service of the state and their status in Venetian society. It was only at the end of the century, as patricians increasingly began to see themselves as an aristocracy, that this pattern started to change.

Patricians played a central role in the creation of their city. Their decisions determined the form and style of the prime images of state power and their influence in the *scuole* was extensive. They also played a leading, although not exclusive, part in the other numerous schemes that embellished the city in the fifteenth century. The stylistic choices they made for state projects were echoed in their visual preferences as private citizens. Elaborate and ornate Gothic, the style of the Doge's Palace, underlined their membership of the ruling élite. The revival of Byzantine traditions during the second half of the century provided an unambiguous statement not only of their patriotic desire to assert their distinctive heritage but also of their Christian beliefs. The close ties between Church and State, fundamental to Venetian culture, made it difficult to distinguish clearly between religious beliefs and state loyalties. Expansion on the Italian mainland and the loss of her authority in the eastern Mediterranean had a direct impact on the lives of Venetians. Opportunities for international trade shrank and the rich started to invest their fortunes in land. Others benefited from the increasing number of administrative jobs to be had in the new Italian possessions. As the patriciate began to change from a mercantile élite to a land-based aristocracy at the end of the fifteenth century, their projects became more grandiose and increasingly preoccupied with individual achievement. Above all, political upheaval and social change were given visual expression in the development of uniquely Venetian solutions to artistic style in the city's architecture, sculpture and painting.

Fifteenth-century Venetians spent their money in a religious context. This was an essential part of their Christian obligations and it could take several forms. In his will of 1438, Jacopo Bernabò, a rich non-patrician merchant from the parish of San Giovanni Crisostomo, asked to be buried in his chapel in the Augustinian church of San Stefano, leaving the convent 1,000 ducats of state loans, 3 ducats a year for a mass on the anniversary of his death and 1 ducat a year for its building fund.[1] He left 100 ducats to the nuns of Santa Croce to pray for his soul and 10 ducats to the building fund of Sant'Alvise. His largest bequest, 8,000 ducats, was to his *scuola*, the Misericordia. To his parish church he left 1 ducat a year to the building fund and his altarpiece of the Virgin, for which he wanted an altar built. Bernabò's will was typical. It was customary to leave money for prayers for one's soul, although widespread membership of *scuole* made the need to make private arrangements far less pressing in Venice than in other places. Franceschina, the wife of the patrician Pietro Pesaro, left money for masses for her soul to be said in over ten different churches.[2] Charitable bequests to a favoured religious order or to one's *scuola* were common, as was the practice of leaving to a church an altarpiece which had been commissioned for private devotion at home. It was also common practice to leave money to church building funds. Stefanela, the wife of a Ser Cristoforo, in 1448 left all her goods to the building fund of Santi Giovanni e Paolo.[3]

Venice's churches were prominent features in the religious, cultural, social and, above all, visual fabric of the city. Seventy-two parish churches, each with its *campo*, or square, and a well for drinking-water, were the centres of community life for the ordinary Venetian. Around sixty convents and monasteries provided a focus for the wide range of cults associated with the many religious orders represented in the city. State control was pervasive and permission was required for new churches as well as for the rebuilding of existing ones. The fifteenth century saw a boom in construction and decoration, stimulated above all by the same powerful motives of religious reform and renewal as lay behind the foundation of new *scuole*. When the Carthusians took over the convent of Sant'Andrea della Certosa, they were ordered to restore its buildings.[4] San Giobbe was rebuilt to commemorate the canonization of the Franciscan reformer and fiery critic of materialism, St Bernardino of Siena (d. 1444; canonized 1450), whose cult had become particularly popular in Venice after he had stayed in the attached hospice in 1443. The new church of Santa Maria dei Miracoli was financed wholly by pious donations made to its miraculous image of the Virgin (see below).

Patricians, as heads of the main convents and monasteries in Venice, took charge of the rebuilding of their churches. But major construction projects for parish churches were delegated to procurators elected, like the committees in charge of state projects, to oversee the expenditure of the funds raised for the work and draw up contracts with suppliers, employ a workforce and appoint a *proto*. Composed of prominent parishioners, these committees usually included patricians. The three parishioners elected as procurators for the rebuilding of San Giovanni Crisostomo by its priests and chapter in 1495 were all patricians.[5]

Gothic church architecture had been introduced into Venice in the thirteenth century by the two great reformist movements, the Dominicans and Franciscans. The austere, unadorned forms of their plain brick churches provided powerful visual statements of their anti-materialist beliefs and desire to return to the poverty and spirituality of Christ and his Apostles. Later Venetian churches continued this theme. Above all, they were quite distinct from both the ornate Gothic of the Doge's Palace and the opulent Veneto-Byzantine style of San Marco. One of the first churches to move away from this tradition was San Giobbe, begun *c*. 1450. Its Observant Franciscan friars chose a design that derived from St Bernardino's own church near Siena and emphasized their links with his reformist zeal.[6] But the revival of Veneto-Byzantine styles and motifs in church architecture conveyed a very different message. This radical stylistic change visibly demonstrated Venice's unique traditions and asserted her identity in the context of mainland Italy. But it also unmistakably associated the city's churches with the prime image of patrician rule, San Marco.

Two conventual churches, significantly both with patrician patrons, were in the forefront of the development of these new ideas. San Michele in Isola (fig. 37) was rebuilt by its patrician Abbot, Pietro Donà (begun 1469). Its façade was expensively clad in gleaming white Istrian stone and crowned by a semi-circular lunette that held clear resonances of San Marco. Over the high altar was a huge dome on pendentives, another distinctive feature of the great basilica. Codussi is usually credited with the design of the church, but the abbot's assistant, Pietro Dolfin, saw the situation very differently. His letters to Donà reported progress on the church, and it is clear from them that Codussi was in charge of construction. Dolfin's praise

37.   Codussi, San Michele in Isola, Venice, begun 1469

for the church was directed not at Codussi but at Abbot Donà, whom he
saw as responsible for the building's visual impact.[7] The Abbess of San
Zaccaria, a convent of patrician nuns, employed Codussi as *proto* in
1483[8] on the later stages of the rebuilding of her church. Markedly more

elaborate, it displayed the same semi-circular lunettes on the façade and the same domes on pendentives inside. Private patrons began to commission burial chapels with square plans crowned by these domes, the standard eastern form for mausoleums. By the end of the century, the Byzantine fashion had extended to church plans. A group of churches begun around 1500 were all based on the San Marco plan of a Greek cross with five domes: Santa Maria Formosa, Sant'Andrea della Certosa, San Salvatore and San Giovanni Crisostomo.[9]

The history of Santa Maria dei Miracoli provides a fascinating insight into the process of patronage, design and construction in fifteenth-century Venice.[10] In 1409 Francesco Amadi had commissioned a painting of the Virgin, which was displayed in a prominent position on the outside of a house, a common practice in Venice. In 1480 the image began to work miracles: a man was found alive after falling into a canal while washing and then staying underwater for half an hour and a woman, stabbed by muggers and left for dead, was later discovered not to have a mark on her. The image attracted much attention. It also attracted much money. Five procurators, Francesco Diedo, Marco Soranzo, Francesco Zen, and Alvise and Angelo Amadi, all prominent local patricians, were elected to take charge of the funds. In July 1480 a local shopkeeper, Marco Rasti, was startled to be told by a passer-by that he would not be there by the end of the year. Asking the old man what he meant, Rasti was reassured that he would be alive but that there would be a church in place of his shop. Two months later, the procurators bought Rasti's shop as part of the site for a chapel to house the image. Granted permission by Pope Sixtus IV and the Patriarch of Venice to dedicate it to the controversial doctrine of the Immaculate Conception of the Virgin, the procurators promised that they and their heirs would be responsible for maintaining both image and cult. In March 1481 they contracted Pietro Lombardo to construct the chapel. Angelo Amadi recorded in his diaries what he saw as the important details of the contract. Lombardo was to provide all the materials to build the chapel, to face it with coloured marbles and to make statues of the Virgin and two angels for the main door. His price was fixed at 1,000 ducats. He referred to a design lodged with Francesco Zen but did not mention a designer, and established Lombardo's credentials by commenting that the stonemason had just finished the tomb of Doge Pietro Mocenigo in Santi Giovanni e Paolo (see below).

Meanwhile, money and gifts continued to pour in. In late 1481 a wealthy Milanese merchant who had been cured of a terminal liver disease donated 1,000 ducats in grateful thanks. Sixtus IV, a keen supporter of the cult of the Immaculate Conception,[11] granted indulgences to the church. By 1485 the procurators had decided to enlarge the shrine with an altar chapel and to build a convent for Franciscan nuns. A new contract was needed with Pietro Lombardo, who drew up designs for the extension. Piecework was clearly inappropriate for the ambitious scheme now under way and he was hired as *proto* at a salary of 70 ducats a year. The procurators undertook to pay for materials and labour. The church was consecrated in 1489 and the convent was finally completed by 1502. In design and articulation, this tiny jewel of a church recalled San Marco. Its barrel vault could be seen in the basilica's chapels. The façade was crowned with a semi-circular lunette and decorated with multi-coloured marble inlays in the style of San Marco's floor mosaics and wall decoration. The overtly extravagant use of Carrara marble and other costly materials on its exterior testified to the piety of the Venetians, their devotion to the Virgin and to the cult of her Immaculate Conception. But the church was also an explicit statement of patrician power.

Wealthy Venetians, like Jacopo Bernabò, took over patronage of chapels and altars in the city's churches, endowing them with funds for services and paying for their furnishings and altarpieces. The pattern was broadly similar to that in Florence but there were striking differences between the two centres. Money was far less of an issue in Venice. The Adoration of the Magi, one of the few Biblical celebrations of material wealth and very popular in Florence, had little appeal for the Venetians. Their preferences were for their patron saints and, above all, for the Virgin, who embodied not only their religious piety but, as one of the principal images of Venice herself, also their patriotic loyalties.

One of the most distinctive features of Venetian patronage is that the building and decoration of these chapels or altars was also often part of a patron's testamentary bequests. But he did not intend to commission it himself. On the contrary, that role was left to the executors of his will. Like participation in the corporate projects of the *scuole*, this practice avoided the charge of self-glorification. It was Vettor Cappello's sons who commissioned a new portal for Sant'Elena, decorating it with a relief of St Helen and their father, who died fighting the Turks in 1467.[12] The enormously wealthy Federigo Corner, one of the richest men in Venice, left the huge sum of 3,000 ducats for the construction of a burial chapel in the Franciscan church of the Frari for himself and his brother.[13] It was commissioned in 1417 by Federigo's son, Giovanni, at much the same time as Palla Strozzi was planning his father's burial chapel in Florence (see Chapter 3). But while Palla Strozzi made explicit visual references to his own part in the project, Giovanni Corner did not; his inscription referred only to the memory of his father.

These testamentary requests stipulated the details that mattered to the patron, such as the subject of an altarpiece or the location of a tomb.

Tomaso Arnaldi, a non-patrician merchant, asked his executors to commission an altarpiece for his parish church, San Giovanni Crisostomo. His will (1457) gave explicit instructions not only for its subject matter but also for its layout, specifying the Virgin and Christ flanked by Saints Thomas, Victor, Catherine and Ursula with smaller figures of Christ, St John the Baptist and St Sebastian in panels above.[14] The will of Giorgio Diletti (1494), another parishioner of San Giovanni Crisostomo, requested his executors to pay for a new chapel in the church dedicated to St Jerome, St Louis and St Christopher and to commission an altarpiece of the patron saints, which was finally ordered from Giovanni Bellini in 1513.[15] In an unusual display of modesty, Pietro Priuli's will (1491) explicitly rejected anything elaborate, requesting a plain stone with no coat of arms for his tomb in San Michele in Isola.[16]

Franceschina Pesaro's burial chapel in the Frari was not the result of a testamentary bequest but commissioned in her memory after her death (1478) by her three sons, Niccolò, Benedetto and Marco.[17] It was also intended to serve as the funeral chapel of their branch of this prominent patrician family. Originally completely frescoed, only a few details of the original decoration and the altarpiece survive. One of the loveliest Venetian Renaissance paintings, Giovanni Bellini's triptych of the *Virgin and Child with Saints* (1488) (fig. 38) is also one of the few still *in situ* on the altar for which it was intended. Set in an elaborate gilded frame, the four saints chosen by the brothers were Peter, Mark, Benedict and Nicholas, the name saints of Franceschina's husband and sons. The setting, often described as old-fashioned, was deliberately designed to recall the Veneto-Byzantine tradition of San Marco with its apse decorated with gold mosaic and marble inlaid throne. Above all, the face of the Virgin was a type, popularized by Bellini, that revived Byzantine icon traditions.

At work renewing the paintings in the Great Council Chamber and employed by the *scuole* on their narrative cycles, Giovanni Bellini (and his shop) was also a prolific producer of a distinctive type of Marian image. The type followed a standard format.[18] The Virgin was shown half-length, often behind a parapet, and separated from a rural background by a curtain or screen and she held her Child in a style that deliberately recalled the *Hodegetria* type of icon which was believed to have been invented by St Luke. Above all, these images were modern versions of the *Theotokos Nikopeia*, the prized Byzantine icon in San Marco looted from Constantinople and thought by the Venetians to have been painted by St Luke. Exploiting the potential of oil as a medium, Bellini's gentle Virgins were intended as images of idealized beauty, with perfect oval faces, delicate noses and small mouths. With their resonances of Byzantine traditions, they were in great demand from patrons in the patriotic atmosphere of late

38. Giovanni Bellini, *Virgin and Child with Saints* (Frari triptych). Venice, Santa Maria dei Frari, 1488

fifteenth-century Venice both for public display in church altarpieces and private devotion in their palaces.

The really impressive and eye-catching monuments in Venetian churches were commemorations of state service, erected to honour her naval and military heroes and, above all, her Doges. Since the mid-fourteenth century, they had not been put up in San Marco but in one of the other main churches, notably the Dominican church of Santi Giovanni e Paolo or the Franciscan church of the Frari. They were not state commissions in the ordinary sense. While the state gave permission for their erection, they were usually paid for by funds provided in wills and commissioned by the testator's executors. But they were intended to honour public office rather than serve exclusively as displays of individual achievement. Ordinary Venetians were not commemorated in such conspicuous fashion.

Vettor Pisani, the heroic patrician admiral who lost his life in the Battle of Chioggia in 1380, was buried with state honours in the transept of Santi Giovanni e Paolo. Paolo Savelli, a Roman *condottiere* who died in 1405 of the plague while leading the Venetian armies in their conquest of Padua, Vicenza and Verona, was given a monument (c. 1415-20) in the Frari with a lengthy inscription detailing his campaigns. In form, it followed the north Italian medieval practice of honouring military prowess with an equestrian statue, a tradition that had its roots in ancient Rome. The state also gave permission for two other equestrian monuments to *condottieri* leaders of the Venetian armies, Erasmo da Narni (1370-1443) better known as Gattamelata, and Bartolommeo Colleoni (1400-76). Gattamelata's statue was put up in front of Sant'Antonio in his home town of Padua. It was to be cast in bronze, requiring skills not available in Padua and his executors commissioned a Florentine sculptor, Donatello.[19] Colleoni's monument was also bronze and commissioned from a Florentine, Verrocchio. Colleoni had left 100,000 ducats in his will to the state on the condition that he was given a statue in the piazza San Marco. There was no precedent for a monument in this prestigious arena, but the state gave permission for the statue to be erected in front of the Scuola di San Marco, beside Santi Giovanni e Paolo.[20]

But the grandest monuments were those erected to the city's Doges, the holders of the highest public office to which a patrician could aspire. Stylistic and iconographic developments in their design during the fifteenth century illustrated the changing nature of ducal power as the distinction between the office and its holder became less clearly defined and the Doge began to adopt a more princely style. Earlier ducal tombs had been relatively simple monuments, decorated with Gothic detail, often including a votive portrait and an explanatory inscription. Above all, they emphasized the religious context. On his monument in the Frari, Doge Francesco

Dandolo (1329–39) and his wife Elisabetta were offered to the Virgin and Child by their name saints, Francis and Elizabeth of Hungary.[21] The tomb of Francesco Foscari (1423–57), also in the Fari, was commissioned by his nephew (c. 1460) and was considerably grander.[22] Covered with the family coat of arms, it showed an effigy of the Doge lying beneath a canopy accompanied by a relief of the Ascending Christ and statues of St Francis, St Mark and the seven Virtues. An inscription listed the towns that charted the success of his policy of expansion on the Italian mainland. Doge Nicolò Tron (1471–3) was buried opposite Foscari in a tomb that was twice the size and a far more overt commemoration of the man. Commissioned by his son in 1476, it included not only a recumbent effigy on a sarcophagus in the centre but also a standing figure of the Doge at ground level flanked by Charity and Prudence. The architectural setting was no longer Gothic, its crowning semi-circular lunette an unmistakable quotation from the façade of San Marco.

One of the few Doges not to have his monument in the Frari or Santi Giovanni e Paolo was Cristoforo Moro (1462–71). He preferred a more explicit association with the Observant Franciscans and church reform. As a private citizen, Moro had been involved in the rebuilding of the church.[23] After his election, an event apparently foreseen by St Bernardino, he included the saint as one of the city's protectors.[24] In his will he left funds for enlarging the church with a presbytery to hold both the high altar, dedicated to St Bernardino, and his tomb. In size and elaboration, the chapel testified to the wealth of its patron. This huge space with its dome resting on pendentives and a massive decorated arched entrance also conformed to current Byzantine taste and it made direct reference to San Marco with small windows inserted above the base of the dome.

Patterns of increasing grandeur were accompanied by imagery that not only glorified the holder of the office but was also becoming less exclusively Christian. A German Dominican friar travelling via Venice on pilgrimage to Jerusalem was shocked by the extravagance of the materials on the tombs he saw in Santi Giovanni e Paolo and, above all, by the statues of pagan gods and other allegorical figures that decorated them.[25] He described with disgust the monument (1476–81) to Doge Pietro Mocenigo (1474–6) by Pietro Lombardo with its figure of Hercules wrestling with the Hydra, antique soldiers and *putti*. This combination of religious, military and classical imagery was standard by the end of the century and formed the basis for the decoration of the monument (1492–5) to Doge Andrea Vendramin (1476–8), commissioned probably from Tullio Lombardo, Pietro's son, for Santa Maria dei Servi (now in Santi Giovanni e Paolo). In this, the grandest of the fifteenth-century ducal tombs, Vendramin's effigy was placed inside a huge triumphal arch ornamented with a votive relief of the

Virgin and Child, allegorical figures and all'antica shield bearers. Prominent on the tomb were Adam and Eve (now lost), carved in a style clearly inspired by ancient Greek sculpture.[26]

Venetian interest in classical antiquity grew slowly. Her Christian and Byzantine heritage was a potent force and the close ties between Church and State were fundamental to her culture.[27] Venice saw herself as the heir of Constantinople and, since the Turks had taken that city, the last surviving link with the Christian Empire that had replaced pagan Rome. The Doge was the heir of Constantine not of Augustus. But Venice's growth as an Italian power and exposure to Italian culture opened new horizons. Venetians began to see themselves as the successors to Roman authority in Italy. By the end of the century, the historian Sanudo described Doge Agostino Barbarigo as the new Augustus and some patricians began to boast descent from famous ancient Roman forbears.[28] But Venice was, above all, a major centre for Greek studies. In 1495, the printer Aldo Manuzio began to publish the Greek classics. In 1499 he printed one of the most bizarre Renaissance texts, the *Hypnerotomachia Polifili* by Fra Francesco Colonna. The book, the 'dream-love-fight of Polyphilus', was a romance in the medieval tradition that told the story of the friar's unrequited passion for a nun. Disguising the nunnery as a Temple of Diana, Colonna also incorporated extensive descriptions of classical buildings based on the ancient Roman texts of Vitruvius and Pliny.[29] By the end of the century classical architectural styles and imagery had become prominent features in Venetian art.

Two patrician wills from around 1500 illustrate the changing attitudes to monuments that blatantly commemorated the individual and the new fashion for all'antica forms and details. Benedetto Pesaro, Procurator of St Mark and Admiral of the Venetian fleet (1500-3), was one of the sons of Franceschina Pesaro, who had commissioned Bellini's altarpiece in the Frari. In his will (1503), he left 1,000 ducats for his tomb in the family chapel, stipulating that it was to include marble columns and an inscription recounting his achievements.[30] His monument, over the entrance to the chapel, was grandiose. Above stood Pesaro with his standard of office between fluted Composite columns beneath a pediment that enclosed an image of the Virgin and Child, the only unambiguously religious detail on the tomb. In a deliberate statement of his prowess, Mars and Neptune, the Roman gods of war and the sea, stood with reliefs of Cephalonia and Leucadia, scenes of his victories over the Turks, the Lion of St Mark, armour and weapons. Cardinal Giovanni Battista Zen's monument was much grander and built according to the very precise instructions in his will (1501).[31] Granted the exceptional privilege of a tomb in San Marco in return for leaving his fortune to the state, Zen left 5,000 ducats for a bronze monument and the embellishment of its altar with four bronze fluted columns and life-size bronze statues of the Virgin holding Christ, St Peter, St John the Baptist and, above, figures of God and angels. An inscription was to include Zen's name and the whole work was to be gilded. He asked his executors to employ a good sculptor and, unusually, specified that it was to be as antique as possible. He also left 1,600 ducats for furnishing the altar with a silver crucifix, six candelabra and other items, all bearing his coat of arms.

A votive portrait to commemorate state office was a new pictorial type developed in response to the desire to celebrate personal achievement. Previously confined to tombs, it had become standard practice by 1500 for a Doge to commission a votive picture of himself for the Doge's Palace.[32] One of the earliest surviving examples showed Doge Giovanni Mocenigo (1478–85) with St Christopher and St John the Baptist presenting him to the Virgin and Child.[33] Depicted in his robes of state and wearing the ducal *biretta*, the Doge's curious horn-shaped hat, Mocenigo held the banner of office given him at his coronation. The focus of the painting was an altar carrying an inscription that emphasized his role as a servant of the Venetian people. Doge Agostino Barbarigo's votive portrait (1488) (fig. 39), commissioned from Giovanni Bellini, was similar in type and showed him being offered to the Virgin by St Augustine, his name saint, and St Mark.[34] But Barbarigo's image was more overtly princely. There were no references to public duty and, wearing a *biretta* encrusted with pearls and rubies, the

39. Giovanni Bellini, *Virgin and Child with SS Augustine and Mark*. Murano, San Pietro Martire, 1488

Doge knelt before the Virgin in the manner of an absolute ruler.

The practice also spread to other state offices. One enigmatic image commissioned by three patricians showed their initials and coats of arms held by *putti* in front of an arch carrying an inscription promoting public duty and the arms of the reigning Doge, Nicolò Tron (1471–3). The lack of portraits was striking, but this soon changed. Giovanni Bellini's portrait of three Procurators of St Mark with St Peter and St Mark presenting them to the Virgin (1510) displayed no such modesty. Nor did Jacopo Pesaro show modesty when he commissioned a painting to commemorate his role as leader of the papal navy in the victory over the Turks at Leucadia in 1502. The picture showed him being presented to St Peter by Pope Alexander VI.[35] For this commission Pesaro chose the little-known Titian, who was to become the city's leading artist later in the sixteenth century.

Private palaces of patricians lined the Grand Canal, the city's most prestigious address and the preferred site for those who were rich enough to build their homes there. Commissioned by wealthy Venetians from the twelfth to the twentieth centuries, these palaces provide one of the great visual feasts for the modern tourist. Venetian palace design was distinctive and reflected the unusual demands of site and function.[36] The main entrance on the canal brought the visitor by boat into an interior courtyard raised above water level. In the courtyard, those who could afford it sank

40.   Ca' d'Oro, Venice, begun 1424

their own private well for fresh drinking water. Windows in the courtyard admitted more light into the main rooms that stretched back from the façade. Exterior staircases, often decorated, gave access from the courtyard to the main rooms on the upper floors. One of the special features of Venetian palaces, and one that much impressed foreign visitors, was the extensive use of glass. Still famous today, Venetian glass was made from superior soda ash imported from Syria and of exceptionally high quality by fifteenth-century standards.[37]

The patron's prime attention was fixed on the Grand Canal façade. There was much he intended to be read from it. A large window and balcony readily identified the location and size of the main reception room, the *salone*, on the *piano nobile*. Clearly visible from the canal, this window was on one side of the façade of smaller palaces and centrally positioned only in the grandest buildings (figs. 40 and 41). Prestigious palaces might have a second reception room on the floor above, its windows slightly less elaborately decorated. The style and extravagance of the decoration on the façade made, above all, a conspicuous statement about its owner.

There are over forty fifteenth-century palaces on the Grand Canal. Coats of arms proclaimed ownership but the extensive use of heraldic emblems as decorative patterns, so common in Florence, was rare here. The palaces varied in size, in plan and in minor details; but most of those built before *c*. 1475 displayed a strikingly uniform feature: the windows and balconies of their main rooms were decorated with the same distinctive style of tracery. This ornate tracery was also clearly visible on another Venetian building, the Doge's Palace. The choice of style and uniformity were clearly intentional. The palaces clearly proclaimed their owners' wealth and, even more importantly, their family's membership of the city's ruling élite.

One of the most exquisite of these palaces is the Ca' d'Oro, literally the House of Gold and so called after the gilding that originally decorated the traceried façade (fig. 40). Its patron was Marin Contarini, a Procurator of St Mark and a highly successful merchant. The palace is one of the few for which detailed building accounts survive and it is clear that Contarini was closely involved with both design and construction.[38] Like the records of Filippo Strozzi and Giovanni Rucellai in Florence (see Chapter 5), Contarini's books make no mention of an overall designer and it was he who co-ordinated the contributions of his various craftsmen. He drew up separate contracts with a builder for its structure, two different workshops of masons for stonework and a French painter for the gilding. Work on the palace began in 1424. The previous year, Contarini had arranged with Giovanni Bon, his son and two apprentices for the supply of stonework for the palace, unusually not paying them piecework but employing them all for 140 ducats a year.[39] When work started, he kept a careful record of other jobs they took on, deducting sums accordingly.[40] They were responsible for much of the decorative stonework commissioned for the palace, including the single windows and balconies on the façade and the pinnacles that crown its skyline. The six-bay window on the *piano nobile* was ordered from the workshop of Matteo Raverti. Ornamented with the cusped pointed arches and quatrefoil roundels of the Doge's Palace, this window was an unambiguous statement of his patrician status. Contarini's wealth was easily visible in his extravagant use of ultramarine and gold-leaf, which picked out not only the stone details but also his coat of arms.

A much grander palace was built by Doge Francesco Foscari on the site of an old Byzantine house which had been given to Francesco Sforza by the state for his services as a *condottiere*.[41] It was re-appropriated after the outbreak of war between Milan and Venice and sold to the Doge in 1452. Foscari's new palace was conspicuously grander than Contarini's, four rather than three storeys high, and its size allowed a centrally-placed *salone* with eight rather than six windows. But it incorporated the same decorative details inspired by the Doge's Palace, along with a panel of Istrian stone bearing his coat of arms.

The first palace to show signs of breaking with this pattern was never finished. Begun in 1457 on a grand scale by a wealthy patrician, Andrea Corner, work stopped when he was exiled and his brother, Marco, sold it to Francesco Sforza, Duke of Milan, in 1460.[42] Sforza, again in favour with Venice since the Peace of Lodi (1454), had been given another palace (now the Palazzo Corner at San Polo) to replace the one sold to Foscari. This was not on the Grand Canal and Sforza arranged to exchange it for Corner's partly built structure. Known as the Ca' del Duca in his memory, Sforza was advised by his agents that it would cost 14,000 ducats to complete. Very little was done before the deed of sale was annulled in 1466 and all that remains is the massive diamond rusticated basement, quite unlike anything seen at this date in Venice. By 1480 tastes had changed. The ornate Gothic tracery of the earlier palaces disappeared to be replaced by round-arched window arcades, decorated pilasters and roundels of multi-coloured stone, all of which were features of the new east wing of the Doge's Palace. But the most striking change was a move away from uniformity in favour of more individualized façades.

One of the most unusual palaces on the Grand Canal is the tiny Ca' Dario (fig. 41), commissioned by a successful *cittadino*, Giovanni Dario, a civil servant, secretary to the Senate and one of the key figures in the peace negotiations with Sultan Mehmed II (1479).[43] State business took him all over the Middle East, even to Persia. In 1484 he wrote to Doge Giovanni Mocenigo complaining that he was 70 years old and stout and would

41. Ca' Dario, Venice, begun c. 1487

like to come home! As *Gran Guardian* of the Scuola di San Giovanni
Evangelista in 1493, he was involved in its projects. His palace (begun
c. 1487) was small but unique. Dedicated by its inscription to the spirit of
the city, its façade was covered with marble inlay and decorated with

multi-coloured patterns that were taken from San Marco. None of the patrician palaces made such a clear association with Venetian tradition and the religious imagery of the state.

Andrea Loredan, a member of a prominent patrician family, built himself a palace (now the Palazzo Vendramin-Calergi) unprecedented in its individuality (fig. 42). Although the layout of its windows followed tradition, with paired columns separating the central *salone*, their form was new. Similar windows had appeared in the drawings of Jacopo Bellini (*c*. 1460), on the Palazzo Corner-Spinelli (*c*. 1480), in the clerestory of San Zaccaria and in Carpaccio's *Dream of St Ursula*. But they were not common. Moreover, Loredan made the unprecedented move of introducing free-standing classical columns onto his façade, fluted Corinthian on the main floor and plain Corinthian above. And easily visible on the ground floor was an inscription, *Non nobis Domine, Non nobis*, the first words of Psalm 115, 'Not unto us, O Lord, not unto us, but unto thy name give glory'.[44]

Loredan was not the only patron who felt obliged to make some consciously religious sign on the exterior of his palace to make it clear that, although they had chosen a highly individualized design ornamented with classical detail, they had not been motivated by the desire for self-glorification.[45] Grand palaces had been built, for example by Francesco

42.   Palazzo Vendramin-Calergi, Venice, begun *c*. 1502

Foscari, but his choice of the Gothic tracery of the Doge's Palace followed the standard format for the display of patrician power. Loredan's palace did not. Not only was it ornamented with pagan detail but it was also different and suggested conspicuous self-glorification. In the changing climate of late fifteenth-century Venice standing out of the crowd was still not acceptable and required some explanation.

As in other private houses of the period, Venetian palace interiors were sparsely furnished and pictorial decoration was overwhelmingly religious. All had their images of private devotion, sometimes a figure of Christ but more often a painting of the Virgin and Child. Bellini's modern versions of Byzantine icons were especially popular. But the fifteenth century also saw a growing taste for secular themes. Francesco Corner commissioned Mantegna to paint a *Triumph of Scipio* which gave visual expression to his family's claim to be descended from the Roman republican hero, Publius Cornelius Scipio, whose military successes had included the defeat of Hannibal.[46] A particularly Venetian innovation that appeared around 1500 was the image of a sleeping female nude.[47] Now primly described as Venuses, they were commissioned to decorate bedrooms.[48] Patrons also began to commission landscapes and allegories, forcing painters to widen their repertoire and change their style.

One of the leading painters in this new development was Giorgione, who died of the plague aged 34 in 1510. His most famous painting, the *Tempesta* (fig. 43), probably commissioned by the prominent patrician Gabriel Vendramin, had little in common with fifteenth-century tastes. This delicately painted landscape with figures of a soldier and a nursing mother dominated by a terrible storm was quite unlike the 'eye-witness' style of the Great Council Chamber and the *scuole* or Bellini's Byzantine Madonnas. Its imagery has long puzzled art historians, who have endeavoured to read too much into it. In contrast to Florence, there was no tradition of complex allegorical programmes for paintings in Venice.[49] Recent research has shown that the key features of Giorgione's canvas can all be related to the appalling psychological impact of the city's defeat by the armies of the League of Cambrai. Venice's defeat at the Battle of Agnadello in 1509 changed her overnight from a major Italian power to a city that seemed unlikely to survive. The League's armies took all her mainland possessions, reaching Padua, less than twenty miles away. Income from her dominions ceased abruptly and the city was plunged into a major financial crisis. One art historian has suggested that the *Tempesta* showed the birth of Plutus, the god of riches, to Ceres, and Zeus's anger at her union with a mortal, as an allusion to the transience of fortune.[50] Plutus was later brought up by Peace and the story would clearly have had a direct relevance to Venice's sudden fall from grace and the hopes and fears of

43. Giorgione, *Tempesta*. Venice, Accademia, *c*. 1509–10

her citizens for their future. Other art historians have related the canvas more precisely to the Battle of Agnadello.[51] The poorly dressed soldier, the nursing mother and the ruined buildings in Giorgione's painting all portrayed the effect of war. The city in the background has been convincingly identified as Padua.[52] The flash of lightning across the sky, a traditional sign of God's wrath, and the sombre threatening mood of the painting reflected the atmosphere in Venice as her citizens tried to come to terms with this dramatic change of fortune.

Part Three
The Italian Courts

11

The Italian Courts

I n June 1473 Eleonora of Aragon, daughter of the King of Naples, stayed
in Rome on her way to Ferrara to marry Duke Ercole d'Este. In a letter
home, she described the lavish banquet given in her honour by Cardinal
Pietro Riario, how they sat on silk chairs at a table covered with four
layers of tablecloths, listened to poems composed specially for the occasion and ate their way through over twenty-five courses interspersed
with frequent handwashing in a variety of scented waters.[1] The food,
recounted in minute detail, included gilded almonds and pomegranate
seeds, a whole goat, chicken, peacock, pheasant and a series of sugar
fantasies and puddings decorated with the d'Este and Aragon coats of
arms. The direct relationship between the obviously enormous cost of the
banquet and the level of honour done to herself, to Naples and to Ferrara
was unmistakable. Neither Eleonora nor her family would have been
impressed by a simple, modest meal. Extravagance was not only the principal way of showing power; it was also the recognized formula to convey
respect. The belief that ostentatious display was the key component of
status and prestige was deeply entrenched in fifteenth-century society,
especially in the secular courts.

Despite the prominence given by art historians to Florence, Venice and
Rome, most of Renaissance Italy was controlled by the absolute rulers of
the peninsula's numerous independent states. The collapse of the Roman
Empire during the fifth century had removed Italy's centralized government
and destroyed its political and cultural unity. The vacuum was filled by a
succession of powers whose ultimate goal was Rome and domination of
the spiritual heart of Christian Europe. The Goths, Byzantine Emperors,
Charlemagne and his Lombard armies and the Normans all tried to
establish their authority in Italy. Naples was under the dynastic control of
the French Kings of Anjou from 1266 to 1435, while the towns of northern
Italy, nominally fiefs of the Holy Roman Empire, took advantage of the
lack of effective imperial leadership to gain their independence, officially
recognized in the Peace of Constance of 1183. The dramatic revival of trade

in the eleventh and twelfth centuries created a powerful mercantile élite which challenged the tradition of inheritance as the basis of power and led to the formation of communal elected governments. Florence was one of the few to survive into the fifteenth century. For the majority, the pressures of economic recession and civic unrest made the prospect of a single powerful ruler appear very attractive. Five secular courts stood out in fifteenth-century Italy as prominent centres of Renaissance culture: Milan, Naples, Ferrara, Urbino and Mantua.

Despite the broad similarity in political systems, these states varied enormously in history, size, prosperity and, above all, in character. Milan and Naples, which had both been important centres in Roman times, were two of Europe's largest cities and their rulers enjoyed prestige throughout the continent. Mantua, Ferrara and Urbino were tiny, all smaller than Pavia, the second city in the Milanese state. In theory, the princes, dukes and marquises who ruled the Italian courts were feudal lords, paying annual dues and owing military service to the Emperor in the case of Milan and Mantua or to the Pope in the case of Ferrara, Urbino and Naples. But in practice they were independent and exercised absolute power over their dominions. They formed alliances through diplomatic links and above all through marriage. Ludovico Sforza, Duke of Milan, was related by marriage to all the leading Italian rulers. His parents-in-law were Ercole d'Este, Duke of Ferrara, and Eleonora of Aragon, daughter of King Ferrante I of Naples. His sister-in-law, Isabella d'Este, was married to Francesco, Marquis of Mantua, and Francesco's sister was the wife of Guidobaldo, Duke of Urbino. Ludovico's second cousin was Louis XII, King of France, though this relationship was to prove disastrous (see Chapter 12). Competition played a vitally important role as these rulers jostled for prestige. Inspired by the really illustrious courts of northern Europe, they surrounded themselves with the trappings of aristocratic power and created centres of Renaissance culture that rivalled their models in ostentation, scale and magnificence.

The culture of these secular courts was essentially military. Many of the rulers earned their living as *condottieri*, or mercenary soldiers selling their military skills to the major Italian powers, especially Venice and the Papacy. Like their counterparts in France or Burgundy, they educated their children in the arts of war, giving them an entirely different outlook on life from that of the sons of wealthy businessmen in Venice or Florence. Chivalry was a central component of their culture and it provided unmistakable evidence of their association with the aristocracies of northern Europe. The Este of Ferrara traced their ancestry back to the knights of King Arthur's Round Table, and Alfonso I of Naples adopted the Siege Perilous as one of his devices. His son, Ferrante I, founded the Order of the Ermine, in imitation of the chivalric companies of knights such as the English Order of the Garter, the French Order of the Star or the Burgundian Order of the Golden Fleece. Poets, writers and musicians used their talents to relate the heroic exploits of the quest for the Holy Grail, the Romance of the Rose and other medieval legends. Horses, essential for fighting, played a prominent role in life at court. Jousts and tournaments were used both to foster and to display military talent. Hunting was the sport of kings. The marshes around the Gonzaga court at Mantua were ideal for hawking and the family was famous for breeding falcons as well as horses and dogs. The Este Dukes of Ferrara employed 52 huntsmen,[2] and the King of Naples paid salaries to over 200 huntsmen and falconers.[3]

Many of these Italian courts were prominent centres of humanism. Milan and Naples were particularly important: it was deliberate political policy on the part of both Francesco Sforza and Alfonso of Aragon to employ humanists to provide propaganda for the legitimacy of their régimes. Humanists made excellent chancellery officials and diplomats, while their histories and biographies were potent material in the fight for power. While humanists in Florence concentrated on eulogizing the superiority of their city, their contemporaries at secular courts promoted the achievements of their individual rulers. Cicero's republican idealism was entirely inappropriate for the support of absolute rule, but his writings provided a powerful new language to advertise status and prestige. There is a tendency to see chivalry as part of an old medieval tradition, inimicable to the new humanism of the fifteenth century; but it was the combination of these two languages that gave each of the Italian courts its distinctive culture, entirely unlike those developed in Florence, Venice and Rome.

The essential component in princely magnificence was conspicuous expenditure. The absolute rulers of the Italian courts felt few moral curbs on their extravagance and they were far less inhibited than patrons in Florence or Venice in their ostentatious display of wealth and prestige. Wedding celebrations provided outstanding opportunities for pageantry celebrating not only the dynastic context of the event but also the uniting of two houses and their future political ambitions. State visits were another occasion for the demonstration of importance. When Eleonora of Aragon's sister, Beatrice, visited Ferrara on her way to marry Matthias Corvinus, King of Hungary, Ercole d'Este elaborately refurbished the ducal apartments in his palace to a standard befitting a future queen.[4] Fifteenth-century rulers travelled with huge entourages of courtiers (often expensively dressed for the occasion in new uniforms) as well as their servants, musicians and even their dogs. Emperor Frederick III came to Italy for his coronation in 1452 with a retinue of 2,000 and was lavishly entertained by the Pope, Alfonso I of Naples and Borso d'Este. When Christian I of

Denmark visited Italy in 1474, he stayed with his brother-in-law, Ludovico Gonzaga, in Mantua, and with Galeazzo Maria Sforza in Milan, where he was shown the Sforza's impressive collection of relics and other precious items, which included the body of a Holy Innocent, the arm of Mary Magdalen, a tooth of St Christopher and some of the Virgin's hair, each displayed in costly gilded and bejewelled reliquaries.[5] Not all rulers were impressed with the expenditure made in their honour. While a Florentine chronicler praised the elaborate festivities arranged for the visit of Pope Pius II in April 1459, the Pope himself commented that the city had spent little money or effort on entertaining him beyond staging a lion fight.[6]

The ritual of court life revolved around the castles, hunting lodges and villas of their rulers, whose principal image of power was a fortress in the city centre, its defensive exterior deliberately designed to convey a message of invulnerability. The building housed kitchens, bakeries and storerooms, armouries and prisons, quarters for guards, servants and courtiers, the principal offices of government, the state treasury, huge reception halls for entertainment, smaller rooms for private audiences and the prince's private apartments. Status and rank were strictly defined. Lavish decoration testified to its owner's wealth and power. Tapestries, gold-leaf and ultramarine covering stone, stucco and woodwork, time-consuming intarsia decoration, clothes of silk, gold or silver brocade and valuable collections of jewels, manuscripts, cameos, curiosities and relics – all were recognizably costly. Like their northern counterparts, fifteenth-century Italian rulers shared a taste for expensive Flemish tapestries and talented Flemish musicians, many of whom were employed at the Italian courts.[7] Flemish painters were sought by the Dukes of Milan and Urbino. The preeminent status we give to painting was not shared by the fifteenth-century kings, dukes and marquises who wanted to display their prestige in conspicuous expenditure. Painting was cheap, but it was a useful, and popular, medium for giving visual expression to the distinctive character of each dynasty, its prestige and achievements, its heritage and ambitions.

The Renaissance courts developed imagery very different from that of Florence, Venice or Rome. This was not surprising; they each had an entirely different message to communicate. The themes of republican idealism, Byzantine heritage or papal primacy meant little to any of the courts. In Milan, the Sforza Dukes were anxious to establish the legitimacy of their position as the rightful heirs to the Visconti regime. The Aragon Kings in Naples made little reference to their Angevin predecessors whom they had ousted from power, but celebrated their own recent victories. The Gonzaga rulers in Mantua, the Este in Ferrara and the Montefeltre in Urbino were more concerned with promoting the prestige of their small courts as rivals to the more powerful states of Milan and Naples. Arthurian legends and chivalric romance provided unambiguous links with the ruling aristocracies of northern Europe. Fresco cycles depicting life at court could display dynastic ambitions and promote the image of a wise, powerful ruler. Expensive new churches and convents testified not only to Christian piety but also to the scale of wealth. And the culture of classical antiquity, above all the culture of imperial Rome, provided new and potent imagery for the expression of absolute power. It was the distinctive combination of secular, religious, imperial and courtly themes that enabled each ruler to proclaim his own power and aspirations.

12

Milan

M ilan was the largest city in fifteenth-century Italy and she had a long
history. Surrounded by the fertile soils of the Po valley and in a
position to control the trade routes over the Alps to France and northern
Europe, the city had been a major administrative centre of the Roman
Empire. It was here that Constantine had signed the Edict of Milan in
313 making Christianity the official religion of his Empire. As Bishop of
Milan (374–97), St Ambrose had made the city an influential centre of
early Christianity. After the collapse of Roman authority, Milan and
the nearby city of Pavia became the heart of the Holy Roman Empire's
Lombard kingdom and the focus of imperial ambitions in Italy. Milan's
buildings testified to her power and prestige.[1] Milan Cathedral (begun
c. 350) was as old as Constantine's basilica of St Peter's in Rome and almost
as large. The huge fourth-century church of San Lorenzo with its massive
entrance colonnade was once the palace chapel of the imperial court. The
Baptistery and the churches of Sant'Ambrogio, San Simpliciano and San
Nazaro had all been founded by St Ambrose. Sant'Ambrogio had been
rebuilt from the ninth century onwards to provide a magnificent setting for
imperial ceremonial.

Milan achieved independence from imperial rule under the terms of the
Peace of Constance (1183). But autonomy brought conflict between the old
imperial nobility and a powerful new mercantile class.[2] The civil wars that
ensued were decisively won by the nobility, who, under the leadership of
the archbishop, Ottone Visconti, imposed aristocratic rule on Milan in
1277. The Visconti were a prominent noble family and the election of
Matteo Visconti as *Capitano* in 1287 marked the start of their dynastic rule.
Milan prospered and grew, extending her control over the surrounding
region. By 1349 the Visconti controlled the rich commercial centres of
Pavia and Brescia, and their authority stretched to the foothills of the Alps
to include Alessandria, Asti, Como, Novara, Bergamo and Cremona. The
Visconti began to develop ambitions in the broader arena of European
politics and, by the late fourteenth century, they had established links with

the ruling houses of northern Europe. Galeazzo II (1355–78) married his daughter to Lionel, Duke of Clarence, son of Edward III of England, and his son, Giangaleazzo, to Isabella of Valois, daughter of John II of France. Giangaleazzo, in turn, married his daughter to Louis, Duke of Orleans, son of Charles V of France, an act that was to have disastrous repercussions later on and form the basis for the French claim to Milan in 1499.

Powerful and ambitious, Giangaleazzo Visconti (1385–1402) embarked on a military campaign to extend his authority in northern Italy. Moving east towards Venice, he seized Verona and Vicenza in 1387 and Padua, Bassano and Belluno in 1388. He then turned south and, by 1402, controlled Perugia, Assisi, Pisa and Siena. But he met stubborn resistance in Florence and died of the plague while besieging the city (see Chapter 1). With their independence and national identity at stake, Florentine humanists condemned his imperial ambitions, but Giangaleazzo's own propagandists proudly promoted his aim of establishing an Italian monarchy.[3] In recognition of his new status, he was granted the title of Duke of Milan by Emperor Wenceslaus in 1395. At home he organized an efficient centralized administration and set up a privy council along the lines of the monarchic governments of France and England.[4] And his court rivalled those of northern Europe in its grandeur and magnificence. Like them, its chivalric culture was explicitly associated with the military ethos of aristocratic rule and not the mercantile values promoted in Florence or Venice.

Giangaleazzo provided ample evidence of the extent and nature of his power in a series of ambitious building projects. He started cathedrals in Monza and Como. In Pavia, he began construction of a Carthusian monastery, the Certosa, planning his mausoleum in the church which was finished by his successors (see below). He completed and decorated the castle in Pavia, started by his father.[5] Built around an enormous courtyard 142 m. square with four imposing corner towers, its walls were heavily castellated and it was surrounded by a deep moat with a fortified drawbridge. This potent image of defence was one of the most impressive settings for the display of courtly power in Italy. Its rooms were frescoed with scenes of hunts, jousts and other courtly entertainments.[6] One room, known as the Hall of Mirrors, was decorated with panes of coloured glass painted in gold with figures, animals and flowers.[7] The Visconti library housed valuable manuscripts of Christian and classical authors, including Vitruvius's treatise on architecture, copies of Dante and Petrarch, exquisitely illustrated missals and books of hours, Arthurian legends and other chivalric romances.[8] Rich, ornate and conspicuously expensive, Giangaleazzo's castle with its decoration and furnishings provided unmistakable evidence of his political and cultural links with the courts of northern Europe.

The prime statement of Giangaleazzo's power and prestige was his decision to replace the old early Christian cathedral in Milan with a magnificent
modern building (fig. 44). The project was supervised by a committee of
deputies representing the cathedral and the city's administration; but, like
the city itself, ultimate control lay with the Duke. The new cathedral was
a massive undertaking, providing steady employment for craftsmen and
new challenges for engineers. Stone was transported in barges from quarries near Lago Maggiore, down the river Ticino and into the city on the
Naviglio Grande, a canal designed to supply fresh water and irrigate the
surrounding land. To cope with these demands, the canal was improved
with crude locks, probably the first in Europe.[9]

Giangaleazzo decided to build the new cathedral in the elaborate Gothic
style of the great churches of northern Europe, deliberately ignoring local
traditions. Started in 1386, its huge nave of pointed arches was crowned
with ribbed vaults and flanked by four side aisles. The high altar was
enclosed by an ambulatory in the French fashion. Outside, flying buttresses
crowned with pinnacles supported the structure. Giangaleazzo's choice
caused enormous problems for the cathedral authorities and for the Duke
himself.[10] The issue was not so much the radically new style of the
building but rather the innovative structural techniques involved. North
European builders had exploited the potential of combining pointed arches,
rib vaults and flying buttresses to create a structure that would carry the
weight of the building in much the same way as a modern steel-frame sup-
ports a skyscraper. Like the skyscraper, the method allowed northern
cathedrals to reach enormous heights, unheard of in Italy. The French and
German masters employed by the Duke to take charge of construction
attempted to build a high nave and low side aisles with the buttresses acting
as stabilizers. But their efforts were undermined by the local workforce,
who were used to the more traditional system of supporting structures on
heavy masonry walls and believed that a lower nave supported by the
flanking side aisles would be more solid.

Relationships between the foreigners and the locals deteriorated. The
detailed cathedral records reveal astonishing levels of anger and resentment. Experts called in from north of the Alps and Italians from Bologna,
Venice and Piacenza gave their opinion of the progress of the building
and unanimously described it as unstable. In 1399 Jean Mignot arrived
from Paris and submitted a report to the authorities. The following year a
meeting was held with the local masters to hear their side of the story. There
was far more at stake than the very real problems of the building. In answer
to Mignot's comment that the buttresses were not strong enough, the locals
replied that their stone was twice as good as French stone. Mignot then
attacked their lack of scientific knowledge, adding that workmanship was

44. Cathedral, Milan, begun 1386

useless without it. The discussion soon degenerated into a petty squabble. Mignot arrogantly insisted that the locals were stubborn and ignorant, and demanded an audience with the Duke. Giangaleazzo clearly sided with him. He criticized the workforce, ordered them to get back to work and insisted that the cathedral authorities continued to pay Mignot's salary. But the Italians had the last laugh. They compiled a list of trivial mistakes made by Mignot, all of which had cost money, and he was sacked in 1401. Not completed until after 1500, the final appearance of the building reflected the dispute; for, despite Giangaleazzo's determination to construct a Gothic cathedral, its squat outline betrays the inability of the local masters to come to terms with the new structural techniques developed in France and their insistence on continuing Lombard building traditions.

Giangaleazzo's new empire disintegrated soon after his death. His son, Giovanni Maria (1402–12), possessed neither the political acumen nor the military skills of his father. He was succeeded by his brother, Filippo Maria (1412–47), who made a determined attempt to re-impose Milanese authority in northern Italy and stem Venetian expansion, recovering most of the city's Lombard territories. Milan never achieved the same size that it had had under Giangaleazzo, but the state remained a powerful force in Italian politics throughout the fifteenth century.

Like his father, Filippo Maria spent conspicuously on ducal projects, and he concentrated on continuing Giangaleazzo's buildings, notably the Duomo and the Certosa at Pavia. But he moved his court back to Milan and established himself in the old Visconti stronghold, the Castello, rarely going out in public. He commissioned Pisanello, one of the leading Italian International Gothic artists, to paint frescos inside the castle (subject unknown)[11] and also to make a portrait medal of himself. Medals (which were a new Italian fashion popularized at the courts of Ferrara and Mantua, see Chapters 15 and 16) reflected the growing interest in the culture of imperial Rome as a precedent for their absolute power. Filippo Maria also employed humanists as propagandists for his widely unpopular régime. Milanese humanists in his service promoted the benefits of monarchical rule in preference to the less stable elected government of Florence and they praised his patronage of the arts as evidence of Visconti power and prestige. Pier Candido Decembrio devoted two chapters of his biography of the Duke to his architectural projects and Francesco Filelfo wrote a defence of his extravagance, based on the Aristotelian concept of magnificence as an essential virtue of the very rich and powerful.[12]

Filippo Maria Visconti died without an heir and amongst those with a claim was the ambitious and talented *condottiere* Francesco Sforza, who was married to the Duke's illegitimate daughter, Bianca Maria. But the day after his death the initiative was seized by the Milanese nobility, who installed themselves at the head of a new republic dedicated to the city's patron saint, St Ambrose.[13] The castle in Milan and other images of Visconti power were destroyed. But the pressures on the new government were formidable. Foreign powers, notably Venice, had taken advantage of the power vacuum and Milan's dominion had begun to collapse. Revenues from subject cities stopped. The new government abolished unpopular taxes but failed to establish other sources of income. Rich merchants would not put patriotism before good business sense and invest in the new economy. In the face of financial disaster and growing civic unrest, the ruling élite increasingly defected to support Francesco Sforza. By 1449 Sforza had manoeuvred himself into a strong position. Employed by the republic to defend the rapidly disintegrating dominion, he had successfully captured many of Milan's subject cities and in 1448 signed a treaty with Venice for her help in realizing his ambitions in Milan. He now blockaded the city, cutting off her supplies of food and water. The starving population was forced to surrender and he established himself as head of state in 1450.

Francesco Sforza (1450–66) speedily secured his new régime, consolidating power with concessions to the nobles who had supported his rise to power and by diplomatic alliances abroad.[14] The pattern of government remained unchanged, but the key personnel were all now Sforza men. The ducal administration and chancery was put into the hands of Cicco Simonetta, an old comrade of Sforza's from his early soldiering days.[15] Another old companion, Bartolomeo Gadio, was given charge of the ambitious building projects that were to give visual expression to his new power and prestige.[16] He secured his border fortresses with trusted *condottieri*.[17] Others were appointed as resident diplomats to the major courts of Europe.[18] The new régime was marked by a change in foreign policy. Milan turned away from her traditional links with northern Europe and sought political ties in Italy. Prominent amongst her new allies was Florence. Cosimo de' Medici had strong political motives for opening a branch of his bank in Milan in 1452. The easy credit that allowed Sforza to secure his position also cemented his links with the Medici. Cosimo appointed Pigello Portinari as manager, a trusted employee who had worked for the Medici since 1434 and who was later given a place on Sforza's privy council.[19] Portinari was in charge of commissioning an ostentatious palace to house the bank's offices and he justified the enormous costs incurred in building and furnishing it as a deliberate attempt to impress the Milanese.[20]

Sforza's most pressing problem was establishing the legitimacy of his position. He stressed his links with the Visconti régime. A deed was forged to claim that he had been given power by the old duke, his father-in-law, and he adopted the Visconti coat of arms.[21] But Sforza had no mandate from the Emperor, and could only promote himself as the man his people recognized as Duke and whose military power had saved them from disaster.[22] Humanists employed at his court turned a blind eye to the legal issue and provided powerful propaganda for the new régime by stressing Sforza's conquest.[23] Cicco Simonetta, the new chancellor, drew up the basic framework for a biography of Sforza outlining his road to power.[24] The work was started by Francesco Filelfo, who had worked for Filippo Maria, and continued by Chancery officials, all humanists, including Cicco's brother, Giovanni.[25] Filelfo's principal work for Sforza was the *Sforziade*, an account of his military career based on Homer's *Iliad*, the story of Achilles' heroic exploits in the Trojan war.

Sforza demonstrated his legitimacy above all with permanent symbols and embarked on a huge programme of architecture, sculpture and painting to display his new authority and testify to his links with the old Visconti régime. He brought economic and strategic benefits to Milan by improving the canal system around the city, adding two new canals with more sophisticated sluice gates and locks.[26] He commissioned the vast Ospedale Maggiore (begun 1456). He reinforced his connection with the Visconti by continuing their projects, notably Milan Cathedral and the Certosa in Pavia, where he commissioned richly decorated cloisters for the monastery. Plainly distancing himself from the unpopularity of his father-in-law, he did not restore the Visconti castle in Milan which had been destroyed by the Ambrosian Republic, but built a garrison on the site.[27] He moved back to Giangaleazzo Visconti's castle in Pavia and, in a striking statement of continuity, chose not to replace the dilapidated frescos commissioned by Giangaleazzo fifty years before, but to restore the scenes of hunting and jousting to their former glory.[28]

In a move designed to appeal to popular sentiment and enhance Sforza power in the Church in Milan, Francesco and Bianca Maria undertook the construction of a number of convents, all associated with the growing movement for Church reform. Bianca Maria's evident involvement in many of these projects again testified to the legitimacy of Sforza's position. They rebuilt the church of San Sigismondo in Cremona (begun 1463) to commemorate the site of their marriage in 1441 and transferred the monastery from the somewhat easy-going Vallombrosans to the Hieronymites, a newly-founded strict flagellant movement (approved 1406).[29] Francesco and Bianca Maria also built Santa Maria Incoronata in Milan (begun 1451) as the headquarters of the Lombard Congregation of Augustinian Hermits, a reform movement that was rapidly expanding in northern Italy.[30] One of the most extraordinary examples of fifteenth-century church design, this church had a double façade with, inside, two naves and two altars, one dedicated to the Virgin (on the left) and the other to St Nicholas of Tolentino, a recently canonized member of the Augustinian Hermits. This church became a popular site for the tombs of Sforza's courtiers. Francesco and Bianca Maria established an Observant Dominican community at Santa Maria delle Grazie in Milan and financed a new church (begun 1463). They also supported a new reformist Franciscan movement, the Amadeiti, founded by Amadeo da Silva around the middle of the century, rebuilding Santa Maria di Bressanoro at Castelleone for them (begun c. 1460)[31] and financing their new church in Milan, Santa Maria della Pace (begun c. 1465).

Francesco Sforza was a conspicuous spender. The cost of building the garrison in Milan was reputedly 300,000 ducats.[32] The Medici bank proved a useful source of funds to finance the costs of displaying his power and prestige. The accounts for the year 1459–60 showed that 42 per cent of the bank's profits had come from the sale of expensive silks, brocades and jewels to Sforza's court and the interest on his loans of 53,000 ducats amounted to 35 per cent of the profits.[33] By 1467 Sforza's debt had risen to 179,000 ducats.[34] His building projects were administered by his old comrade-in-arms, Bartolomeo Gadio, who authorized the payments for wages and materials and liaised between Sforza and the craftsmen on the sites. The workforce was supervised by a chief craftsman. Sforza's principal foremen were two Florentines, Benedetto Ferrini, and Antonio Filarete, who had worked for Pope Eugenius IV on the bronze doors for St Peter's and, since 1451, had been employed by Sforza in Milan on the Ospedale Maggiore and other projects.

The most prestigious job for a stonemason in Milan was serving as one of the chief craftsmen on the cathedral. In 1451 Sforza forced the reluctant deputies to give the post to Giorgio degli Organi, son of Filippino da Modena (d. 1450), who had held it under the Visconti and had been sacked for political reasons during the Ambrosian Republic.[35] His request specifically cited Filippino da Modena's service to Bianca Maria's father. When Giorgio degli Organi died in 1452, the deputies promoted one of their own men, Giovanni Solari, and Sforza arranged that Filarete should be appointed as well.[36] Filarete was sacked in 1454 and Sforza's bid to get him reinstated was unsuccessful.[37] When the next post became available, Giovanni Solari's son, Guinforte, was appointed.[38] When Guinforte died in 1481, his place was taken by his son-in-law, Giovanni Amadeo.[39] This system of family succession, unthinkable in Florence, reflected the importance of dynasty and the nature of ducal rule in Milan.

Sforza took a close interest in the design of his projects. In 1456 he sent Filarete to see whether the Ospedale Santa Maria Nuova in Florence could provide the basis for his new hospital and, later in the same year, Cosimo de' Medici sent him a model for the building that he had had made, probably by Bernardo Rossellino.[40] It is clear from the correspondence with his agent in Venice regarding the purchase and completion of Marco Corner's palace on the Grand Canal that Sforza had firm ideas on what he wanted (see Chapter 10).[41] As the hospital was finished much later and the Ca' del Duca in Venice was never completed, it is difficult to be certain of Sforza's original intentions. But his important religious commissions significantly showed no striking change of style from those of his Visconti predecessors. The pointed arches in Santa Maria delle Grazie, Santa Maria Incoronata and the Certosa at Pavia were Gothic. It is clear that Sforza considered visual continuity a key element in underlining his right to rule. One patron in Milan was conspicuously different. When Pigello Portinari, manager of the Medici bank, commissioned his burial chapel in Sant'Eustorgio, he chose a deliberate statement of his nationality and his political allegiances by basing it on the Medici sacristy in San Lorenzo, Florence (see Chapter 3).[42]

There is evidence that Sforza was being encouraged by his advisers to adopt a radically new style for his projects. Filarete, with the help of the humanist Filelfo, wrote a treatise on architecture (1461-4)[43] for Sforza that told the story of how an architect and his patron, unmistakably Filarete and Francesco Sforza, built two cities, Sforzinda and Plousiapolis. (A final chapter was added on Medici patronage, see Chapters 4 and 5.) The Greek content of the text reflected the central role of Filelfo in its creation.[44] Plousiapolis was Greek for 'rich city'. Plato was the principal source for the treatise's dialogue form and for the general appearance of the two cities, which Filarete based on Athens and the lost city of Atlantis. Deliberate clues linked Sforzinda to Milan. The names of the patron's architect and his court scholar were anagrams of Antonio Averlino (Filarete) and Francesco da Tolentino (Filelfo). The city's gates were named after Sforza's family. Above all, Filarete described the architect teaching his patron about a better style of architecture based on the adoption of classical forms, and praised Ludovico Gonzaga as an example of a patron who had done so (see Chapter 16). Following Alberti, whose treatise had been aimed at a wider audience (see Chapters 16 and 18), Filarete set out to persuade Francesco Sforza of the advantages of the classical language of architecture and how it could be used to indicate status. His highly individual reading of the orders is confusing but his application of them is a fascinating insight into the preoccupations of courtly society. In describing the buildings of Sforzinda, he showed his patron how the orders could be used to denote status and how they could function alongside the more traditional methods of scale and elaboration to make the distinctions in rank that were so important in Milanese society.[45]

Filarete's treatise also throws light on the process of design at the Sforza court and, clearly, he did not consider it the exclusive province of the architect. Some buildings were designed by the architect, their plans submitted for the patron's approval. On other occasions, the patron detailed precisely what he wanted and the architect drew up the ideas. Drawing was essential. Filarete's architect taught his patron's son how to draw, so that he could follow the precedents of Roman Emperors and design his own buildings.[46] He illustrated his ideal patron with some intriguing metaphors. The patron was like a man in love: he would not care about the cost. He described the relationship between patron, architect and building as that of a father, mother and child: both patron and architect were indispensable in the creation of a building but it was the mother who gave birth to it.[47] While Alberti had described the job of the architect as that of an expert designer (see Chapter 16), the architect in Filarete's treatise was essentially that which Filarete himself knew well, chief foreman on a building site.[48] The close relationship he envisaged between architect and patron was highly idealized and should be seen as a comment on the difficulties Filarete experienced in dealing with Sforza through his agents and secretaries.

Francesco was succeeded by his 21-year-old son, Galeazzo Maria Sforza (1466–76), who surrounded himself with the external manifestations of princely prestige. Cicco Simonetta stayed head of the Chancery and Gadio remained in charge of ducal projects but Galeazzo Maria sacked most of his father's courtiers and replaced them with his own friends.[49] He was not popular and was finally assassinated. His court was famous for its extravagant entertainments and displays. Under his leadership, Milan became a major centre of Renaissance music and he instructed his agents in Flanders, England and Naples to find talented performers.[50] In 1471 he travelled on a state visit to Florence with a retinue that included courtiers, dressed in specially designed outfits embroidered with gold and silver thread, priests, secretaries, servants and musicians plus over 1,000 horses and pack mules, 5,000 pairs of hounds and 12 covered carriages.[51] With no pretensions to his father's military talents and with a direct blood link to his Visconti predecessors, Galeazzo Maria testified to the legitimacy of his rule as the rightful heir of the powerful Giangaleazzo Visconti and adopted his great-grandfather's coat of arms.[52] On one occasion, he ordered the ladies at court to adopt the hairstyles and fashions of one of Giangaleazzo's frescos in the castle at Pavia.[53] According to the Mantuan ambassador, they looked very charming!

Galeazzo Maria continued his predecessors' projects, working on the cathedral, churches, the Ospedale Maggiore and the Certosa. But his energy was directed towards the prime symbols of his position, the castles in Pavia and Milan, which he embellished to create fitting settings for his magnificent court. He tried, unsuccessfully, to buy some of the treasures from Pope Paul II's collection.[54] In his will he left the enormous sum of 25,000 ducats for the building of two churches; one he specified was to be clad in multi-coloured marble like the baptisteries in Florence and Pisa and to contain his expensive bronze tomb.[55] Costly gold and ultramarine were prominent in the elaborate fresco decorations he commissioned for chapels in the castles at Pavia and Milan.[56] But his main preoccupation was the detailed planning of fresco cycles for these two castles.

In 1469 Galeazzo Maria requested a survey of the state of the decorations in the castle at Pavia and drew up a programme for new paintings to replace much of the older work, commissioned by Giangaleazzo Visconti ninety years before.[57] But, like his father, Galeazzo Maria had no intention of destroying these vital visual links with the Visconti dynasty. It was clear from a progress report submitted to Cicco Simonetta that Bonifacio Bembo, one of the painters working on the redecoration, had been instructed to follow the style of the earlier works. Galeazzo Maria's new frescos for the castle's public rooms included scenes of hunting and falconry, his horses and his dogs, as well as a depiction of Giangaleazzo with greyhounds in the main hall. His private apartments were decorated with more personal statements of his prestige, with scenes of him dressing, eating and holding audience. His marriage to Bona of Savoy in 1468 was commemorated in a narrative cycle painted in her apartments, which showed their proxy wedding in Amboise and her journey from France to Milan, her new status clearly marked in a scene showing her exchanging her French clothes for Lombard fashions. In their private bedroom was a group portrait of the couple with their first child, born in 1469 and named, not surprisingly, Giangaleazzo.

Undeterred by warnings from his advisers that the move might be unpopular, Galeazzo Maria moved back to the old Visconti castle in Milan, adding new wings and a second floor to his father's garrison to create a setting for his court as magnificent as that at Pavia.[58] At one stage, he planned to drape some of the main reception rooms with velvet but this was, perhaps, too expensive.[59] He then drew up a scheme for a cycle of frescos, elaborating it in two later versions (1470–1).[60] He was very specific about what he wanted. A deer hunt for the large reception hall was to include his favourite dogs and his horse, Galeso, as well as his courtiers, brothers and huntsmen, who were all listed by name. The final version included his favourite Flemish singer, Petro da Oli. The dynastic cycle for the ducal chamber gave unmistakable evidence of the legitimacy of his rule. Galeazzo Maria did not look far back into Milanese history to promote his power and prestige. On the four walls were frescos of Galeazzo Maria himself and three of his forebears: Giangaleazzo Visconti, Filippo Maria Visconti and his father, Francesco Sforza (Giovanni Maria Visconti was excluded). In a clear statement of dynasty and prestige, each was portrayed with an entourage of family and courtiers. There were some telling gaps. Filippo Maria Visconti's wife was not included as Bianca Maria had been illegitimate, and Francesco Sforza's courtiers were not the ones Galeazzo Maria had sacked but those he continued to employ. Despite the elaborate planning, the project never materialized, perhaps because the painters' estimate of 5,400 ducats was too high.

Galeazzo Maria attached enormous importance to portraiture as a means of indicating the intricate hierarchy of his court. While on a visit to Mantua in 1471, he sent for his principal portrait painter, Zanetti Bugatto, and it seems likely that this was so that Bugatto could see Ludovico Gonzaga's Camera degli Sposi, then in the process of being decorated by Mantegna with scenes of the Mantuan court (see Chapter 16).[61] The three schemes for the castle in Milan (1471–2) contained many modifications as his favours changed.[62] Amongst the courtiers and family surrounding him in the ducal chamber, Galeazzo Maria requested portraits of his brother-in-law, the Marquis of Monferrat and Ludovico Gonzaga, Marquis of Mantua. The painter was instructed to make sure they appeared equal in status.[63] Galeazzo Maria was furious to find that he did not appear in the Camera degli Sposi.[64] He took a close personal interest in the decoration of his castles. It was his choice to imitate the style of the earlier frescos. Bembo had to ask him for more precise details so that he could finish painting Bona of Savoy in her wedding clothes in the Duchess's apartments in the castle at Pavia.[65] He was also involved in the choice of artist and, significantly, he showed far more concern for cost than for quality. He told Gadio to choose the quickest and cheapest of the artists submitting estimates for redecoration in the castle at Milan and the contract went to Pietro de Marchexi.[66] This painter knew the system. For the frescos in the chapel in the castle at Pavia, he offered 175 ducats and was undercut by a team that included Bembo and Bugatto and had the support of Gadio, which offered 160 ducats. Pietro de Marchexi promptly dropped his price to 150 ducats and won the contract.[67]

In 1476 Galeazzo Maria was assassinated, leaving his 7-year-old son, Giangaleazzo, as heir. Bona of Savoy took over as regent and ruled with the Privy Council, which was dominated by Cicco Simonetta and his brother, Giovanni. This precarious situation offered an enticing opportunity for Galeazzo Maria's ambitious brother, Ludovico, who seized control of the council in 1479 and ruled in Giangaleazzo's name.[68] Cicco Simonetta was executed (1480), his brother was exiled and Bona of Savoy left the city. In 1491 Ludovico married Beatrice d'Este, sister of Isabella d'Este, wife of Francesco Gonzaga (see Chapter 16). In 1493 he persuaded Emperor Maximilian to marry his niece for the massive dowry of 400,000 ducats and over 100,000 ducats worth of valuables.[69] The Emperor was now finally obliged to recognize the Sforza claim to be Dukes of Milan and, with the death of Giangaleazzo in 1494, Ludovico assumed the title. Until that date, he claimed legitimacy as the son of Francesco Sforza and the grandson of Filippo Maria Visconti.[70] In 1483 Ludovico published four hundred copies of the biography of his father, written in the Chancery under the auspices of Simonetta, printing more copies in 1486 and an Italian translation in 1490.[71] Prefaced with a eulogy of Ludovico's talents that promoted him as heir to his father's military and political skills, the book was a blatant attempt to legitimize his *de facto* position as head of state.

One of Ludovico's major projects was a huge bronze equestrian monument of his father, probably planned for the courtyard of the castle in Milan.[72] The tradition of celebrating military prowess with an equestrian monument was well established in northern Italy. Two famous Venetian *condottieri*, Gattamelata and Colleoni, had both been commemorated in bronze statues (see Chapter 10). But Ludovico's plans were far more ambitious. Leonardo took over the commission in 1490 and his notebooks included many anatomical sketches of horses in various poses. The clay model of this colossal statue, never cast, was 24 feet high and showed Francesco Sforza sitting on a rearing horse.

Determined to imprint his authority in Milan, Ludovico rivalled his

45. Bramante, choir, Santa Maria presso San Satiro, Milan, begun *c.* 1478

brother, father and even great-grandfather as a patron of architecture, sculpture and painting. He continued the Visconti-Sforza projects. He commissioned new decorations for the castle in Milan and re-invigorated work at the cathedral. He also began a major programme of urban renewal in Milan that provided clear evidence of the political order he imposed on the city. He removed street obstructions and encouraged citizens to rebuild the façades of their houses to a uniform height and cleared large piazzas in front of the cathedral and the castle.[73] He commissioned repairs and additions to many of the city's churches, notably Sant'Ambrogio, Santa Maria presso San Satiro (fig. 45), Santa Maria presso San Celso and Santa Maria delle Grazie (fig. 46). He instituted urban renewal schemes in Pavia, Cremona and, above all, in his birthplace, Vigevano (see below). In Cremona, he completed his parents' church, San Sigismondo. In Pavia he started a new cathedral and embellished the interior of the Certosa with paintings and expensive intarsia choir stalls. He commissioned Bergognone to paint a fresco of the *Coronation of the Virgin* for the left transept with portraits of himself and his father as donors and another fresco of Giangaleazzo Visconti presenting a model of the Certosa to the Virgin for the right transept (1488).

The system of patronage, design, construction and decoration of Ludovico's projects followed the pattern of that of his predecessors. But there were subtle changes. While Galeazzo Maria had shown a preference for local artists and choosing the cheapest estimates on offer, Ludovico looked further afield and wanted quality. Answering a request for information about good painters in Florence (c. 1490), his ambassador there sent details of four: Botticelli, Perugino, Ghirlandaio and Filippino Lippi.[74] The letter compared the styles of the artists and, in reference to their status, added that three of them had worked in the Sistine Chapel and all had worked for Lorenzo de' Medici. Ghirlandaio was specially praised for his speed. Ludovico's court attracted the talents of two artists, Bramante and Leonardo. Both of them were trained as painters but Ludovico expected far more from his court artists.

Ludovico employed Bramante principally on his architectural projects. With no grounding in the building crafts, Bramante did not fill the same role as Filarete, the chief craftsman working on the site, nor was he the ducal agent in charge of finance and administration. His role was a significant innovation, one that involved quality control and, above all, design. Lorenzo de' Medici and Ercole d'Este preferred to retain personal control over the design of their projects (see Chapters 5 and 15). Ludovico Gonzaga was one of the few patrons to have turned to an expert in classical style, Alberti, for the design of some of his projects but Alberti was not an employee (see Chapter 16). Ludovico Sforza's decision to employ an expert

46.   Bramante, Santa Maria delle Grazie, Milan, begun 1492

draughtsman with a knowledge of classical style to take responsibility for the final appearance of his buildings was a significant step in the emergence of the modern architect.

Ludovico's employment of Leonardo was more conventional. Leonardo's letter asking for employment at the Sforza court laid heavy stress on his skills as a designer of military machines, listing portable bridges, cannons, explosives and transport. These are not talents we would expect from a painter, but they were what Ludovico and other Renaissance princes wanted. The range of Leonardo's commissions in Milan was typical of the court artist. He painted a portrait of Ludovico's mistress, Cecilia Gallerani, designed temporary decorations for court festivals, made a model for the tower of Milan cathedral (see below) and worked on Ludovico's military projects. Leonardo's notebooks included a scheme for representing the Duke as Good Fortune protecting his people from Poverty.[75] The Confraternity of the Immaculate Conception commissioned Leonardo to paint an altarpiece, known as the *Madonna of the Rocks*.[76] And the security of court employment gave Leonardo the freedom to experiment. His architectural drawings were some of the first to show buildings from above.[77] His oil-based frescos may have been dismal failures but his use of oil to develop a *sfumato* technique was an important innovation.

Above all, Ludovico broke decisively with the stylistic choices used by his father and brother to display their visual links with the Visconti dukes. As his employment of Bramante suggested, Ludovico was keen to exploit the potential of the culture of imperial Rome to provide imagery for his rule. Milan had been an important centre of the Roman Empire and, at one stage, the capital of the Christian Empire. Ludovico took up this imperial theme. The elaborate decorations erected for the celebration of Giangaleazzo's marriage to Isabella of Aragon in 1489 included a massive triumphal arch decorated with reliefs showing scenes of Francesco Sforza's career as well as other temporary structures that combined references to imperial Rome and early Christian Milan[78] to make manifest the nature of Sforza power in the city. Ludovico commissioned Leonardo to decorate the Sala delle Asse in the castle at Milan with trees and vegetation (repainted in 1901) in imitation of the natural woodland settings painted in Roman palaces as described by Pliny and other classical authors.[79] Bramante designed a Corinthian canonica for Sant'Ambrogio, and two cloisters, one Ionic, the other Doric. There was no room for a real coffered barrel-vaulted choir at Santa Maria presso San Satiro and Bramante's design was painted *trompe l'oeil* onto the flat wall (fig. 45). Bramante's crypt for the Duomo at Pavia was built with pumpkin vaults of a type that could be seen in Emperor Hadrian's villa at Tivoli.[80]

Santa Maria delle Grazie had been started by Francesco Sforza and

Ludovico embellished the convent (fig. 46). He commissioned the tomb of his wife, Beatrice (d. 1497), from Cristoforo Solari.[81] Bramante designed a new cloister and sacristy for the church as well as an ambitious extension of the main chapel (begun 1492), which was intended as his mausoleum. Its massive forms and round arches were in striking contrast to the Gothic nave built by Ludovico's father. It had far more in common with the huge church of San Lorenzo built in the fourth century. Santa Maria delle Grazie was also the site of Ludovico's most famous project, the *Last Supper* (1496–7), commissioned from Leonardo for the refectory of the convent (fig. 47). Leonardo's experiments with oil for this fresco were not successful and the painting began to deteriorate immediately after completion. His interpretation of the subject, the traditional choice for refectories, was strikingly innovative. In contrast to other fifteenth-century depictions of the Last Supper, this one did not show the institution of the Eucharist but the more dramatic moment earlier in the story when Christ announced that one of the disciples was going to betray him. The painting was in a deep perspective setting and light from the window behind emphasized the lone

47. Leonardo, *Last Supper*. Milan, Santa Maria delle Grazie, refectory, 1496–7

figure of Christ. It has been convincingly shown that the separation of the Apostles into four distinct groups reflected the division of contemporary choirs into treble, alto, tenor and bass to provide an expression of the interest in music at the Sforza court.[82]

The issue of stylistic choices became crucial with the cathedral. By 1480 it was nearing completion and decisions had to be taken regarding the form of the tower, or *tiburio*, that was to crown the crossing (fig. 44). Letters to the town councillors of Strasbourg asking if the foreman of their cathedral could come to Milan to advise on progress were unproductive.[83] The chief craftsman of Freiburg cathedral, Johannes Nexemperger, agreed to come to Milan and signed a contract (1483) allowing him to bring up to ten of his own masons, a carpenter and a smith.[84] But this arrangement did not work and Nexemperger left the following year. Ludovico now turned to Italian experts. In March 1487 Ludovico Gonzaga's builder, Fancelli, came over from Mantua and the landlord of the Stag was paid for his eight-day stay.[85] Fancelli spent the rest of the year in Milan assessing various models that had been submitted for the tower.[86] He was highly critical of the building, which he described in a letter to Lorenzo de' Medici (August 1487) as lacking bones and rationality.[87] The arguments dragged on. During the next few years, models were submitted by many different talents: local builders and stone workers, including the two chief craftsmen on the cathedral, Amadeo and Dolcebuono, as well as one of Italy's best-known engineering experts, Francesco di Giorgio, a Dominican friar and two other non-builders, Bramante and Leonardo. Bramante also submitted a written opinion that concentrated on stylistic issues and ignored the structural repercussions.[88] Finally, in June 1490, a meeting was held in the Duke's presence to make a final decision. Given the long history of friction between design ideals and the realities of building practice on Milan cathedral, it is not surprising to find that Bramante's report was rejected in favour of the plans of Amadeo and Dolcebuono, which were based on local Lombard building traditions and conformed visually to the rest of the building.[89]

It was at Vigevano, his birthplace, that Ludovico was able to exploit the imperial theme most freely. The transformation of this town and its old Visconti castle was his most ambitious project.[90] He had pressing political motives. Started in the 1480s, shortly after he had seized control of the Privy Council but before his position in Milan was secured, this massive scheme was designed to create a focus for his personal power outside Milan. Like Pope Pius II at Pienza, his involvement in the town was not limited to architecture. He tried unsuccessfully to get city status for Vigevano, using his brother Cardinal Ascanio Sforza as an intermediary with the Pope.[91] He invested in the local economy and made profits for himself, building new irrigation canals, planting groves of mulberry trees, introducing new breeds of sheep from Provence and setting up stables for horse breeding.[92] An inscription over the entrance to the castle recorded his agricultural improvements and his architectural projects in the town. He imposed order on Vigevano with a radical programme of urban renewal, building new streets, churches and houses. Bramante and Leonardo were two of the many craftsmen involved in the ambitious remodelling of the castle, which included a new tower, a drawbridge, stables, and decoration of the ducal apartments.

The focus of the new town was a magnificent central piazza, the space cleared by demolishing the old town hall and houses along the wide old market street, to create a vast open space, over 120 yards long and 45 yards wide (134 × 48m).[93] In imitation of an imperial Roman forum, the piazza was lined with arcades on three sides, broken by two triumphal arches and frescoed with *all'antica* decorations. The fourth side was closed by the church and an imposing ramp gave access from the piazza to the castle. Ludovico's coat of arms were prominent, even appearing on the façade of the new town hall alongside those of the commune.

But storm clouds were gathering. Milan had been ruled by two of Giangaleazzo Visconti's great-grandsons for over thirty years when, in 1498, a third was crowned King Louis XII of France. With no taint of illegitimacy, his claim to Milan was superior to that of Ludovico's and he decided to enforce it. In 1499 his armies ousted the Sforza dynasty and Ludovico died a prisoner in France in 1508.

13

Naples

I n 1524 the critic, Pietro Summonte, summarized the achievements in Neapolitan art during the fifteenth century.[1] He had little positive to say. He related with horror the destruction of Giotto's frescos in the chapel of Castel Nuovo and claimed that the Aragonese kings had not been interested in art, but preoccupied with war, hunting, jousting and outfits for their horses. His judgement was unfair and he ignored the fact that the particular historical, economic, political and social situation facing the rulers of fifteenth-century Naples forced them to develop solutions for the visual expression of their power that were distinctively different from those elsewhere in Renaissance Italy.

Naples had a heritage richer and more diverse than any other state in fifteenth-century Italy. Ancient Greeks had settled in southern Italy and Sicily and the area had become an important centre of Hellenistic culture. Naples was a prosperous city of the Roman Empire, as were the local towns of Pompeii and Herculaneum before they were destroyed by the eruption of Vesuvius in A.D. 79. The Bay of Naples was a favourite spot for the seaside villas of wealthy Romans and Emperor Tiberius built a retreat on nearby Capri. With the collapse of the Roman Empire, Byzantine and Lombard powers filled the vacuum in southern Italy, while Sicily was conquered by the Arabs. During the twelfth century the Normans unified the area, establishing a kingdom which was recognized by the Papacy and given the status of a papal fief. The Normans were ousted by the Holy Roman Emperor, Henry VI (1194–7), whose son, Frederick II (1198–1250), inherited his father's title and dominion over Germany, southern Italy and Sicily. A formidable ruler, he adopted the image of Emperor Augustus as propaganda for his imperial ambitions and created a glittering court noted for the revival of the culture of classical antiquity. He built new cities and castles, commissioned all' antica medals and sculpture, and erected an imposing triumphal arch in Capua (1233–40). But his efforts to assert authority on a broader scale in northern Italy brought him into direct conflict with Pope Innocent IV. The growth of a powerful state so close to

Rome was a threat to papal independence and this issue was to play a key role in the history of fifteenth-century Naples.

After the death of Frederick II, imperial authority in southern Italy and Sicily disintegrated and the kingdom passed, with papal assistance, to Charles I of Anjou (1266–85), son of Louis VIII of France. In 1288 a violent revolt against him in Sicily, the so-called Sicilian Vespers, led to the rebels proclaiming Peter of Aragon as their king and the old kingdom split. The Angevins and Aragons were now rival powers. The Angevins, who ruled in Naples until 1435, imposed the political and cultural values of the French court on their kingdom. But by 1400 their power was on the decline as a string of ineffective rulers failed to cope with corruption and civic unrest. Joanna II (1414–35), after an argument with her heir, Louis III of Anjou, replaced him with Alfonso V, King of Aragon and Sicily (1416–58). She changed her mind again, this time disinheriting Alfonso in favour of Louis III's brother, René of Anjou. Joanna II's death in 1435 was followed by war between the rival Aragon and Angevin claims for the succession (1435–42) and it was Alfonso of Aragon who emerged victorious.

Alfonso's route to power had involved far more than his military skills and owed much to his political cunning. Appreciating the importance of papal support for his ambitions, he had backed Pope Martin V's election and sided prominently with Pope Eugenius IV against the Council of Basle (1431–7). The Pope was quick to recognize Alfonso's victory and in 1444 created his chief adviser, Alfonso Borgia, a cardinal. But there had been problems. At the outset of the war, René of Anjou's allies had decisively defeated Alfonso at the Battle of Ponza (1435) and he had been imprisoned by Filippo Maria Visconti, Duke of Milan. But he had persuaded Visconti that a Spanish king in Naples was preferable to a French one and turned the defeat to his own advantage.[2] He finally conquered Naples in 1442 and on 26 February 1443 made his triumphal entry into the city. He had reason to be proud. This ambitious man was now ruler of Aragon, Catalonia, Valencia, Sicily, Sardinia and southern Italy. Only the King of France could boast a larger united dominion in Europe.

Alfonso I's triumphal entry into Naples was carefully planned to display his authority and the nature of the new regime.[3] Drawing deliberately on the imagery of imperial Rome, he rode into the city in a chariot with a huge procession of his soldiers and courtiers through specially-decorated streets and squares that culminated in an imposing triumphal arch, the Roman symbol of military victory, and his conquest was 'legitimized' by a figure representing Julius Caesar.[4] A Catalan who was present sent a report of the pageant home to Barcelona. In it he described the King's gilded chariot, the rich and costly materials of his clothes, the elaborate floats accompanying the cavalcade and the Neapolitan barons doing homage to their new

Spanish ruler.[5] He made much of the prominent symbol of the Siege Perilous of Arthurian legend, the seat at the Round Table left empty for the knight who succeeded in the Quest of the Holy Grail and death for anyone else. The Siege Perilous was one of the significant and suggestive devices adopted by Alfonso I after his conquest of Naples; another was the imperial Roman eagle, a symbol which had also been used by his powerful thirteenth-century predecessor, Frederick II.[6]

With a population of nearly 100,000, Naples was much the same size as Milan. But it was not prosperous. Angevin economic policies had discouraged the growth of an urban middle class and the civil war had damaged the city's economy as well as its architecture. The old feudal aristocracy, many of whom had supported the Angevin claim, were not overjoyed at the prospect of a Spanish King. Alfonso I secured alliances with the barons by marrying his son and heir, Ferrante, to Isabella da Chiaromonte, niece of the influential Prince of Taranto and his daughter Eleonora to Marino Marzano, son of the Duke of Sessa. He appointed the local nobles to the prestigious offices of the old Angevin regime, but these posts, although they had a prominent ceremonial role, carried little influence in Alfonso I's government.[7] He largely ignored Borso d'Este's advice to give his Italian subjects more power, a policy that was to have serious repercussions for his successors.[8] He imposed his Aragonese government and household on Naples and installed trusted Spanish courtiers in all the important positions in his kingdom.[9] But Alfonso I was far from hostile to Italian culture. His cosmopolitan court was dominated by Spaniards but it also included Flemish musicians and painters as well as Italian humanists employed as secretaries in his administration. Alfonso I was an outstanding supporter of humanism, holding regular intellectual discussions that provided a forum for the exchange of ideas unparalled at other Italian courts. Under his leadership, Naples became one of the major centres of humanism in the fifteenth century.[10]

Above all, Alfonso I's humanists provided propaganda to legitimize his position as King of Naples which was insecure at a variety of levels. Recognition from Italian powers came slowly. Initially, only the Este rulers of Ferrara established links with the new régime: Leonello d'Este married Alfonso's daughter, Maria (1444) and sent his younger brothers to train at the court. Florence and Venice finally recognized Alfonso I in 1450. His Spanish court was unpopular with his Italian subjects and his authority in Naples was unstable. Problems soon surfaced in his relationship with his overlord, the Pope, and René of Anjou refused to renounce his claim to the kingdom. Like Francesco Sforza (see Chapter 12), Alfonso I had a compelling need for effective propaganda and humanism became a potent political tool of the Aragon dynasty.[11] He appointed Bartolomeo Fazio to write his official biography (1448–55)[12] and another of his humanists, Lorenzo Valla, exposed the Donation of Constantine as an eighth-century forgery (c. 1440), a political act that toppled the principal basis of papal claims to temporal power in Italy. Panormita (Antonio Beccadelli), a secretary employed by Alfonso to deal with diplomatic affairs, wrote a biography of the king that stressed his religious devotion, military skills and political acumen while underlining the success and power of ancient Roman Emperors who had been born in Spain, notably Trajan and Hadrian, as precedents for his rule in Italy.[13]

The insecurity of his régime gave Alfonso I a compelling motive for conspicuous expenditure to assert his power and prestige. His entertainments were lavish. When Emperor Frederick III visited Naples with an entourage of 2,000 in 1452, Alfonso reputedly spent 100,000 ducats on hospitality and diversions, including fountains that spouted wine, the promise to pay for all purchases made by his guests in the city and a ceremonial hunt with stags, deer, bears, boar and porcupines.[14] Above all, he commissioned buildings that would not only give visual expression to his new authority but also defend it. He was preoccupied with fortifications, initiating repairs to castles throughout the kingdom. He built a new castle at Gaeta, on his northern border, and its account books reveal an average expenditure of 5,000 ducats a year between 1448 and 1454.[15] Another stronghold was built at Castellammare di Stabia (begun 1451) on the Bay of Naples and he restored the defences of the city itself. In contrast to other Italian rulers, he spent surprisingly little on religious foundations. The focus of his attention was the building of the principal image of his power, Castel Nuovo.

The old Angevin castle on the Bay of Naples had been the main target of Alfonso I's punishing attack on the city and he decided to rebuild the badly damaged fortress, enlarging it into a magnificent royal residence that would provide an impressive setting for the display of his power. The new castle was a mighty image of defence. Ringed by a moat, its walls were dominated by five massive cylindrical towers, two of which flanked the entrance. The building incorporated many defensive features designed to resist attack by the cannon and gunfire of modern warfare and it was these innovations that most interested the Milanese ambassador when he reported on its progress to Francesco Sforza.[16] Inside, were elaborately decorated reception rooms and private apartments, as well as government offices, weapon stores and facilities for casting cannon. The project also included a grand park laid out under the supervision of a Spanish gardener and ornamented with fountains and pavilions.[17]

Work started immediately after Alfonso's conquest of Naples and he appointed Spaniards to take charge of the project. Initially in the hands of the castellan, Arnaldo Sanz, this massive enterprise needed its own separate administration, set up under the control of Francisco Bonshoms in 1444.[18] The workforce was largely local, though it also included royal slaves and prisoners.[19] At first, the foreman in charge was an Italian, Pertello de Marino, but this post was transferred to a Spanish stonemason from Majorca, Guillermo Sagrera in 1449.[20] Alfonso I's outlay was enormous, and it has been estimated that he spent well over 250,000 ducats on the structure alone.[21] By 1451, mounting costs and the problems inherent in employing a large workforce persuaded Alfonso of the need to control expenditure and make the system more efficient so the decision was taken to put the rest of the project out to contract. Three contracts were drawn up: for completing the structure, for building and decorating the prime reception room, the Sala dei Baroni, and for the triumphal arch at the entrance to the castle. Alfonso I's choice of artists reflected the distinctive combination of imagery that he planned to give visual expression to his authority.

The four stonemasons commissioned to finish the construction were all local and had been working on the project at salaries of 12 ducats a month.[22] Their contract (1451) stipulated in detail what had been completed and what still had to be done. Above all, they were involved in building the defensive features planned by the King from his technical knowledge of warfare. One peculiarity of the castle was a gallery running round the outside walls, a detail common in Spanish fortifications.[23] Other features were the direct result of his own experiences during the war of succession. Alfonso I's combination of Italian and Spanish elements of military architecture was designed not only to make the castle look impregnable but also to ensure that it actually was.[24]

Sagrera, with his largely Spanish workforce, was commissioned (1452) to build a grand hall inside the castle for official receptions, known as the Sala dei Baroni.[25] The hall was huge, 90 feet square, and, in both style and materials, was decidedly Spanish. Stone was imported from Majorca.[26] Elaborate tierceron Gothic rib vaults decorated with bosses displaying the coats of arms of the lands under Aragonese rule and ornate traceried windows in the tradition of the Aragonese court emphasized Alfonso's position as one of Europe's most powerful rulers.

The third contract, for an elaborate sculptured gate to fit between the two massive towers that marked the entrance to his palace, was given to Italian sculptors from outside his realm.[27] In 1452 he wrote to Ragusa asking for the services of a stonemason, Pietro da Milano, and work was underway in 1453 when payments made to him, Francesco Laurana, Paolo Romano and thirty-three other workers.[28] A preliminary drawing for the gate by the International Gothic artist, Pisanello, with its decorative Gothic detail suggests that Alfonso originally intended this public statement of his power to have a visual association with the courts of northern Europe.[29] But the arch that was built was classical, drawing on the imperial traditions of ancient Rome and carrying strong resonances of Frederick II's arch at Capua. Ornamented with reliefs of Alfonso, his family, his military commanders and courtiers, the arch included the figure of the King seated in the Siege Perilous. A striking contrast to the Spanish decoration commissioned for the Sala dei Baroni, the style of the arch was manifestly intended to impress his Italian subjects. It certainly impressed the Milanese ambassador, who mentioned its antique style in a letter to Francesco Sforza,[30] and Alfonso's humanists were unstinting in their praise.[31]

The lavish display of wealth inside Castel Nuovo testified to Alfonso's prestige as a major European ruler, to his imperial pretensions and, above all, to his Spanish origins. He collected Roman imperial coins and commissioned a medal of himself (1449) from Pisanello, which depicted his portrait between the helmet of conquest and the crown of kingship.[32] The medals made by Cristoforo di Geremia, employed at the Neapolitan court in the 1450s, made significant advances in the revival of antique imagery.[33] Alfonso also commissioned his portrait bust from a local sculptor, Domenico da Montemignano, for which he paid 70 ducats.[34] But his preferences seem to have been for Flemish and Spanish decoration. He sent agents to Flanders to buy expensive tapestries for the castle; Andreu Pol, who as *comprador* was in charge of supplying the royal household with items ranging from meat and vegetables to hangings and paintings, bought tapestries there depicting the story of Nebuchadnezzar.[35] A set of tapestries of Solomon and the Queen of Sheba, which had once decorated the hall of Alfonso I's predecessor, Joanna II, now hung in the Sala dei Baroni.[36] Bartolomeo Fazio described a Passion of Christ series designed by the Flemish artist, Rogier van der Weyden, which reputedly cost 5,000 ducats.[37] Amongst the devotional paintings in Alfonso's private apartments was an Annunciation by the Flemish painter, Jan van Eyck.[38] Alfonso wrote to a Catalan artist offering him work in Naples[39] but the most distinctively Spanish feature in the castle was its floors, laid with Hispano-Moresque tiles brought over by boat from Valencia. The quantities were enormous.[40] In 1446 he commissioned 13,458 tiles decorated with the royal arms, the Siege Perilous and other personal devices; 30,000 more were ordered in 1449 and in 1456 Alfonso sent his secretary to Valencia to oversee the production of 200,000 similar tiles for the Sala dei Baroni.

One of the problems in assessing the achievements of Alfonso I and his fifteenth-century successors is that so little of their work has survived intact. They were followed by Spanish viceroys (1503–1734) and then by the Bourbon dynasty (1734–1860), who remodelled or demolished much of the remaining Renaissance city. And the Allied bombardment of 1944 inflicted major devastation on Naples, destroying many buildings as well as the state archives. Much of our knowledge of Castel Nuovo comes from pre-war art historians who published details of their research into the account books, contracts and letters relating to the project. More information has been gleaned from humanist biographies and orations. But little private correspondence has come to light and, in contrast to Milan, Mantua or Ferrara, we have little personal contact with the Aragonese Kings.

Alfonso died in 1458 and he was succeeded in Naples by his illegitimate son, Ferrante I (1458–94). Alfonso's Spanish kingdom was inherited by his brother, Juan II, and it was the marriage of Juan's son, Ferdinand of Aragon, to Isabella of Castile that united Spain and created a powerful new force in the European political arena. Ferrante I faced serious challenges to his authority. He had been recognized by Pope Eugenius IV as the lawful heir in 1443 but Pope Calixtus III, once Alfonso I's chief adviser, refused to acknowledge the succession. As had happened in the past, fear of a powerful state so close to the borders of Rome persuaded the Pope to divide and rule. Calixtus III now encouraged René of Anjou to revive his claim. Calixtus died in 1458 and, although Pius II favoured Ferrante I, the Angevins pursued their right to the title. They had powerful allies in the Neapolitan barons, who had been excluded from power by Alfonso I and now rebelled openly against Ferrante (1459). War followed and Ferrante I was kept out of Naples until his decisive victory at the Battle of Ischia (1465).

Ferrante I now established alliances with the major Italian powers, marrying his heir, Alfonso, Duke of Calabria, to Ippolita, daughter of Francesco Sforza (1465). Another son, Giovanni, was created a cardinal by Sixtus IV (1477). Eleonora was married to Ercole d'Este (1473) and Beatrice was married to Matthias Corvinus, King of Hungary (1476). Ferrante sided with the Papacy in the war against Florence following the Pazzi conspiracy but, when Lorenzo de' Medici came to Naples to sue for peace in 1479–80, he established a firm friendship with the Florentine statesman which was to form the basis of the alliance between Naples, Florence and Milan that maintained the largely undisturbed peace between the Italian powers until 1494. But Ferrante's problems continued. The growing power of the Turks in the eastern Mediterranean, which had robbed Venice of her maritime Empire, was now threatening Ferrante I's kingdom. In 1480 the Turks conquered Otranto, on the heel of Italy, which was soon retaken by Ferrante's armies, but it forced the King to strengthen his defences. At home, continuing resentment amongst the old feudal nobility blew up in the Barons' Revolt (1485–7) which was led by Ferrante's brother-in-law, Marino Marzano, and supported by Pope Innocent VIII. This direct challenge to his position was ruthlessly suppressed but it underlined the need for powerful propaganda to bolster the Aragonese régime. Ferrante and his son, Alfonso, initiated a massive programme of architecture, painting and sculpture that was clearly designed to testify to their hold on power.

When Ferrante I returned to Naples in 1465, he immediately resumed work on the prime image of his power, Castel Nuovo. He completed his father's arch, embellishing it with more sculpture.[41] He also commissioned decorative ironwork, a new clock, glass windows, and a statue of Justice for the Sala dei Baroni.[42] He adorned the castle park with pavilions, an aviary and marble fountains.[43] The palace chapel, one of the few parts of the old Angevin castle left intact by Alfonso I, had been badly damaged in an earthquake in 1456 and Ferrante I redecorated it with a new rose window, sculpture, woodwork and wall paintings to replace frescos by Giotto, which had been ruined.[44] He commissioned the so-called Tavola Strozzi, a visual record of his triumphant return after the Battle of Ischia. His victory over René of Anjou and the Neapolitan barons was affirmed more publicly in the scenes decorating the huge bronze doors he commissioned from the court cannon expert, Fra Guillaume of Paris, for the entrance to Castel Nuovo.[45] Above them, he placed a relief of his coronation (1468).[46] The imagery was an unmistakable statement of Ferrante's claim to power and authority in his realm.

Although the distinction between the patronage of father and son is blurred, it is clear that it was Ferrante I's son, Alfonso, who was the principal force behind this ambitious programme.[47] Known as the Duke of Calabria, the traditional title for the heir to the Neapolitan throne, Alfonso was his father's right-hand man, prominent in government and leader of Ferrante's armies. He had commanded the Neapolitan forces against Florence, playing an important part in the battles for Castellina (1478) and Poggio Imperiale (1479). He had also been responsible for pushing the Turks out of Otranto (1481). Alfonso's court was one of the most magnificent in Europe and famous for its lavish banquets and jousts, spectacular triumphs and the revival of classical theatre. Pontano, Leostello and other humanists provided forceful propaganda for the Aragon cause. Extending classical themes beyond the straightforward imperial parallels sanctioned by Alfonso I, they promoted the Duke as heir to a long line of Neapolitan rulers which stretched back into Roman mythology, stressing the tradition of loyalty of the Neapolitan subjects to their leader and the loyalty of the city to Rome.[48] This contained a potent message to Ferrante's two main antagonists, the rebel barons and the Pope; Alfonso's projects gave it visual expression.

Alfonso initiated an ambitious scheme of urban renewal in Naples and built extensive fortifications throughout the kingdom. He remodelled and redecorated the old Angevin stronghold, Castel Capuano, his official residence. He also built two villas, La Duchesca in the garden of Castel Capuano[49] and, his major project, Poggioreale (see below). Alfonso I had been keen to emphasize the Spanish nature of his court, but this was no longer an issue for Ferrante and his son. The craftsmen responsible for the work on their projects were exclusively Italian.[50]

Alfonso and Ferrante's plans for Naples were impressive and included new walls and improvements to the water supply.[51] A massive gate, the Porta Capuana, was built with classical pilasters enclosing a huge arched entrance (c. 1488). Like the entrance to Castel Nuovo, the Porta Capuana was crowned with a statue of Ferrante's coronation (removed by Emperor Charles V in 1535 and replaced with his imperial eagle). In an unambiguous statement of Aragonese authority, Alfonso and Ferrante planned the Palazzo dei Tribunali, a vast new building to house the offices of government near Castel Nuovo.[52] Alfonso financed works in the city's churches, such as the new coffered ceiling for Sant'Eligio built to a design by Giuliano da Maiano (1488).[53] The Duke's presence was particularly conspicuous in Sant'Anna dei Lombardi where he commissioned the Modenese sculptor, Guido Mazzoni, to make a group of eight life-size terracotta statues representing the Lamentation of Christ, with himself as Joseph of Arimathea, making an oblique reference to his grandfather's choice of the Siege Perilous as his personal device after his conquest of Naples.[54] He encouraged the members of his court to build grand palaces and his humanists were also active as patrons.[55] Pontano's chapel (1492) dedicated to the Virgin and St John the Evangelist, was designed in imitation of the temples of ancient Rome. Pontano and other humanists praised Alfonso's embellishment of the city. Leostello justified his enormous expenditure on the unusual grounds that he had given so much employment to craftsmen that there were now some in Naples who could afford dowries for four or even five daughters![56]

It was at his magnificent villa of Poggioreale, now destroyed, that Alfonso most effectively displayed his image as heir to the imperial tradition of Rome. Its classical grandeur deliberately rivalled descriptions of the seaside retreats of ancient patricians. Built on the site of an old Angevin residence, Alfonso's new villa was a huge rectangular block with corner towers.[57] Inside was an arcaded courtyard, formed like an amphitheatre with seating around a sunken stage and cunningly hidden pipes enabled it to be flooded for mock naval battles. It was, above all, a pleasure palace set amid beautiful gardens with cooling fountains, where Alfonso could indulge his taste for entertaining. Pontano wrote an eloquent description of the ideal villa garden, its topiary hedges and lemon trees providing a pleasant setting for banquets.[58]

Work had begun at Poggioreale by 1484[59] but the major remodelling only started after 1487, when two models of the palace were brought by carrier from Florence.[60] The design of Poggioreale has long been attributed to Giuliano da Maiano, who was probably in charge of its construction.[61] But intriguing evidence exists to suggest that it was Lorenzo de' Medici who was responsible for the creative ideas behind the building. In a letter to Lorenzo (1489), the Florentine ambassador in Naples, Baccio Ugolini, reported that Alfonso had invited him to Poggioreale, which, Ugolini wrote, Maiano had built from Lorenzo's model.[62] Luca Pacioli, writing c. 1500, was also clear that Maiano had carried out Lorenzo's ideas.[63] Lorenzo's architectural expertise is well documented and the temple façade on his villa at Poggio a Caiano (mid-1480s) was a major landmark in the revival of classical style (see Chapter 5). He was certainly capable of offering suggestions for the design of Poggioreale and he had close connections with the Neapolitan court. While, with his approval, Florentine bankers financed Ferrante's wars against the Turks and the barons,[64] Lorenzo made political capital out of the persuasive image of Florence's cultural superiority so assiduously promoted by her citizens and his own reputation as a connoisseur. His assistance to the Duke of Calabria, sending a design and a craftsman to supervise its construction, should be seen as evidence not only of Lorenzo's reputation as an expert but also of his determination to maintain his alliance with Ferrante and Alfonso.

Alfonso's buildings were decorated with imagery designed to reinforce the continuing power of the Aragonese régime. In imitation of ancient Roman coins and medals, heads of Ferrante's predecessors were placed in the courtyard at Poggioreale.[65] Antique sculptures emphasized the imperial context. At La Duchesca there was a statue of Parthenope, the mythical founder of Naples, with water spouting from her nipples into the mouths of *putti* who then urinated it into the fountain basin.[66] Above all, Alfonso stressed the military achievements of his father's reign. The Siege of Poggio Imperiale, one of Alfonso's victories, was recorded for the Duke by Francesco di Giorgio, the Sienese engineer and painter who had been in Alfonso's service during the war with Florence.[67] La Duchesca was decorated with scenes of the Battle of Otranto[68] and the bones of the dead from the battle were brought to the villa where Alfonso erected a martyrs' chapel to house them.[69] And, to underline Aragonese authority in Naples, the story of the Barons' Revolt was frescoed on the walls of both La Duchesca and Poggioreale.[70]

With the constant threat of attack and insurrection hanging over them, fortifications were a prime concern for Ferrante I and the Duke of Calabria, as they had been for Alfonso I. Alfonso I's defence expert, Fra Guillaume of Paris, had been paid 400 ducats a year, considerably more than the 144 ducats paid to Sagrera, the man in charge of the construction of the Sala dei Baroni.[71] Ferrante I kept the Frenchman on, increased his salary to 600 ducats a year and made him a royal councillor.[72] Luciano Laurana, who had worked on Federigo da Montefeltro's palace in Urbino (see Chapter 14), was tempted to Naples as a master of artillery for a salary of 200 ducats a year (1472–5).[73] Military architects were much in demand at Ferrante's court. Fra Giocondo was employed by the Duke of Calabria on the design of fortresses.[74] And the most famous defence expert in late fifteenth-century Italy, Francesco di Giorgio, made a number of trips to Naples between 1484 and 1495.[75] Francesco di Giorgio wrote extensively on architecture and military engineering (see Chapter 14) and dedicated the second draft of his treatise to the Duke of Calabria.[76] A copy of the third draft, which consisted of four books on defence and three on architecture, was made in Naples and Fra Giocondo was paid for the drawings (1492).[77] Francesco di Giorgio's value as a military architect was soon to be proved very effectively.

The pressures were growing on the Aragonese régime. Dissatisfaction amongst the barons was a constant threat to internal stability. The Turkish navies menaced the southern Italian coastline and in 1492 the Duke of Calabria wrote to the Commune of Siena to apologize for not allowing Francesco di Giorgio to return as promised because of the danger of their attack.[78] But the biggest problem was the revival of the Anjou claim. René of Anjou had died in 1480 without an heir and the claim passed to his great-nephew, now Charles VIII, King of France, who was determined to enforce it. Ferrante I died in January 1494 just before the French armies entered Italy. In February, Alfonso, now the King, asked the Sienese government to send Francesco di Giorgio back to Naples.[79] In January 1495, Alfonso II abdicated in favour of his son, Ferrante II (1495–6) and Charles VIII conquered Naples the following month. Ferrante II launched a counter-attack in July 1495. He finally retook the city after a long battle culminating in an assault on Alfonso I's impregnable Castel Nuovo, after Francesco di Giorgio had blown away its defences by detonating a charge of gunpowder in a tunnel dug under the castle walls (November 1495).[80]

Ferrante was succeeded by his uncle, Federigo (1496–1501). By 1498 Naples had become the battle ground for supremacy between the two leading European rulers, Louis XII of France, heir to the Angevin claim, and Ferdinand of Spain, nephew of Alfonso I of Aragon. Spain proved stronger and in 1503 Ferdinand united Naples to his Spanish kingdom.

14

Urbino

H igh up in the mountains of central Italy, the tiny fortress town of Urbino was an unlikely setting for one of the leading centres of the Italian Renaissance. The town was not prosperous but, situated on the northern border of the papal states, it was strategically important. Urbino was nominally a papal fief, owned by the Montefeltre who had acquired it in lieu of debts owed to them by the Papacy.[1] The family were famous as soldiers, earning their living as *condottieri*. The succession of Federigo da Montefeltro as Count of Urbino (1444–82) marked a turning point in Urbino's fortunes and the transformation of this insignificant hill-top town into one of the outstanding courts of fifteenth-century Italy.

Federigo da Montefeltro had been educated at the Gonzaga court in Mantua where he had been taught by the humanist, Vittorino da Feltre. He inherited his father's company of troops and embarked on an immensely successful career as a *condottiere*, fighting at various times for Venice, Naples, Florence and the Papacy.[2] Francesco Sforza employed him for 60,000 ducats a year in peace time and 80,000 for war.[3] He accepted an offer of 165,000 ducats for himself and his troops to fight in the War of Ferrara (1482–4) and was reputed to have turned down a bid of 80,000 ducats for his neutrality from Venice.[4] His considerable talents and prestige were rewarded when Pope Sixtus IV created him Duke of Urbino in 1474 and Edward IV of England made him a Knight of the Garter in the same year.[5] The loss of his right eye in a tournament gave him a striking appearance and contemporaries described him as well read. One of his employers, Pope Pius II, reported a conversation they had had on the subject of classical warfare, adding that he disagreed with Federigo's derisive judgement on the Trojan war.[6] By all accounts he was prudent, practical and cunning as a fighter and a benevolent ruler.[7] He died in 1482 of a fever, possibly malaria, at the age of 60, while fighting in Ferrara.

Federigo had travelled widely in Italy and he had been a comrade, or opponent, of many of the rulers of the peninsula's secular courts. His ducal status put him on a level with the Este in Ferrara or the Gonzaga in Mantua. But Urbino lacked the grandeur expected of someone of his rank. Federigo set out to acquire the trappings of princely prestige and to create a court that would impress his peers. He employed humanists to advertise his reputation. Unlike the Sforza regime in Milan or the Aragonese kings in Naples, Federigo had no compelling need to legitimize his power. But he did need to display his achievements and promote his prestige. The humanists attached to his court wrote laudatory accounts of his career and promoted him, with reason, as a major patron of the arts. Federigo spent conspicuously on grand architecture and lavish decoration. He commissioned a programme of church building and decoration in Urbino and dramatically enlarged his family palace. He built ducal residences in Gubbio, Urbania (now Castel Durante), Sant'Agata Feltria and other smaller towns under his rule. New fortresses were constructed and he remodelled the castles scattered throughout his state. With funds estimated at 50,000 ducats a year at his disposal after financing the running of his court,[8] Federigo was immensely rich. And he used his wealth to effect.

One of the most important components of princely prestige was a library and Federigo's was one of the most impressive in fifteenth-century Italy. Begun from nothing, it contained over 1,100 books by 1482, many in lavish gold and silver bindings.[9] Vespasiano, the Florentine bookseller who supplied many of the manuscripts, claimed it cost 30,000 ducats. Its contents revealed much about Federigo's personal interests and reflected his preference for scientific facts rather than literary theories.[10] Besides the standard texts of Greek, Roman and Christian authors that a visitor would expect to find in a library of the period, Federigo owned an exceptional number of works, ancient and modern, on the art of war and defensive machinery. He also owned copies of Vitruvius's and Alberti's treatises on architecture, Piero della Francesca's book on perspective and Francesco di Giorgio's architectural treatise which dealt extensively with military matters (see below).

Federigo's programme of church building and decoration testified to his Christian devotion, but its principal aim was to embellish Urbino with the grand convents, monasteries and cathedrals that were the definitive mark of a great city. He began a new cathedral and built the convent of Santa Chiara. He financed a new portal for San Domenico and commissioned a relief of the Crucifixion, with a portrait of himself as donor, for Santa Croce.[11] His portrait also appeared in the altarpiece he commissioned from Justus of Ghent for the church of Corpus Domini, depicting the Institution of the Eucharist, with predella panels by Uccello of the miracles performed by the Host.

His main religious work was the renovation of the Observant Franciscan convent of San Donato. The convent had been founded in 1425 by his

48.   Piero della Francesca, *Battista Sforza*. Florence, Uffizi, after 1474

49.   Piero della Francesca, *Federigo da Montefeltro*. Florence, Uffizi, after 1474

father, Guidantonio, who had been buried in the church and commemorated with a massive stone slab showing him dressed in the habit of
a Franciscan.[12] Federigo added a much grander church to the convent,
dedicated to the Observant Franciscan St Bernardino who had been
canonized in 1450.[13] With its plain brick façade and simple whitewashed
interior, the church gave deliberate visual expression to the austere and
reformist idealism of its patron saint. Vespasiano, in his biography of
Federigo, praised him for his devotion to the Observant Franciscans[14] and
it is probable that Federigo intended the church, begun some time between
1477 and 1481, as a mausoleum for himself and his heirs.[15] The church
was not finished, however, when he died and his coffin was placed in the
old church of San Donato next door.[16]

The main focus of Federigo's ambitious scheme for Urbino was the
Montefeltro palace in the centre of the city. In the patent (1468) appointing
Laurana as chief supervisor of the building (see below), Federigo was very
clear about his motives for transforming the unprepossessing family home
into a magnificent ducal residence. He wanted, he said, to build a beautiful
and dignified palace that would do honour to the status and fame of
his family as well as his own prestige.[17] The new building did, indeed,
create a setting worthy of a ruler of rank. Vespasiano was fulsome in its
praise[18] and two major fifteenth-century patrons, Lorenzo de' Medici and
Federigo Gonzaga, were impressed enough to request drawings of the
palace.[19]

The remodelling of the old palace was under way by 1450, and by 1470
a massive extension to the north and west of the original building had been
begun.[20] Work continued throughout Federigo's life and he must be seen as
the major force behind its design. The new palace was carefully planned to
proclaim Federigo's military prowess, his authority as a ruler and his
cultural aspirations. Seen from the mountains, the massive walls, ramparts
and turrets of the west façade were visibly defensive. By contrast, the east
front, which faced into the city, was not. Here, large windows and doors
flanked by decorative pilasters and elaborately carved stone frames
testified to Federigo's wealth and power. Inside was a vast courtyard, surrounded by arcades supported on Composite columns, its inscription
proudly boasting the Duke's achievements (fig. 50). The lettering, like the
capitals, was conspicuously classical, a stylistic choice that manifestly
associated Federigo with cultural traditions of imperial Rome and the
prestige of his contemporaries, notably Pope Pius II and Ludovico Gonzaga.

On arrival in the courtyard, the visitor entered the palace proper up an
imposing stone staircase to the official reception rooms inside. Federigo
built halls, private apartments for himself and his wife, a garden, a chapel
and all the other requirements of formal court life. He spent lavishly

50. Courtyard, Palazzo Ducale, Urbino, *c.* 1475

on detail, commissioning expensive intarsia doors set in ornately carved frames, and decorative marble fireplaces. One particularly impressive fireplace was embellished with a gilded frieze of *putti* playing musical instruments. His coat of arms and other devices were visible everywhere, as were the letters FE DUX proclaiming his ducal status. Like his rivals in Ferrara, Mantua and Naples, he hung the walls of important rooms with costly tapestries. Despite his disdain for the Trojan War as a battle, he recognized its value as propaganda for an aspiring ruler. The Flemish weaver, Jean Grenier of Tournai, who was known for producing tapestries displaying the pageantry and chivalric imagery so popular at the courts of northern Europe, was commissioned to make a set of eleven tapestries (1476) of this epic struggle between the Greeks and the Trojans. They cost the Duke 2,557 ducats in 1476.[21]

One of the most expensively decorated rooms in the palace was Federigo's tiny, exquisite studio.[22] Its ornate and gilded coffered ceiling was decorated with Federigo's arms and devices and an inscription, dated 1476, recorded his many titles. Following the medieval tradition of decorating libraries with portraits of famous men, Federigo commissioned twenty-eight paintings of Christian and pagan figures with inscriptions explaining his reasons for their choice. The selection ranged widely. It included the Greeks Homer, Plato and Aristotle, the Roman writers Cicero and Virgil, the Old Testament heroes Moses and Solomon, and two leading medieval theologians, the Dominican St Thomas Aquinas and the Franciscan Duns Scotus; modern achievement was represented in figures of Dante, Petrarch, his own teacher, the humanist Vittorino da Feltre, and Popes Pius II and Sixtus IV. But the most striking feature of the room, and its most costly element, was the elaborate intarsia decoration on the lower levels of the walls (fig. 51). The fictive woodwork was designed to suggest the walls of a study with latticed cupboards, open doors revealing a parrot in a cage or a muddle of books and oddments, a sword leaning against the wall, musical instruments, a chessboard, ducal devices, and, one of the most enchanting details, a squirrel cracking a nut in front of a loggia with views of the landscape beyond.

As far as we know, Federigo did not commission any large fresco cycles for his palace. But he did commission many portraits of himself and his family to testify to his dynastic ambitions as well as to his wealth, status, military skills and cultural aspirations. His principal court painter was the Flemish artist, Justus of Ghent, whose two surviving portraits of the Duke combined martial, intellectual and dynastic imagery. Unlike Borso d'Este, Federigo preferred to be portrayed in modest clothes. In one of Justus's portraits (1475), he was shown reading a manuscript, dressed in armour, his badge of the Order of the Garter tied below his left knee, with his young son beside him ostentatiously clad in glittering costly materials.[23] The other showed Federigo and his son listening attentively to an oration, the duke in his robes of state and, once again, his son, not himself, adorned in expensive jewels.[24]

For us, the best-known creator of the Duke's image was Piero della Francesca, a painter from Borgo Sansepolcro, near Urbino. His interest in the laws of perspective and his application of strict mathematical rules to form and pictorial composition was an approach which would have appealed to the down-to-earth Federigo. Piero wrote a treatise on perspective and one on the five regular solids which was dedicated to the Duke and was in the Urbino library.[25] In his double portrait of Federigo and his wife, Battista Sforza (figs 48 and 49), Piero showed a stern man, dressed in plain scarlet robes, while Battista displayed his wealth in her costly necklace and elaborate *coiffure*. Amongst his other commissions from the Duke was the *Flagellation of Christ*. This enigmatic painting in its overtly classical setting has long posed problems for art historians. It has been suggested that it was intended for Federigo's studiolo[26] but neither its original location nor the identities of the three men standing prominently on the right of the picture have so far been convincingly explained. There are also problems in establishing Federigo's plans for his votive altarpiece, commissioned from

51.   Studiolo, Palazzo Ducale, Urbino, *c*. 1476

Piero, possibly for San Bernardino.[27] Piero's picture (c. 1472-4), known as the Brera altarpiece, showed the Duke in armour kneeling before the Virgin and Child with Saints John the Baptist, Bernardino of Siena, Jerome, Francis, Peter Martyr and Andrew beneath an ostrich egg suspended from the ceiling. A traditional symbol of miraculous birth, the ostrich egg had particular importance for Federigo. Not only was it one of his personal devices, but his wife had died in 1472 giving birth to Federigo's son and heir, Guidobaldo.[28]

Our knowledge of the process of patronage, design and construction of Federigo's palace is hampered by a lack of surviving documentation. One of the few existing records is the patent of 1468 appointing Luciano Laurana to take charge of building work and specifying his duties.[29] Laurana's responsibilities were considerable by fifteenth-century standards. Besides supervising the workforce, he was also given the power to engage and dismiss his craftsmen and to choose whether to pay them piecework rates or daily wages. Above all, he was given power over the ducal agents in charge of the administrative side of the project. Unlike the chief foreman in Milan or Ferrara, Laurana was clearly the figure in direct contact with the Duke, a significant fact that underlined Federigo's central role in the design of his palace. Laurana left and was probably working in Naples in 1472.[30] The next piece of information dates from 1477, when the Sienese painter, Francesco di Giorgio, now the chief supervisor of Federigo's projects, drew up a contract with an artist for the decoration of a room in the Duke's palace in Gubbio.[31]

The scope of Francesco di Giorgio's career reveals much about the demands placed on fifteenth-century craftsmen by their employers.[32] He trained and practised as a painter in Siena, but he was also one of the city's technical experts responsible for maintaining the complex systems devised for supplying water to this hill-top site. Working for Federigo, Francesco di Giorgio was certainly involved on the palace, where, he said, he had designed stabling for 300 horses[33] and fixed the chimneys so that they did not smoke.[34] He also acted as a diplomatic envoy for Federigo.[35] Above all, the combination of Federigo's knowledge of warfare and Francesco di Giorgio's technical skills was used to powerful effect in the design of a series of innovative fortresses constructed throughout the state of Urbino.

Francesco di Giorgio's stay in Urbino (1447-87) was formative in his emergence as one of the leading architectural and defence experts in late fifteenth-century Italy. He wrote down his ideas in a number of works. The earliest, the so-called opusculum (c. 1475), was dedicated to Federigo, and consisted of drawings of technical devices, including artillery, pumps, water mills and a mechanical saw as well as methods for scaling walls.[36] Three more drafts of his treatise exist dating from c. 1476-90,[37] and they reveal a wholly different approach to architecture than that found in the works of Alberti and Filarete. Francesco di Giorgio devoted much of his texts to the discussion of the problems faced by the modern military engineer, the design of fortresses, explosives, catapults and siege machines. Less in awe of the achievements of antiquity, he emphasized that classical texts were of little use in planning defences that could withstand the new power of gunpowder. His practical approach to his subject was evident in the numerous explanatory diagrams and illustrations provided with his text. After leaving Urbino, Francesco di Giorgio returned to Siena, where he was employed as the city's principal engineer during the 1490s. But his skills were now in demand throughout Italy and he travelled to Milan (1490) to advise on the cathedral (see Chapter 12) as well as to Naples to work for Alfonso, Duke of Calabria (see Chapter 13).

Federigo had transformed Urbino into a major centre of Renaissance culture and created an impressive architectural setting for the display of his achievements. But the state's enormous income dried up after his death (1482). Federigo was succeeded by his 10-year-old son, Guidobaldo (1482–1508), who was faced with the political turmoil that accompanied the French invasions of Italy, and Urbino became the target of the ambitious Cesare Borgia, who occupied the city in 1502–3. Guidobaldo died without an heir and Urbino passed to his nephew, Francesco Maria della Rovere. The city never again achieved the same prestige as it had enjoyed under Federigo.

15

Ferrara

F errara was the centre of a small state, sandwiched between the dominant powers of Milan and Venice, that had been ruled by the Este family since the thirteenth century. Members of the old imperial nobility, the family had risen to power as lords of Este, near Padua, in the eleventh century. Taking advantage of the disputes between Pope and Emperor, they had gradually extended their authority and established control of a part of the broad and fertile Po valley, which included not only the imperial fiefs of Modena and Reggio but also the papal fief of Ferrara. Their income derived from taxes, tolls on commercial traffic through their territory, income from their agricultural estates, and, above all, from funds earned by selling their skills as *condottieri*.

Fifteenth-century Ferrara was ruled by Nicolò III (1393–1441) and his three sons, Leonello (1441–50), Borso (1450–71) and Ercole (1471–1505). Apart from the failed coup attempted by Leonello's son, Nicolò, in 1476, the régime was stable. Nicolò III and his sons may have lacked the political influence of their powerful neighbours in Milan or Venice, but, through judicious marriages, skilful diplomacy, efficient administration and especially through conspicuous expenditure, they established Ferrara as an important centre in fifteenth-century Italy and the city grew in size and prestige as the century progressed. Nicolò III persuaded Pope Eugenius IV to hold his Council in Ferrara in 1437, though the threat of the plague and the forceful arguments of Cosimo de' Medici led to its removal to Florence in 1438. Visiting rulers were lavishly entertained in Ferrara, including Emperor Frederick III on his way to his coronation in Rome (1452) and Pope Pius II on route to the Congress of Mantua (1459–60). Nicolò III's sons established close ties with the Aragon régime in Naples. Leonello was one of the first Italian rulers to recognize Alfonso I as King of Naples and he married Alfonso's daughter, Maria (1444). Ercole was educated at the Neapolitan court and married Eleonora of Aragon, Alfonso I's grand-daughter.

Following the pattern of the prestigious rulers in Naples and Milan, the

Este adopted the language of Italian absolute power. They combined the courtly and chivalric imagery of northern European aristocracies with the culture of ancient Rome to provide effective propaganda for the status of their court. The family boasted an ancestry that went back to the Knights of King Arthur's Round Table and Nicolò III named Borso after Sir Bors, one of those on the quest of the Holy Grail.[1] Nicolò also employed the eminent humanist, Guarino of Verona (1374–1460), as tutor to his elder son, Leonello. Nicolò III's three sons were very different personalities, each developing their own distinctive style of leadership, and this had a formative impact on the evolution of the arts in Renaissance Ferrara.

Much of the architecture, painting and sculpture commissioned by Leonello, Borso and Ercole is now lost behind the remodelling and rebuilding ordered by their successors. Relatively little has survived intact. But the state archives are a mine of information. The survival of huge quantities of account books, contracts, letters and inventories recording the minute details of Este patronage has enabled art historians to reconstruct the appearance of the city and, above all, to examine the personal involvement of the fifteenth-century Dukes in their projects in a way that is impossible for their contemporaries in many other centres.

Ferrara was dominated by the buildings belonging to the court and the principal symbols of Este power were the Castello Vecchio and the Palazzo del Corte. The fourteenth-century Castello Vecchio with its massive towering walls unadorned except for castellations and machicolations was one of the most imposing images of defence in Italy. The Palazzo del Corte, facing the cathedral across the city's central piazza, provided the main setting for the ostentatious display that was a hallmark of Ferrarese culture. On the eastern side of the city stood the magnificent Palazzo Schifanoia. Nicolò III built two fortified castles on the banks of the tributary that linked Ferrara with the Po, the Castello Thealdo (1395) and the Castello Nuovo (1425–32).[2] The Este also owned hunting lodges and castles outside Ferrara, notably the villa Belfiore and Belreguardo, started by Nicolò III.

After his father's death, Leonello (1441–50) continued to embellish these images of family power and prestige. He commissioned expensive intarsia decoration for his studios in the Palazzo del Corte, Belreguardo and Belfiore and the sacristy of Santa Maria degli Angeli, one of his father's religious foundations.[3] He acquired an impressive collection of engraved gems, jewels, tapestries, paintings and sculpture.[4] He commissioned portraits (1441) from the leading International Gothic artist, Pisanello, and from the Venetian painter, Jacopo Bellini, and Pisanello also worked for him at Belreguardo (1445).[5] We do not know how far he was involved in the equestrian monument to his father (1443); but its base with two Composite columns supporting a heavy and antique entablature was an important landmark in the revival of classical style. It is traditionally attributed to Alberti, who had close links with Leonello's humanist court.[6]

Inspired by the influence of Guarino and the literature of antiquity, humanists at Leonello's court developed important new attitudes to patronage and to art. They promoted Leonello as a connoisseur and expert rather than as a prolific builder, the image more generally preferred by Italian princely patrons. Leonello's views on art formed the principal theme of an unusual dialogue, *de politia litteraria*, written by one of his humanists, Angelo Decembrio.[7] He described the contents of his ideal library with its celestial sphere, pictures and sculptures of gods and heroes, and specially recommended the image of St Jerome writing in the desert as an inspiration to study.[8] The text stressed Leonello's knowledge of both ancient and modern art as well as a lack of interest in ostentation. He criticized the tapestry weavers of northern Europe, and, by implication, their patrons, for their preoccupation with opulence and what he saw as the frivolous themes of courtly power.[9] His discussion of the relative merits of his portraits painted by Pisanello and Jacopo Bellini was stimulated by classical literary precedents and it was an important step in the emergence of the idea of the creative artist.[10] Above all, Decembrio's text suggested a desire to imbue the imagery of the Ferrarese court with more subtlety than the traditional, and easily recognizable, link between display and cost.

Leonello's projects reflected his interest in the culture of classical antiquity. Before decorating his studio at Belfiore with paintings of the nine Muses, he asked Guarino for advice and his old tutor's reply (1447) gave details of the attributes he considered appropriate for each of them.[11] Leonello's liking for the bronze coins of ancient Rome ornamented with profile heads of Emperors inspired him to have his own medals similarly designed, many commissioned from Pisanello. According to the humanist, Flavio Biondo, he had over 10,000 made.[12] This was a significant development and such medals soon became the fashion with other rulers, notably Alfonso I of Naples and Ludovico Gonzaga in Mantua (see Chapters 13 and 16).[13] The medals were decorated with explanatory inscriptions, a profile head on one side and a design on the reverse that might commemorate an individual or an event. Their imperial connotations made them distinctive statements of absolute power, and they were far less popular amongst the merchants of Venice and Florence.

Under Borso (1450–71), the Este court took on an entirely different character. Borso's preferences were for conspicuous expenditure and ostentatious display. And he used his talents in this field to great success in consolidating the family's authority and prestige. Lavish entertainments, expensive presents and the promise of political support encouraged Emperor Frederick III to raise the status of the imperial fiefs of Modena and Reggio to a dukedom (1452) and he also persuaded the Pope to grant him the title of Duke of Ferrara (1471). With a taste for extravagance, Borso was famous for his costly clothes and jewels, and the entourage that accompanied him to Rome for his investiture as Duke included not only his courtiers, doctors and priests but also his grooms and huntsmen, dressed in ducal uniforms, together with his falcons, leopards and 320 hounds.[14]

Borso spent conspicuously on the visual symbols of his power in Ferrara and his territories.[15] He embellished the Palazzo del Corte with lavish tapestries, including a particularly magnificent set of Flemish hangings, bought in Venice for 9,000 ducats, which depicted the medieval chivalric Romance of the Rose embroidered on blue velvet.[16] His Bible, with its ornate miniatures and gilded bindings, cost over 2,200 ducats (5,507 lire) and was one of the most expensive books produced in fifteenth-century Italy.[17] He repaired and renewed the fortresses on the borders of his state and began work on an impressive new Certosa and its adjoining palace in Ferrara (begun 1452). He initiated extensive renovations to the Este villas at Belreguardo (see below) and Belfiore, where he commissioned elaborate intarsia work and paintings for the studio that had been started by Leonello.[18] He also began a scheme of urban renewal, extending the city to the south-east and building a new set of enclosing walls. But his principal project was the rebuilding of the Palazzo Schifanoia.

The new Palazzo Schifanoia was impressive. The doorway with its fluted Corinthian pilasters flanking an arch carried on Composite piers was ornately decorated with *all'antica* motifs and surmounted by a massive plaque bearing the Este coat of arms. Gilded stucco ceilings and intarsia woodwork testified to the expense of decorating the interior rooms.[19] The main hall of the palace was vast, measuring 40 × 80 feet. Known as the Salone del Mesi, or the Hall of the Months, its walls were frescoed by Francesco del Cossa and his assistants with an impressive cycle that combined chivalric themes of aristocratic rule with classical imagery of imperial Rome. The decoration (completed by 1470) was divided into three levels: at the top were triumphs of the Gods who presided over each month, in the middle, allegories of the zodiacal signs and below, where they were most easily visible from the floor, were scenes of court life.[20] The combination was inspired by the books of hours so popular at the French court, but the interpretation was Ferrarese. August, the month of harvest, for example, was presided over by Ceres, the Roman goddess of corn, with an allegory of Virgo below. At the bottom, Borso himself could be seen receiving an ambassador. Indeed, all the scenes at ground level included the figure of the opulently-dressed Borso, surrounded by smiling courtiers and servants, receiving letters, dispensing justice, hunting and generally fulfilling the role of the perfect ruler. Like Ludovico Gonzaga's Camera degli Sposi in Mantua or Galeazzo Maria Sforza's frescos in the Castello in Pavia, Borso's cycle provided a permanent, if idealized, record of life at his court.

Borso's stylistic preferences are well-illustrated by the decoration of his chapel at Belreguardo, a smaller project than the vast Salone del Mesi, but far more elaborate. A contract (1469) was drawn up with Borso's court painter, Cosimo Tura, which detailed the responsibilities of the two parties.[21] Borso agreed to advance funds for the considerable quantities of gold and ultramarine to be used on the project, and the amount was to be deducted from the final payment for the work, which was assessed by a panel of experts. The subject matter was to be specified later by the Duke. In November, Borso made arrangements to send Tura to Brescia to see Gentile da Fabriano's St George and the Dragon (c. 1414-19), presumably so that Tura could imitate the painter's elegant and highly decorative International Gothic style.[22] The new chapel was decorated with ornate gilded stucco work and painted with figures of God the Father, together with the four Evangelists and the four Doctors of the Church in the vaults. Borso's choice of style and his conspicuous use of expensive colours gave clear expression to his belief in the importance of the ostentatious display of wealth and power.

The account books kept in Ferrara still survive and they reveal a concern for detail exceptional even by the meticulous standards of the fifteenth century. Some of the books are even in Borso's own hand.[23] It is the incredibly precise valuation of Tura's chapel, long since destroyed, that allows us to reconstruct its appearance.[24] The principal concern of the assessors was estimating its cost and the whole work, down to each individual piece of cornice, was measured and valued. Painting was the cheapest part of the decoration. While the cost of gold, ultramarine and other colours came to over 330 lire, the nine figures painted in the chapel only cost 280 lire. Painters in Ferrara were usually paid by the square foot, their rates depending on skill and materials involved, which they had to buy. Cossa, who earned the same rate of 10 soldi as the others painting in the Salone dei Mesi, wrote to Borso arguing that he should be paid more because he was better known and had used higher quality materials.[25] But the sum of 1,058 lire that Borso spent on decorating his ornate chapel or the estimated figure of 2,300 lire for the fresco cycle in the enormous Salone dei Mesi were modest in contrast to the 5,507 lire he spent on his Bible.[26]

Under Ercole (1471–1505), the nature of Este propaganda changed once again. Ercole preferred plainer clothes to the flashy cloth of gold worn by his brother.[27] But, even so, he was a conspicuous spender. He commemorated his marriage to Eleonora of Aragon (1473) with a set of silver serving dishes decorated with his coat of arms and *all'antica* motifs. Designed by Cosimo Tura and another painter, Girardo Costa, the service was made by a Venetian goldsmith and cost over 7,000 ducats.[28] Ercole's court was less ostentatious than Borso's, but it was nonetheless impressive. He was an important patron of the revival of classical theatre.[29] The *de triumpho religionis* (mid-1490s), written by the humanist, Giovanni Sabbadino degli Arienti, promoted Ercole as a Christian prince and the embodiment of virtues such as magnanimity, liberality, magnificence, justice and patience.[30]

Venetian ambitions on the mainland posed a real threat to Ferrarese authority. Seeking allies for his campaign against Naples, Pope Sixtus IV elicited the support of Venice in return for papal fiefs held by Ferrara, which the Venetians quickly occupied (1483). The dispute soon escalated. Spain declared for Naples while Milan and Florence joined Ferrara. Sixtus IV opted out of the deal but the Venetians, determined to retain their new territory, threatened to call on France to support her claim and the prospect of a European war compelled the parties to sue for peace. But the event emphasized the insecurity of Ercole's position in the face of the ambitions of more powerful rulers and he reinforced his links with the major Italian courts. He married his daughters Isabella and Beatrice respectively to Francesco Gonzaga (1490) and Ludovico Sforza (1491). His heir, Alfonso, was married to Anna (1491), a daughter of Francesco Sforza, and another son, Ippolito, was created a cardinal (1493). After Anna Sforza's death (1497), Ercole was persuaded by Pope Alexander VI, in return for an enormous dowry that included 100,000 ducats cash, land, jewels and other valuables, to marry Alfonso to the Pope's daughter, the infamous Lucrezia Borgia (1501).

Above all, he concentrated his energies on commissioning visual symbols of his prestige and transformed the appearance of Ferrara. Ercole d'Este was one of the most impressive patrons in fifteenth-century Italy, though sadly little of his work has survived.[31] We know from Sabadino of paintings at Belreguardo depicting the story of Cupid and Psyche.[32] He also commissioned fresco cycles that charted his family's achievements, including the arrival of Eleonora of Aragon in Ferrara in 1473 which was painted at Belfiore.[33] But his principal projects were architectural. He remodelled the Palazzo del Corte and the Castello Nuovo, commissioned decorations for Belreguardo and rebuilt Belfiore after it was burnt down by the Venetians during the war (1483). He dramatically enlarged the city to the north-east with the so-called *Addizione Ercole*, laying out new streets and a piazza. He encouraged members of his court to build palaces in the new extension. But the focus of Ercole's plans were his religious projects. He rebuilt his father's foundations of Santa Maria degli Angeli and the Certosa, and commissioned additions to the cathedral and at least four other churches. In a striking statement of piety and power, he also founded over twelve new churches in Ferrara, many of which were in the *Addizione Ercole*. Ercole's expenditure on buildings formed the principal theme of Sabbadino's discussion of his magnificence.[34] Drawing on the Aristotelian tradition that had inspired other humanists to justify the extravagant expenditure of patrons like Cosimo de' Medici, Sabbadino emphasized that Ercole's unstinting outlay on architecture, like the money he spent on lavish wedding celebrations, was an essential component of the wealthy and powerful ruler.

To cope with this massive building campaign, Ercole streamlined the various organs in charge of ducal projects, uniting them under the control of a central office of works which took charge not only of the construction but also of the furnishing and decoration of palaces, castles and villas throughout the territory.[35] Like the administration of the state, the organization of the office of works was designed for efficiency. A ducal agent was appointed to administer the building projects and overall control of construction was delegated to a chief supervisor. This position was held by Pietro de Benvenuti (1469–83) and after his death taken over by his assistant, Biagio Rossetti (1483–1505). Foremen were contracted to take charge of work at each site, a position Rossetti also held for some of Ercole's churches, while the rest were done by other builders.[36] The relationship between the agent and the supervisor was formalized in a document of 1475, which stipulated their areas of responsibility.[37] The agent was to keep the accounts, receive daily reports from the foremen from each site and to organize the supplies of materials and labour. The supervisor was required to visit the sites, to liaise with the foremen, to authorize payments and to ensure that the work was up to stardard. Petty theft was a major problem, and various stratagems were included to avoid malpractice. The supervisor was responsible for ensuring that all the materials sent had been used, while the agent was required to check the loading of carts of bricks, tiles and lime to make sure that the kiln workers did not cheat.

Ercole's interest in architecture was exceptional and well documented. By 1495 he owned copies of both Vitruvius's and Alberti's treatises on architecture.[38] He was also curious to know about Filippo Strozzi's new palace in Florence (begun 1489) (fig. 12) which had roused considerable interest in Ferrara, where many members of the Strozzi family had settled after their exile in 1434. Giovanni Strozzi, writing to his brother in Florence, reported that the Duke had asked for details of its dimensions and decoration, the number of floors, the size of the main rooms, whether there was to be a courtyard and loggias and if Filippo was planning to use any Carrara marble.[39] Strozzi added significantly that the Duke took great pleasure in building and in making designs. While away fighting in 1479, Ercole sent back plans for new work on the Palazzo del Corte together with instructions for his foreman, Pietro de Benvenuti[40] and Sabbadino's account of Ercole's projects specifically attributed their design to the Duke.[41] Ercole's wife, Eleonora, loyally described him as an excellent architect.[42] Like Lorenzo de' Medici, Pope Pius II and Ludovico Gonzaga, Ercole was one of a number of patrons in fifteenth-century Italy who played a central role in the design of their projects. The contract drawn up with Biagio Rossetti for the construction of Santa Maria in Vado (1495)[43] referred to designs by the court painter, Ercole de' Roberti, but it is also possible that Roberti had been responsible for formalizing Ercole's ideas.

Work on remodelling the Palazzo del Corte began soon after Ercole assumed power and, apart from an interruption during the Wars of Ferrara, it continued throughout his reign.[44] His ambitious schemes included new courtyards and gardens, an imposing staircase, a covered walkway linking the palace with the Castello Vecchio, a chapel, balconies, apartments for himself and his duchess and, an important innovation, a purpose-built theatre. The two equestrian monuments commissioned by the town council to commemorate Nicolò III and Borso were moved to the façade.[45] Unlike Ercole's churches, which were largely built of local brick, much of the work on the Palazzo del Corte was done in expensive imported stone.[46] The interior of the palace was magnificent. Hung with splendid tapestries, the main reception halls in the palace were known as the *Camere Dorate* from their ornate gilded stucco decoration.[47] Carrara marble and tiles, painted with Este arms and devices, decorated the floors and elaborate intarsia work was commissioned for the palace doors.[48] One of the prominent images in the palace was the figure of Hercules: three Labours of Hercules were painted on the covered corridor to the Castello Vecchio and Ercole also commissioned two bronze statues of the god to decorate the grand marble staircase.[49] The subject of Hercules had provided the theme for the decoration of the main reception room in the Palazzo Medici in Florence (see Chapter 5). The Duke's choice, which was likewise intended to convey the message of a wise ruler and opponent of tyranny, also of course made a more direct reference to Ercole himself.

The Este Dukes created an impressive setting for the display of their power and prestige. Under their initiative, fifteenth-century Ferrara became one of the major centres of Renaissance art. Their state weathered the political chaos following the French invasions and the family continued as the rulers of their dukedom until Napoleon invaded northern Italy in 1796.

16

Mantua

M antua was effectively an island in the river Mincio that flowed from Lake Garda to the Po and it was surrounded on three sides by mosquito-infested swamps. Damp and foggy in winter and humid in summer, the city had grown up at a strategic point in the fertile Lombard plain on the trade route that linked Italy with Germany through the Brenner pass. With a population of around 25,000, Mantua was about the same size as nearby Ferrara and far smaller than their powerful neighbours, Milan and Venice.

Mantua could claim historical fame as the birthplace of the Roman poet, Virgil. After the collapse of the Roman Empire, the city had become part of the feudal territories on the Lombard plain under imperial authority. In 1183 it gained independence with the Peace of Constance and a communal government which disintegrated when Pinamonte Bonacolsi seized power in 1273. In 1328 Luigi Gonzaga, a member of a local landowning family, took control of the city, establishing the basis for Gonzaga rule in Mantua which lasted until 1627. Like nearby Ferrara, fifteenth-century Mantua was politically stable and this was a significant factor in its cultural achievement. Through judicious marital alliances, skilful diplomacy and, above all, through the creation of an illustrious court, the fifteenth-century Gonzaga rulers achieved a level of distinction for their city out of all proportion to its size.

The focus of Gonzaga power in Mantua was their huge palace, now known as the Palazzo Ducale. Once the Palazzo del Capitano of the old commune, it had been enlarged and embellished by the fourteenth-century Gonzaga rulers as the prime symbol of their authority. Francesco I (1382–1407) had added the Castello San Giorgio, a fortified tower overlooking the Ponte San Giorgio, the bridge linking Mantua with the mainland. Like the ducal palaces in Ferrara and Urbino, its defensive aspect contrasted with a more open urban façade. The principal front of the palace faced the city's central piazza. Its castellated skyline, brick façade, pointed-arched arcade at ground level and elegant Gothic windows provided an impressive image of political stability, and one that was very different from the impregnable stronghold erected by the Visconti and Sforza rulers in Milan or the Aragon castle in Naples. Also on the piazza was Mantua's cathedral with an expensive marble façade covered in ornate Gothic detail, which had also been commissioned by Francesco I (c. 1400). The city's commercial district centred on Mantua's other principal church, Sant'Andrea. Almost as large as the cathedral, it possessed a famous relic of the Blood of Christ which attracted pilgrims from far afield.

Francesco I was succeeded by his son, Gianfrancesco (1407–44), whose investiture as Marquis of Mantua by the Holy Roman Emperor in 1433 marked an important turning point in the fortunes of both the family and the city. In contrast to the rulers of Milan or Ferrara, the Gonzaga looked towards the Empire to establish political links. Gianfrancesco's heir, Ludovico, married Barbara of Brandenburg (1433) and Ludovico's son, Federigo, Margaret of Bavaria (1463). Gianfrancesco was a prominent supporter of humanism, inviting Vittorino da Feltre to teach his children and take charge of his library (1423). He continued to embellish Mantua, commissioning work on the Palazzo Ducale, completing Santa Maria delle Grazie, founded by his father (begun 1399), and started a new church, Santa Maria degli Angeli (1429). He also built the Gonzaga castle at Marmirolo. But it was his son, Ludovico, who took the initiative in transforming this insignificant and unhealthy city into one of the most famous centres of the Renaissance.

Ludovico (1444–78) took advantage of the collapse of Milanese power in Lombardy following the death of Filippo Maria Visconti (1447). He fought as a *condottiere* in turn for the Visconti (1445), Florence (1447), Venice (1448), Naples (1449) and Francesco Sforza (1450).[1] He acquired a reputation as a skilful soldier and an astute politician, as well as bringing in much-needed funds to the state coffers. Ludovico now exploited his connections with the imperial court in Germany to persuade Pope Pius II to hold his forthcoming Congress (1459–60) on the crusade at Mantua, tempting him with the promise that Frederick III would attend.[2] Although the Emperor never arrived, the papal court spent nine months resident in the city. Ludovico also exploited his imperial links as the political lever to get his son created a cardinal.[3] Francesco acquired his red hat in 1461 and soon proved a very useful ally at the papal court (see below).

Ludovico was one of the most impressive patrons of fifteenth-century Italy and the survival of much of his correspondence in the Mantua archives enables us to appreciate the enormous personal interest he took in his projects. His ambitious programme of urban renewal decisively changed the appearance of the city centre. He commissioned extensive repairs and renovations to the Palazzo Ducale, including a new set of apartments in the

Castello San Giorgio. Outside the city, he remodelled and redecorated the Gonzaga castles and hunting lodges at Cavriana, Goito, Gonzaga, Marmirolo, San Martino di Gusnago and Saviola. In Florence he contributed towards the rebuilding of Santissima Annunziata, adding 2,000 ducats to a bequest of 200 ducats made by his father to the church.[4] But the projects that have made Ludovico really famous were the fresco cycles he commissioned from Pisanello and Mantegna for the Palazzo Ducale and two churches in Mantua, San Sebastiano and Sant'Andrea, both built to designs by Alberti.

Ludovico's first major project was to engage Pisanello to decorate the main reception hall of the Palazzo Ducale (c. 1447–8).[5] Although it was never completed, the preparatory sketches and some of the paintings still survive (fig. 52). Pisanello was one of the best-known painters of the

52.   Pisanello, Sala del Pisanello, Palazzo Ducale, Mantua, c. 1447–8

elegant International Gothic style favoured by the leading courts of Europe and the fresco cycle was to depict the Knights of the Round Table, taken from a thirteenth-century French Arthurian romance in the Gonzaga library. The remains of the frescos showed knights in armour doing battle with lances and swords, their horses caparisoned in the Gonzaga colours. Huge fortified castles towered in the background and the frieze above was decorated with the Gonzaga devices. Both style and theme were typical of current tastes for the visual expression of aristocratic rule.

Sometime during the 1450s Ludovico decided on a radical change of image to promote his prestige and this decision should be seen as part of his broader political policy to enhance his power by strengthening links with the Empire and the papal court. In place of courtly Gothic and chivalric themes, he opted for the classical language of ancient Rome. This was a bold step and Ludovico must have been influenced by the example of Sigismondo Malatesta, Lord of Rimini, who had started to remodel the church of San Francesco in Rimini (begun *c.* 1450) according to a design by Alberti, based on the architecture of antiquity.[6] Like Malatesta, Ludovico was the ruler of a small, relatively uninfluential state and he needed powerful propaganda to advertise its status in competition with Italy's leading rulers, notably Francesco Sforza in Milan (see Chapter 12). Sforza's preference was for Gothic. Ludovico's choice of style enabled him to appear both different and impressive. Above all, the language of antiquity made a manifest association with a grand, imperial power.

As early as 1447, Ludovico had taken up Leonello d'Este's passion for *all'antica* bronze medals and commissioned several from Pisanello, who also worked for the Ferrarese ruler (see Chapter 15).[7] His next step was far more significant. By 1457 he had persuaded the Paduan painter, Mantegna, to work for him, and the artist took up permanent residence in Mantua in 1460.[8] Mantegna's work had little in common with the courtly imagery of northern Europe. In response to the demands of his humanist patrons in Padua, he had developed an *all'antica* style with figures derived from antique reliefs and settings that revived the architectural language of ancient Rome. Mantegna's first commission for Ludovico was a series of panels of the Adoration of the Magi, the Circumcision, the Ascension and the Death of the Virgin, for the chapel in Castello San Giorgio. His major project for Ludovico was the decoration of the Camera degli Sposi, the audience chamber in the Castello San Giorgio (1465–74).[9]

Ludovico's ideas on the themes appropriate for an important palace reception room had dramatically changed since his commission to Pisanello twenty years before. Instead of the ideal of knightly chivalry, he commissioned Mantegna to paint a cycle of frescos that gave visual expression to the prestige of the Mantuan court and stressed its association with the

53.   Mantegna, *Ludovico Gonzaga and his Court*. Mantua, Palazzo Ducale,
Camera degli Sposi, 1465–74

imperial traditions of ancient Rome, not the courts of northern Europe. On
the walls were frescos of Ludovico, his family and courtiers (fig. 53). Gonzaga devices were everywhere. The vaults were painted to look like stucco
moulding with portrait medallions of the first eight Roman Emperors and
lunettes with fictive reliefs of stories from classical mythology. In the centre
of the ceiling, Mantegna painted what appeared to be an oculus open to the
sky surrounded by a parapet, with court ladies and *putti* looking down into
the room (fig. 54). Amusing details, like the precariously balanced plant pot
or the cherub about to drop an apple contrasted with the seriousness of the
room beneath. The wall frescos were filled with identifiable portraits. In the
Court Scene (fig. 53) sat Ludovico and Barbara of Brandenburg, their
children and the court dwarf together with courtiers dressed in the Gonzaga

54.   Mantegna, ceiling, Camera degli Sposi, Palazzo Ducale, Mantua, 1465–74

colours. Ludovico, a letter in his hand and his dog under the chair, was conferring with a secretary. In the Meeting Scene with Ludovico and his son, Cardinal Francesco Gonzaga, were portraits of two European rulers, the Holy Roman Emperor Frederick III and King Christian I of Denmark, Barbara of Brandenburg's brother-in-law.[10] This was not the record of a particular event. Christian I was in Mantua in 1474 but Frederick III never visited the city and Ludovico had to ask his agent in Milan to send a drawing of the Emperor for Mantegna to use.[11] The inclusion of these two rulers testified to Mantua's links with European power. Dynastic and imperial, the themes chosen for the chamber provided impressive propaganda for the Gonzaga court.

Mantegna was Ludovico's court artist, and his job involved a wide range of commissions, from designs for pageants and tapestries to portraiture and the decoration of his patron's many palaces and villas.[12] His salary of 180 ducats a year, supplemented by living accommodation, grain to feed six people and firewood, made him a member of Mantua's prosperous middle classes, on a par with the tailor, the builder and the linen merchant who were among the witnesses of his will.[13] The surviving letters between Mantegna and Ludovico reveal that his salary was not always promptly paid and that lack of ready funds forced Ludovico to reward his painter with grants of land instead.[14] They also show Mantegna's difficult and litigious nature: he took a neighbour to court for allegedly stealing 500 apples and accused an engraver of sodomy whom he suspected of stealing his designs.[15]

Ludovico's new image had a far-reaching effect on the fabric of Mantua itself. The city had not impressed the members of the papal court in Mantua for the Congress and Pius II had criticized its muddy streets and scruffy appearance.[16] Ludovico's response was to initiate a massive programme of urban renewal, largely rebuilding the city centre. He paved the streets, restored the old Merchants' Loggia and the town hall (the Palazzo del Podesta), began a new clock tower, planned work on the Romanesque church of San Lorenzo (never carried out), founded the church of San Sebastiano and rebuilt Sant'Andrea. Seeking advice on designs that would give visual expression to his new image, Ludovico turned to Alberti (1404–72), a papal abbreviator in Mantua for the Congress and a recognized expert on the architecture of classical antiquity. He provided plans for San Sebastiano, San Lorenzo and the Palazzo del Podestà (1460)[17] and Sant'Andrea (1470).[18]

Alberti's churches of San Sebastiano and Sant'Andrea were designed on the monumental scale of ancient Roman architecture in striking contrast to the elegant detail of the Gothic buildings in Mantua and other secular courts. The imposing temple façade of San Sebastiano, set on an arcade of heavy piers, was crowned by a classical pediment split by an arch, a detail that could also be seen on the Roman arch at Orange. Not everyone liked it. Ludovico's son, Cardinal Francesco Gonzaga, was less than complimentary when he commented in 1473 that it was difficult to tell whether the building was a church, a mosque or a synagogue.[19] However, the church was still unfinished in 1500 and its present appearance is the result of dubious restoration work carried out in the 1920s. There is considerable debate amongst art historians as to Alberti's original intentions.[20] Alberti's design for Sant'Andrea has posed far fewer problems.[21] Its façade was based an a triumphal arch, topped by a triangular pediment. The vast open interior was designed to hold large crowds of pilgrims venerating the church's famous relic of the Blood of Christ. Alberti adapted the three apses of the Basilica of Maxentius in Rome to provide three huge chapels opening off each side of the massive nave. Both nave and chapels were covered by antique coffered barrel vaults. The building was overtly classical, but Alberti's source was not entirely pagan; the Basilica of Maxentius had been completed by the first Christian Emperor, Constantine. The pilasters and arches lining the nave repeated the design of the façade in both size and form, reflecting Alberti's theories on the unity of design,[22] a decisive change from the medieval practice of treating façade, nave and chapels as separate units.

Ludovico's decision to rebuild Sant'Andrea was part of a wider scheme to take over the monastery and its lucrative revenues.[23] He ran into opposition from the Abbot and the Pope. In 1460, Ludovico and his agents started a smear campaign questioning both the personal conduct of the Abbot and the general state of religious observance at the monastery. But the old Abbot was stubborn and it was only after his death in 1470 that Ludovico could begin to realize his ambition. He now started to organize funds for rebuilding and Alberti provided a design for the new church (1470).[24] With Cardinal Francesco as a valuable ally in Rome, Ludovico lobbied the Pope for permission to start. Pope Paul II (1464–71) was evasive, but his successor Sixtus IV (1471–84) was more amenable and, soon after his election, Ludovico urged Francesco to renew the request. In January 1472, Francesco wrote to say that the Pope had agreed and work started the following month. In June 1472, Sixtus IV issued a Bull transferring the monastery from the Benedictines to a new collegiate foundation under the authority of Cardinal Francesco.

Ludovico's association with Alberti was a major step in the development of the relationship between a modern patron and his architect.[25] The illegitimate son of an exiled Florentine noble, Alberti belonged to the upper echelons of Renaissance society. He never held the post of chief foreman on a building site: his background and scholarly training made him entirely unsuitable for the job. Nor was he paid a salary for his work: Ludovico returned his help with favours, lending him the Gonzaga villa at Cavriana[26] and intervening on his behalf with Paul II after the Pope had abolished his job in the College of Abbreviators in Rome.[27] Alberti had established himself as an expert on classical architecture with his treatise, de re aedificatoria (1452). Aimed at patrons, it showed them how the architectural language of ancient Rome could be adapted to their requirements for churches, palaces, castles and other impressive buildings that were the hallmarks of powerful cities. Above all, Alberti revived the Roman concept of an expert in architectural design, emphasizing his own suitability for the role and making a clear distinction between the intellectual qualities of the architect and the manual skills of the craftsmen who built his design.[28] This was an enormously innovative idea. The modern concept of an architect did not exist in early fifteenth-century Italy, where the range of talents involved in architectural design was vast and the patron, who had the greatest concern for his building's final appearance, played a central role in the process.[29] Like other Renaissance patrons, Ludovico was closely involved in the design of his projects[30] and his correspondence with Alberti showed that he had his own ideas to contribute to Sant'Andrea.[31] But there is no doubt that it was Alberti who was the principal force behind the design of San Sebastiano and Sant'Andrea. Ludovico's decision to seek the advice of an expert in design reflected not only the importance he attached to these two major symbols of his prestige and their radically new forms, but also his recognition that this expert could play a prominent role in the creation of an impressive image of power.

The foreman in charge of constructing Ludovico's projects was Luca Fancelli, a Florentine stonecutter who had worked for him since the early 1450s.[32] Unlike Francesco Sforza, Ludovico did not employ an agent. When problems arose on San Sebastiano, he sent Fancelli to Alberti for instructions,[33] but he himself usually took the decisions affecting the final appearance of his buildings. Fancelli kept Ludovico regularly informed of progress on the projects underway. His many surviving letters to Ludovico, and their prompt replies, reveal much about how Ludovico's plans were realized, the problems they faced and what life was like in fifteenth-century Mantua. Above all, their correspondence shows how closely Ludovico was personally involved in the process. We can read, for instance, of how work at San Sebastiano was severely hampered in the winter of 1463–4, first by an outbreak of the plague, then heavy rain and finally snow,[34] of Fancelli's effort to uncover fraud on Sant'Andrea[35] and of the frenzied activity at the castle of Gonzaga in preparation for the visit of Galeazzo Maria Sforza and Bona of Savoy.[36] The Duke and Duchess of Milan were expected in July 1471 and work gathered pace as the date approached. In March Fancelli reported that the site was like Babylon with 150 craftsmen at work. At the end of the month he asked Ludovico to hurry up with the materials and to send more men. Rainstorms in April held up work for a few days. In June he wrote that carved wooden cornices had arrived but that the ultramarine, bought specially in Venice to decorate them, had been rejected by Mantegna as of poor quality. Ludovico contacted Mantegna directly and sorted out this dispute. Later in June Fancelli asked Ludovico to organize the gold needed for the ceilings. In July, Ludovico asked Fancelli to measure the sizes of the beds so that he could order their mattresses. A few days later, Fancelli reported that he was worried about who was paying the forty-five builders, forty-three carpenters and eighteen painters at work on the site. He sent a list of what was ready with his own suggestion that some of the walls should be painted with fictive coloured marble instead of panelled with the wood which Ludovico had ordered. Ludovico tactfully replied that the wood would be better for his visitors' health! On 20 July, just before the visitors arrived, Ludovico's chief steward reported that the workforce had been up until three in the morning getting the castle ready. The letters reveal an affectionate relationship. When Fancelli fell down in

Sant'Andrea and hurt a testicle, Ludovico replied that God allows men to teach themselves a lesson in the place where they have made mistakes.[37] Ludovico emerges as an efficient, interested and level-headed man, while Fancelli comes across as hard-working, fussy, and, like many of his contemporaries, obsessed with avoiding illness.

Ludovico was succeeded by his rather solid and uninspiring son, Federigo (1478–84), who continued work on his father's projects, his plans for urban renewal, San Sebastiano and Sant'Andrea. He also initiated work on the Gonzaga castles at Due Castelli, Sermide and Gonzaga, where he commissioned Mantegna to paint a fresco cycle (now destroyed).[38] But his principal project was an extension to the Palazzo Ducale, the *Domus Nova*. Work on the foundations had started by 1480[39] and the following year Federigo wrote to Urbino asking for a drawing of Federigo da Montefeltro's palace.[40] He later wrote directly to Francesco di Giorgio to ask for his help in designing fireplaces that did not smoke.[41] Federigo kept Fancelli as chief supervisor of his building works, but the old direct relationship that had existed between Ludovico and Fancelli disappeared. Federigo employed an agent to oversee construction and to keep him informed of progress. It was to the agent that Fancelli now directed his requests for materials. And, in an implied criticism of Fancelli, the agent recommended to Federigo that work should be put out to contract to save money (1481).[42]

The succession of Federigo's 18-year-old son, Francesco (1484–1519), opened another exciting chapter in the visual and cultural history of Mantua. Francesco, also confusingly known as Gianfrancesco II, was an important patron and his marriage to Isabella d'Este (1490) introduced a second prodigious spender to the city (see below). Francesco had a distinguished career as a *condottiere*, commanding the Venetian armies in 1489–98 and fighting for both Louis XII of France and Pope Julius II. He played a prominent role in the Battle of Fornovo (1495) against the French armies of Charles VIII, which was claimed by both sides as a celebrated victory and marked the end of Charles VIII's activities in Italy. Francesco's stables were renowned throughout Europe and he made a welcome present of four Gonzaga horses to Henry VIII of England (1514).[43] The prizes won by his racehorses were recorded in an elaborately-decorated manuscript ornamented with illustrations of his favourites.[44] He died of syphilis aged 53.

Francesco continued work on Sant'Andrea and commissioned extensive decorations for the family castles at Gonzaga and Marmirolo. He stopped work on his father's *Domus Nova* and concentrated instead on building himself a new palace near San Sebastiano using the materials intended for the church.[45] His tastes were extravagant. The lavish decorations of the

Palazzo San Sebastiano included expensive tapestries and gilded brocades. His own bed was covered with crimson velvet embroidered with pearls and one of the rooms was frescoed with pictures of his horses.[46] At Marmirolo he commissioned pictures of cities, a fashion also adopted by Pope Innocent VIII at the Villa Belvedere (see Chapter 20) that derived from literary descriptions of the villas of ancient Roman patricians.[47] Above all, Francesco promoted himself as a military leader, and displayed a distinctive preference for the martial imagery of ancient Rome. His medals showed him in armour[48] as did his portrait bust (c. 1498) by Giancristoforo Romano.[49] The bust, with its tapering base directly recalling the imperial style of ancient Rome, was markedly different from the Florentine preference for busts which were cut off in a horizontal line below the shoulders.[50]

Francesco's power and prestige was celebrated in the theme of military prowess. The Battle of Fornovo was advertised as his victory and the court humanist, Battista Spagnuoli, commemorated it in epic prose.[51] Francesco began a votive chàpel at San Simone, which he dedicated to the Madonna of Victory,[52] and commissioned Mantegna to paint an altarpiece, the *Madonna della Vittoria* (1495), portraying Francesco as the donor, dressed in his armour, in the company of two warrior saints, Michael and George. The chapel was never built but a pageant was organized to commemorate the first anniversary of the battle on 6 July 1496, and the altarpiece was carried to San Simone in a magnificent procession, accompanied by Mantuan citizens playing the parts of God, angels, prophets and the twelve Apostles as living adjuncts to the painted image.[53] Francesco promoted the military achievements of himself and his ancestors in a series of Gonzaga triumphs. He sent a painter to Fornovo to make an accurate study of the site of his own triumph.[54] The first in the series was a dramatic portrayal of the struggle with the Bonacolsi family which had brought the Gonzaga to power in 1328. Domenico Morone's scene, the *Expulsion of the Bonacolsi*, was set unmistakably in the piazza in front of the Palazzo Ducale with the opponents dressed in late fifteenth-century armour.[55]

Francesco's most famous commission continued the theme of military triumph. Mantegna's nine canvases of the *Triumphs of Caesar* were in the Palazzo San Sebastiano by 1508, though they were probably painted for the Palazzo Ducale (c. 1484–1506).[56] On a visit to Mantua in 1486, Ercole d'Este saw the works in progress and was impressed.[57] Based on accounts of Roman triumphs in Appian and Plutarch, the paintings were intended to represent Julius Caesar's triumphal return to Rome after his conquest of Gaul.[58] Mantegna portrayed the pageantry of this ancient Roman spectacle in elaborate detail, showing slaves and soldiers laden with booty, elephants, trumpeters, prisoners and senators moving in procession across the nine canvases. The ambitious cycle provided unambiguous evidence of Francesco's desire to be associated with Julius Caesar, one of the most highly revered military leaders of antiquity.

Francesco's wife, Isabella d'Este (1474–1539), presented an entirely different image. The daughter of Ercole d'Este and Eleonora of Aragon, she had been brought up in the cultured court of Ferrara. Moving to Mantua in 1490, she was determined to make her mark on her adopted city.[59] She planned a monument to Virgil, Mantua's most illustrious Roman citizen, with a bronze statue of the poet in a toga and antique sandals.[60] She also planned a shrine to Beata Osanna Andreasi, a local mystic whose cult was especially popular in the city.[61] Neither of these two projects was ever finished and Isabella focused her attention on her private apartments in the Palazzo Ducale.

Isabella d'Este was one of the most prolific collectors in sixteenth-century Italy and the bulk of her achievement, after the death of Francesco, is outside the scope of this book. She had what she herself described as an insatiable desire for old things.[62] But she did not limit herself to antiques and her agents scoured Italy for precious objects. She bought gems and cameos, sculpture, paintings and high-quality editions of classical texts printed by Aldo Manuzio in Venice.[63] She commissioned ceramics from Ferrara and Faenza and glassware from Venice.[64] Her collection included both antique sculptures and modern reproductions. She acquired statues of Cupid by both Praxiteles (in 1505) and Michelangelo (in 1502).[65] The sculptor, Antico, was commissioned to make a cast of his *Spinario*, a copy of an ancient Roman bronze, and a gold statue of St John the Baptist.[66] Mantegna was persuaded to part with his ancient Roman bust of Faustina which he loved dearly but was forced to sell to pay off his debts.[67] She commissioned portraits from Leonardo and Lorenzo Costa.[68] Her image also appeared on her many medals. Notoriously vain, she kept a gold version of one of her favourites, set in diamonds and enamels, with an antique cameo of Emperor Augustus and his wife, Livia.[69]

Isabella's apartments in the Castello San Giorgio have now disappeared but much of their decoration was incorporated into her new suite, built after Francesco's death, in the Palazzo Ducale.[70] They were lavishly furnished. The *grotta*, where she kept her collection, was covered by a barrel vault decorated with *all' antica* stucco reliefs.[71] Her *studiolo* (begun c. 1492) had a floor paved with ceramic tiles decorated with Gonzaga devices[72] and walls embellished with expensive intarsia woodwork. But it was the five paintings commissioned for the walls that most clearly revealed Isabella's tastes, her attitude to art and her relationship with her artists. Mantegna's *Parnassus* (finished 1497) and his *Expulsion of the Vices* (1502), Perugino's *Battle of Love and Chastity* (1505) and Lorenzo Costa's

Allegory (1504–6) and his *Reign of Comus* (after 1506) were all commissioned to detailed programmes devised by Paride da Ceresara, Isabella's literary adviser.[73] All drew on the literature of classical antiquity. Mantegna's *Parnassus* showed Mars, not as the god of war, but as Venus's lover with the nine Muses dancing below. The image of cultural creativity was deliberately designed to foster Isabella's image as a patron of the arts. But the precise meaning of this and the other panels has never been convincingly explained.

We are, however, very well informed on how the paintings were commissioned. Isabella's intention, as she pointed out in a letter to her agent in Florence, was to get the best artists in Italy to produce paintings in competition with each other.[74] This somewhat commercial approach was designed to achieve excellence. Writing to her agent in Florence about her offer to Perugino, Isabella was not worried about the quality of his work; she was sure that he would not want to compare badly with Mantegna.[75] She tried, unsuccessfully, to persuade Leonardo and Giovanni Bellini to paint panels for the *studiolo*.[76] She knew exactly what she wanted. In order to achieve a basic uniformity, the painters were given very precise instructions covering not only the size of the canvas, the medium for paint and the position of the light source but also the scale of the principal figures. Like many patrons of the period, Isabella's principal interest was the content of the paintings, not their style, and she issued exceptionally detailed instructions of what was to be painted.[77] Bellini refused the commission because he needed more freedom of composition.[78] Perugino's contract (1503) shows how little scope Bellini was offered.[79] He was to paint Pallas and Diana fighting Venus and Cupid; Pallas was to look as if she were beating Cupid, while Diana and Venus were to appear to struggle equally. The clothes for each figure were specified. In the background, Perugino was to paint nymphs fighting fawns and satyrs, a broad stream with white swans and images of mythological assault, including Jupiter as a bull raping Europa, Pluto kidnapping Persephone and Apollo chasing the unwilling Daphne. There was a diagram explaining the composition and Perugino was allowed to leave out some of the lesser scenes if there was too much for the panel!

Isabella ran into serious problems with Perugino's panel. She wrote to her agents for progress reports and they, in turn, pestered the painter. Perugino for his part proved a master of excuses and procrastination. In 1504 one of her agents reported that he thought some of the figures badly designed; Isabella immediately sent others to check.[80] She was really worried when she heard that Perugino had painted Venus nude, as this, she said, would change the whole meaning of the picture.[81] Perugino then disappeared for two months and neither his family nor servants would say where he had gone.[82] Once back, there were more delays but the picture was finally delivered to Isabella in June 1505,[83] two and a half years after the contract had been signed.

Attitudes to art at the Mantuan court had changed since Ludovico Gonzaga appointed Mantegna as his court painter. Inspired by literary accounts of the rulers of antiquity who were praised by contemporaries for their ability to recognize creative talent, Francesco drew a parallel between his own patronage of Mantegna and Alexander the Great's patronage of two of the greatest artists of the classical world, the painter Apelles and the sculptor Lysippus.[84] The artist was no longer just a craftsman. The central role he played in creating an image for his patron had significantly altered the relationship between them. It was the patron's prestige that was now enhanced by the quality of his artists. Isabella may have treated her artists rather badly, but she was keen to be seen to have commissioned quality. Francesco was fully aware of the honour that reflected on him by having an artist of the calibre of Mantegna at his court. He recognized that the *Triumphs of Caesar* was Mantegna's creation and he was proud to own them.[85]

Part Four
Rome

17

Rome: City of the Popes

O nce the capital of an Empire that stretched half across the world, medieval Rome was a mere shadow of her former self. But she was now the centre of the Christian world. It was here that St Peter and St Paul had preached and died for their faith and thousands of nameless believers had been killed for the entertainment of pagan emperors. The city's two oldest and most important basilicas, San Giovanni Laterano and St Peter's, had been built by Emperor Constantine, whose adoption of Christianity as the religion of the Roman Empire in A.D. 313 had ensured its survival. At San Giovanni Laterano, pilgrims could see the table where Christ and his Apostles had eaten the Last Supper and climb the staircase of Pontius Pilate's house where Christ had received his sentence of death (brought from Jerusalem by Constantine's mother, Helena). At St Peter's, built over the tomb of the first Pope, they could marvel at the miraculous imprint of Christ's features on the towel with which St Veronica had wiped Christ's face on his way to his Crucifixion. In the hundreds of churches throughout the city, many with traditions dating back to the earliest days of Christianity, pilgrims could see and believe in the sites of Christian legend. These churches, designed to impress and decorated with gilded altarpieces, costly sculpture and mosaics, provided visual proof of the enduring power of the Christian faith. Above all, Rome was the city of the Pope. Elected to a line of succession that stretched back to St Peter, his authority as the Vicar of Christ on earth was absolute. Papal power also had a secular dimension. As heir to Constantine and the imperial tradition, he was the temporal ruler of the papal states in Italy.

The beginning of the fifteenth century saw the Papacy in the throes of a crisis that threatened its very survival. Demands that the Pope should abandon his secular role and return to the pure spirituality of the age of the Apostles had become increasingly vociferous. And now the Papacy also faced a challenge to its supreme position at the head of the Church. The roots of this crisis were to be found in the means adopted by the medieval Papacy for its own survival.

Constantine had created a division between the temporal power of the Emperor and the spiritual authority of the Pope, moving his capital from Rome to Constantinople in A.D. 330. The fall of Italy in the fifth century left the Pope as sole heir to the old régime in the West. Imperial unity crumbled and Europe was politically divided. Rome remained the religious centre of Christendom but she had lost her Empire and, with it, the ability to enforce her authority. The unprotected city was a tempting target for those who wanted control of the Christian leadership of Europe. Determined to retain its independence, the Papacy claimed the right to temporal rule in Italy on the basis of the Donation of Constantine. This document, forged during the eighth century, justified the claim as a gift to Pope Sylvester I from Constantine after the Emperor's miraculous recovery from leprosy by baptism. But much of Italy was under Lombard control and Rome sought help from the powerful Frankish kingdom in northern Europe to enforce its right. Charlemagne's defeat of the Lombards in A.D. 774 and his coronation by Pope Leo III as Holy Roman Emperor in A.D. 800 recreated, in spirit at least, the old split between the Pope as religious leader and the Emperor as secular ruler. But the division was ambiguous. While the Papacy tried to assert its spiritual authority over Christian Europe, Charlemagne and his successors appointed their feudal nobles to bishoprics and other ecclesiastical posts. Rome had lost her independence and the balance of power had shifted to northern Europe.

Rome proved surprisingly resilient. During the eleventh and twelfth centuries the Papacy exploited political divisions in Europe to reassert its influence. A series of reforms freed the Church from outside interference. Papal elections were put in the hands of papal appointees, excluding the traditional rights of the Roman nobility and the Emperor. Clerical marriage was abolished, freeing priests from dynastic ambitions. The foundation of Cluny established a monastic order that owed its allegiance to Rome rather than to secular rulers and associated the Papacy with much-needed monastic reforms. Most importantly, the Papacy finally won the long Investiture Contest with the German Emperors in 1122 and claimed the right to appoint major church figures. By 1200, Rome was once again a potent force on the European political scene. But the nature of papal power had changed. Its renewal had been engineered by a series of worldly and politically astute Popes, not by religious ascetics, and the papal court increasingly resembled its secular rivals.

The renewed power and prosperity of Rome highlighted a real dilemma concerning the wealth of the Church. The history of Christianity included two conflicting traditions. On the one hand, the New Testament provided a forceful reminder of the spirituality and poverty of Christ and his Apostles. But this image proved manifestly inappropriate for the official religion of the Roman Empire. The plain table at which the early Christians had worshipped now became an elaborate altar. Modest houses were replaced by grandiose basilicas. The simple breaking of bread and blessing of wine became an elaborate, hierarchical ceremony. The image of Christ had changed from Saviour of the Poor to Emperor of Heaven and acquired all the trappings of Roman imperial power. The belief that conspicuous expenditure was fundamental to the expression of prestige was also deeply entrenched in medieval culture. The Church establishment was no exception. Throughout Europe, vast monasteries and cathedrals decorated with gilded sculpture and other extravagances provided visual evidence of its authority. In Rome the patronage of medieval Popes reached levels of ostentation that matched the days of Empire. Costly mosaics testified to their wealth and the themes of these images proclaimed the supremacy of their power.

The contrast between the poverty and morality of the *vita apostolica* and the opulent lifestyles of the Pope and prelates provided the focus for deep-rooted animosity and it was an issue that was fundamental to the history of the medieval Church. Critics condemned the extravagance of the buildings which provided the setting for ecclesiastical power, the elaborate ceremony that surrounded both Pope and prelates and, most of all, the corruption that materialism brought in its wake. Inspired by Christ and his Apostles, new religious orders emerged that rejected the growing secularization of traditional Benedictine monasticism and sought new solutions to the dilemma of reconciling practical needs with the desire to avoid ostentation. The Cistercians (founded 1098) demonstrated their moral way of life in an architectural style that was conspicuous for its simplicity and lack of sculptural decoration. A century later, the Cistercians had abandoned many of their former ideals and were themselves criticized for their lavish lifestyle by St Dominic, a zealous opponent of heresy and the founder of the Dominican Order (approved 1216), which insisted on a life of evangelical poverty and preaching for its members. The same desire to recreate the simple life of Christ and his Apostles formed the basis for the Franciscan Order (approved 1210) and both orders proclaimed their belief in poverty and morality by rejecting costly sculpture and mosaics and issuing statutes aimed at controlling the scale and elaboration of their churches. But each side of the argument had its supporters. When St Bernard of Clairvaux, a Cistercian and a leading critic of corruption in the medieval Church, launched an attack on the opulence of Abbot Suger's embellishment of St Denis, Paris (c. 1140), Suger justified it on the grounds that the money was spent to glorify God and the greater the cost the greater the glory. This was the dilemma for the Church: wealth and extravagance or poverty and morality. Like Suger, the medieval Papacy was competing in the secular world, where prestige and authority were most effectively expressed by conspicuous expenditure. Moreover, the basis of its power was firmly rooted in the imperial tradition of Constantine. Beyond giving recognition to the Cistercians, Franciscans and Dominicans, the medieval Papacy showed little appetite for changing its own lifestyle nor its goal of real power in the temporal sphere of European politics.

By the middle of the thirteenth century, a confident Papacy had begun to exploit the ambivalent distinction between its spiritual and temporal power so as to expand its influence in the political sphere and enforce its authority over the increasingly influential secular rulers of northern Europe. The conflict broke out into open hostility when Boniface VIII (1294–1303) issued his Bull *Unam Sanctam* (1302). This unambiguous statement of papal supremacy not only stressed his role as head of the Church but also asserted that it was a precondition for salvation for everyone to be subject to him. This claim to overlordship in the temporal realm was rightly seen as an infringement of the rights of secular rulers and so infuriated the French King Philip IV (1285–1314) that he captured the Pope, who died soon after. Factional feuds and civic unrest in Rome forced Clement V (1305–14) to leave the city and he set up his court in Avignon. Dante's inclusion of both Boniface VIII and Clement V amongst those suffering the torments of Hell reflected the widespread contemporary disgust felt towards the increasing secularization of the Papacy. Moreover, although Avignon was not actually in France, it was part of the wider French hegemony and, despite the efforts of Clement V and his successors to maintain their impartiality, the election of an ex-chancellor of France as Clement VI (1342–52) identified Avignon with French interests. Throughout Europe, the Pope was now seen as a tool of the French King.

Established in a huge and sumptuously decorated fortified palace, the papal court in Avignon soon acquired all the outward trappings of a secular state. But the costs of installing and maintaining this splendour highlighted inefficiencies in the management of papal affairs. Major financial and administrative reforms were designed to raise revenues and to bring the government of the Church more directly under papal control. The reorganization of the Curia created the largest bureaucracy in medieval Europe, dealing with petitions from all over Christendom, dispensations, indulgences and other spiritual grants of favour as well as issuing papal bulls and letters of appointment and governing the papal states. The opportunities for gain were considerable. Traditionally, papal revenues were divided into two categories: spiritual and temporal. Spiritual sources ranged from the charges made on issuing bulls, dispensations and other favours to the taxes (services) raised on benefices granted by the Pope. Temporal sources, which included levies paid by the papal states in Italy and taxes on goods imported into Rome, were less easy to collect from Avignon and the Curia concentrated on enhancing spiritual income by extending clerical taxation, by expanding the sale of indulgences from voluntary contributions into a major source of funds and by developing new sources of revenue, in particular, the sale of non-spiritual posts in the papal administration.

By the mid-fourteenth century, the calls for the Papacy to leave Avignon were becoming increasingly urgent. As the centre of the Christian world, Rome was the rightful seat of the successor to St Peter. St Catherine of Siena spent three months in Avignon convincing Gregory XI (1370–8) of the necessity to return and restore his spiritual credibility. But the demands were not exclusively religious. Rome had financial reasons for wanting the return of the papal court as her economy had suffered in its absence. Above all, the demands had a political dimension and reflected growing resentment towards French influence over the Papacy. Gregory XI finally returned to Rome in 1377 just before his death and his successor, Urban VI (1378–89) was, significantly, an Italian. But the French cardinals, eleven out of the total of sixteen, declared his election invalid and elected Clement VII (1378–94) in his place. Clement VII moved back to Avignon, inaugurating the Schism which was to split Europe for forty years. Political issues dominated the split from the start. While Urban VI's court in Rome was supported by England and rulers in Germany, Central Europe and most of Italy, the Avigon Pope Clement VII was recognized by France, Burgundy, Naples, Scotland, Spain and Portugal. Negotiations proved futile. Neither Pope, nor their successors, were prepared to surrender power. Finally, under strong pressure from secular rulers, the Cardinals of each obedience summoned the Council of Pisa in 1409 with the specific purpose of ending the Schism. But neither Pope would attend, nor abdicate, and the Council elected a third Pope Alexander V (1409–10).

The credibility of the Church was at a very low ebb. Three Popes now claimed legitimacy as the true successor to St Peter, their supporters openly split into political, not spiritual factions. Critics contrasted their extravagant and secular life styles with the spirituality and poverty of Christ and his Apostles. Attacks on the corruption of the clergy were intensifying. Neither criticism was new but, in the context of the Schism, they acquired added force. Radical reform movements, under John Wyclif (c. 1320–84) in England and Jan Hus (1373–1415) in Bohemia, rejected the ecclesiastical hierarchy in favour of the Bible as the supreme source of Christian doctrine, calling for confiscation of Church wealth and questioning the role of the Pope as head of the Church. Wyclif's ideas, in particular, had a political dimension that reflected the anti-French feelings generated in England during the Hundred Years War (1337–1453) towards the excessive French influence over the Papacy and the growing resentment at sending money to Avignon or, as the English saw it, to France. Europe was drifting into chaos. Under strong pressure from the rulers of Germany, France and England, the Pisan Pope, John XXIII (1410-15) was forced to summon the Council of Constance (1414-18) with the strict intention of responding to demands for reform and ending the Schism.

The Council of Constance was presided over by Emperor Sigismund and its participants included not only cardinals, theologians and leaders of the religious orders, but also representatives of secular rulers. United in their desire to end the Schism, the Council agreed that all three Popes should abdicate and, in 1417, they elected Cardinal Oddo Colonna as Martin V (see Chapter 18). But the Council was less unanimous on the issue of Church reform. The radical changes demanded by the followers of Wyclif and Hus were perceived by all to be a threat to established authority, secular as well as spiritual, and condemned as heresy. Hus was burned. Church reform had a political dimension and the conservative faction in the Council ensured that little progress was made towards changing the secular nature of papal power or reforming clerical corruption. But significant moves were made to regulate the government of the Church. The decree *Frequens* (1417) attempted to curb papal sovereignty by insisting on the superiority of the Council over a Pope and requiring Martin V to hold Councils that would deal with the problem of reform at regular intervals in the future. This unprecedented attack on the supreme authority of the Papacy was to have important ramifications for Martin V and his successors.

The institution of the Papacy faced a serious crisis at the beginning of the fifteenth century. The Schism had eroded much of its credibility and had had a devastating effect on its financial resources. The Papacy had lost its independence in the political arena. Its extravagant life style, the key indicator of its power and prestige, was under attack. Above all, its spiritual authority was in danger of being severely curtailed. Martin V and his successors responded to the conciliar movement by largely ignoring it. Determined to reassert their former supremacy in the Christian world, they repeatedly refused to submit their authority to that of a Council. Indeed, the democratic institution of a Council can have had little appeal to rulers who could claim to be the heirs of St Peter and the Emperors of ancient Rome. Faced with the awesome task of repairing the damage caused by the Schism, they concentrated on restoring papal authority in Europe. Based firmly in Rome, all but one of the fifteenth-century Popes were Italian. The exception, Calixtus III, was a Spaniard with close links to the Neapolitan court of Alfonso I of Aragon. Only two non-Italians have been elected since: Hadrian VI (1522-3) and John Paul II (1978-   ). Half the cardinals at the Council of Constance were Italian but the twenty-three who elected Alexander VI in 1492 included only one non-Italian. Dominated by Italian interests, the Papacy became increasingly involved in the political affairs of the peninsula.

The absence of the Popes in Avignon and the Great Schism had seriously eroded their authority in the Italian papal states and regaining control of this territory was as much a financial as a political priority. Their financial problems were exacerbated by the breakdown of the efficient organization of spiritual revenues established in the Avignon period. Decreasing revenues from the provinces forced the fifteenth-century Popes to seek other sources of funds and they expanded the sale of indulgences and venal offices in the Curia on a scale that far exceeded that of their Avignon predecessors.

The conciliar movement failed and, in the interests of unity, the urgent issue of Church reform was effectively shelved. Critics attacked abuses within the Church with renewed vigour, disgusted at the sacrifice of spiritual leadership for secular power. Extravagant and conspicuous expenditure on the part of the Papacy was condemned, as was corruption in the Curia. It was the sale of indulgences to finance the rebuilding of St Peter's that finally forced Luther to nail his theses to the church door in Wittenberg in 1517. But to see the fifteenth-century Papacy as a rotten and degenerate régime is to succumb to Protestant propaganda. Martin V and his successors certainly underestimated the scale of the demand for Church reform but their target was the restoration of the power and authority of the Papacy.

The arts provided persuasive propaganda for their cause. In a period of declining political influence, financial resources and spiritual authority, the Renaissance Popes found new sources of income and spent conspicuously, above all in Rome. And the principal themes that they chose for their buildings, sculptural projects, fresco cycles and altarpieces were the two controversial issues of papal primacy and Church wealth. Above all, they applied themselves to the transformation of Rome into a magnificent city, a fitting setting for the capital of Christendom, the seat of the successors to St Peter as well as the imperial tradition of ancient Rome.

18

The Return of the Papacy

Martin V made his triumphal entry into Rome on 28 September 1420 and his return heralded a new era in the fortunes of the city. Rome was again the undisputed centre of the Christian world. But visitors who expected a magnificent capital, one that befitted the seat of the heirs to St Peter and the Emperors of ancient Rome, would have been disappointed. The city was a mess. With a population that had slumped to 17,000, Rome was now smaller, and scruffier, than Paris, London, Venice, Naples, Florence or Milan. The huge area enclosed by the ancient walls was largely empty, and provided pasture for animals or land for crops. The churches and palaces that had impressed the medieval pilgrim were now dilapidated. St Peter's had huge cracks in its walls. Other churches had collapsed. Buildings were shabby, bridges broken, aqueducts ruined and there was rubbish everywhere. Few streets were paved. It was not surprising; apart from the damage caused by riots and factional fighting, little money had been spent on the upkeep of the city's monuments or its infrastructure since 1305. Improving the appearance of Rome was a major priority for the fifteenth-century Popes, not least because of the practical needs of the city's inhabitants and temporary visitors. But the prime motivation was propaganda. As the context for a Papacy determined to reassert its supreme authority over the Church, Rome in 1420 signally failed to impress.

Martin V, 1417–31

Two factors had influenced the Council of Constance in its decision to elect Cardinal Oddo Colonna as Martin V: his staunch support of its call for reform and his family background. As a reformer, he proved a disappointment, though he did attempt to suppress Hussite heresy. And, while he did bow to popular demand and call the Councils of Pavia (1423) and of Basle (1431), he firmly refused to surrender his supreme power. As a result, the Council of Pavia was ineffective and he died just before the Council of Basle opened. His family background was an important factor in re-establishing the Papacy in Rome and restoring its tarnished image. As a member of the powerful Roman Colonna clan, he had a secure base in the city and the influence to enforce his authority.

Martin V was faced with daunting tasks. Inheriting almost empty coffers from his Roman and Avignonese predecessors together with two sets of curial officials and bureaucratic systems, he was forced to institute a major reorganization of papal finances and administration. The Schism had badly affected the income of the Holy See. Spiritual revenues had been increasingly appropriated by secular rulers in northern Europe and reversing this loss had complex political ramifications. Martin V concentrated on regaining his lost temporal income, embarking on a military campaign in the papal states to oust those rulers who had taken advantage of the absence of the Papacy in Avignon and the political vacuum caused by the Schism. His success had financial benefits. The annual income of Gregory XI (1370–8) is estimated to have been between 200,000 and 300,000 florins, of which one-quarter came from the papal states. Martin V's income in 1426–7 was around 170,000 florins, of which half was from the papal states.[1] But the decision to install his Colonna relations in key positions of authority was to pose political problems for his successors.

The appalling appearance of the city of Rome demanded attention. In 1425 Martin V issued new statutes for the *maestri di strada*, a body of officials that had existed during the Roman Empire and the Middle Ages to take charge of cleaning, maintaining and repairing the city's streets, squares, bridges, aqueducts and sewers. The statutes included orders for the sweeping of main thoroughfares every Saturday and a ban on dumping rubbish in the streets (it was to be thrown into the Tiber instead).[2] Financial constraints restricted Martin V's options and his patronage of the arts was limited but conspicuous. He enlarged the Palazzo Colonna by Santi Apostoli but he concentrated his efforts on repairing the major pilgrimage attractions, the four main basilicas in the city: San Giovanni in Laterano, St Peter's, Santa Maria Maggiore and San Paolo fuori le Mura. At two of them, San Giovanni in Laterano and Santa Maria Maggiore, Martin V also commissioned decorative programmes.

The frescos commissioned by Martin V in San Giovanni Laterano were destroyed during the seventeenth century when the basilica was rebuilt, but we know the basic details of the programme painted by Gentile da Fabriano and completed after his death in 1427 by Pisanello. Between the windows of the clerestory, Gentile painted a series of Old Testament prophets in imitation of marble statues set in niches and, along the wall of the nave, a cycle of scenes from the life of St John the Baptist, to whom the church was dedicated. Neither narratives nor prophets made any explicit statement about papal primacy, a theme which had been common during the thirteenth century and which was to be central to the projects of later fifteenth-century Popes. Martin V's position was perhaps too vulnerable for such directness. But, as the first large-scale decorative scheme commissioned by a Pope since the end of the thirteenth century in Rome, it did make an unmistakable reference to the revival of papal fortunes. This was reinforced by the new pavement commissioned for the basilica in the traditional early Christian and medieval pattern of inlaid marble.[3] San Giovanni Laterano was the seat of the Pope as the Bishop of Rome and the Lateran Palace was his official residence. Martin V's decision to have his tomb placed there emphasized the importance he attached to it.

The painting Martin V commissioned from Masolino for the Colonna chapel in Santa Maria Maggiore was a traditional double-sided altarpiece, with the *Miracle of the Snow* flanked by St John the Baptist, St Jerome, St John the Evangelist and St Martin of Tours on the side facing into the church. On the reverse was the *Assumption of the Virgin*, flanked by Pope Liberius (?), St Matthias, St Peter and St Paul.[4] Masolino's *Miracle of the Snow* was an unambiguous depiction of the legendary founding of the basilica by Pope Liberius after a dream in which the Virgin told him to build a church where the snow fell on the night of 5 August. An obvious theme for Santa Maria Maggiore, it underlined the papal links with the church. But the altarpiece also referred directly to the Colonna family. As evidence of the family's prestige, its coat of arms was conspicuous on the cloak of St Martin and implied in the unusual addition of a column (Italian: *colonna*) supporting the Cross held by John the Baptist.

Martin V's painters were foreign. With virtually no work for artists in fourteenth-century Rome, the city had lost its resident population of painters, sculptors and building workers. Gentile da Fabriano and Masolino were both active in Florence, while Pisanello worked for the Gonzaga in Mantua. It is no coincidence that Martin V had spent most of the first three years of his pontificate in these two cities and reasonable to assume that he was impressed by what he saw. But what is more important is that all three artists had established reputations and traditional styles. Elaborate compositions, elegant poses and courtly imagery were the hallmarks of International Gothic, a style popularized in the courts of northern Europe. By definition, this choice associated Martin V with the secular ruling élite.

Eugenius IV, 1431–47

The conclave following the death of Martin V was dominated by the issue of Church reform. All the cardinals swore that, if elected, they would abide by the decrees of the Council of Constance and respond to the increasingly urgent demands for reform at the forthcoming Council of Basle. But the election of Eugenius IV effectively halted any prospect for reform. Created cardinal by his uncle, the Roman Pope Gregory XII, at the age of 25,

Gabriel Condulmer had personal experience of the Schism and had taken part in the Council of Constance. Like Martin V, his apparent desire for reform evaporated at the prospect of exchanging supreme papal power for the dictates of a Council.

Eugenius IV's response to the Council of Basle was to dismiss it. But the Council refused to disperse and he was forced to recognize it. Round One may have gone to the Council but Round Two unquestionably belonged to Eugenius IV. His banner was union with the Eastern Church, another issue of prime importance at Basle and, more compellingly, an ideal opportunity to promote papal supremacy. Eugenius IV succeeded in persuading most of the Council to transfer to Ferrara to meet the Greek clergy, moving to Florence where the new Council officially opened in 1438. The Act of Union, *Laetantur coeli*, was signed in 1439, and the Eastern Church agreed to recognize the primacy of the Pope and major dogmas of the Western Church, notably the concepts of Purgatory and the Eucharist.

Meanwhile, the remainder of the Council of Basle passed decrees severely restricting papal claims to nominations and, above all, to revenues from benefices. Charles VII of France ratified these decrees as the Pragmatic Sanction of Bourges (1438). In November 1439, Eugenius IV was deposed and the Council elected a successor, Felix V. But political manœuvring averted another schism. In December Eugenius IV created seventeen cardinals to give him a majority in the College. These included nominees of the Kings of France, England, Portugal, Spain, Germany, Poland and Hungary as well as two Greeks, Bessarion and Isidore of Kiev, who underlined his success in Florence. Felix V's adviser, Piccolomini, defected to Eugenius IV's camp. Alfonso of Aragon was persuaded by his adviser, Borgia, that his claim to the kingdom of Naples would be realized by judicious support of the Pope and not the Council (Eugenius IV recognized the claim in 1443). Piccolomini and another papal legate, Parentucelli, were instrumental in convincing the German King, Frederick III, to change sides. As a reward, Parentucelli and Borgia were made Cardinals and, with Piccolomini, were Eugenius IV's successors to the Papacy. Eugenius IV emerged victorious from his battle with the Council over the issue of papal supremacy and set the pattern for the rest of the century. The efforts of the Council to attack corruption and introduce reforms had strikingly failed and, many historians would argue, the Protestant Reformation was just a matter of time.

Eugenius IV spent very little of his pontificate in Rome. Born into a Venetian patrician family, he commanded no particular loyalty from the Colonna rulers installed by Martin V in the papal states and his efforts to replace them led to a Colonna-backed revolt (1434). Eugenius IV was forced to escape, according to a contemporary account in a boat down the Tiber disguised as a friar,[5] not to return until 1443. He also had financial problems. Papal revenues for 1436 have been estimated at 60,000 florins, a significant drop from the 170,000 florins received by Martin V in 1426.[6] Charles VII's Pragmatic Sanction (1438) further reduced papal income and Eugenius IV was forced to increase the sale of indulgences to offset the loss.

Despite a lack of funds, Eugenius IV went in for show. Ghiberti described a papal tiara that he made for the Pope with sapphires, rubies, emeralds and pearls (six as big as walnuts) that was valued at 38,000 florins.[7] Work continued on Martin V's projects, the repairs to St Peter's and the fresco cycles in San Giovanni Laterano. Eugenius IV also restored other churches, including Santo Spirito in Sassia and Santa Susanna.[8] He also made an attempt to introduce some of the benefits of a modern city, clearing the piazza in front of Santa Maria della Rotonda (the Pantheon).[9] But by far his most conspicuous and prestigious projects were for St Peter's: Donatello and Michelozzo's tabernacle for the Eucharist and Filarete's bronze doors.

The massive bronze doors for the main entrance into St Peter's were designed to impress. Filarete had come to Rome in 1433 to cast the tomb of Martin V and set up a bronze foundry, the first in the city since the thirteenth century.[10] Bronze was the most expensive material available for large-scale sculpture and, although relatively common in the wealthy city of Florence, rare in impoverished Rome. Eugenius IV's choice of material was a conspicuous statement of prestige but it was the imagery of the doors that contained the keynote of his pontificate, an unambiguous message of papal primacy. The two panels were divided into three levels, with Christ and the Virgin at the top, St Peter and St Paul in the middle and scenes representing their deaths below. After 1439 and the Union with the Eastern Church, Eugenius IV decided to add four small panels depicting the events of the Council of Florence and underlining the supreme authority of the Pope as head of the Church.

Filarete's doors are usually described as stylistically old-fashioned and compared unfavourably with Ghiberti's two sets of doors for the Baptistery in Florence. It is true that Filarete's panels have little of the elegance, realism and detail of Ghiberti's compositions. But this is in itself significant. Filarete's massive figures of Christ, the Virgin, St Peter and St Paul were not intended to be subtle; they were designed for instant impact. The message of papal primacy was contained in the image of St Peter offering a huge set of keys to a much smaller figure of Pope Eugenius IV. Conveying status by scale may have been old-fashioned by Florentine standards but tradition was the essence of the papal claim to supremacy.

Nicholas V, 1447–55

By all accounts, Eugenius IV's successor, Tommaso Parentucelli, had risen through the Church hierarchy on merit. After studying theology, he had become secretary to Cardinal Albergati, attended the Council of Florence and was sent by Eugenius IV to lobby the German princes for their support in his battle with the Council of Basle. His success was rewarded with a cardinal's hat in 1446. Less than three months later, he became Pope Nicholas V. His unexpected election, no doubt influenced by his reputation, reflected the need to find a compromise candidate to appeal to both the pro- and anti-Colonna factions in the conclave. With a majority of Italian cardinals in the conclave for the first time since the Schism, the split also reflected political alliances in Italy and the growing domination of Italian affairs in papal elections.

Nicholas V's prime political aim was to repair the complex network of relationships with rulers in Italy and northern Europe that had broken down during the pontificate of Eugenius IV. The image of a mediator had financial as well as political benefits for the Pope. After recognizing the petty rulers of various papal states, he summoned a congress of all Italian states to work out a peace agreement. Although the congress failed, it did lead to a non-aggression pact, the Peace of Lodi (1454) between Milan, Venice and Florence which was joined by Naples and the Papacy the following year. He took the same approach to the rulers of northern Europe. The German King Frederick III was crowned Emperor in St Peter's (1452). Peace was negotiated with Charles VII of France and the Council of Basle and he also attempted to implement the reforms demanded by the Council, sending the formidable churchmen, Nicholas of Cusa and Giovanni Capistrano, to Germany to examine claims of corruption.

In Rome, Nicholas V made a concerted effort to re-establish political stability, instituting reforms that increased the autonomy of the city's municipal government[11] and proclaiming a Holy Year for 1450 to attract a major influx of pilgrims to Rome and provide a much needed boost to the city's economy. The institution of the Holy Year, started in 1300 by Boniface VIII (1294–1303), derived from the Old Testament descriptions of the Jubilee that occurred every fifty years and required the Jewish community to free slaves, to return to its original owners land purchased since the last Jubilee and other acts of restitution.[12] In the Christian context, the Jubilee took on a spiritual meaning and the Pope granted a plenary indulgence, a full pardon for sins committed, to all those true repentants who visited and prayed in a prescribed manner in the major churches of Rome. Up to a million pilgrims could be expected to visit Rome during a Holy Year, bringing economic benefits to the city but also straining its resources to breaking point. Above all, it reinforced the role of Rome as the capital of the Christian world.

Nicholas V's role as a mediator was also reflected at an intellectual level in his support for three distinct areas of theological learning: the traditional Scholastic theology of medieval Europe, patristic studies of the early Christian Fathers from the Eastern Church and the humanism of modern Italy.[13] Nicholas V's own interest in patristic studies had led him to look for manuscripts in monastic libraries in the 1420s.[14] The growing importance of the subject was stimulated by direct contact with Eastern theologians at the Council of Florence. Nicholas V was an ardent promoter of patristic studies, commissioning translations of Greek texts and supporting scholarship in the field. His library became the largest collection of patristic texts in the West.[15] His support of humanism had important implications for the development of the intellectual life of Rome. With their skills in Latin and Greek, their concern for accuracy and their knowledge of the classical world, humanist scholars were ideal translators of patristic texts. But Nicholas V's support went further than that. His employment of many Florentine humanists in the Curia should be seen as part of a deliberate policy to make Rome the intellectual capital of Christendom and the focus of a modern, Christian learning that incorporated the culture of classical antiquity into the traditions of early Christian patristic studies and medieval Scholastism.

Nicholas V's ambitious plans for a new capital of Christendom were not just intellectual, they were also visual. Martin V and Eugenius IV had both made cosmetic improvements to the city but it was Nicholas V who made the first real attempt to transform Rome into an appropriate setting for the display of papal prestige. According to his secretary and biographer, Giannozzo Manetti, Nicholas V justified his extensive patronage of architecture on the grounds that magnificent buildings were more effective than the arguments of intellectuals in convincing ordinary people of the supreme authority of the Church and in confirming their faith.[16] Surrounded by the ruins of the massive buildings of imperial Rome and the imposing churches of his medieval predecessors, he was fully aware of the power of the arts as propaganda.

Nicholas V's programme of urban renewal was extensive. He repaired the Aqua Vergine, thus improving the water supply, widened streets and mended bridges. The powers of the *maestri di strada* were strengthened and brought under papal control (1452). He made major improvements to the city harbour at Ostia and, as part of his reorganization of the city's municipal government, undertook a comprehensive restoration of its buildings on the Capitol, giving the Palazzo del Senatorio a new façade.[17] Like his predecessors, he continued restoration work on the major basilicas of San Giovanni Laterano, San Paolo fuori le Mura and St Peter's (see below) but he also repaired many less prestigious churches, including Santi Apostoli, San Celso, Sant'Eusebio, San Lorenzo fuori le Mura, Santa Maria in Trastevere, Santa Prassede, San Salvatore and Santo Stefano Rotondo.[18] His interest in the Eastern Church was reflected in the rebuilding of San Teodoro, a church with close ties to the Greek community in Rome.[19]

Recent research has shown that Nicholas V was closely involved with the development of the area around the church of San Celso, south of the Ponte Sant'Angelo.[20] During 1450 the Ponte Sant'Angelo had collapsed under the weight of pilgrims jostling on the only direct access to St Peter's from the city proper. Over two hundred pilgrims died. Nicholas V rebuilt the bridge and commemorated the disaster with two chapels on the city side of the bridge dedicated appropriately to Mary Magdalen and the Holy Innocents.[21] With the Pope's direct support, the area to the south of the bridge was developed by wealthy bankers, merchants and curial employees into a prestigious business and residential district. Subsidies were offered to house builders.[22] Improvements were made to the three main streets which linked the Vatican with the main centres of Rome and a piazza was cleared where they met by the Ponte Sant'Angelo.

The focus of Nicholas V's new Christian capital was over the river, at St Peter's and the Vatican. He made extensive renovations to the Castel Sant'Angelo and strengthened the fortifications that surrounded the Vatican area. Repair work on St Peter's continued and, if Manetti's account is to be believed, Nicholas V planned an imposing new choir behind the shrine of the first Pope. But his most conspicuous project was the expansion of the Vatican Palace. The original palace, started by Innocent III (1198–1216) and enlarged by Nicholas III (1277–80) and Nicholas IV (1288–92), was a single block, housing the Great Chapel used for papal elections, three council halls, a smaller chapel and modest papal apartments. Nicholas V added a three-storeyed wing containing a new set of private apartments, his own private chapel, office space and a library for his impressive collection of books.[23]

Most importantly, he established the Vatican as the official residence of his Papacy. This was a significant move. Ever since Constantine had made Christianity the religion of the Roman Empire, the official seat of the Pope had been the Lateran Palace, by San Giovanni Laterano, the cathedral of the Pope as Bishop of Rome. Like his medieval predecessors, Innocent III, Nicholas III and Nicholas IV, Nicholas V deliberately disassociated himself from the connotations of imperial power that were so resonant at the Lateran, preferring instead to emphasize his spiritual role as successor to St Peter and supreme head of the Church at the Vatican.

Manetti's account of Nicholas V's patronage described a much more ambitious scheme for St Peter's, the Vatican and the area between the basilica and the river known as the Borgo.[24] If realized, it would indeed have created a magnificent focus for the capital of the Christian world. According to Manetti, Nicholas V planned a grandiose palace with gardens to replace the modest medieval building. The dilapidated structure of St Peter's was to be restored with new exterior walls and a modern choir to replace the apse of Constantine's basilica. The piazza in front was to be embellished with an ancient Egyptian obelisk standing on the south side of the church and thought to contain the ashes of Julius Caesar. (It was finally moved into the piazza in 1586.) The piazza was to become the focus of three triumphal roads from the Ponte Sant'Angelo that would not only provide an imposing approach to St Peter's but would also transform the slums of the Borgo into a prestigious neighbourhood. Although Manetti explained that Nicholas V's death had put a halt to this ambitious project, it is doubtful that it went beyond the stage of wishful thinking. It was certainly true that the neglected Borgo was hardly a fitting approach to St Peter's and the Vatican Palace; but, apart from Manetti's text, there is no evidence that the project was begun and, moreover, Manetti ignored many of Nicholas V's actual schemes, notably the San Celso project.[25] His account should be seen as an ideal rather than an actual programme for urban renewal.

Typically in accounts of fifteenth-century patronage, Manetti made no mention of any designer. Indeed, he attributed the design of the Borgo project to Nicholas V himself, naming Bernardo Rossellino, a Florentine sculptor, as the executor. But art historians continue to discuss the identity of the creative genius that they assume must have been behind it. Central to the debate is the extent to which Alberti was involved. The issue is not clear. On the one hand, he was in Rome, closely associated with the papal court and a known authority on architecture. But no evidence links him directly to the scheme beyond the fact that he dedicated his treatise on architecture, *de re aedificatoria*, to Nicholas V. In it Alberti makes some interesting remarks on town planning. A large and powerful city, which Rome certainly could claim to be, should have straight and broad streets[26] and he also recommended that continual changes of view and impressive structures would enhance its beauty.[27] The Borgo project, as outlined by Manetti, attempted to create this effect. Like Nicholas V and Manetti, Alberti was explicit in his recognition of the impact that architecture could have on the viewer and, more importantly, explicit in saying that it could be manipulated by careful design. The idea was not new. Those responsible for the layout of the imposing piazzas in Venice, Florence, Siena and other medieval cities were aware, however subconsciously, of designing for deliberate effect. What was innovatory was the theoretical approach. Both Alberti's general treatise and Manetti's specific project are of major significance in the development of the theory of urban planning. But they also illustrate the compelling importance that the subject had in mid-fifteenth-century Rome for a Papacy determined to create an impressive setting for the exercise of its supreme power.

There was another, arguably more fundamental, reason why Manetti devoted so much of his biography to Nicholas V's architectural projects.

Nicholas V had been criticized by contemporaries for his extravagant and conspicuous expenditure. Indeed, Manetti's text can be read as a justification for this expenditure, and he emphasized the fact that it was not designed to gain personal fame but rather for the glory of the Church.[28] That the scale and grandeur of Nicholas V's projects far superceded the achievements of the ancient world was seen as a Christian achievement. Manetti stressed the superiority of Nicholas V's library of Christian books over those of pagan rulers of the past.[29] His references to Nicholas V as a new Solomon drew associations with that fabulously wealthy but wise ruler of the old religion whose impressive palace with its magnificent Temple was one of the few massive buildings to earn unqualified praise in the Bible. But Manetti's parallel had a more direct Christian message: Nicholas V's new church and palace surpassed Solomon's projects in the same way, and to the same degree, as the new Christian religion was superior to the old Jewish faith.[30]

Nicholas V's attitude to the controversial issue of papal wealth was proclaimed in his private chapel in the Vatican, painted by the Florentine Dominican friar, Fra Angelico, with scenes from the lives of the martyrs, St Stephen and St Laurence (1447–50). St Laurence had been roasted on a grid by the Roman authorities after his refusal to hand over the wealth of the Church that had been entrusted to him by Sixtus II. When interrogated, he had insisted that it was with the poor and the sick. Both saints were shown handing out alms. The combination of these two saints was traditional and one that was especially popular with the Franciscans for whom the rejection of the personal ownership of property was basic to their beliefs. Nicholas V's choice of subject matter, like Manetti's biography, emphasized that papal wealth should not be used for personal gain but for the good of the Church. Both saints were also shown receiving their diaconate, St Stephen from St Peter himself in Jerusalem and St Laurence from Pope Sixtus II in Rome. But the architectural settings were both strongly resonant of Constantine's basilica of St Peter in Rome. Moreover, the entablatures supported by massive columns and piers had little in common with the delicate arches and elegant columns of the settings of Fra Angelico's Florentine paintings. This deliberate choice of architectural setting gave visual expression to an association, also made in Manetti's text, of Nicholas V as a new Solomon, or of Rome as a modern, Christian Jerusalem.

Other aspects of the decorative scheme emphasized the theme of papal primacy and had obvious links with Nicholas V's theological interests. Apart from the traditional depiction of the Four Evangelists in the spandrels of the vault, Fra Angelico also painted portraits of the early Christian Fathers (Saints Augustine, Ambrose, Gregory the Great, Jerome, Leo the

Great, Athanasius and Chrysostom) and the medieval Scholastic theologians, the Franciscan St Bonaventura and the Dominican St Thomas Aquinas. Moreover, Chrysostom and Athanasius were both strong supporters of the concept of papal primacy in the early Church[31] and the pontificate of Leo the Great had established papal authority over the Church.[32]

Calixtus III, 1455–8

The fall of Constantinople in 1453 had brought the threat of an expanding Turkish Empire in the eastern Mediterranean sharply into focus. It was a key issue in the conclave following the death of Nicholas V and the election of a non-Italian Cardinal, Alfonso Borgia, reflected his enthusiastic support for a crusade. A Spaniard with a reputation for austerity and integrity, Borgia had been private secretary to Alfonso V of Aragon and had moved to Naples with the King when he became Alfonso I of Naples (1442). He was a lawyer by training and had been closely involved in negotiations between the King and the Councils of Constance and Basle. Eugenius IV had made him a cardinal in 1444 as a reward for his steadfast defence of papal supremacy. Calixtus III's call for a crusade met with a lukewarm response from the rulers of northern Europe, who were less directly affected by the Turkish advance. His main contribution to the appearance of Rome was to pave the piazza in front of St Peter's but his prime concern was the crusade. A massive fund-raising campaign brought in enough to build and equip a fleet that had modest successes in the Aegean. In addition to his sale of indulgences and non-spiritual posts in the Curia, Church treasures and even, reputedly, the valuable bindings of manuscripts from Nicholas V's library,[33] Calixtus III also stopped work on Nicholas V's extension to the Vatican palace, saving around 1,000 ducats a month on household expenses.[34] Nicholas V had spent conspicuously on building a new Christian capital, but Calixtus III devoted his short pontificate to its protection.

In the forty years from the election of Martin V to the death of Calixtus III, Rome had begun to change. Order was being imposed on the scruffy city and it had begun to expand. The growth of the papal court had brought new intellectual energy to Rome and stimulated her economy. Above all, Nicholas V had established a standard for papal patronage, planning on a scale unprecedented since the heights of papal prestige during the Middle Ages. But it was the next generation of Popes who were to develop a new visual language in which to express their supreme power and authority.

19

A New Language

Humanism provided potent propaganda with which to counter critics of clerical abuse and papal extravagance, and, above all, to defend the Pope's claim to supreme authority in the Church. The Papacy had a long tradition of employing keen intellects and fifteenth-century Popes recognized the urgent need to develop a new language for promoting their power. By the middle of the century, the Curia was dominated by humanists. Poggio Bracciolini (1380–1459), whose searches in the monastic libraries of northern Italy unearthed forgotten manuscripts of Cicero, Vitruvius and other Roman authors, was secretary to the Pisan Pope John XXIII and a leading critic of clerical abuse at the Council of Constance.[1] Serving under Eugenius IV, he attacked those who supported the Council of Basle against the Pope.[2] Eugenius IV appointed Alberti as an abbreviator in the papal Chancery.[3] His secretaries included the humanists Enea Silvio Piccolomini, later Pope Pius II, and Flavio Biondo (1392–1463) whose *Roma instaurata* and *Roma triumphans* were landmarks in the growing interest in ancient Rome.[4] Lorenzo Valla (1407–57), who had exposed the Donation of Constantine as a forgery (1440) while working for the King of Naples, later moved to Rome as one of Calixtus III's secretaries. A critic of the increasing secularization of the Papacy, he remained a strong supporter of its supreme spiritual authority.[5]

Humanism in Rome developed along distinctive lines. Cicero's belief in the virtues of republican rule, central to the evolution of humanism in Florence, was inappropriate for the defence of absolute power.[6] It was not in the interests of humanists in the Curia to challenge either the structure of authority within the Church or the Pope's position at its head. But they obliquely attacked simony, nepotism and materialism in funeral orations, dialogues and biographies, using the language and rhetoric of Cicero to lavish praise on their patrons, eulogizing them as ideal churchmen, pious Christians who had obtained their post by merit rather than by money or family connections and who put their wealth to charitable use.[7] Above all, Roman humanists provided propaganda for the papal claim to supreme power in the Church by giving new weight to the old tradition of promoting the Papacy as the heir to ancient Rome.

The city's imperial past was a potent image and one that had been central to the political ambitions of the Papacy since the collapse of the Roman Empire. Medieval Popes had presented themselves as successors to the first Christian Emperor, Constantine, giving visual expression to their claim in buildings and decorative schemes that were manifestly and deliberately resonant of early Christian Rome.[8] But the humanists went further, exploiting the links between the Renaissance Popes and the Emperors of pre-Christian Rome to bolster up papal power. Moving away from the medieval attitude of pagan vice versus Christian virtue, they emphasized the continuity between the two cultures and the idea that Rome's glorious past could be reborn into an even more glorious Christian present. For Valla, the principal evidence of this continuity was Latin, once the language of imperial Rome and now the universal language of Christendom, particularly since humanists had revived classical Ciceronian Latin to replace what they saw as the debased Latin of the medieval Church.[9] Alberti showed how the classical language of architecture tempered with Ciceronian morality could be adapted to the requirements of a Christian society.[10] Manetti likened Nicholas V's buildings to the monuments of antiquity but stressed their Christian superiority (see Chapter 18). Biondo described the Pope and his cardinals as the heirs of Caesar and the Senate, and recommended the revival of Roman triumphal processions with St Peter, St Paul, St Michael and St George taking the place of Jupiter, Neptune, Juno and Mercury.[11] And it was in this context that an increasingly confident Papacy, which had weathered the storms of the Councils, revived the architectural styles of ancient Rome.

Pius II, 1458–64

The first humanist Pope, Enea Silvio Piccolomini came from a noble Sienese family, but one politically unpopular in his city. A poet and an historian, he was also a skilled diplomat with a broad experience of European politics.[12] He had been a prominent defender of the Council of Basle against Eugenius IV and served as secretary to Felix V, the Pope elected by the Council after it had deposed Eugenius IV in 1439. Later he was employed by Frederick III in Germany (1442) and, once it was obvious that Eugenius IV had reasserted his power over the council, Piccolomini reconciled himself with the Pope (1445), who appointed him as a personal secretary.[13] He now applied his talents to the papal cause and was instrumental in persuading Frederick III to recognize Eugenius IV. As Pope, he strengthened the papal position by issuing a Bull, *Execrabilis* (1460) that condemned appeals to a council as heresy. He recorded his experiences in his *Commentaries*, a unique insight into the politics of fifteenth-century Europe, which documented, amongst other things, his horror at the austerity of Scotland in mid-winter, his admiration for Joan of Arc (d. 1431), the political scheming behind his own election and the beauty of the southern Tuscan landscape.[14]

The recovery of papal finances from their nadir under Eugenius IV had been dramatic. Pius II's estimated income in 1461-2 was 471,694 florins, nearly eight times Eugenius IV's income in 1436.[15] The discovery of rich deposits of alum, a mineral essential in the textile industry, at Tolfa (1462) was worth 50,000 ducats a year by 1480.[16] But much of the increase derived from the exploitation of indulgences, dispensations and curial posts as financial assets. Increasing the sale of non-spiritual offices in the Curia, Pius II also founded a college of seventy abbreviators (1463) for the Chancery, which brought in around 30,000 ducats.[17] Pius II's main preoccupation was stemming the growing power of the Turks in the eastern Mediterranean and he tried to raise support for a crusade by inviting European rulers to the Congress of Mantua (1459). But political issues divided the participants. Pius II's support of Aragonese rights in Naples after the death of Alfonso I (1458) angered the French, who backed the rival Angevin claim. The German rulers promised an army, but backed out after Pius II refused to submit to a Council. Despite the lack of support, Pius II continued his efforts and appealed to Sultan Mehmed II to renounce Islam and become a Christian. Finally, with the very real threat of a Turkish army that had conquered Serbia in 1459 and Bosnia in 1463, Venice and Hungary joined Pius II's crusade, which he intended to lead in person, but he died in Ancona as Venetian galleys came into sight.

In Rome Pius II concentrated on restoring St Peter's, the prime image of his supreme authority in the Church. The approach to Constantine's basilica, shrine of the first Pope, was far from impressive. The area in front was a mess, the old marble steps up to the church were worn down and its façade was dilapidated. In contrast to the imposing public squares in Venice, Florence or Siena, deliberately designed for maximum impact, the area in front of St Peter's could in no way impress the visitor. Pius II determined to create a more fitting approach.[18] Immediately on his return from Mantua in 1460, he ordered all obstructions to be cleared from the piazza and surrounding houses to be pulled down. Marble was ordered for a new set of steps up to the entrance of the basilica (1460). Massive statues of St Peter and St Paul holding gilded keys and sword were commissioned from Paolo Romano (1461) and placed on either side of the staircase on pedestals bearing the Piccolomini coat of arms and inscriptions recording Pius as patron. And, deliberately orchestrating maximum impact, the number of steps was increased form twenty-eight to thirty-five. A new entrance embellished with gilded Piccolomini coats of arms was commissioned for the adjoining papal palace and a fountain was laid out in the piazza.

The focus of Pius II's plans was an imposing new entrance front for St Peter's. Only the first four of eleven bays were completed and it was used as the papal Benediction loggia until it was destroyed during the rebuilding of St Peter's in the sixteenth century. The most striking feature of the new façade was its wholesale adoption of the architectural language of ancient Rome. The huge arches carried on piers and decorated with applied half-columns and classical capitals would have been recognizable as a direct quotation from the Colosseum. And, testifying to the birth of a more glorious Christian Rome, the materials were taken from ancient Roman buildings: the columns from the Portico of Octavia and the marble for the steps from the Colosseum. Pius II's adoption of the style of imperial Rome for such an important project was a deliberate piece of propaganda and announced the Papacy as the heir of the Emperors of ancient Rome.

Renaissance Rome was literally built from the ruins of the ancient city. From Petrarch onwards, humanists had lamented the sad state of once proud monuments. Much of the destruction was the direct result of papal building campaigns. Practical considerations outweighed any nostalgia for the past. The ruins provided medieval and Renaissance Popes with a ready-made quarry of cut stone that could either be used whole or burnt for lime. Who could blame Eugenius IV or Nicholas V for cutting costs and allowing their foremen to take the stone by the cartload from the Colosseum?[19] Many early Christian and medieval churches had been built with columns from older buildings. Pius II was the first Pope to take serious steps to halt the demolition.[20] Like other humanists, he had deplored the habit of treating the ruins as a quarry and forecast that there would be nothing left in three hundred years.[21] Once Pope, he issued a Bull (1462) prohibiting destruction without special licence[22] and most of the marble for his project came from outside Rome.[23] But the destruction continued and it was only in the sixteenth century, with the development of a more archaeological interest in the ruins, that the practice ceased.

By Easter 1462 the piazza had been smartened up and a temporary wooden façade erected in front of St Peter's for the official reception of the relic of the head of St Andrew, brother of St Peter, which two years before had been saved from the Turks invading Greece.[24] As an excellent opportunity to attract visitors, Pius II organized an elaborate parade for the occasion, culminating at St Peter's and his new piazza. His detailed account of the event left little doubt as to the importance he attached to the relic.[25] He met the procession bringing it from Ancona to Rome at the Milvian Bridge, the site of Constantine's victory over Maxentius, and commemorated the event in a marble tabernacle with a statue of St Andrew and a lavish inscription detailing his role in the relic's history.[26] He built a chapel for the relic in St Peter's, embellishing it with a tabernacle, ornamented with classical columns, and an elaborate reliquary. In an unprecedented display of papal power, the Pope also designated the chapel for his own tomb.[27]

Alberti, a member of Pius II's court, has long been credited with the design of the Pope's projects, especially the new front for St Peter's. But the surviving building accounts throw more light on the issue and make it clear that the key figures in the project were Pius himself, his agent, Francesco del Borgo, and the main contractor, Manfredino da Como. As foreman in charge of the workforce, Manfredino supervised the construction of the façade, the staircase, the chapel of St Andrew and the new portal for the Vatican Palace.[28] Francesco del Borgo, a *scriptor* in the Curia, was appointed by Pius II to administer the work, authorize all payments and keep accounts.[29] He also drew up contracts with suppliers and craftsmen, with the masons preparing the marble and the carriers transporting it, and with Fra Jacopo da Gaeta, who designed and made the cranes for hoisting the columns for the façade.[30] Biondo described Francesco del Borgo as the man in charge of the work.[31] He was certainly the central figure on the project, co-ordinating labour, supplies and execution, a position that has led one art historian to assume he was responsible for its design as well.[32] But Pius II must also have played a leading part in this innovative scheme, with or without the help of Alberti. The Pope's interest in the culture of antiquity was well recorded in his writings.[33] In Mantua, he had requested a copy of Vitruvius's *de architectura*.[34] Above all, his contemporaries saw Pius II as the principal force behind the new façade. There can be little doubt that he was closely involved in deciding the final appearance of this prestigious project and the bold choice of a decisively new language for the visual expression of papal authority.

Pius II's most ambitious scheme was the visual and economic renewal of his birthplace, Corsignano, near Siena.[35] He injected funds into the local economy[36] and elevated the town to a bishopric (1462), renaming the new city Pienza in honour of himself. Pius II was involved at all levels. In addition to financial aid, he rebuilt the cathedral and the Palazzo Piccolomini and encouraged others to participate in the scheme. He persuaded the Sienese government to pass a law (1460) forcing vendors to sell land and houses.[37] His two sisters bought properties and Jacopo Ammanati, an honorary member of the family and Pius II's private secretary, paid 488 lire for four houses and a garden (1460).[38] Pius II also coaxed members of the papal court to build.[39] Francesco Gonzaga and Jean Jouffroy, who had both been created cardinals in 1461 along with

55. Duomo, Pienza, begun *c*. 1460

Ammanati, were patrons of new palaces. The wealthy vice-chancellor, Rodrigo Borgia, built the Bishop's Palace on a site acquired by Pius II.[40] A landmark in the history of urban planning, the transformation of this small medieval border fortress into an impressive modern centre was not primarily a display of papal power. It was aimed at restoring the wealth and

56. Façade, Palazzo Piccolomini, Pienza, begun c. 1460

prestige of Pius II's family. In return for his investment, the Sienese government had agreed to restore the Piccolomini's rights in Siena.[41]

Pius II's new cathedral (fig. 55) reflected the problems that fifteenth-
century patrons faced in adapting the language of antiquity, a pagan style,
to a Christian building. His detailed description of the building reveals that

this was an issue that had concerned him.[42] He explained that the façade with its Composite columns, arches and statue niches was modelled on classical temples. But the interior was inspired by the hall churches he had seen in Germany and was lit by Gothic traceried windows. He expressly banned by papal Bull any pictorial decoration on the white walls inside as well as the addition of chapels or altars. Manifestly Christian, the simplicity of the interior was in striking contrast to the elaboration and overt classicism of the more secular exterior, which was designed to relate to the other buildings in the piazza (see below).[43]

The Palazzo Piccolomini (fig. 56) was far less inhibited in its adoption of classical forms. The façade was articulated with Doric pilasters on the ground floor, decorative Corinthian pilasters on the main floor and plainer Corinthian ones above. Composite columns decorated the courtyard (fig. 57), which prominently displayed the Piccolomini coat of arms. The design of the façade bears a striking resemblance to the Palazzo Rucellai in Florence and there is much controversy about which came first (see Chapter 5). Pius II's memoirs make no reference to the relationship and his description of the palace concentrated on its practical advantages, its layout, the details of the water supply, the larders, kitchen and dining rooms, the efforts to avoid damp and a description of the wonderful view of the Tuscan landscape from the garden loggia.[44]

Financed by papal funds, work started on the new church and palace in 1459 and both were largely complete when the Pope visited Pienza in 1462.[45] Pius II spent 15,000 lire acquiring property[46] and his memoirs recorded his horror on discovering that the builder, Bernardo Rossellino, had spent 50,000 ducats on the work after estimating only 18,000 ducats.[47] But he was full of praise for the result. Conspicuous expenditure was the essential component of prestige and, while we cannot prove the truth of this anecdote, it shows similar attitudes to Vespasiano's account of Cosimo de' Medici's complaints that his builders were not spending enough (see Chapter 5). Rossellino had been the foreman on Nicholas V's projects and this seems also to have been his role here. Biondo recounted how Rossellino had taken him on a guided tour and, when he concluded that the cathedral was the better building, Rossellino complained that the Pope's agents had insisted on changes.[48] But Pius II's description of the church and palace make it clear that he saw himself as the creative force in their design and, in his lavish praise of the buildings, Biondo described Pius as their author, drawing parallels with learned Roman Emperors like Septimius Severus and Marcus Aurelius, who had rebuilt their homes.[49]

The central piazza of Pienza was trapezoidal in plan and deliberately designed to create maximum effect in this tiny space. Urban planning was not new and the illusion of grandeur devised here had precedents in the

57. Courtyard, Palazzo Piccolomini, Pienza, begun *c.* 1460

medieval piazzas of Siena and Venice. But there were significant innovations in the Pienza scheme. The piazza was surrounded by four buildings
and the carefully planned relationships between their façades exploited the
potential of the classical orders to denote their differences in status and
function.[50] The most prestigious building, the cathedral, was decorated
with Composite columns; Corinthian pilasters dominated the Palazzo

Piccolomini; Ionic columns decorated the loggia of the town hall, and the Bishop's Palace, while grand in scale, was without either columns or pilasters. Pius II's innovative scheme added new dimensions to the medieval tradition of town planning.

Paul II, 1464–71

Pius II's successor was Pietro Barbo, a Venetian patrician, and nephew of Eugenius IV who in 1440 had made him a cardinal at the age of 23. Pope Paul II adopted wholeheartedly the role of a secular prince and Rome now took on the guise of an Italian court. Increasingly elaborate ceremonies and lavish entertainments were laid on for carnivals and state visits, like those of Emperor Frederick III (1468) and Borso d'Este (1471), with horse races in the Corso and public banquets in the piazza San Marco.[51] His coronation reputedly cost 23,000 florins.[52]

Paul II has been much maligned for his attack on humanists employed in the Curia, his abolition of Pius II's College of Abbreviators and his suppression of the Roman Academy (1468). But his action was an attempt to curb the growing power of humanists at the papal court. Many scholars lost their jobs, including Alberti and Platina, who had just bought his abbreviatorship and was understandably furious. He threatened the Pope with an ecumenical council and was imprisoned in Castel Sant'Angelo.[53] But there was another reason. The creation of the college had restricted the influence of the vice-chancellor, Rodrigo Borgia, and by abolishing the college, Paul II restored Borgia's influence over the Chancery.[54] Paul II was far from hostile to the culture of antiquity. He supported patristic studies and his library included the works of classical authors.[55] He restored the arches of Titus and Septimius Severus in the Forum and the equestrian monument of Marcus Aurelius that had long stood outside the papal palace at San Giovanni Laterano.[56]

Above all, he amassed one of the outstanding collections of antiquities and precious objects in fifteenth-century Europe.[57] He owned cameos and marble busts of Roman Emperors, vases of semi-precious stones, antique bronzes, early Christian ivories, Byzantine icons and Flemish tapestries. He acquired the gilded silver reliquary of Montalto, which was encrusted with gems and valued at 800 ducats[58] and the Tazza Farnese, a sardonyx cameo (c. 200 B.C.) elaborately carved with an allegory of Cleopatra I and typical of the opulent taste of the late Hellenistic age. Paul II's enthusiam for collecting led him, reputedly, to offer the inhabitants of Toulouse a bridge in return for a priceless Roman cameo, the *Gemma Augustea*.[59] A list of his treasures compiled after his death included fifty-four silver cups filled with pearls valued at 300,000 ducats, a diamond worth 7,000 ducats, and gold, silver and jewels estimated at 1,000,000 ducats.[60]

Paul II's most conspicuous association with secular rather than spiritual power was his decision to move out of the Vatican and into the palace he had built as a cardinal at San Marco, which he now enlarged into the papal residence. He justified this unprecedented action in a Bull (1466) that tenuously linked St Mark to the Petrine tradition by describing him as a disciple of St Peter.[61] The move created a new focus for the display of papal prestige. The Vatican Palace was on the western edge of the city, but Paul II's palace was in central Rome. It stood on the Corso, the street that led from the main gate for visitors from the North, the Porta del Popolo, down to the Capitol, the old seat of Roman government. His schemes for urban renewal centred on this area. He encouraged commercial development and improved the road leading from San Marco to the Castel Sant'Angelo.[62] As part of the palace project, he rebuilt the church of San Marco and commissioned restorations on the nearby Santa Maria in Aracoeli.[63] At the Vatican, he continued Pius II's Benediction loggia, adding a second storey.[64]

Paul II's new palace at San Marco, known as the Palazzo Venezia, provided a grandiose setting for the display of papal power.[65] The building he had started as a cardinal (1455) was clearly inadequate for its new function and Paul II began his ambitious scheme by enlarging it to form the main block of the papal palace (east wing, begun 1465). He rebuilt the attached church of San Marco (begun 1465) and commissioned a one-storey Benediction loggia for its façade (begun 1466). He added a separate court to one side of the east wing, known as the Palazzetto (begun 1466),[66] and a new extension for grand reception rooms to the other side (north wing, begun 1467). There is evidence that the grand garden court (fig. 59) was planned by Paul II, but it was built after his death by his nephew, Marco Barbo, whom he had appointed Cardinal of San Marco soon after his election (see Chapter 21). The papal court moved into its new quarters in 1466, long before the building was finished.

A piazza, formed by the east wing and the adjoining Palazzetto, opened off the Corso in front of the palace like the entrance façade at Urbino (see Chapter 15). Visitors were left in no doubt of the magnificence of their host as they entered through a huge barrel-vaulted doorway in the east wing. Inside were the Pope's private apartments, a garden decorated with ancient statues, huge reception halls, robing rooms and audience chambers decorated with gilded coffered ceilings. The palace was embellished with Paul II's coat of arms and its windows were inscribed with his name. Borso d'Este's enthusiastic description of the building (1471) specifically mentioned a grand marble staircase, rooms decorated with tapestries and showcases displaying Paul II's treasures.[67]

58.   Benediction Loggia, San Marco, Rome, begun 1465

The fortified appearance of the Palazzo Venezia conformed to current
Roman tastes in palace design, but, significantly, was much larger. Facing
the street was the massive block of the east wing with a tower on the south
end. Its crenellated roofline was continued across the walls of the Palazzetto
which enclosed a courtyard lined by arcades supported by octagonal piers
on the ground floor and Ionic columns above. But the the design of the
Benediction loggia (fig. 58) on the façade of San Marco was very different.
Here Paul II chose to make a clear connection with Pius II's new façade for
St Peter's by constructing a three-bay loggia with arches supported on piers
and applied Composite half-columns. Paul II had preferred a traditional
Roman image to give expression to his power in the city, but it was the
architectural style of ancient Rome that testified to his supreme spiritual
authority in the Church.

This ambitious scheme was financed by the Apostolic Chamber headed
by Paul II's nephew, Cardinal Marco Barbo, and additional funds were
raised from indulgences granted for the rebuilding of San Marco.[68] Paul II
appointed Francesco del Borgo to take charge of the project.[69] He was
imprisoned for a short period in 1467 on a charge of embezzlement but
was released on papal orders[70] and served until his death in 1468, when he
was replaced by another curial employee, Antonello da Albano.[71] Many
of the craftsmen employed on Pius II's projects joined the huge workforce

59.   Garden Court, Palazzo Venezia, Rome, 1480s

working on the Palazzo Venezia, including Manfredino da Como, who was again a major contractor on the site. As before, Francesco del Borgo was the central figure on the Palazzo Venezia project and, again, the extent to which he was responsible for its final appearance is unclear.[72] The contract he drew up with Manfredino da Como and his team for the Palazzetto (1466) reveals a lot about the design and construction of the Palazzo Venezia.[73] It offered piecework terms, stipulating that the builders were to dig the foundations, construct the walls, roofs, doors and windows out of specified materials at their own expense, and to ensure good craftsmanship. One fascinating clause, reflecting the unusual conditions of working in the ruins of ancient Rome, obliged them to hand over all gold and silver, coins, images, columns and other pieces of marble, stone and metal that they found. All the details of the design were to be provided by the Pope on whose behalf Francesco del Borgo drew up the contract. While this did not necessarily mean that Paul II himself drew up the plans for the building, it does show how closely he was involved in determining the appearance of his new palace.

With their innovative use of the classical language of architecture, Pius II and Paul II had introduced a new style for the display of papal authority and prestige and taken a significant step in the development of the arts in Rome. But it was a step that Paul II's successor did not endorse.

20

Morality and Extravagance

Wealth and extravagance or poverty and morality? Ever since Constantine adopted Christianity as the religion of the Roman Empire, replacing the simplicity of the *vita apostolica* with the ceremonial trappings of imperial power, the nature of the true Christian life style had never been far below the surface, above all, for the display of papal authority. In the increasingly secular climate of the late fifteenth century, the issue again assumed prominence. The Pope was under attack for neglecting the spiritual importance of his position in favour of the materialist values of princely rule. But he was also faced with the compelling need to assert his position as the supreme head of the Church. Conspicuous expenditure was recognized throughout Renaissance Europe as the key component in the display of status and prestige. There were many ways of advertising papal power. Pius II and Paul II had chosen to promote themselves as the heirs of Rome's glorious imperial past and revived the architectural language of antiquity as visual evidence of their authority. But the traditionalists within the Church did not consider this image appropriate for the successor to St Peter. The last three Popes of the century had widely different responses to the debate.

Sixtus IV, 1471–84

Francesco della Rovere was a Franciscan. The son of a modest trader from Savona, he had acquired a reputation as a reformer and an intellectual on the traditional side of Church politics.[1] He defended the Franciscan view on controversial issues of Church doctrine in treatises and took part in a public debate before Pius II on the divinity of the Blood of Christ (1462). As Minister-General of his Order (1464–9), he had attacked corruption and laxity in Franciscan convents and his appointment as cardinal by Paul II (1467) had been popular amongst reformers. His poor background and his Franciscan career had given him little influence in European politics and he had no power base at the papal court. These were major factors in his election as Pope. As the ideal compromise candidate, each faction felt it could control him. They could not have been more mistaken; for Sixtus IV proved a formidable opponent.

Like his predecessors', Sixtus IV's policies concentrated on imposing his authority in the Christian world. He announced crusades to counter the increasing power of the Turks in the Mediterranean and consolidated his control of the papal states by putting trusted relatives in key positions of power. He acquired Imola from the Sforza, appointing his nephew, Girolamo Riario, as its new Vicar. This event sparked off a major war with Florence (1478–80). The Medici saw the expansion of papal control as a threat to the balance of power in Italy and refused to advance the Pope the funds he needed to buy Imola. The loan was arranged through the Pazzi family, rivals of the Medici who, with the powerful backing of Girolamo Riario, then attempted to kill Lorenzo de' Medici and his brother and oust the Medici from Florence. They failed but the ensuing war between Florence and Rome seriously damaged relations between the two states for the remainder of Sixtus IV's reign.

Sixtus IV established his own power base in Rome. Like Eugenius IV (see Chapter 18), he filled the College of Cardinals with his own appointees. To establish good relations with European rulers, he created cardinals for Portugal, Spain, France, Burgundy, Germany, Naples and Milan. He promoted the cardinals who had supported him in conclave, including the influential vice-chancellor, Rodrigo Borgia, whose son, Cesare Borgia, he legitimized.[2] He also installed his nephews in key administrative posts in Rome and created several of them cardinals. This was standard practice. It enabled the Pope to surround himself with men he could trust; but it also left him open to the charge of nepotism, a prime target of Church reformers. Eugenius IV, Pius II and Paul II each had three relatives in the College. Sixtus IV appointed six, though never more than four served at once. The promotion of so many della Rovere and Riario relations to positions of power created a new dynasty in Rome, notorious for extravagance and ostentation. Many were outstanding patrons who made a significant impact on their adopted city (see Chapter 21). But Sixtus IV himself was far less prominent. He moved back to the Vatican and, underlining his role as spiritual head of the Church, left the lavish entertainments that were such a feature of his pontificate to his nephews. At the centre of his glittering court, Sixtus IV continued to wear his Franciscan habit under his papal vestments and spent long hours praying to the Virgin.

Sixtus IV made a determined effort to respond to the demands for Church reform. A Bull (1471) aimed to curb laxity in his own order.[3] He supported the Amadeiti, a reformist Franciscan movement founded by Amadeo da Silva, appointing him his personal confessor.[4] He attempted to limit the excesses of the increasingly worldly College of Cardinals, drawing up plans which, not surprisingly, met fierce opposition in the College and were never published.[5] He vastly increased the privileges of his order[6] and canonized a number of Franciscans including the theologian, St Bonaventure (1482). He extended the Feast of St Francis to the whole Church and banned the representation of saints other than St Francis with the stigmata.[7] Above all, he greatly increased the prominence given to the Virgin. Her cult was an essential element of popular piety, and the Franciscans attached particular importance to her position as the Mother of Christ. He extended the Feast of the Visitation (1475) and introduced the Presentation of the Virgin as a feast for the entire Church (1472).[8] Most importantly, he introduced the Feast of the Immaculate Conception of the Virgin (1476) which had been observed by the Franciscans since 1263 but strenuously opposed by the Dominicans. A highly controversial issue in the fifteenth-century Church, it was only finally accepted as a dogma of the Church in 1854.[9]

In his attitudes to the culture of pagan antiquity, Sixtus IV forcefully promoted traditional Church views. The humanists employed at his court used their talents to promote the Christian context of his position.[10] Platina, who had been imprisoned by Paul II (see Chapter 19), was now appointed as the Vatican librarian and he wrote a history of the Popes from St Peter to Sixtus IV. In a highly visible gesture that supported his belief in the separation between the Christian papacy and the classical heritage of the city of Rome, he donated the ancient bronze statues which had long stood outside the papal palace at San Giovanni Laterano to the traditional seat of Roman government on the Capitol.[11] He dispersed Paul II's valuable collection of antiquities for political and financial gain. One of the beneficiaries was Lorenzo de' Medici, who acquired busts of Roman Emperors and the priceless Tazza Farnese.[12]

Sixtus IV testified to his beliefs in the supremacy of Christian culture and Rome as the principal city in the Christian world in a programme of buildings and decoration that was unprecedented in scale. Art historians may argue about the quality, but, in terms of quantity, Sixtus IV must rank as the leading patron of fifteenth-century Italy. By the end of his thirteen-year pontificate, the appearance of Rome had been decisively transformed in a massive scheme of urban renewal. Unlike Paul II, Sixtus IV spent conspicuously on public and religious commissions, new streets, church building, a charitable hospital (the Ospedale Santo Spirito), work in St Peter's, a new Vatican library and the Sistine Chapel. But he was careful to emphasize that the expenditure was not for his own glory. His only private commission was a burial chapel for his parents in San Francesco, Savona. A fresco in the Ospedale Santo Spirito commemorating his patronage showed the Pope presenting his projects to God and the inscription underneath stressed that he had built for the glory of God and the city of Rome.[13] Above all, he decisively rejected his predecessors' image of the Papacy as heir to Rome's pagan imperial past and chose instead to revive the visual language of early Christian Rome.

The Jubilee Year of 1475 provided the spur for his ambitious programme of urban renewal to smarten up the city.[14] New legislation extended the powers of the *maestri di strada*, enabling them to order compulsory purchases and give permission for building. They were put under the direct authority of the papal chamberlain, Cardinal Guillaume d'Estouteville, who had the influence to enforce unpopular decisions. Main roads and piazzas were cleared of obstructions, widened and paved in brick. Repairs were made to the aqueducts supplying the city with water. Fines were imposed for unauthorised dumping of rubbish. The city's principal market was moved from the Capitol to the piazza Navona, the site of the ruined Stadium of Domitian, which Sixtus IV, unhampered by nostalgia for the glories of ancient Rome, tore down. He built a new bridge over the Tiber, the Ponte Sisto (1473), to link the Campo dei Fiori with Trastevere and provide a second route to the Vatican. His legislation encouraged new building. Reluctant vendors could now be forced to sell properties in bad condition and he changed the laws on inheritance to enable members of the papal court, whose property had previously been claimed by the Church after their death, to pass it on to their heirs.[15]

As part of the scheme of urban renewal, Sixtus IV also commissioned the repair and reconstruction of Rome's numerous religious buildings.[16] He restored over twenty churches, adding to them plain travertine portals with triangular pediments and inscriptions recording his action. Many of the churches were early Christian foundations and he issued a Bull to protect all such churches.[17] He returned the magnificent fourth-century porphyry tomb of Emperor Constantine's daughter, Constantia, to her church of Santa Costanza from San Marco where Paul II had used it as an altar.[18] He built two new churches, both significantly dedicated to the Virgin: Santa Maria del Popolo (begun c. 1472) and Santa Maria della Pace (begun 1482). A conspicuously visible project, Santa Maria del Popolo was the first church seen by visitors entering Rome through the Porta del Popolo, and Sixtus IV encouraged members of the papal court to take over patronage of its chapels (see Chapter 21). An inscription on the façade of the church promised indulgences to visitors offering prayers on the major Marian feasts, including that of the Immaculate Conception.

Sixtus IV stopped work on the Benediction loggia of St Peter's and concentrated on the interior. For the high altar, he commissioned an ornate tabernacle decorated with scenes of St Peter and St Paul.[19] His burial chapel in the south aisle was dedicated to the Virgin and the Franciscan saints, Francis of Assisi and Antony of Padua.[20] In the apse was a fresco, commissioned from Perugino, of St Peter presenting Sixtus IV to the Virgin with the chapel's two Franciscan patron saints. His magnificent bronze tomb was commissioned by his nephew, Giuliano della Rovere (see Chapter 21).

Sixtus IV spent money on a massive scale. His ambitious plans for the transformation of Rome were only a part of his outlay which also included financing two crusades and the costly war with Florence. In January 1472, the manager of the Rome branch of the Medici bank, Giovanni Tornabuoni, informed Lorenzo de' Medici that the loans to the Pope totalled 107,000 florins.[21] In an effort to raise funds, Sixtus IV doubled the number of non-spiritual posts available for sale and put the Datary in charge of fixing prices and collecting the money.[22] Flavio Biondo's son paid 1,400 ducats for his post of scriptor.[23] More money came in from re-opening the College of Abbreviators, founded by Pius II and closed by Paul II. He appropriated taxes on wine (normally used to pay university salaries) to help finance urban renewal, an act that provoked fury amongst humanists like Infessura, who lost his job and wrote a vitriolic attack on the Pope's extravagance.[24]

Little documentation has survived for Sixtus IV's projects and the meagre archival material must be supplemented by literary accounts of his activities in the biographies of Platina and others. The ubiquitous inscriptions on streets, piazzas, churches and buildings throughout the city testify to the extent of his patronage. The foreman in charge of his works in the Vatican was Giovannino de' Dolci, a Florentine carpenter who had worked for Nicholas V, Pius II and Paul II on the Vatican palace and the Palazzo Venezia.[25] But the impetus for the striking change in style could only have come from Sixtus himself. His three major projects, the Ospedale Santo Spirito, the Vatican Library and the Sistine Chapel, deserve closer attention.

The Ospedale Santo Spirito had been founded by Pope Innocent III in 1198 to care for foundlings, pilgrims, the sick and destitute. It had fallen into disrepair and been badly damaged by fire in 1471. Sixtus IV's decision to revive this prominent charitable institution involved not only a new building but also substantial endowments of land and money to finance its operations.[26] Significantly, Sixtus IV was the only fifteenth-century Pope to embark on such a conspicuous statement of his Christian beliefs and duties. The building consisted of two long rectangular wards, male and female, separated by a central entrance with a chapel crowned with an octagon. It was large, as it needed to be, but it was far from grand. Built of brick, its travertine marble details were limited to door and window frames, each inscribed with Sixtus IV's name and his coat of arms. Surrounding the huge block was a single-storey portico, its long row of arches carried on piers with Doric pilasters. The use of an undecorated Doric order carried strong moral overtones[27] and its austerity was a manifest comment on the extravagant use of the Composite and Corinthian orders by his predecessors. Doric was not a feature of Roman imperial architecture and one of the few Doric buildings in Rome was Sixtus IV's own cardinal church of San Pietro in Vincoli built in the fifth century.[28] And further evidence of the Christian function of the building could be seen in its most overt and costly detail, the elaborate Gothic tracery in the windows of the octagon above the chapel.

Inside, the two wards were frescoed with forty-six scenes of the lives of Innocent III and Sixtus IV.[29] The poor quality of the paintings was in striking contrast to the impressive decoration of the Sistine Chapel (see below), and, perhaps, reflected a desire to appeal to a less sophisticated audience.[30] Innocent III had a particular importance for the Franciscans. It was his dream of St Francis propping up San Giovanni Laterano that had persuaded the Pope to allow the friar and his companions to preach and start the order. This scene appeared in the hospital with others recording his role in its foundation. The parallel between Innocent III confirming the Franciscan way of life and Sixtus IV bringing Franciscan morality to the Church was clear.[31] The life cycle of a patron was unprecedented in fifteenth-century Rome and it established Sixtus IV's credentials as a pious Christian from a poor background chosen by God for special destiny, the theme also of Platina's biography. The scenes showed his mother dreaming of St Francis and St Antony of Padua offering her son the Franciscan habit, his birth, his miraculous escapes from disasters and predictions of his future greatness. But the cycle concentrated on Sixtus IV's pontificate. Scenes of European rulers doing homage to the Pope underlined papal supremacy and others recorded his patronage of the hospital, the Ponte Sisto, Santa Maria del Popolo, the Vatican library and Santa Maria della Pace. And the format of rectangular scenes with prominent inscriptions below could also be seen in the major early Christian basilicas in Rome, notably in the decoration of Santa Maria Maggiore.[32]

Sixtus IV's contribution to the Vatican library was immense. It grew from 2,527 volumes in 1475 to over 3,500 in 1484.[33] The impressive collections amassed by the Medici or Federigo da Montefeltro only totalled about 1,000 volumes. Unlike secular libraries of the period, the Vatican library contained no vernacular works but concentrated instead on the texts that were the basis of Christian learning with Bibles and works of the early Church Fathers forming the principal element. The humanist Platina was appointed librarian in 1475 with the handsome salary of 120 ducats a year and his staff included copyists and a book-binder.[34] Sixtus IV converted a suite of store rooms on the ground floor of Nicholas V's palace block into a magnificent setting for his new library. Following tradition, the Latin and Greek texts were housed in separate halls and other rooms held the private papal collection, the archives and apartments for the librarian and his staff. The rooms were lavishly decorated. Work began in 1475[35] and Platina drew up contracts with craftsmen for new bookcases, desks, chains for manuscripts, rods, locks and keys.[36] The Latin Library was decorated with gilded wooden intarsia panelling and fictive draperies.[37] Above were portraits of twelve men representing Christian learning: six pagan philosophers whose works had been incorporated into the Christian tradition and six leading theologians, St Augustine, St Ambrose, St Jerome, St Gregory, St Thomas Aquinas and St Bonaventure, a Franciscan who was canonized by Sixtus IV. Prominently displayed opposite the entrance was a fresco (1474-7) by Melozzo da Forlì (fig. 60) commemorating the foundation of the library with the Pope and four of his nephews. In the centre, Platina was portrayed pointing down to a poem written by him that outlined Sixtus IV's contribution to the changed face of the city and drew special attention to his library.

Sixtus IV's principal project was the Sistine Chapel (fig. 61) which he built to replace the Great Chapel built by Nicholas III (1268).[38] Demolition of the old chapel began in 1477 and construction started using the earlier foundations.[39] By 1481 the interior decoration was under way and the new building was inaugurated on the Feast of the Assumption of the Virgin on 15 August 1483. It is difficult to overstate the importance of the building. The focus of papal ceremonial, it was above all the site where God spoke directly to Man in the conclaves to elect a new Pope. The chapel was clearly visible from the piazza in front of St Peter's and its prominent position next to the basilica underlined the enormous significance of the building in the context of papal authority. Vasari named Baccio Pontelli as the architect of the building[40] and art historians have disputed the attribution ever since. But it is clear that Sixtus IV was the creative mind behind the project.

The Pope's choice of architectural style and pictorial decoration were indicative of the importance he attached to Christian tradition and to his own position at the head of the Church. Like Nicholas V, he drew parallels between himself and the Old Testament King Solomon: the proportions of the chapel were the same as the Biblical description of the Holy of Holies in Solomon's great Temple in Jerusalem that housed the Ark of the Covenant,[41] and there were other references to Solomon inside (see below). The massive and austere brick walls of the exterior crowned by a crenellated parapet displayed none of the classical style of Pius II's new

TEMPLA DOMVM EXPOSITIS·VICOS·FORA·MOENIA·PONTES·
VIRGINEAM TRIVII·QVOD·REPARARIS·AQVAM·
PRISCA·LICET·NAVTIS·STATVAS·DARE·COMMODA·PORTVS·
ET·VATICANVM·CINGERE·SIXTE·IVGVM·
PLVS·TAMEN·VRBS·DEBET·NAM·QVAE·SQVALORE·LATEBAT·
CERNITVR·IN·CELEBRI·BIBLIOTHECA·LOCO·

60.   Melozzo da Forlì, *Sixtus IV, his Nephews and Platina*, 1474–7

façade to the basilica next door. For the architectural historian tracing the
revival of antiquity in the Renaissance, the building seems old-fashioned
and it is usually relegated to the status of a box that houses a notable
fifteenth-century fresco cycle. But it is highly unlikely that Sixtus IV saw

61.   Sistine Chapel, Rome, begun 1477

it in this light. His preference for a highly fortified exterior was calculated and was probably intended to recall the traditions established by earlier papal palace chapels at the Vatican, at San Giovanni in Laterano and at Avignon.[42]

62. Botticelli, *Temptation of Christ*. Rome, Sistine Chapel, 1481

Inside, Sixtus IV was more explicit in his rejection of the pagan connotations of the language of ancient Rome as adopted by his predecessors. The interior was filled with early Christian allusions[43] designed to emphasize his position as heir to Constantine, not the Emperors of pagan Rome. A costly inlaid marble floor, divided by an elaborate choir screen, imitated the *opus alexandrinum* pavement and *iconostasis* of early Christian basilicas. The decoration of the walls was divided into three levels. At the top between the windows were portraits of the first thirty Popes with St Peter and St Paul above the main altar. In the middle were narratives of the lives of Christ and Moses with inscriptions beneath painted by five of the leading artists of the day, Botticelli, Ghirlandaio, Rosselli, Perugino and Signorelli. The paralleling of Old and New Testament scenes with explanatory inscriptions was common in early Christian churches and so was the use of fictive gold and silver brocade hangings that were painted on the lower levels of the Sistine Chapel walls and decorated with the della Rovere coat of arms. A similar format could also be seen in San Francesco, Assisi, the mother church of the Franciscans.[44] And the vaults of the chapel, like those of the upper and lower churches at Assisi, were decorated with a blue sky covered with gold stars. The building was dedicated to the Assumption of the Virgin and an altarpiece of the subject by Perugino stood on the high altar. To a Franciscan, this image was the prime symbol of her

63. Perugino, *Christ's Charge to Peter*. Rome, Sistine Chapel, 1481

Immaculate Conception and it suggests that Sixtus IV associated the chapel with this highly controversial doctrine.[45]

But the main theme of the chapel's pictorial decoration was the issue of papal primacy.[46] The carefully chosen scenes of Moses and Christ were linked by their inscriptions to provide visual and verbal propaganda for its legitimacy. The life of Moses provided Old Testament prefigurations of Christ's ministry. Botticelli's *Temptation of Christ* (fig. 62), opposite the papal throne, had the events of Christ's temptation in the upper part of the painting, but its central focus was a scene of sacrifice that deliberately stressed Christ's own sacrifice of his Blood and the Eucharist as the basis of Christian faith. In the background, the Temple of Jerusalem bore a striking resemblance to Sixtus IV's Ospedale Santo Spirito and early Christian churches in the city.[47] The scene of *Christ's Charge to Peter* (fig. 63), by Perugino, emphasized that the Pope's authority came directly from Christ and was not subject to Church Councils. Behind, two massive triumphal arches flanked another version of Solomon's Temple. They carried a telling inscription: 'You Sixtus IV have dedicated this temple, unequal to Solomon in your wealth but superior in your religion'.[48]

Sixtus IV combined the themes of his pontificate in his new chapel. Early Christian morality, Franciscan austerity, the Virgin, papal primacy and the problem of wealth for the Church were all marshalled to make clear the power of the Christian faith and supreme authority of the Pope at the head of its Church. His two successors had a different attitude to the nature of papal power, preferring to promote themselves as secular rulers rather than as spiritual leaders of the Church.

Innocent VIII, 1484–92

Innocent VIII was a complete contrast to the determined Franciscan friar. Giovanni Battista Cibò was the son of a Roman senator and educated at the Neapolitan court. He had served as deputy to the Datary, the official in charge of fixing prices for the sale of offices in the Curia, for two years (1472–3),[49] before being created a cardinal by Sixtus IV in 1473. Innocent VIII inherited vast debts from his predecessor and further increased the sale of offices to finance his enterprises, setting up new Colleges of Notaries and Secretaries which brought in 62,400 ducats.[50] He repaired papal relations with Florence and cemented the new alliance by marrying his son, Franceschetto, to Maddalena, the daughter of Lorenzo de' Medici. He also created Lorenzo's 14-year-old son, Giovanni, a cardinal. Pleasure-loving and by all accounts fairly ineffectual, Innocent VIII was the least forceful pope of the fifteenth century. He promoted the secular rather than the spiritual aspect of his position and under his leadership the Vatican increasingly took on the appearance of a princely court.

Innocent VIII was not a patron on the scale of his predecessor and much of what he commissioned has been lost behind the projects of his successors, notably Julius II (see Chapter 22). He continued the programme of urban renewal started by Sixtus IV, financed restoration work on San Giovanni Laterano, Santa Balbina, Santa Croce, Santa Prassede and other churches, contributing 400 ducats towards the rebuilding of Santa Maria in Via Lata.[51] He also started work on a new prison.[52] At the Vatican, he built an extension to the palace and enlarged the entrance portal built by Pius II, decorating it with his own coat of arms.[53] He also embellished the fountain in the piazza in front of St Peter's.[54] Inside the basilica, he commissioned a burial chapel dedicated to the Virgin. Following the precedent set by Pius II, he combined his tomb with an ornate tabernacle for an important relic, the Holy Lance, the spear with which the Roman centurion, Longinus, had pierced Christ while he was on the Cross. Innocent VIII had acquired this relic from Sultan Bajazet together with 40,000 ducats in return for the safekeeping of the Sultan's brother, Jem.

Innocent VIII's principal project was the construction and decoration of the Villa Belvedere, designed as a pleasant retreat on the hill behind the Vatican. Heavily castellated in a style similar to Paul II's Palazzo Venezia, this imposing villa was lavishly decorated inside with imagery derived from descriptions in classical literature of the palaces and villas of the rulers of ancient imperial Rome. The rooms were painted with illusionistic furniture and curtains with a parrot in a cage and other frivolous details.[55] He commissioned views of Rome, Milan, Florence, Venice and Naples to decorate his loggia (now the Galleria delle Statue in the Vatican Museum), set in a fictive framework of painted arches and pilasters.[56] He persuaded Francesco Gonzaga to part with Mantegna for two years (1488–90) to decorate the villa's chapel.[57] We know little about the details of this commission, but Mantegna wrote home describing life at Innocent VIII's court and, in particular, the gross eating and drinking habits of Sultan Bajazet's brother, who apparently walked like an elephant![58]

Alexander VI, 1492–1503

Innocent VIII's successor was Rodrigo Borgia, elected Pope the same year as Columbus sailed for America. Born in Valencia, he had moved to Italy with his uncle, Alfonso Borgia, chief adviser to Alfonso V of Aragon (Alfonso I of Naples).[59] Alfonso's election as Calixtus III secured his nephew's future: the 26-year-old Rodrigo was appointed vice-chancellor of the papal court. Rich and immensely influential, he wielded enormous power in Rome for over thirty years (see Chapter 21). He was not a pious churchman, and openly flaunted his mistress, Vanozza Catanei, and their four children. As Pope, he ignored demands for Church reform. He dramatically enlarged the College of Cardinals with new creations that included six of his relations and his son, Cesare, as well as many others from Naples and Spain. His election as Pope may seem strange to us, but it is clear that the conclave considered an astute and worldly politician to be best suited to deal with the problems now facing the Papacy, in particular, the threat posed to the balance of power in Italy by the emergence of France and Spain as dominant forces in European politics.

Alexander VI was a skilful manipulator and successfully exploited the differences between France and Spain for the benefit of the Papacy and, even more, for his family.[60] France and Spain both claimed to be the rightful rulers of Italian states; as successors to the rival Angevin and Aragon rulers of Naples, they disputed the right to the Neapolitan throne (see Chapter 13) while France also asserted her right to Milan (see Chapter 12). In the first of a series of foreign invasions of the peninsula, Charles VIII of France and his armies entered Italy (1494) in pursuit of the Angevin claim to Naples. His successor, Louis XII, conquered Milan (1499) as the legitimate descendant of the Visconti Dukes but was denied the throne of Naples by the invasion of Ferdinand of Spain (1504). Behind this brief outline was a complex pattern of alliances that changed with bewildering rapidity. Charles VIII was forced out of Italy in 1495 by a coalition of Alexander VI, the Holy Roman Emperor, Ferdinand of Spain and Milan. Pursuing an anti-French policy, the Pope then excommunicated Savonarola (1498), the principal force behind Florence's pro-French policy. But in 1499, faced with an alliance of France and Spain, the Pope quickly changed sides. He now exploited Louis XII's need for papal sanction to allow him to divorce his wife and marry the widow of Charles VIII, the wealthy heiress to Brittany. In return, Alexander VI needed the French armies to help him enforce his authority in the papal states and to expand them into the Romagna for his son, Cesare. The French got Milan and Cesare Borgia carved out an impressive territory for himself in the Romagna. France and Spain now became increasingly hostile over their rival claims to Naples and, just as Alexander VI seemed to be preparing to change sides to support Spain, he died.[61]

Alexander VI asserted papal power in a series of prestigious and eye-catching projects. He drew up an ambitious scheme for replanning the Borgo, building a new street from the Castel Sant'Angelo to the entrance of the Vatican Palace. For one of Rome's principal churches, Santa Maria Maggiore, he commissioned an expensive gilded coffered ceiling prominently decorated with the Borgia rosettes and bulls. The tradition that the gold for the ceiling was the first brought to Europe from Peru and given to the Pope by Ferdinand and Isabella of Spain is sadly a seventeenth-century myth.[62] Alexander VI also commissioned work on other Roman churches, including San Giacomo degli Spagnoli in the piazza Navona and San Giovanni Laterano.[63] At St Peter's he commissioned repairs to the basilica's roof[64] and added a second storey to Pius II's Benediction loggia, where he narrowly missed being hit by an iron candlestick during a bull-fight in the piazza (1500).[65] He also embellished the fountain in the piazza with Borgia bulls.[66]

In a highly visible gesture, and one which clearly demonstrated the military preoccupations of his pontificate, Alexander VI commissioned extensive alterations to the papal stronghold of Castel Sant'Angelo, adding new fortifications, towers, a gateway, water tanks and dungeons.[67] As further evidence of the growing threat of attack, Alexander VI also commissioned work on several papal strongholds outside Rome and built fortresses at Tivoli, Civita Vecchia and Viterbo.[68] Inside Castel Sant'Angelo, he commissioned fresco decorations (now destroyed) for the papal apart-

64. Pinturicchio and assistants, *Rhetoric* and *Geometry*. Vatican Palace, Sala dei Arti Liberali, 1492–5

ments. One of the artists involved in the scheme was Pinturicchio, who was paid for his labours with a leasehold on farms.[69] The embellishments included a life cycle of the Pope himself.[70] Unlike Sixtus IV's project in the Ospedale Santo Spirito, which related episodes covering the whole life of the Pope and celebrated his Christian piety and the spiritual authority of his position as head of the Church, Alexander VI's cycle depicted only his achievements as Pope, promoting him as a secular ruler and military leader of the papal state.

Alexander VI's main project was the enlargement of Nicholas V's Vatican Palace with a tower, the Torre Borgia, and the decoration of his private suite of apartments. Ostentatiously expensive, the walls and ceilings glittered with their gilded stucco details. The floors were laid with ornate ceramic tiles and the Borgia bulls were noticeably prominent (fig. 64). The frescos in the apartments were commissioned from Pinturicchio and his assistants (1492–5).[71] The themes were essentially Christian with rooms decorated with Sibyls and Prophets, with the Liberal Arts (fig. 64) and with the Mysteries of the Faith, where Alexander VI himself appeared kneeling, dressed in magnificent pontifical robes, before the Christ of Resurrection (fig. 65).

The so-called Sala dei Santi was decorated with the Visitation and events from the lives of St Anthony Abbot and St Paul the Hermit, St Catherine of Alexandria, St Barbara, St Susanna and St Sebastian. The scenes

65.   Pinturicchio and assistants, *Resurrection*. Vatican Palace, Sala dei Misteri della Fede, 1492–5

depicted all carried the same message of deliverance. The Feast of the Visitation had been instituted during the Schism in an attempt to promote Church unity and had been invoked by Sixtus IV for the crusade against the Turks.[72] It has been convincingly shown that Alexander VI's programme for the room celebrated amongst other things the recent fall of Muslim Granada to the powerful Christian armies of Ferdinand and Isabella of Spain (1491).[73] But the most bizarre aspect of the room was the theme of the ceiling decoration. Contrasting oddly with the overwhelmingly Christian imagery of the walls, Alexander VI chose to depict the ancient Egyptian deities, Isis and Osiris. The unusual subject had a specific meaning for Alexander VI: his personal secretary, Annius of Viterbo, had traced the descent of the Borgias to Osiris[74] and the theme of the vault was explicitly dynastic, lending force to Alexander VI's image as a secular ruler.

One of the most striking innovations in the Borgia apartments was the appearance of grotesques. These elaborate and imaginative details on friezes and pilasters were inspired by the extravagant stucco and painted decoration, discovered in the 1490s in the buried ruins of the Golden House of Nero by the Colosseum. The excitement of the discovery of authentic Roman painting must have been tremendous and it had a radical effect on the decorative vocabulary of late fifteenth-century Rome.[75] The anonymous Milanese author of an account of the city commented that the place was full of painters.[76] Many of them left their signatures on the walls. He also described his own visit down into the narrow passages excavated beneath the vaults, crawling on his stomach with his bread and wine. Grotesques fast became the modern fashion and this ornate decorative style appealed to Alexander VI's lavish tastes.

21

The Papal Court

In June 1462 the papal court celebrated the Feast of Corpus Christi in Viterbo and the elaborate festivities arranged by the Pope and his cardinals were graphically described by Pius II in his memoirs.[1] The cardinals had each decorated a section of the main street where they built ornate gold and silver altars, flew banners showing their coats of arms, hung curtains and tapestries over the walls of the houses and stretched canopies of blue material painted with gold stars across the rooftops. There were arches garlanded with flowers, choirs of boys singing like angels and fountains of wine. The Dominican, Juan Torquemada, stressed the religious content of the feast with a representation of the Last Supper and the Institution of the Eucharist. Rodrigo Borgia, the urbane vice-chancellor, forcefully drew attention to the supreme authority of the Pope by staging a lavish and colourful entertainment with five kings who initially refused to open their gates to Pius II but changed their minds when angels told them the Pope was 'Lord of all the World'. The presence of the papal court in this small town must have been dazzling and it illustrated the central role played by the cardinals in the complex ritual of the Church as well as the ostentatious display that testified to its power.

Whatever our perceptions of the correct role for a cardinal may be, it is essential to recognize that the enormous prestige they enjoyed in Renaissance Europe was not exclusively spiritual. Accorded the rank of dukes and princes, they wielded immense power in the political arena. Many of them were hugely wealthy and lived in great style surrounded by households of servants and secretaries. Some were members of Europe's ruling élite and had been brought up at aristocratic courts. Those from more modest backgrounds had a powerful incentive to display their worldly success. But there were also cardinals who were critical of what they saw as secular and materialist values. The contrast between Torquemada's piety and Borgia's worldliness, clearly brought out in the pageants for the celebrations in Viterbo, reflected two extremes in Church thought. These factors were also evident in the architecture, sculpture and painting commissioned by cardinals in Rome.

Flavio Biondo's claim that the Pope and his cardinals were the heirs of the Emperor and the Senate of ancient Rome was not far from the truth.[2] The College of Cardinals was essentially an advisory body, its power limited by the supreme authority of the Pope, but its members played a significant part in formulating papal policy. Above all, they were central figures in the complex network of political power and patronage that dominated Renaissance Rome and extended throughout Europe. Their influence was enormous. Prelates hoping for promotion, petitioners seeking papal dispensations and humanists pursuing a curial career in Rome, all lobbied cardinals for their influence. Corruption and bribery gave opportunities for financial gain on a massive scale. Not all cardinals were corrupt but many were rich. Appointed for life, they had the opportunity of rising to high office within the papal administration. Promotion depended largely on papal favour. Success required a bit of luck but mainly a shrewd political mind and the ability to recognize and support a future Pope from amongst their colleagues. And they also had the real chance of election to the papacy itself.

The Council of Constance (1414–17) had fixed a maximum size for the College of twenty-four, a limit that was largely ignored and the number of cardinals increased as the century progressed. Martin V had inherited a College of thirty-one, which grew to thirty-three under Eugenius IV, reached thirty-six under Sixtus IV and was dramatically enlarged to forty-eight by Alexander VI (1500).[3] Cardinals were appointed for a variety of reasons, not necessarily for their Christian devotion. The Franciscan Minister-General, Francesco della Rovere (the future Pope Sixtus IV), and the Dominican, Juan Torquemada, were both prominent theologians. But many were promoted as political favours for secular rulers keen to have their own trusted agents in the College. All the major courts of Europe were represented and, by the end of the fifteenth century, so were the Italian powers. Galeazzo Maria and Ludovico Sforza, Alfonso d'Este, Federigo Gonzaga and Alfonso of Calabria in Naples all had brothers who were cardinals. Lorenzo de' Medici had to lobby hard, but he finally secured the promotion of his son, Giovanni. Above all, Renaissance Popes promoted their relatives and countrymen to secure a power base in the College. Five of the eleven Popes elected between 1417 and 1503 had been nepotist creations: Eugenius IV, Paul II, Alexander VI, Pius III and Julius II. Church reformers were highly critical both of political appointments and of nepotism, but they were really incensed by the age of some of those elected to lead the Church: Rodrigo Borgia was 25 when he was created a cardinal by his uncle, Calixtus III; Pietro Riario, the nephew of Sixtus IV, was 26; and Giovanni de' Medici (later Pope Leo X) was only 14.

The really powerful cardinals were those heading the three departments of the Curia: the Chancery, the Apostolic Chamber and the Penitentiary.[4] The most prestigious post was that of vice-chancellor, head of the Chancery, who acted as the Pope's deputy when necessary, directed the notaries, scriptors, abbreviators, masters of the seal and archivists and issued, copied and filed the official bulls and letters of the Holy See. The chamberlain, head of the Chamber, supervised the collection of papal revenues, handled the political affairs of the Papal States and was the Pope's chief policy adviser. The grand penitentiary ran the department that dealt with grants of spiritual favour, notably indulgences, and their growing importance as a source of papal revenue made this job particularly lucrative. Immensely influential and offering ample scope for financial gain, these three posts were invariably given to close confidants.

It is difficult to be precise about a cardinal's income; it could vary from as little as 2,000 ducats to over 20,000 ducats a year. Martin V had recommended a minimum of 6,000 ducats and those who could make 12,000 ducats a year were wealthy.[5] The basic source of a cardinal's wealth was his share of papal revenues distributed for attendance in Consistory, the official meetings of the College, and a register for 1460–70 showed average annual amounts ranging from 125 florins to over 1,200 florins.[6] Cardinals were each appointed to titular churches that provided additional, though small, funds and benefits but these sums were hardly adequate to pay for the opulent life style expected from a prince of the Church. The prestigious posts of vice-chancellor, chamberlain and penitentiary all paid 6,000 ducats a year plus considerable extras besides. Most rich cardinals had incomes from bishoprics, abbacies and other benefices acquired through family connections or papal favour. Francesco Gonzaga's earnings included revenues from numerous religious foundations around Mantua[7] and the nepotist cardinals were showered with benefices by their papal uncles. Some had private means, like Ascanio Sforza who in 1484 received 13,500 ducats from ducal revenues in Milan.[8] And there were other lucrative ways of making money. Bishoprics and secretarial posts, indulgences and papal dispensations – all favours were for sale at the right price. Both bribes and tips were customary methods of ensuring goodwill in the corrupt bureaucracy of Renaissance Rome.[9]

The cardinals were conspicuous spenders in Rome and prominent amongst them were nepotist appointments. Often elected at a young age and enriched by their indulgent papal relatives, they had the time, the money and, above all, the incentive to display their new rank. It was the cardinals and other members of the papal court, not the Popes, who took over patronage of chapels in Rome's numerous churches, embellishing them with fresco cycles, altarpieces and tombs. Some concentrated on their titular churches. Others preferred to emphasize their association with one of the many religious orders or to display their patriotism in churches with particular national affiliations. The prime focus of a cardinal's patronage was his palace, the setting for his court and the clearest indicator of his prestige.[10] While a few built separate residences, most cardinals' palaces were attached to their titular church, like Pietro Barbo's palace at San Marco, which he converted to the papal residence after his election as Paul II (see Chapter 19). In contrast to Renaissance patrons elsewhere in Italy, a cardinal did not build his palace as a statement of family status and power. Tied to the Church, it usually passed on to the next incumbent. Rodrigo Borgia's palace was successively occupied by Ascanio Sforza, Galeazzo della Rovere and Sisto della Rovere, his successors as vice-chancellor, and the palace at San Lorenzo in Lucina, built by its titular cardinal, Jean Rochtaillée, was extended and embellished by his successors, Filippo Calandrini, Jorge da Costa and Fazio Santorio.[11] It is a striking fact that few of those responsible for the development of the arts in the city were Roman. Civic pride, such a powerful motive in Florence and Venice, played little part in motivating expenditure in Rome. Cardinals spent on statements of personal achievement, of piety, of national interests or of religious beliefs; but their patronage was designed, above all, to proclaim their wealth and prestige as members of the papal court.

One of the major problems in examining the architecture, sculpture and painting commissioned by the cardinals of fifteenth-century Rome is that so much of it has vanished behind later schemes, especially the sumptuous Baroque projects that transformed Rome in the seventeenth century. The palace at San Lorenzo in Lucina has been completely rebuilt, Francesco Piccolomini's palace is now the site of Sant'Andrea della Valle and Guillaume d'Estouteville's residence, possibly the grandest of all fifteenth-century palaces, has completely disappeared. Moreover, there is a serious lack of documentation, making it difficult to be precise about dates and artists or to analyse the process of patronage, design and construction. However, the surviving monuments, supplemented by literary sources, correspondence and descriptions of the city, provide enough material to testify to the style and scope of the artistic activities of Renaissance cardinals.

Martin V had returned in 1420 to a dilapidated and depressing city (see Chapter 18). The absence of the papal court in Avignon followed by the political and financial problems arising from the Schism had not encouraged many builders in fourteenth-century Rome. The fabric of the illustrious old medieval city had decayed with disuse and, apart from the churches, the most prominent buildings were the towers and strongholds of the Roman feudal nobility, like that of the Orsini family built in the ruins of the Theatre of Marcellus. We have little information on the first attempts to smarten up the city, but it is clear that cardinals were active. One of the major palaces of the period was built by Martin V's influential vice-chancellor, Jean Rochtaillée, at his titular church, San Lorenzo in Lucina (c. 1430).[12] Giordano Orsini, a wealthy Roman cardinal, decorated his palace on Monte Giordano with a fresco cycle depicting famous men that included Biblical characters, heroes from classical history and more modern figures, notably Tamburlaine (d. 1405).[13]

Another cardinal active in early fifteenth-century Rome was Branda Castiglione, appointed by the Pisan Pope John XXIII and a prominent advocate of Church reform at the Council of Constance (1414–17).[14] He built an imposing palace at Sant'Apollinare[15] and commissioned the Florentine painter, Masolino, to paint a fresco cycle in his titular church of San Clemente (late 1420s).[16] The altar wall was dominated by a huge Crucifixion, and he chose events from the lives of St Ambrose and St Catherine of Alexandria to decorate the side walls. The St Catherine cycle included a scene of the saint protesting vigorously against the worship of idols (fig. 66). Masolino's depiction of the idol was both in pose and form unmistakably a classical statue, and the association was a deliberate and

66.   Masolino, *St Catherine of Alexandria and the Idol*. Rome, San Clemente, late 1420s

potent piece of Christian propaganda. Castiglione's principal project was the transformation of his small home town of Castiglione Olona, outside Milan, with a family palace, a new church and other buildings (1420–43).[17] His attitudes to the culture of antiquity were expressed by a colleague, Francisco Pizzolpasso, who wrote an account (c. 1432) of the new buildings, in which he described the columns in the church as Doric.[18] It is clear from the Gothic leaf capitals in the building that Pizzolpasso did not mean classical Doric but was referring to the moral qualities of the order as outlined by Vitruvius.[19] Neither Pizzolpasso nor Castiglione considered the classical language of antiquity appropriate for his Christian building but, like generations of medieval theologians, they were interested in the moral values contained in classical literature and Pizzolpasso used them to provide a justification for Castiglione's extravagance.

The transformation of Rome really got under way after 1450. With the papal court firmly established in Rome and Eugenius IV's battles against the Council of Basle finally over, his successors, Nicholas V, Pius II and Paul II, embarked on ambitious schemes of urban renewal designed to advertise the renewed power and prestige of the Papacy (see Chapters 18 and 19). The cardinals also played a significant role, initiating building projects that contributed to the reconstruction of the old medieval centre of the city.[20] Eugenius IV's three fellow Venetian cardinals, two of them relatives, now all began new palaces (c. 1455): Ludovico Trevisan at his titular church of San Lorenzo in Damaso, Francesco Condulmer nearby in the Campo dei Fiori and Pietro Barbo at his titular church of San Marco. The Roman cardinal, Domenico Capranica, built a palace (begun c. 1450) near the Pantheon. Four of Pius II's creations, Jean Jouffroy, Francesco Gonzaga and two relatives, Francesco Piccolomini and Jacopo Ammanati, built or embellished palaces in central Rome. Ammanati, Jouffroy and Gonzaga also all built palaces in Pius II's home town of Pienza (see Chapter 19). The remains of the palaces of Barbo and Capranica suggest that they all followed a similar format. With their unadorned façades, crenellations and massive square corner towers, they bore an explicit resemblance to the fortified strongholds of medieval Rome. These new palaces were landmarks in the dilapidated city and a manifest indication of the revival of her fortunes. Pius II's account of the procession of the relic of St Andrew's head charted its progress past these grand residences, hung with expensive tapestries and other elaborate displays but he reserved his especial praise for the magnificent palace of Rodrigo Borgia.[21]

Calixtus III had created his 25-year-old nephew, Rodrigo Borgia, a cardinal in 1456 and the following year gave him the premier post of vice-chancellor, which he held until his election as Pope Alexander VI in

1493.[22] Borgia was one of the most powerful figures in fifteenth-century Rome. Influential and wealthy, his vast income derived from numerous benefices, including the archbishopric of Valencia, the bishoprics of Cartagena and Majorca and the abbeys of Subiaco and Fossanova. Borgia's titular church, San Nicola in Carcere, was outside the city centre. Planning a more conspicuous site for his residence, he paid 2,000 ducats for the old mint near the Campo dei Fiori, where he constructed one of the most impressive palaces in the city (c. 1460).[23] Borgia's palace was traditional in style and built round an interior courtyard with arches supported on octagonal columns. But, to parade his status and ambitions, it was noticeably grander than the palaces of his contemporaries and its interior was lavishly decorated. Cardinal Ascanio Sforza's description of the palace in a letter (1484) to his brother, Ludovico Sforza, listed expensive tapestries, bed canopies of crimson satin, gold brocade and Alexandrian velvet, carpets and a valuable collection of gold and silver dishes.[24]

Extravagance and ostentation was the formula recognized throughout Renaissance Europe for the display of power; but it was not universally accepted as the appropriate language for the leaders of the Church. In the increasingly secular climate of fifteenth-century Rome, the cardinals were strongly attacked by church reformers for their materialism and unclerical life style. Rodrigo Borgia, who lived openly with his mistress and their four children, was not unique. Lorenzo de' Medici warned his son that Rome was a den of vice.[25] Attempts were made to justify conspicuous expenditure. Pizzolpasso's letter reflected Castiglione's desire to explain that his motive for building was not self-glorification.[26] One of Eugenius IV's secretaries, Lapo di Castiglionchio, wrote a dialogue (1438) claiming that the cardinals were compelled to spend lavishly because that was the most effective way of promoting the power of Christianity.[27] Some cardinals implicitly criticized the behaviour of their more secular colleagues by concentrating on performing their duties as Christians. Juan Torquemada gave dowries to poor girls and founded the Confraternity of the Annunciation at the Dominican church of Santa Maria sopra Minerva, commissioning an altarpiece for his chapel in the church which showed him offering these women to the Virgin.[28] Domenico Capranica's palace was also a college, endowed by him for teaching clerics. The Portuguese cardinal, Antonio Martinez de Chavez, built the church of Sant'Antonio dei Portoghesi with a hospice for pilgrims.[29] But many stepped over the thin line between exalting the Church and advertising their own prestige. Sixtus IV was the only fifteenth-century Pope to undertake a prominent charitable commission, the Ospedale Santo Spirito (see Chapter 20), and the cardinals were equally reluctant to spend conspicuously on charity. Most of them preferred more visible demonstrations of their own importance. Their splendid palaces, titular churches and chapels may have testified to the power of the Church but, even more importantly, such projects advanced their own individual prestige, and competition between these worldly cardinals stimulated patterns of increasing magnificence as the century progressed.

Sixtus IV's massive programme of urban renewal provided a further spur to the cardinals. His legislation stimulated palace building and the restoration of dilapidated houses.[30] Cardinal Stefano Nardini's impressive palace can be dated to 1475 from an inscription above the main entrance.[31] Sixtus IV allowed Marco Barbo tax exemptions to enable him to continue work on his uncle's magnificent palace at San Marco.[32] The Pope's ambitious scheme of church repair was augmented by cardinals like Pedro Ferriz, who remodelled his titular church, San Sisto,[33] the Franciscan Gabriel Rangone, who commissioned a chapel dedicated to St Bonaventure in Santa Maria in Aracoeli[34] and Marco Barbo, who added a portico to Santa Balbina.[35] Sixtus IV also encouraged religious building by religious and national groups. He transferred Santo Stefano in Vaticano to Coptic monks, who then restored the church,[36] he gave the site of San Pietro in Montorio in 1472 to Fra Amadeo da Silva and his Amadeiti for their new church,[37] and he allowed the German community in Rome to rebuild Santa Maria della Pietà by St Peter's (c. 1473).[38]

Perhaps Sixtus IV's greatest contribution to the visual transformation of Rome stemmed from his promotion of six relatives to the College of Cardinals and their endowment with lucrative benefices and jobs: his nephews, Pietro Riario, Giuliano della Rovere, Girolamo Basso della Rovere and Raffaello Riario, and two distant relatives, the brothers Cristoforo and Domenico della Rovere.[39] The sudden elevation of these men from modest backgrounds to unimagined wealth and influence gave them a powerful motive for conspicuous display. Pietro Riario, a Franciscan like his uncle, was created a cardinal in August 1471 and given benefices that brought in over 50,000 ducats a year.[40] He spent astonishing amounts on setting up a magnificent court at his titular palace of Santi Apostoli and died in January 1474 with debts of over 60,000 ducats.[41] Domenico della Rovere, created a cardinal (1478) after the death of his brother, built a magnificent palace near St Peter's, now the Palazzo Penitenzieri, decorated with frescos by Pinturicchio (c. 1485),[42] though the motto SOLI DEO which he inscribed on its windows was deliberately intended to show that the building was for the glory of God not himself.[43] He also commissioned a new cathedral in his home town, Turin, with a façade which bore a marked resemblance to Sixtus IV's church of Santa Maria del Popolo in Rome. Girolamo Basso della Rovere created a splendid court at Jacopo Ammanati's palace near the Ponte Sant'Angelo[44] and commissioned Melozzo da Forlì to decorate the four sacristies in the Sanctuary of the Holy House at Loreto.[45] Raffaello Riario was a major figure in the revival of classical culture in Renaissance Rome (see below). But the greatest patron of Sixtus IV's extravagant nephews was Giuliano della Rovere.

Sixtus IV created Giuliano della Rovere, also a Franciscan, Cardinal of San Pietro in Vincoli in 1471 and gave him the additional title of Santi Apostoli after the death of Pietro Riario.[46] His impressive string of benefices must have brought in an income similar to his cousin's and he was also appointed grand penitentiary (1476). Rich and influential, like his rival, Rodrigo Borgia, Giuliano wielded enormous power in late fifteenth-century Rome and was elected Pope Julius II in 1503. Conspicuous expenditure testified to his prestige. He restored the early Christian church of Sant'Agnese fuori le Mura, acknowledging his relationship to Sixtus IV in an inscription over the door (1479)[47] and commissioned his uncle's tomb for St Peter's (see below). At Ostia he built a fortress and the Canonica Sant'Aurea with his expenditure again commemorated in clearly visible inscriptions. He commissioned the Palazzo della Rovere in his home town of Savona, an unmistakable statement of the new prestige of his family, and its austere Doric façade reflected his uncle's deliberately moral use of the order on his Ospedale Santo Spirito.[48]

Giuliano della Rovere directed his prime attention at his two titular churches, San Pietro in Vincoli and Santi Apostoli, commissioning extensive renovations and repairs on both churches. At Santi Apostoli he continued the projects begun by Pietro Riario, financing new vaults, the choir, two cloisters and a new two-storey portico across the façade (1473–8)[49] which, according to Platina, the papal librarian, was built to his own design.[50] He commissioned Melozzo da Forlì to paint the new choir with a fresco of Christ in Glory and erected tombs to his father, Raffaello della Rovere, and Pietro Riario in the church. At San Pietro in Vincoli he commissioned new vaults, cloisters as well as a portico like that at Santi Apostoli.[51] Both porticoes were supported on octagonal piers with leaf capitals emblazoned with the oak tree, the della Rovere coat of arms. Porticoes across the front of the church were also common on fourth- and fifth-century churches in Rome[52] and Giuliano was clearly identifying himself with his uncle's determination to revive early Christian models for his own projects (see Chapter 20). Giuliano della Rovere also commissioned palaces attached to each church, both similar in style, with his name clearly inscribed in the windows of the main floor. We have no knowledge of their interior decorations and can only guess at their magnificence.

Another prominent patron during Sixtus IV's pontificate was his rich and powerful chamberlain, Guillaume d'Estouteville.[53] One of the wealthiest cardinals of the fifteenth century, d'Estouteville was related to the French royal family and created a cardinal by Eugenius IV in 1439. His benefices included the archbishopric of Rouen, one of the few really lucrative sees in Europe. As Cardinal-bishop of Ostia (1461–83), he was the most senior cardinal in the College. He was one of the most prolific patrons in fifteenth-century Rome. He contributed funds for the rebuilding of San Luigi dei Francesi, the French church in Rome,[54] and commissioned major repairs to one of the city's grandest churches, Santa Maria Maggiore, financing new vaults and windows,[55] and leaving money in his will for rebuilding the choir.[56] He commissioned the Florentine sculptor, Mino da Fiesole, to carve an elaborate ciborium (1474), a tabernacle for the high altar decorated with reliefs depicting the legendary foundation of the basilica after a snowstorm in August.[57]

But the main focus of d'Estouteville's patronage was improving the area around his palace at Sant'Apollinare, just off the piazza Navona. The palace, inherited from Branda Castiglione (see above), has long since vanished and we know little about it except that it was one of the grandest in Rome.[58] As chamberlain (1477–83), d'Estouteville was in charge of Sixtus IV's ambitious scheme of urban renewal and he was closely involved with the plans to clear the ruins of the Stadium of Domitian, now the piazza Navona, to provide a new site for Rome's principal market.[59] He also commissioned a new church near his palace. Sant'Agostino, begun in 1479, was part of a large convent, financed by d'Estouteville for the Augustinians.[60] Its plain travertine façade bore a marked resemblance to Sixtus IV's Santa Maria del Popolo (begun 1472) but its Corinthian and Composite pilasters were conspicuously more decorative and d'Estouteville's name and titles were prominently displayed in an inscription in the frieze across the façade. This enormous undertaking was designed, above all, to testify to the wealth of its patron.

Santa Maria del Popolo was an important focus of expenditure for members of the papal court.[61] With the della Rovere cardinals taking the lead, others also acquired patronage rights to its chapels and altars, embellishing them with painting and sculpture. The church soon became a fashionable site for burial. Amongst the many tombs in the church were those of Cristoforo della Rovere (d. 1478) (fig. 67) and his brother Domenico (d. 1501), Giovanni Mellini (d. 1478), Ferry de Cluny (d. 1483), Pietro Foscari (d. 1485) and Jorge da Costa (d. 1508), all cardinals appointed by Sixtus IV. Other tombs included those of Giovanni Montemirabile, an abbreviator in the Curia, and Juan Gomiel, the papal Datary (1502–3).[62] Rodrigo Borgia took over patronage of the high altar, commissioning an ostentatiously expensive marble relief of the Virgin and Child set in an elaborate triumphal arch with statues of saints in its niches and the Borgia bulls prominently displayed on shields held

67.   Tomb of Cardinal Cristoforo della Rovere (d.1478), Santa Maria
del Popolo, Rome

by *putti* (1473).[63] Cardinal Girolamo Basso della Rovere acquired his
chapel in 1484 and commissioned Pinturicchio to paint frescos of scenes
from the life of the Virgin for the vaults, her Assumption on the left wall
and an altarpiece of the Virgin and Child with St Augustine and St Francis
(fig. 68).[64] The grisaille scenes of Saints Augustine, Catherine, Peter and
Paul below the window and the elaborate carving on the pilasters flanking
the altarpiece were fashionably *all'antica*. The chapel also contained the
tomb he commissioned for his father Giovanni Basso (d. 1483). Domenico
della Rovere took over patronage of a chapel dedicated to the Virgin and
St Jerome for the tomb of his brother, Cristoforo (d. 1478) (fig. 67). He also
commissioned Pinturicchio to paint his altarpiece of the Nativity and scenes

68. Cappella Basso della Rovere, Santa Maria del Popolo, Rome, c. 1485

from the life of St Jerome in the vaults (c. 1488–90).[65] The grotesques painted on the pilasters flanking the windows of Domenico's chapel (fig. 68) were inspired by the recently discovered decoration in the Golden House of Nero (see Chapter 20) and displayed the Cardinal's taste for the new fashion sweeping Rome in the 1490s. Domenico sold another chapel to Jorge da Costa for 200 ducats in 1488,[66] which Costa endowed with a house to provide income for its upkeep and embellished it with an extravagant marble altarpiece of St Catherine with St Vincent and St Anthony of Padua.[67]

Although it was usual practice for a cardinal to be buried in his titular church, many preferred to make an explicit association with a particular religious order. Domenico Capranica, Pedro Ferriz and Juan Torquemada were all buried in the Dominican church of Santa Maria sopra Minerva, and Gabriel Rangone was buried in his chapel in the Franciscan church of Santa Maria in Aracoeli. The choice of Santa Maria del Popolo was more a statement of status at the papal court. The medieval tradition of floor slabs was replaced in the fifteenth century by more elaborate wall tombs, decorated with statues of saints, inscriptions and an effigy of the cardinal. As the century progressed, the tombs became more ornate but the religious imagery remained essentially unchanged. Pietro Riario's tomb in Santi Apostoli, commissioned by his cousin, Giuliano della Rovere, displayed Riario's effigy on a fancy antique sarcophagus flanked by Franciscan saints. Cristoforo della Rovere's tomb in Santa Maria del Popolo (fig. 67) was covered with expensive carved all'antica detail but its only imagery was a relief of the Virgin and Child. Most fifteenth-century tombs were marble, though the Venetian Cardinal Pietro Foscari was commemorated with a costly bronze effigy in Santa Maria del Popolo. The French Cardinal Jean de Bilhères de Lagraulas commissioned Michelangelo to carve the exquisitely finished and poignant Pietà (1497) (fig. 69) for his tomb in the chapel of the King of France in St Peter's.[68]

By far the grandest burial monuments in Renaissance Rome were the tombs of the Popes, usually commissioned by their cardinal nephews. Many of them were cast in expensive bronze. Martin V's bronze tomb was in San Giovanni Laterano, the church of the Pope as Bishop of Rome, but his successors preferred to associate themselves more explicitly with the Petrine tradition and built their burial chapels in St Peter's. Pius II was commemorated in his chapel, which contained the head of St Andrew (see Chapter 19), with a marble wall monument commissioned by Francesco Piccolomini and decorated with panels depicting the arrival of the relic in Rome.[69] Paul II's marble tomb, commissioned by Marco Barbo, carried reliefs of the life of St Peter carved in a style that was unmistakably derived from ancient Roman sculpture.[70]

Sixtus IV's tomb (c. 1490), commissioned by Giuliano della Rovere from the Florentine sculptors, Antonio and Pietro Pollaiuolo, was exceptional both in style and format.[71] This massive bronze monument was designed not for a wall but to lie in the centre of the Pope's chapel in St Peter's, his recumbent effigy surrounded by the Virtues and the Liberal Arts. It was one of the most opulent monuments in fifteenth-century Italy and its decoration celebrated Sixtus IV's Franciscan background and his theological expertise.

69.   Michelangelo, *Pietà*. Rome, St Peter's, 1497

There was a long tradition of depicting the Virtues on papal tombs, and they appeared on the monuments of both Pius II and Paul II. But the Liberal Arts were unprecedented, and their iconography, chosen by Giuliano della Rovere, related directly to the medieval Aristotelian traditions in Franciscan thought. Innocent VIII's tomb (1492–8), commissioned by Lorenzo Cibo from the Pollaiuolo brothers, also broke with tradition.[72] This magnificent bronze wall monument displayed the effigy of Innocent VIII on his sarcophagus, but its central focus was a seated figure of the Pope, his hand lifted in the gesture of benediction that would have been familiar to anyone in the basilica from the revered thirteenth-century bronze statue of St Peter, attributed to Arnolfo di Cambio.

Francesco Piccolomini also financed a more emphatic celebration of the life of his uncle, Pius II, in a library attached to the cathedral in Siena. It was traditional to decorate libraries with portraits of famous men, the theme chosen by Federigo da Montefeltro in his palace at Urbino (see Chapter 14). But Piccolomini gave this tradition a distinctly dynastic twist by commissioning ten large scenes for the walls of the Siena cathedral library that depicted the political and ecclesiastical career of Pius II together with his achievements as Pope. Piccolomini's contract (1502) with the painter, Pinturicchio, was very detailed.[73] Pinturicchio was to be paid 1,000 ducats for this ambitious cycle and given free accommodation in Siena, though the amount of flour, wine and oil consumed by his household was to be deducted from the final payment. The high price also included the cost of the large quantities of gold and ultramarine that Piccolomini wanted to testify to the expense of the project. The scenes were all to be chosen by Piccolomini, and the contract specified that Pinturicchio was to paint all the heads in the frescos. Interestingly, Piccolomini requested that the vault was to be decorated with grotesques, then the height of fashion in Rome. He also stipulated that the backgrounds were to be ornamented with trees, landscapes and cities. It is obvious from the finished frescos that the scenes were not intended to be realistic; for they occurred in places as far afield as Scotland and Germany, as well as Rome, and the uniform grandeur of the architectural settings enhanced the success of Pius II's route to power.

There were many strands to the revival of antiquity in Rome. Since the beginning of the century, humanists had used the literature of antiquity to provide propaganda in support of papal supremacy and had promoted the concept of the cardinals as heirs to the patrician senators of ancient Rome (see Chapter 19). Castiglione had exploited Vitruvius's theories to justify his expenditure, but he had used the visual language of antiquity to criticize non-Christian beliefs.[74] The humanist funeral orations of Cardinals Ludovico Trevisan (d. 1465) and Domenico della Rovere (d. 1501) compared them to Lucullus, an extravagant patron of the arts in ancient Rome, to convey the notions of wealth and lavish expenditure, not necessarily their stylistic preferences.[75] Pius II and Paul II had adopted the classical language of architecture to promote the Papacy as the heir of imperial Rome, but Sixtus IV had decisively rejected this image in favour of the imagery of early Christianity. His cardinal-nephews followed his lead, tempering their ostentatious life styles with austere and traditional visual forms. In the more secular climate of the pontificates of Innocent VIII and Alexander VI, *all'antica* detail proliferated and the discovery of the Golden House of Nero added to the classical decorative vocabulary. By the end of the century, there were overt signs to show that the cardinals increasingly wanted to display their association with the patrician culture of ancient Rome.

In direct imitation of their patrician forbears, wealthy cardinals assembled collections of sculpture which they displayed in the gardens of their palaces.[76] While patrons in other centres had to be content with reproductions of antique statues, the cardinals could acquire the real thing. The building boom in fifteenth-century Rome had unearthed considerable quantities of antiquities. Paul II had been careful to stipulate in a contract that anything found by the builders digging the foundations for his palace was to belong to him.[77] As early as 1435, Cardinal Prospero Colonna had displayed the Torso Belvedere in his garden.[78] By the end of the century it was common practice. Domenico Grimani and Giuliano Cesarini, who claimed descent from Julius Caesar, both had impressive collections in their palaces.[79] Francesco Piccolomini owned a statue of the Three Graces as well as an impressive library of Greek and Latin manuscripts.[80] Raffaello Riario bought a Cupid by Michelangelo for 200 ducats, thinking it was an antique, to add to his impressive collection[81] and Giuliano della Rovere owned the famous statue of the Apollo Belvedere, which he displayed in the garden of his palace at Santi Apostoli (*c.* 1489).[82] Others commissioned modern sculptors to carve statues. Michelangelo and Jacopo Sansovino were both commissioned to carve statues of Bacchus for wealthy patrons in Rome.[83] They reveal very different attitudes to wine! While Sansovino's Bacchus (1506) extolled its virtues, Michelangelo's (1497) was a dissolute figure barely able to keep his balance (fig. 70).

The cardinal's adoption of the image of ancient Roman patricians also had a decisive impact on the appearance of the city as they increasingly adopted the classical language of architecture to give visual expression to their heritage and prestige. Two patrons made significant contributions to this development: Raffaello Riario and Oliviero Carafa.

Raffaello Riario had been created a cardinal in 1477 by his uncle, Sixtus IV, who later appointed him to the influential post of chamberlain

70.   Michelangelo, *Bacchus*. Florence, Museo Nazionale, 1497

(1483–1521).[84] He played a prominent role in the revival of ancient Roman drama, staging performances of classical theatre in his palace.[85] The first printed edition of Vitruvius's treatise on architecture, *de architectura* (1487) was dedicated to him, a gesture that reflected both his interest in the culture of antiquity and his political importance in late fifteenth-century Rome. And his palace, the Cancelleria (1487–1511) (fig. 71), was the first in Rome to display prominently the classical orders on its façade.[86] The palace was attached to his titular church of San Lorenzo in Damaso, an early Christian basilica which had been restored earlier in the century by Ludovico Trevisan, who had also built a palace there. Riario's ambitious project involved the destruction of both the old basilica and Trevisan's palace to make way for what was undoubtedly the most sumptuous cardinal's residence in late fifteenth-century Rome. The inscription on the façade of the new palace, which had two courtyards and gardens, proclaimed Riario's status and wealth. He was reputed to have financed the project from gambling winnings taken from Franceschetto Cibo, son of Innocent VIII.[87] Riario's choice of design was innovative. Its rusticated façade was ornamented with Corinthian pilasters, a far cry from the austere unadorned façades of earlier palaces. Instead of the traditional use of octagonal piers, the two-tiered arcade in the main courtyard was supported on Doric

71. Palazzo della Cancelleria, Rome, 1487–1511

columns.[88] The new style was soon taken up by other patrons, notably Adriano Castellesi, who built his palace (begun *c.* 1503) on Alexander VI's new street in the Borgo by St Peter's.[89]

Oliviero Carafa was another influential figure in the Roman Curia.[90] Born into a prominent Neapolitan family, he had been created cardinal by Paul II in 1467. He had commanded Sixtus IV's papal fleet in the crusade (1472) and had been appointed cardinal-protector of the Dominicans (1481). A series of expensive commissions in Naples and Rome proclaimed his rank and prestige.[91] His Roman projects included a magnificent villa on the Quirinal, restoration work at the early Christian basilica of San Lorenzo fuori le Mura and at the Franciscan church of Santa Maria in Aracoeli. He also took over patronage of a chapel in the Dominican church of Santa Maria sopra Minerva dedicated to the Virgin and the Dominican theologian, St Thomas Aquinas (1486).[92] He commissioned the Florentine painter, Filippino Lippi, to paint an altarpiece of the Annunciation, which showed St Thomas Aquinas presenting Carafa to the Virgin. On the walls, Lippi frescoed scenes from the life of the Dominican saint and the Assumption of the Virgin (fig. 72). Rich and lavish, the chapel testified to Carafa's Dominican associations and to his wealth. The chapel also illustrated the role of politics in artistic patronage. Lippi had been recommended to Carafa by Lorenzo de' Medici, who had persuaded the painter to stop work on an important commission in Florence in order to go to Rome. Carafa was immensely proud of getting Lorenzo's recommendation for Lippi[93] and did him a favour in return. Lorenzo wanted to get his son made a cardinal and Carafa, who had initially opposed the scheme, now used his considerable influence to support Lorenzo's ambition.[94]

Carafa's other major project in Rome was a new set of cloisters for the convent of Lateran Canons at Santa Maria della Pace (1500).[95] This was just one aspect of his patronage of the order, to which he left his library.[96] Carafa's involvement was prominently displayed in an inscription around the cloisters (fig. 73) and his choice of design was an important step in the revival of classical architecture. The articulation of the two storeys of the cloisters involved the unprecedented use of all four classical orders: Doric piers and Ionic pilasters on the ground floor and Corinthian piers with Composite columns above. The cloisters also marked an important step in the emergence of the modern concept of a patron and his architect. The designer of this innovative project was Bramante, who had just arrived in Rome after his previous employer, Ludovico Sforza, had been expelled from Milan by the French in 1499 (see Chapter 12). Like Sforza, Carafa chose to employ an expert in classical architectural design and Bramante's subsequent career in Rome, working for Julius II (see Chapter 22), saw this practice established as the norm.

72. Filippino Lippi, Carafa Chapel, Santa Maria sopra Minerva, Rome, begun 1488

73.   Cloisters, Santa Maria della Pace, Rome, begun 1500

Bramante's next project in Rome was a tiny votive chapel by the church
of San Pietro in Montorio on the site where St Peter was believed to have
been martyred (fig. 74). We know little about this commission, which produced the Tempietto (1502),[97] one of the major landmarks in Renaissance
architecture. The convent belonged to the Franciscan reformers, the
Amadeiti, and the chapel was financed by Ferdinand and Isabella of Spain.
The circular form of the Tempietto was traditional for a martyrium, but its
articulation was strikingly new. Attitudes to the antique had changed since
Pizzolpasso had assigned the moral values of classical Doric to the Gothic
leaf capitals in Branda Castiglione's church at Castiglione Olona. The
design of the Tempietto showed how classical Doric itself could be used to
convey a Christian message. The central *cella* of the martyrium was surrounded by a peristyle of Doric columns with a correctly proportioned
classical Doric frieze ornamented with metopes and triglyphs. Vitruvius
had recommended the Doric order for strong, masculine deities[98] and its
use here was clearly intended to convey St Peter's role as the first Pope. But
Bramante's use of the Doric order was not pagan. Instead of the details normally found in classical metopes, he had inserted the attributes of St Peter,

74.   Bramante, Tempietto, San Pietro in Montorio, Rome, 1502

especially the papal symbol of the crossed keys. This new style, which translated the classical language of antiquity into a modern Christian context, was to prove a powerful tool in the hands of Pope Julius II.

22

The Triumph of Rome

The election of Giuliano della Rovere as Julius II (1503–13) was a landmark in both the political and the cultural history of Rome. Created cardinal by his uncle Sixtus IV in 1471, Giuliano had been close to the centre of papal power for over thirty years, acquiring enormous wealth and influence as well as a reputation for conspicuous expenditure (see Chapter 21). The Venetian ambassador described him as stubborn, impatient and argumentative, but credited him with grand vision.[1] Another contemporary, Erasmus, was appalled at his extravagance.[2] Modern historians blame his ambitious policies for precipitating the Protestant Reformation, but the art world heaps praise on him as the patron of Bramante's project for a new St Peter's, Raphael's series of frescos in the papal apartments in the Vatican and, above all, Michelangelo's ceiling in the Sistine Chapel. Julius II exploited the potential of art and architecture as propaganda for the Church and the Papacy on an unprecedented scale. His projects had an irreversible impact on Rome and the stylistic changes he introduced mark the beginning of what art historians describe as the High Renaissance.

Alexander VI had been succeeded in 1503 by Francesco Piccolomini who, as Pius III, reigned for less than a month before dying. Julius II had been Alexander VI's rival in the Curia for twenty years, and the animosity between them reputedly extended to the new Pope's refusal to enter the lavishly decorated Borgia apartments in the Vatican. Julius II was faced with the daunting task of repairing the damage caused by Alexander VI's policies and his territorial ambitions for his family. He inherited a bankrupt treasury and papal states in which all authority had disintegrated. His election was a bitter blow to Alexander VI's son, Cesare Borgia, who was compelled to resign his control of the Romagna, and Julius II embarked on a ruthless military campaign to restore order throughout the papal states. He led his own armies in the reconquest of Perugia and Bologna (1506). To regain Faenza, Rimini and Ravenna, which had been seized by Venice, he joined the Holy Roman Empire, Spain, Mantua and Ferrara in the League of Cambrai. All the members of the League had reasons for stemming

Venetian expansion on the Italian mainland and they launched a savage attack on Venice, defeating her at the Battle of Agnadello (1509) (see Chapter 10). But the presence of the French armies in Italy was a threat to Julius II's independence and in 1511 he allied himself with Venice, Spain and Henry VII of England in a Holy League which successfully forced the French out of Italy. Julius II had used his political cunning and military skills not only to regain control of the papal states but also to expand them with the addition of Parma, Piacenza and Reggio Emilia.

In Rome he forcefully established a power base in the College to balance the Borgia cardinals and their allies appointed by Alexander VI. He founded a permanent papal army, the Swiss Guard, whose uniform was designed by Michelangelo. Under heavy pressure from his political enemies and critics of clerical abuse, he called the Fifth Lateran Council (1512–17) to institute reforms in the Church. Above all, his policies had a beneficial effect on the papal treasury. Consolidation of his authority in the papal states secured existing income and conquest brought in extra revenues.[3] He also instituted economic reforms, revaluing the currency and introducing a new coin, the *giulio*, which increased the real revenue from taxes and bribes charged on granting papal favours.[4] And he expanded the system of venal offices, founding the College of Archivists with 101 members. A price list of 1514 specified figures of 2,700 ducats for a scriptor in the Chancery, 6,000 ducats for a master of the Seal and 10,000 ducats for clerks in the Chamber.[5]

Julius II's choice of name was highly significant. While he may have been referring to the forceful pontificate of Julius I (337–52), a vigorous defender of the Nicene orthodoxy against Arianism, it is clear that he intended to draw a deliberate parallel between himself and his illustrious imperial predecessor, Julius Caesar. The campaign medal celebrating his victory in Bologna was inscribed *IULIUS CAESAR PONT II* and the Augustinian Minister-General, Egidio of Viterbo, hailed the Portuguese victories in the Indian Ocean as a triumph for the Church boasting that Julius II now owned lands unknown to Julius Caesar.[6] Not all were so complimentary. In a witty and biting attack on the Pope (*c.* 1511), Erasmus imagined Julius II being refused entry into Heaven by St Peter and described how well the Pope's name suited him: he was a tyrant, he had ignored the Gods and forced his country into war. But there was one difference, Julius II came from a far more modest background.[7]

If the name of Julius was strongly reminiscent of the military and political strengths of Julius Caesar, it also evoked parallels with the ambitious conqueror's grandiose building projects. Suetonius's life of Julius Caesar recounted his many projects planned for the embellishment of Rome, including the Temple of Mars, the largest in the world, on the site of the circus where mock naval battles had been staged, and an enormous theatre sloping down from Tarpeian Rock on the Capitol Hill.[8] Julius II's new St Peter's, built on the site of Nero's Circus, was to be the largest church in Christendom. His extension to the Vatican Palace was not on the Capitol, but it did slope down from Innocent VIII's Villa Belvedere to provide an impressive setting for spectacular extravaganzas. But it was Julius II's deliberate adoption of the classical language of imperial Rome that was to provide the strongest parallel and signify the rebirth of the city's majestic past into an even more glorious Christian present.

Julius II planned to make Rome a truly impressive centre, one that would clearly demonstrate his vision of the renewed power and prestige of the Pope as supreme head of the Church. His ambition had a dramatic impact on the appearance of the city.[9] Following the example of his uncle, Sixtus IV, Julius II embarked on a massive programme of urban renewal. He repaired roads, sewers, aqueducts and bridges, and built the via Giulia, linking the Ponte Sisto to the Ponte Sant' Angelo. He added to Alexander VI's schemes to fortify the Castel Sant' Angelo. He comissioned repairs to many churches in the city, including Santa Maria Maggiore and San Celso. He remodelled San Biagio della Pagnotta and built Santa Maria di Loreto in the Forum of Trajan.[10] He commissioned the papal goldsmith, Caradosso, to make gilt bronze doors for the reliquary holding St Peter's Chains in his old titular church of San Pietro in Vincoli and a papal tiara, which was valued in 1521 at the staggering amount of 62,430 ducats.[11] At Santa Maria del Popolo he built a new, and larger, choir for the church, commissioning expensive stained glass for its windows from Marcillat, an elaborate painted coffered ceiling from Pinturicchio and tombs to Cardinal Ascanio Sforza (d. 1505) and to his cousin, Cardinal Girolamo Basso della Rovere (d. 1507) from Andrea Sansovino.[12] He began an enormous palace to house the law courts and notaries' offices, the Palazzo di Giustizia, built to a design by Bramante around the church of San Biagio della Pagnotta.[13] Outside Rome, Julius II planned an elaborate and expensive marble casing for the Casa Santa, reputedly the house of the Virgin, which was conserved inside the church at Loreto. The work was designed by Bramante but only executed after the death of both Julius II (1513) and its architect (1514). In a clear statement of his new authority in the papal states, he commissioned extensive repairs to fortresses at Civita Vecchia, Ostia, Forlì, Imola, Viterbo and Bologna. Soon after his conquest of Bologna (1506), Julius II commissioned Michelangelo to design a bronze statue of himself, three-times life size, which he erected on the façade of the city's principal church, San Petronio.[14] The statue provided the focus for an angry mob of Bolognese citizens, who destroyed this symbol of his overlordship, and it was eventually cast into a cannon by Alfonso d'Este and named La Giulia.[15]

Above all, Julius II directed his main attention to the buildings at the heart of papal authority, St Peter's and the Vatican, where the new church, the extension to the palace, the decoration of the Sistine Chapel ceiling and the embellishment of his private apartments radically altered the setting for the display of papal sovreignty and prestige. There can be no doubt that Julius II was the prime force behind these projects, but the significant innovations in style and form that they introduced make it clear that his principal artists, Bramante, Raphael and Michelangelo, played more than an executive role in the creation of the Pope's impressive image of power.

It is difficult to overstate the enormity of Julius II's decision to rebuild St Peter's. His plans involved the total demolition of the old basilica built by Emperor Constantine in the fourth century.[16] Although dilapidated, its age and historical associations made it one of the most venerable buildings in Christendom. Julius II's action was not universally popular. While Sigismondo de' Conti, a prominent member of his court, justified the Pope's actions by criticizing the style of Constantine's church as old-fashioned and inelegant, others denounced Julius II for his destruction of this prime symbol of the triumph of Christianity.[17] To finance this massive project, Julius II urged Christians throughout Europe to contribute funds, offering them the irresistible bait of indulgences on an unprecedented scale and sending an army of commissioners to collect revenues due. It was the widespread abuse of indulgences for this and other projects that provoked Luther to attack the Church establishment, an act which launched the Protestant Reformation. The new St Peter's was far from finished when Julius II died in 1513. The foundation ceremony was held in April 1506 but the building was only finally completed at the beginning of the seventeenth century. The dramatic changes that had taken place in religious attitudes during the Counter-Reformation had had a significant impact on its final appearance, and Bramante's original plans were substantially altered.

Julius II's choice of design for the new St Peter's was radically different from that of the old Constantinian basilica. Built on the massive scale of the monuments of ancient Rome, its grandeur was deliberately calculated to impress. But Bramante's project, known from a ground plan (fig. 75) and a commemorative medal commissioned from Caradosso (1506), was not strictly classical.[18] It was based on a Greek cross plan, crowned by a vast hemispherical dome and with towers at each of the four corners. The centralized plan, dome and corner towers had good Christian precedents, including the enormous fourth-century church of San Lorenzo in Milan, which Bramante knew, and the imperial church architecture of the Byzantine East. The huge piers supporting the dome inside were decorated with Corinthian capitals, like the interior of the old basilica. However,

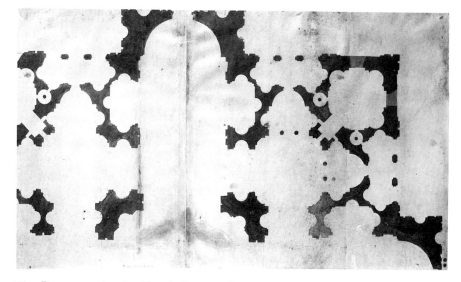

75.   Bramante, plan for New St Peter's. Florence, Uffizi, 1506

Bramante's temporary shrine, erected over the site of St Peter's tomb (fig. 76), was articulated with Doric columns designed, like those of the Tempietto (see Chapter 21), to convey the strong masculine qualities of the first Pope.

Bramante's design for St Peter's gave visual expression to Julius II's intention to erect an essentially Christian monument. The suggestion that the new church should be reorientated so that it faced the ancient Egyptian obelisk to the south of the building (which was believed to contain the ashes of Julius Caesar) was ruled out by the Pope on the grounds that it involved moving the tomb of St Peter.[19] In building St Peter's, Julius II emphasized the parallel between himself and Solomon, the wise ruler who had erected the great Temple of Jerusalem. Like Nicholas V and Sixtus IV, he justified his conspicuous expenditure by reference to this significant Biblical precedent. Egidio da Viterbo compared Julius II's pontificate with the reign of Solomon[20] and the Pope's last Bull, dated 19 February 1513, referred explictly to his intention to emulate Solomon's unstinting efforts to build a temple worthy of God's name.[21]

While St Peter's exuded imperial Christian resonances Bramante's work on extending and embellishing the Vatican Palace was unambiguous in its visual association with the temporal power and prestige of the Emperors of ancient Rome. Julius II commissioned an extensive remodelling of the old palace by St Peter's, adding two new ceremonial staircases, a classical loggia and frescos to decorate his private apartments (see below).[22] Bramante's new Doric window for the Sala Regia with its architrave broken by an arch was derived from an old symbol of imperial power, which

76. Interior of Old St Peter's with new choir and altar house. Hamburg, Kunsthalle, c. 1570

Bramante could have seen at San Lorenzo in Milan or at Hadrian's villa at Tivoli. This stylistic innovation, known as a Serlian or Palladian window, became a popular motif in sixteenth-century architecture.

Julius II's plans for enlarging the Vatican Palace were unprecedented in scale. At a practical level, the extension was needed to provide accommodation for the papal court, which was already the largest bureaucracy in Europe and expanding rapidly. Bramante's design was impressive. Two long parallel three-storeyed blocks linked the old nucleus of the Vatican palace to Innocent VIII's Villa Belvedere up on the hill behind St Peter's. They enclosed an open space that was divided into three sections, each at a different level, to accommodate the slope of the hill from villa to palace. The area formed an impressive setting for theatre, tournaments, military displays and bull fights and could even, according to an engraving, be flooded for mock naval battles, like the circuses of ancient Rome.[23] This ambitious scheme was the greatest single project in the city since the collapse of the Roman Empire and it was manifestly classical in style. The new palace was inspired by descriptions of the palatial villas of Roman

77.   Bramante, spiral staircase, Villa Belvedere, Vatican, *c.* 1511

Emperors in the writings of Tacitus, Suetonius and others, especially that
of the Golden House of Nero, the luxurious palace of one of Rome's
most extravagant Emperors that had included a one-mile-long connecting
colonnade.[24]

Bramante's new entrance to the Villa Belvedere must have surprised
visitors by its novel appearance. It took the form of a spiral staircase
(fig. 77), its architrave supported by columns that started Doric at ground

level and climbed through Ionic and Corinthian to Composite at the top. The visitor arrived in the focus of Julius II's embellishments to the Villa Belvedere, the court that housed his impressive collection of antique statuary. It included works that are still revered as some of the greatest surviving sculptures from antiquity: the Apollo Belvedere which had graced his palace at Santi Apostoli (see Chapter 21),[25] the Laocoön, which had been found near Santa Maria Maggiore in 1506 and quickly acquired by the Pope,[26] the statue of Emperor Commodus as Hercules, found in 1507 near the Campo dei Fiori[27] and the imposing river god, known as the Tiber, found in 1512 near Santa Maria sopra Minerva.[28] Julius donated all these statues to the Church.[29] The combination of the architectural language of antiquity and the sculptural relics of this once-mighty civilization provided unmistakable evidence of Julius II's desire to promote himself not only as the successor to St Peter but also as the heir to the immense power and prestige of the Emperors of ancient Rome.

Julius II planned to give visual expression to his achievements in what would have been unquestionably the grandest papal tomb to date.[30] Intended for his chapel in the new St Peter's, he started planning it long before the foundation stone of the new church had been laid. In 1505 he commissioned Michelangelo to start work on the tomb and the enormous price, 10,000 ducats, testified to its intended magnificence.[31] Michelangelo spent the next six months in Carrara organizing the quarrying of the marble, but the project was dropped the following year, presumably because Julius II needed the funds for St Peter's. It was taken up again after the Pope's death but never completed. Amongst the surviving statues was Michelangelo's famous Moses and a series of partly blocked-out figures, known as the Captives. Despite the problems with the tombs, Julius II must have been impressed with Michelangelo. His next commission for the artist was to redecorate the ceiling of the Sistine Chapel, built by his uncle Sixtus IV (see Chapter 19).

Early in 1504 a crack was noticed in the ceiling of the Sistine Chapel and the mess caused by the repairs encouraged Julius II to redecorate it.[32] By 1506 ideas and artists were being discussed. In a letter to Michelangelo, Piero Rosselli wrote that Bramante had told Julius II that Michelangelo lacked the courage to do the ceiling.[33] Bramante had a point: Michelangelo was a sculptor, not an experienced fresco painter. Nevertheless, he obtained the commission and signed a contract for 3,000 ducats for the job in 1508.[34] Work on constructing scaffolding and preparing the surface began immediately. Although art historians argue about the date of individual parts of the ceiling, they generally agree that the project was finished in 1512, when the scaffolding was finally removed.[35] Michelangelo's original contract was for a series of the Apostles in the twelve spandrels and lunettes

78.   Michelangelo, ceiling, Sistine Chapel, Vatican, 1508–12

of the ceiling, the rest of the vault to be covered with ornamental compartments inspired by ancient Roman schemes. But the plan soon became more ambitious. An alternative, more elaborate, scheme was proposed, which the painter, and presumably also the Pope, preferred (see below).[36] Michelangelo painted an epic sweep through the Old Testament across the ceiling, with scenes and individual figures arranged in an elaborate architectural framework that owed much to Bramante's ideas (fig. 78).[37] In the central section were scenes from Genesis, starting with *God separating Light from Darkness* and ending with the *Drunkenness of Noah*. Flanking alternate panels were medallions in imitation of gilded bronze medals depicting events from the books of Genesis, Samuel, Kings and Maccabees.[38] The medallions appeared to be secured by strips of material held in place by nude figures, the so-called *Ignudi*, many of whom have clusters of oak leaves and acorns, a direct reference to the oak-tree of the della Rovere coat of arms. In each of the four corner lunettes were Old Testament stories on the theme of salvation. The spandrels, above Sixtus IV's cycle of the first thirty Popes, were decorated with the names of the forty ancestors of Christ (Matthew 1: 1–16) embellished with figures of men, women and children. Between the spandrels were figures of seven Prophets and five Sibyls, announcing the coming of Christ.

Art historians have revelled in contriving ever more complex interpretations for the iconography of the Sistine Chapel ceiling. It has been related to Florentine Neo-Platonism,[39] to Dominican theology,[40] to Franciscan thought,[41] to Pentecost[42] and to the Apocalypse prophesied by Joachim of Fiore.[43] This last theory is particularly intriguing because Joachim's ideas can also be found in the other solutions mentioned above.[44] Other ideas include the suggestion that the medallions represent the Ten Commandments[45] and that Julius II got Egidio da Viterbo, the influential Minister-General of the Augustinians, to devise the iconography for the ceiling.[46] In the absence of documentary evidence, it is difficult to be certain of anything beyond the basic theme of the ceiling, that it depicted Old Testament prefigurations for the Christian faith. It is even harder to establish who was responsible for thinking up the ambitious scheme. It has been argued convincingly that the scenes represented in the medallions, many of which were unusual in fifteenth-century religious art, emphasized obedience to the supreme authority of God and, by implication, to his Vicar on earth.[47] Michelangelo based these scenes directly on woodcuts in an early printed edition of the Bible, the so-called Malermi Bible, thus ensuring that they would be easily recognizable.[48] But it is unlikely that Michelangelo was entirely responsible for devising the iconography of the whole scheme, as many art historians would like to believe. It is evident from contracts discussed in preceding chapters that Renaissance patrons were principally responsible for deciding the subject matter of their projects.[49] There is every reason to suppose that Julius II would also have had firm ideas about his ceiling, as he did for his private apartments (see below), and possible that he sought theological advice from an expert. He certainly sought advice from his artist, and Michelangelo played a central role in the planning and execution of this ambitious project.

Julius II's choice of Michelangelo to paint the Sistine Chapel ceiling proved a crucial decision in the history of European art. The extent of Michelangelo's involvement with the iconography of the cycle may be controversial but the stylistic innovations he introduced are clear. Trained as a sculptor, his powerful style had little in common with the elegant courtly imagery of Pinturicchio, who had painted Alexander VI's apartments and undertaken many commissions for cardinals, including Giuliano della Rovere. As Pope, Julius II clearly wanted something innovative and he got it. Michelangelo's interpretation of the events of the Creation differed markedly from tradition. The *Creation of Adam* (fig. 79) showed the dramatic moment just before God endowed the lethargic figure of Adam with life. God himself was depicted moving in an unprecedentedly forceful and energetic manner through the scenes of his creation of the world.

79. Michelangelo, *Creation of Adam*. Ceiling, Sistine Chapel, Vatican, 1508–12

For the decoration of his private apartments in the Vatican, Julius II commissioned a team of artists led by Raphael. Born in Urbino, Raphael had made a name for himself painting altarpieces and portraits for Florentine merchants (see Chapter 6). His commissions for the Pope included a portrait of Julius II as a tired old man at the end of his life, worn out by the labours of his pontificate.[50] His frescos in the papal audience chamber (Stanza d'Eliodoro), the library (Stanza della Segnatura) and the hall of the papal tribunal (Stanza della 'Incendio) established him as one of the leading exponents of the High Renaissance.[51] A contemporary biographer of Raphael, Paolo Giovio, reported that it was Julius II who drew up the scheme for the decoration of these rooms.[52] It was manifestly designed to promote the power of the Christian Church together with the spiritual and temporal authority of the Pope as its supreme leader. Only partly complete when Julius II died, the rooms were completed by his successor, Leo X (1513–21), who appeared in some of the later scenes. Julius II himself was prominent in the rooms. He was depicted as the Pope in the scene of *Pope Gregory IX handing the Decretals to St Raymund* in the Stanza della Segnatura and he appeared twice in the Stanza d'Eliodoro: as a witness to a Eucharistic miracle (see below) in the *Miracle of the Mass at Bolsena*, and again as a witness to the *Expulsion of Heliodorus*, a scene from Maccabees II chosen to justify the Church's right to temporal possessions.[53] And the della Rovere coat of arms could be seen conspicuously throughout the apartments.

Raphael's frescos for Julius II's library, the Stanza della Segnatura (c. 1509–12), followed the medieval custom of decorating libraries with images of famous men of learning.[54] But this was no ordinary cycle of individual portraits. In the ceiling were traditional personifications of the four spheres of Christian learning: Theology, Philosophy, Poetry and Jurisprudence. On the four walls below, Raphael introduced the innovative idea of gathering the authorities in each area into a single convincing setting, combining recognizable figures and unidentifiable onlookers into groups of enthusiastic debaters and lone thinkers. The frescos displayed the ideal of intellectual freedom promoted at Julius II's court. In the centre of the *School of Athens* (fig. 80) were the two giants of classical philosophy, Aristotle and Plato, each gesturing to the source of their inspiration. Plato pointed up to his ideal world, while Aristotle's gesture emphasized his reliance on empiric observation. On the left, Pythagoras was shown writing on a slate, recording his theory of musical harmony. On the right, Euclid demonstrated his geometrical theories with a pair of compasses.

Theology was displayed on the opposite wall in a fresco that focused on the Host, the Body of Christ, set on an elaborate altar. The scene showed the dispute over the Eucharist (fig. 81), a theme also shown in the *Miracle of the Mass at Bolsena*, underlining the importance Julius II attached to this

80. Raphael, *School of Athens*. Stanza della Segnatura, Vatican, 1509–12

key issue of Christian belief. In the *Miracle of the Mass at Bolsena*, Raphael depicted a thirteenth-century miracle when blood had seeped out of a communion wafer to reward the prayers of a priest who had doubts about the Eucharist and the miracle of transubstantiation. In the *Dispute over the Eucharist* he showed Christ with the Virgin and St John the Baptist sitting in Heaven with figures from the Old and New Testaments provided the heavenly proof of transubstantiation. Below, mortals debated the issue. Sixtus IV, Julius II's uncle and a supporter of the doctrine of transubstantiation, stood to the right of the altar, a book at his feet. The concept of intellectual freedom embodied in this fresco had important implications for the Reformation. The issue of whether the Eucharist was a miraculous event, transforming bread and wine into Christ's Body and Blood, or simply represented it, was already controversial in the Church and it was destined to divide Europe.

Attitudes to art and artists at the papal court had changed radically since Julius II had been created a cardinal in 1471. When Alfonso d'Este, Duke of Ferrara, visited Rome in 1512, he was taken at his request on a guided tour of Raphael's apartments and Michelangelo's ceiling.[55] In the Sistine Chapel he climbed up the scaffolding, to where Michelangelo was working. He spent a long time up there looking at the painter's work and offered him

81. Raphael, *Dispute over the Eucharist*. Stanza della Segnatura, Vatican, 1509-12

a commission for a picture which unfortunately the letter does not describe. But the event epitomizes the growing recognition of the creative skill of an artist and the aesthetic value of his work. The status of the artist had also begun to change. Raphael was appointed a scriptor in the Chancery,[56] a post that carried a level of prestige unavailable to painters of a generation before. Pinturicchio had been rewarded by Alexander VI with grants of land.[57] In his description of Rome (1510), Albertini recorded the contribution of Popes and cardinals to the transformation of the city, but he attributed creative responsibility for the paintings they commissioned to their artists.[58]

Like Ludovico Sforza, Francesco Gonzaga and Isabella d'Este, Julius II recognized not only the importance of artists in the fabrication of a successful image for their patrons but also the creative contribution they could make to it. As in Milan, Bramante was not employed as the foreman of Julius II's architectural projects. His role involved the administration and quality control undertaken by Francesco del Borgo for Pius II and Paul II.[59] But it also involved design. Bramante was trained as a painter, and it is significant that it was painters who now took the lead in the design of projects that gave visual expression to the image a patron wished to present.

82.   Bramante, Palazzo Caprini (Casa di Raffaello), c. 1510

When Bramante died in 1514, his post at St Peter's was inherited by Raphael.[60] Michelangelo's long career made him a major figure in sixteenth-century architecture, sculpture and painting, working for Julius II's successors in Rome and the Medici in Florence. He was clearly a very difficult personality. Much of what we know about his work for Julius II comes from his letters, which complain endlessly about money owed to him. The new programme for the Sistine Chapel ceiling, which involved much more work than the first scheme, was not formalized in a contract and he had a protracted argument with the papal treasurers about payment.[61] Looking back in 1542 on his work for Julius II, he blamed the difficulties he had with his patron on the jealousy of Bramante and Raphael, who, he claimed, wanted to ruin him.[62]

Julius II's forceful example was followed by members of his court, who commissioned palaces, villas and chapels, altarpieces, fresco cycles and portraits, proclaiming their own prestige in Rome in the new style sanctioned by the Pope. Bramante and Raphael were much in demand. Caprini, an apostololic protonotary, commissioned Bramante to design his palace (fig. 82), and its use of Doric columns with a frieze of metopes and triglyphs made an obvious reference to Julius II's projects at St Peter's and the Vatican Palace.[63] Its classical formula, its rusticated basement, the use of the orders and pedimented windows with balustrades, set a pattern for the style of a grand town house that was to be imitated down the centuries

83. Raphael, *Madonna di Foligno*. Vatican, Pinacoteca, *c.* 1512

84.   Peruzzi, Sala delle Prospettive, Villa Farnesina, Rome, 1516–17

in places as far afield as London, St Petersburg and Washington. Sigismondo de' Conti, whose career in the Curia had taken off under Sixtus IV and who was a prominent figure at Julius II's court, took over patronage of the high altar in the Franciscan church of Santa Maria in Aracoeli and commissioned Raphael to paint its altarpiece, the *Madonna di Foligno* (fig. 83).[64] This votive image showed its patron being offered to the Virgin by St Jerome, with St Francis and St John the Baptist. Raphael's skill as a portrait painter earned him commissions from numerous patrons in Rome, including Cardinal Tommaso Inghirami and the humanist ambassador from Urbino, Baldassare Castiglione.[65]

One of the outstanding patrons of Julius II's court was Agostino Chigi, the enormously wealthy Sienese papal banker. He commissioned Raphael to paint a series of Sibyls and Prophets for his chapel in Santa Maria della Pace (*c*. 1512–13).[66] He took over patronage of Cardinal Mellini's chapel in Santa Maria del Popolo in 1507 and commissioned Raphael to design costly marble and mosaic decoration which was finished after his death.[67] Chigi's principal project was the Villa Farnesina.[68] Inspired by the vision of rich Roman patricians with their elegantly decorated villas filled with beautiful and valuable objects, so evocatively described in the literature of antiquity, Chigi built his own villa on the banks of the Tiber, between the Vatican and the Ponte Sisto. The Villa Farnesina was designed by Peruzzi, a Sienese painter, in a conspicuously classical style and frescoed by Raphael, Sebastiano del Piombo and Peruzzi. Peruzzi's frescos for the Sala delle Prospettive upstairs combined real and fake architecture to create the impressive effect of an open-ended loggia with views between massive Doric columns out over a landscape (fig. 84). Fictive architectural details suggested a rich variety of expensive marble. Downstairs, in a real open loggia designed to provide a magnificent setting for *al fresco* banquets, Raphael's painting of *Galatea* (*c.* 1512) showed the nymph driving a conch-shell chariot pulled by dolphins.[69] Expensive and overtly classical in both style and decoration, the Villa Farnesina testified to Chigi's desire to be associated with the image of the powerful and cultured patricians of ancient Rome.

Julius II had achieved much in the ten years of his pontificate. In his funeral oration on the death of the Pope, Inghirami contrasted Rome as it had been in 1503 with the city in 1513.[70] Julius II had inherited a rebellious, divided Italy and had reasserted control in the papal states and expanded his temporal authority in Italy. He had found the papal coffers empty and left them full. Above all, Inghirami stressed the concept of a Golden Age under Julius II and his impact on the appearance of Rome. He attributed its renewal to the projects of the Pope, and his uncle, and, for once, the Renaissance *topos* of praising a patron for the transformation of a shabby city into a magnificent centre held more than a grain of truth.

Notes

These footnotes are designed to be of service to the student and general reader, rather than an exclusively academic audience. Many refer to archival documentation and, instead of giving the archival source, I have, except in rare cases, aimed to give references to other texts where the material is published.

Introduction

1. Bullard, *passim*.
2. Gombrich 1960, 280–1.
3. Baxandall 1971, 1–2.
4. Onians 1988, Chs. 8 & 14.
5. Jacopa di Palla Strozzi's dowry was 1,200 florins (Kent 1981, 17), her sister Lena's was 991 florins (Molho 1977, 75).
6. Martines 1979, 312.
7. Martines 1979, Ch. 13.
8. Alberti, prologue, 5.
9. G Manetti, 949–50; Westfall 1974, 33.
10. Burns 1975, 113.
11. Hale 1981, 24.
12. Filangieri 1937, 68.
13. Ibid., 19.
14. Ryder, 216–17.
15. Ibid., 70, 210; on castle see Filangieri 1937, 23–4.
16. Tuohy, 64 n130, 98–9, 124.
17. Jenkins 1970, 163.
18. Hope 1990, 538.
19. Hollingsworth 1984, *passim*.
20. Baxandall 1972, *passim*.
21. Kemp 1977, *passim*.

Chapter 1: Florence: A New Century

1. Bruni, 238–9.
2. Fanelli, 70–1.
3. On Florentine galleys, see Mallett 1967.
4. N Rubinstein 1968, 449.
5. Baron 1966, *passim*.
6. Baron 1966, 61–3.
7. N Rubinstein 1968, *passim*.
8. N Rubinstein 1987, 29–32.
9. Pius II, 103.

Chapter 2: Civic Pride and Guild Prestige

1. Wackernagel, 212.
2. Ibid., Ch. 5; Goldthwaite 1980, 9–11.
3. Brucker 1971, 17; on exchange rates between the lira and the florin, see Goldthwaite 1980, Appendix 1, 429–30; see also Roover 1963, 31–4.
4. Brucker 1971, 90.
5. Battisti 1981, 334 (before 20 August 1434).
6. Roover 1967, 12 n40.
7. Brucker 1971, 90–2.
8. Brucker 1969, 63.
9. Goldthwaite 1980, 208.
10. For examples, see Wackernagel, 213.
11. Hollingsworth 1984, 390–2.
12. See documents in Krautheimer 1982.
13. Hollingsworth 1982, Ch. 12 & Appendix III, table 1.
14. Janson, 12–13 (19 December 1408).
15. Ibid., 13 (8 October 1415).
16. Ibid., 17 (3 April 1411).
17. Krautheimer 1982, 368–9 (doc. 26); Janson, 17 (15 February 1409).
18. Ghiberti, 42.
19. Krautheimer 1982, 46.
20. Ibid., 370 (doc. 36).
21. Ibid., 372–3 (doc. 52).
22. Ibid., Digest 57, 109, 286, 302.
23. Ibid., Digest 157.
24. Ibid., Digest 292.
25. On Orsanmichele, see Zervas 1987, 101–9.
26. Ibid., 107.
27. Ibid., 102–3.
28. Ibid., 108.
29. Janson, 17 (24 April 1411).
30. Doren, *passim*.
31. Janson, 18.
32. Krautheimer 1982, 385–6 (doc. 107).
33. Onians 1982, *passim*.
34. Research on the Florentine Duomo is extensive. Original archival documentation is published in Guasti 1857, Guasti 1887 and Poggi 1909a. Useful studies include Saalman 1980 and Haines.
35. Haines, 92–3.
36. Ibid., 93.
37. Saalman 1964, *passim*.
38. Guasti 1887, 199–205.
39. Saalman 1959, *passim*.
40. Hollingsworth 1984, 399–401.
41. C Smith, 301.
42. Haines, 123.
43. Seymour 1966, 24–7.
44. Janson, 12–13 (19 December 1408).
45. Seymour 1966, 31–5.
46. Janson, 33–5.
47. See entries in Krautheimer 1982, Digest.
48. Janson, 119–21.
49. Krautheimer 1982, 412, Digest 166.
50. Haines, 123–4.

Chapter 3: Merchants and Morality

1. On the structure of Florentine society, see D Kent 1978, D & FW Kent 1982.
2. For details of 1403 *prestanze* and 1427 *catasto*, see Martines 1963, Appendix II, 351–78.

3. Goldthwaite 1980, Appendices I & III.
4. Krautheimer 1982, 376-7 (doc. 81); translation in Brucker 1971, 10-12.
5. On Strozzi's finances, see Molho 1971, 157-60.
6. Bruni, *Commentary on pseudo-Aristotle's Economics*; quoted in Baron 1988, I, 230 n10.
7. On attitudes to wealth in early fifteenth-century Florence, see Baron 1988, I, Chs. 7, 8 and 9; Roover 1967; Jenkins.
8. See note 6.
9. Roover 1967, 14-15.
10. Origo, 280-1.
11. Brucker 1969, 210.
12. Krautheimer 1982, 106, 161.
13. See entries in Doren; Cosimo and Lorenzo were both assessed at 6 florins in the 1422 levy and 20 florins in the 1423 levy.
14. Fra Giovanni Dominici, *Regola del governo di cura famigliare*; quoted in Jenkins, 163.
15. Preyer 1983, 396; on fifteenth-century palace building, see Goldthwaite 1972; Sinding-Larsen 1975; Rubinstein 1980; Preyer 1983; FW Kent 1987.
16. Preyer 1983, 392-3 & fig. 12.
17. On building and furnishing an early fifteenth-century palace, see Origo, 225-44.
18. Ibid., 233.
19. Saalman & Mattox, 336-7.
20. Origo, 239.
21. Ibid., 276-7.
22. Preyer 1983, 387 n4; Wackernagel, 114 n2, 221.
23. Gaston, 122.
24. Borsook, 158, 170.
25. Wackernagel, 338 n1; Borsook, 163.
26. Wackernagel, 340.
27. Krautheimer 1982, 385 (docs. 105, 106); Wackernagel, 338 n1.
28. Baxandall 1972, 11.
29. *Is(te) perfecit opus*; see Gombrich 1960, 287.
30. On Palla Strozzi, see Gregory 1987, 208-14.
31. Inventory in Fiocco, 289-310; there is no evidence of Palla setting up a public library at Santa Trinità (Gregory 1987, 215-17).
32. Gregory 1987, 213.
33. On Strozzi's expenses, see Molho 1971, 157-60; also Molho 1977, 75; FW Kent 1981, 17; Gregory 1987, 214.
34. D Kent 1978, 143.
35. Goldthwaite 1980, 91.
36. The Bartolini family chapel, dedicated to the Annunciation, was decorated with frescos of the life of the Virgin and an altarpiece of the Annunciation by Lorenzo Monaco (Wackernagel, 113). Cante di Giovanni Compagni, a banker who was closely involved with his guild's commission of Ghiberti's *St Matthew* for Orsanmichele (Doren), had his chapel frescoed with scenes of the Vallombrosan St Giovanni Gualbertus (Wackernagel, 114 n2).
37. Davisson, 315-17.
38. Ibid., 327.
39. Middledorf, 76.
40. Krautheimer 1982, 261 n16. A debt of 64 lire 16 soldi, that Ghiberti owed to the Strozzi bank, was cancelled by Palla in 1426 in return for unspecified designs and other services rendered by Ghiberti to Palla (Sale 1978, 356).
41. Another altarpiece, Fra Angelico's *Deposition*, has also been associated with Strozzi's sacristy (Davisson), though not entirely convincingly (Gregory 1987, 217-18).
42. Davisson, 324 & n76.
43. Brucker 1969, 250; Gentile da Fabriano was given a part payment of 150 florins in July 1423 (Christiansen, 162-4).
44. . . . *la capella nostra nuovamente per Nofri mio padre ordinata e facti e fondamenti e per me messa ad executione e compiuta come lasciò per suo testamento et ultima volontà* (quoted in Gregory 1987, 218).
45. D Kent 1978, 37-9.
46. On the Medici Bank, see Roover 1963; Holmes.

47. Martines 1963, Appendix II, 356, 369.
48. D Kent 1978, Ch. 1.
49. Ibid., 40-3.
50. Molho 1979, 27 n52; see also Battisti 1981, 367 (doc. 8).
51. Molho 1979, 27 n51.
52. D Kent 1978, 70-1.
53. Reference to the sacristy and two chapels, all started by Giovanni di Bicci, in document of 13 August 1442 (Battisti 1981, 368-9, doc. 16).
54. Hyman 1979, 199.
55. Burns 1971, 279.
56. Martines 1963, Appendix II, table 8; Molho 1977, 75.
57. On Brancacci's career, see Molho 1977, 74-9.
58. Molho 1977, 83-5; by the time Filippino Lippi was involved (1480s), the chapel had been acquired by a lay confraternity, who paid for its completion (Molho 1977, 83). On Masaccio and the Brancacci chapel, see Beck.
59. The following analysis of the chapel follows Molho 1977, 59-70; for further information on the Carmelites, see C Gilbert 1990.
60. Molho 1977, 52-3.
61. Ibid.
62. Onians 1982, *passim*.
63. On the emergence of the new style, see Baxandall 1972; Burke; Kemp 1978.
64. Alberti, *de pictura*, II, 49; see also Baxandall 1972, 1-27.

Chapter 4: Cosimo de' Medici

1. The best account of the coup is D Kent 1978, Ch. 5; on Cosimo de' Medici, see also Molho 1979.
2. Ibid., 305; see also Roover 1963.
3. Roover 1963, 55 (table 11), 69 (table 17).
4. Ibid., Appendix, 377-9.
5. D Kent 1978, 79-80.
6. Saalman & Mattox, Appendix 9, 344-5.
7. Roover 1963, 70-1; Molho 1979, 30-1.
8. See entries in Doren.
9. On Cosimo's patronage, see Wackernagel; Gombrich 1960; Jenkins.
10. Saalman 1966a, 242-50.
11. Fabriczy 1892, 266-85.
12. Vespasiano, 221-2.
13. Zervas 1988, 467.
14. Wackernagel, 233.
15. Krautheimer 1982, 138-9, 146-8.
16. Wackernagel, 233-4.
17. Text quoted in Gombrich 1960, 284-5.
18. Jenkins, 164.
19. For a general account, see Wackernagel, 231.
20. P F Brown 1981 (the Union subsequently failed).
21. Ibid., 177.
22. Battisti 1981, 173; see also Hyman 1975, 106.
23. Saalman 1978, 361.
24. Battisti 1981, 368 (doc. 15); see also Hyman 1977; Molho 1979, 27 n53.
25. Battisti 1981, 368-9 (doc. 16); see also Hyman 1975.
26. Teubner, 244.
27. Ibid.
28. N Rubinstein 1990, 65.
29. Ibid., 66-7.
30. On S. Marco Library, see Ullman & Stadter.
31. Teubner, 249; Wackernagel, 88-9, 229-30.
32. Onians 1988, 141.
33. Hood 1986, *passim*; Hood 1990, *passim*.
34. Teubner, 246.

35. Ibid., 249; see also Hatfield 1970a, 136.
36. Ibid., 248-9, figs. 9 & 10.
37. Hood 1990, 112.
38. Saalman-Mattox 1985, 331.
39. D & FW Kent 1979, *passim*.
40. Saalman & Mattox, 334.
41. On the Palazzo Medici, see Hyman 1975; Preyer 1990; Elam 1990.
42. Trachtenberg, 568.
43. Hatfield 1970b, 232.
44. Ibid., 232-3.
45. Filarete, f189r.
46. Ibid., f188v.
47. Gombrich 1960, 296; text in Gombrich 1962, Appendix, 223-9.
48. See Gombrich 1960, 296; Preyer 1991, 64-5.
49. Florence, Biblioteca Nazionale, MS Magl VII 1121, *Terze rime in lode Cosimo de' Medici* (1458) f20v; see also Hatfield 1970b.
50. Gombrich 1960, 294-6.
51. Filarete, f188r.
52. Ibid., 189r.
53. Pius II, 101.
54. Rubinstein 1990, 66.
55. Jenkins *passim*.

Chapter 5: For God, Their City and Themselves

1. N Rubinstein 1966, *passim*.
2. Hollingsworth 1982, 106 & Appendix I.
3. Trachtenberg, 568-77.
4. N Rubinstein 1987, 36-8.
5. On the fifteenth-century building boom in Florence, see Goldthwaite 1972; Goldthwaite 1980, 16-22; Fanelli, Ch. 6.
6. Letter quoted in Phillips, 43.
7. Vespasiano, 220-1.
8. Rucellai, 121: *Tutte le sopra dette chose m'ànno dato e danno grandissimo chontentamento e grandissima dolcezza, perchè raghuardano in parte all'onore di Dio e all'onore della città e a memoria di me.*
9. A Manetti, 34.
10. This theme was extensively elaborated in sixteenth-century Florence; see Gombrich 1961; N Rubinstein 1984; Bullard.
11. FW Kent 1987, 52-3.
12. Mack 1983, 261-4.
13. Preyer 1983, 398-400.
14. Goldthwaite 1972, 992-5.
15. Preyer 1983, 398.
16. Goldthwaite 1973, 189-90.
17. Preyer 1981, 156-9.
18. Goldthwaite 1972, 993.
19. FW Kent 1987, *passim*.
20. FW Kent 1977, *passim*.
21. Rucellai, f83v; FW Kent 1981, 13.
22. FW Kent 1987, 46-7.
23. Preyer 1983, 399-400.
24. Phillips, 52.
25. Saalman 1966b, 162; see also Mack 1983, 272.
26. On the Palazzo Scala (late 1470s), see Pellecchia; Parronchi.
27. On the Palazzo Rucellai, see Mack 1974; Preyer 1981.
28. Preyer 1981, 185.
29. The general opinion amongst art historians is that the Pope copied Rucellai but the issue is controversial. Two theories have emerged: firstly, that the five right-hand bays of the façade were begun before the property purchase of 1458, and before Pius II started his

palace at Pienza, after which the façade was extended by three bays to the right (Preyer 1981, 161); secondly, that the whole façade was begun after 1461, so after Pius II began building (Mack 1974).

30. Rucellai, 120–2.
31. FW Kent 1981, 33, 34 n6; Roover 1963, 31.
32. Goldthwaite 1968, 61 (table 5); Goldthwaite 1973, 103.
33. FW Kent 1981, 66.
34. Ibid., 67.
35. On Strozzi's career see Goldthwaite 1968; Goldthwaite 1973, 100–5.
36. For a general account of Rucellai's patronage, see FW Kent 1981.
37. For a general account of Strozzi's patronage, see Goldthwaite 1973, 105–11.
38. FW Kent 1981, 55; Preyer 1981, 203.
39. Mack 1983, *passim*.
40. Preyer 1983, 398.
41. Preyer 1981, 156–61 & plate 5.
42. Goldthwaite 1973, *passim*.
43. Hollingsworth 1984, *passim*.
44. Goldthwaite 1973, 126 & Appendix III.
45. On Cronaca's role, see Goldthwaite 1973, 123–7; see also Hollingsworth 1982, 143–4.
46. Goldthwaite 1973, 122–35 & Appendix I.
47. Rucellai, 60–1.
48. Ibid., 23–4.
49. For a general introduction to classical attitudes to art and architecture, see entries in Pollitt.
50. Baxandall 1972, 115–53; C Gilbert 1980, 185–6.
51. Wackernagel, 262 n23.
52. W Smith, 37–8, Appendix I.
53. Lavin, *passim*.
54. W Smith, *passim*; Lightbown 1989, 120–52.
55. See, for example, Gombrich 1972.
56. Hatfield 1970a, *passim*.
57. Donatello's *David* has long been the focus of energetic and, at times, pedantic, debate amongst art historians, who have disputed the date of the statue, its site, its iconography, and even questioned its subject. For a general outline of research to date, and a lucid account of the statue, see Ames-Lewis 1979 & 1989. More recent research provides convincing evidence that the statue should be dated *c.* 1428–30, that its subject is indeed David and that an inscription, now lost, referred specifically to freedom from foreign oppression (Sperling 1992, *passim*).
58. Ames-Lewis 1979, 141–2.
59. Ettlinger 1978, 164–5 (cat. 44).
60. Müntz 1888; see also Chambers 1970a, 106–11; Wackernagel, 163–8, 253–8.
61. Haskell & Penny, 93.
62. Hatfield 1970a, 136–7.
63. Müntz 1888; see also Wackernagel, 166; Weiss, 188–90.
64. Alberti, V, 15–17.
65. On the myth of the Florentine Academy, see Hankins.
66. Lillie 1984, 90.
67. FW Kent 1981, 81.
68. FW Kent 1979, *passim*.
69. Martelli, 107.
70. Gombrich 1960, 307.
71. Wackernagel, 268–9.
72. Bridgeman, *passim*.
73. Battisti 1981, 222–9, 371–3.
74. Wackernagel, 212.
75. Saalman 1966a, 249; on Salviati and the Medici party, see D Kent 1978.
76. Mack 1983, 262–4; see also Saalman 1966b, 160 n39.
77. Hyman 1975, 101.
78. Ibid.
79. Gaston, 124–5.

80. Wackernagel, 239, 251.
81. Wazbinski, 534-6.
82. On SS. Annunziata, see B L Brown 1978; B L Brown 1981; Zervas 1988.
83. Zervas 1988, 467; B L Brown 1981, 63-4.
84. B L Brown 1981, 63-4.
85. Zervas 1988, 468.
86. Goldthwaite 1980, 283; on the Pucci family's allegiance to the Medici party, see D Kent 1978.
87. Davies, 443-6.
88. Zervas 1988, 468.
89. Gombrich 1960, 299.
90. Fra Domenico Corella, *Theotokon*; excerpts translated in C Gilbert 1980, 149-52.
91. Borsook, 152.
92. Wackernagel, 39; Krautheimer 1982, 256.
93. FW Kent 1981, 41.
94. On Guasparre della Lama, see Hatfield 1976, Ch. 1.
95. Ibid., Ch. 3.
96. FW Kent 1981, 62-5.
97. Wackernagel, 48.
98. On the Strozzi chapel, see Friedman, *passim*.
99. The contract is published in Scharf, 88 (doc. VIII).
100. Roover 1963, 218-24.
101. Simons, 221-6.
102. Ibid., 234.
103. Ibid., 232-3.
104. Ibid., 237; contract translated in Chambers 1970a, 173.
105. Simons, 239.
106. Roover 1963, Ch. 14.
107. On this issue, see papers by FW Kent, Alison Brown, Frank d'Accone, Nerida Newbiggin, Alison Wright, Amanda Lillie, William Connell and Melissa Bullard to be published in *Lorenzo il Magnifico e il suo mondo* (Acts of Conference at Villa I Tatti 1992).
108. The best general overview of Lorenzo's patronage is Gombrich 1960, 304-11; see also Borgo & Sievers; Elam 1978; Foster 1978; FW Kent 1979; FW Kent 1982; see also note 107 above.
109. A Brown, *passim*.
110. Rubinstein 1990, 72; FW Kent 1982.
111. On the via Laura project, see Elam 1978, *passim*.
112. Ibid., 54-8; see also Caroline Elam at note 108 above.
113. See note 40 above.
114. Foster 1981, *passim*.
115. Hollingsworth 1984, 403.
116. Foster 1971, *passim*.
117. Hollingsworth 1984, 403.
118. Sources and further examples cited in Gombrich 1960, 306-7; Wackernagel, 261 n21; Fabriczy 1903, 171; Hollingsworth 1984, 403.
119. Foster 1971, 238-9.
120. . . . *uno modello affatto ffare Lorenzo di piero di chosimo a giuliano da sanghallo che si seghuiti quello e quel più o meno che paressi a detto Lorenzo*; quoted in Fabriczy 1902, 30 (14 August 1489); see also Hollingsworth 1984, 404. On Lorenzo as a designer, see Martelli; FW Kent 1982.
121. On this issue, see Gombrich 1961; N Rubinstein 1984; Bullard.
122. Foster 1978, 221-2.

Chapter 6: Propaganda for the New Republic

1. For detailed account of the establishment of the new government and Savonarola's role in its formation, see N Rubinstein 1960.
2. N Rubinstein 1979, 110.
3. N Rubinstein 1960, 163-4.

4. Wilde 1944, 78.
5. N Rubinstein 1984, 95–6.
6. Landucci, 114 (11 August 1495); translated C Gilbert 1980, 217.
7. Borgo & Sievers, 238–9.
8. Frey, 114–15.
9. Wilde 1944, 76 (documents in Frey, 106, 114–18).
10. See documents in Frey.
11. Wilde 1944, *passim* (documents in Frey).
12. On Savonarola and the Palazzo della Signoria, see Steinberg, 95–100.
13. Steinberg 1977, 95.
14. Wilde 1944, 73–4 (documents in Frey, 120–1, 125–6).
15. Goldthwaite 1973, 176–9 & table 3.
16. Hollingsworth 1982, 257, Appendix III, table 3.
17. Goldthwaite 1980, 327, 443.
18. N Rubinstein 1990, 75; Brucker 1990, 44.
19. Garin, *passim*.
20. N Rubinstein 1960, 165–6.
21. Ibid., 168–9.
22. Friedman, 122–3.
23. On Savonarola's attitudes to art, see Weinstein 1970; Steinberg; Friedman; Hall.
24. Goldthwaite 1980, 87.
25. Davies, 103–8; Weinstein 1968.
26. Zervas 1987, 104–5.
27. Steinberg, 139 n97.
28. FW Kent 1983, *passim*.
29. Friedman, 123–6.
30. Ibid.
31. Wilde 1944, 77–8 (documents in Poggi 1909b, 145–6).
32. Ibid., 78–81.
33. On Michelangelo's *David*, see Seymour 1967 for background and archival documentation.
34. Hall, 509.
35. Seymour 1967 & Levine give two, slightly different, accounts of the meeting.
36. Landucci, 268.
37. Hall, 510.
38. Ibid.
39. Jones & Penny, Ch. 2.
40. Rubinstein 1984, *passim*.

Chapter 7: Venice: Heir of Byzantium

1. On Venice's maritime empire and trade, see Lane.
2. Harrison, 100.
3. Muir 1979, 35–6.
4. Goffen 1986a, Ch. 5.
5. On Byzantine architecture in Venice, see Howard 1980, Ch. 2.
6. P F Brown 1988, 166–8.
7. On the structure of Venetian society, see Chambers 1970b, 74–86; Logan, Ch. 2.
8. Howard 1980, 68; Cracco, 80.
9. Muir 1978, 152–5.
10. Chambers 1970b, 86–93.
11. On religion in Venice, see F Gilbert 1979; Prodi; Logan, 30–3.
12. Howard 1980, 79–80.
13. Ibid., 79–85.
14. On Venetian humanists, see F Gilbert 1979; King.
15. Baron 1988, I, 123–4.

Chapter 8: The Image of the State

1. Burns 1975, 113.
2. A M Schulz, 127.

3. Muraro, 268.
4. A M Schulz, 129.
5. Spencer, 5 n21.
6. Connell, 181.
7. Paoletti 1893, I, 3–4.
8. Ibid., I, 37; contract translated in Chambers 1970a, 66–9.
9. Pincus, 108–9.
10. Paoletti 1893, I, 3–4.
11. Howard 1980, 83.
12. P F Brown 1988, 261–5.
13. Ibid., 37–42.
14. Ibid., 259–60.
15. Pincus, 36; see also Howard 1980, 80–1.
16. A M Schulz, 114.
17. On the image of the Lion of St Mark, see Pincus, Appendix I, 384–401.
18. P F Brown 1988, 11.
19. Muir 1979, 22 n13.
20. F Gilbert 1979, *passim*; King, *passim*.
21. On the Mascoli Chapel, see Muraro; P F Brown 1988, 106–20.
22. Muraro, 270–3.
23. Howard 1980, 104–6.
24. On the building history and imagery of the Arco Foscari, see Pincus.
25. Howard 1980, 108.
26. P F Brown 1988, 273 (doc. XIII,1a).
27. Ibid., 54.
28. Ibid., 275 (doc. XIII,11).
29. Ibid., 274 (doc. XIII,10).
30. Ibid., 273 (doc. XIII,1a) and glossary.
31. Ibid., 276 (doc. XIII,24).
32. Ibid., 273 (doc. XIII,2).
33. Ibid., Chs. 6, 7 & 8.
34. P F Brown 1984, *passim*; see also P F Brown 1988, 79–82.
35. P F Brown 1988, 26–7.
36. Pincus, 390.
37. Ibid., 393–401.
38. Muir 1978, 154.
39. Ibid., 147.
40. Muir 1979, 27; on the staircase, see Howard 1980, 110.
41. Muir 1978, 148–51.
42. Norwich, 79–81.
43. A M Schulz, 128.
44. Ibid., 128–35.
45. Lieberman 1972, 113.
46. Muir 1979, 27.
47. F Gilbert 1980, 27–30.

Chapter 9: The *Scuole*

1. On the *scuole*, see above all, Pullan 1971.
2. On the *scuole* as patrons, see Humfrey & MacKenney; Humfrey 1988.
3. Humfrey & MacKenney, 318.
4. On the *Scuole Grandi*, see Pullan 1971.
5. Pullan 1971, Ch. 2.
6. P F Brown 1988, 22–3.
7. Humfrey & MacKenney, 318.
8. P F Brown 1988, 279–80 (doc. XIV,1).
9. Humfrey 1988, 410.
10. P F Brown 1988, 288.
11. Pullan 1990, 277.
12. For example, Giovanni Bellini's altarpiece for the Scuola di San Giobbe, with Saints

Francis, John the Baptist, Job, Dominic, Sebastian and Louis of Toulouse; see also Humfrey 1988, 410.
13. Humfrey & MacKenney, 325.
14. Howard 1980, 101.
15. Humfrey 1988, 408–9; St Bonaventura was canonized in 1482.
16. Ibid., 407.
17. Pincus, 136–8.
18. P F Brown 1988, 290 (doc. XVIII,1).
19. Humfrey 1991, *passim*.
20. Goffen 1986a, 42–3.
21. For details of Carpaccio's *scuole* commissions, see P F Brown 1988, catalogue XIV, XV, XVII, XVIII, XXII.
22. For a discussion of Carpaccio's style, see ibid., 156–64 & 209–16.
23. Ibid., 210.
24. Ibid., Chs. 8 & 12.
25. Ibid., 293 (doc. XIX, 2b).
26. Ibid., 281.
27. Ibid., 279–80 (doc. XIV,1).
28. Ibid., 57–9.
29. Ibid., 69–70.
30. Ibid., 288.
31. Ibid., 266.
32. Ibid., 268.
33. Sohm 1978, 136.
34. P F Brown 1988, 266.
35. Ibid., 266 (doc. VII,1).
36. Ibid., 267.
37. Ibid., 266–8.
38. Ibid., 268 (docs. VIII, 1–2).
39. Ibid., 269 (doc. X, 1).
40. Ibid., 269–70.
41. Ibid., 291–2; Sohm 1981, 96.
42. Sohm 1978, *passim*.
43. Ibid., 128.
44. Paoletti 1929, 26–8; Sohm 1981, 118–21.
45. Sohm 1978, 132.
46. Ibid.
47. P F Brown 1988, 283 (docs. XV, 2–4).
48. Ibid., 283 (doc. XV, 5).
49. Sohm 1978, 137–9.
50. Ibid., 141.
51. P F Brown 1988, 283 (doc. XV, 6a).
52. Ibid., 140.
53. The following discussion of the miracles is based on ibid., 139–64.
54. Ibid., 285.
55. Ibid., Ch. 12.
56. Ibid., 285.
57. Ibid., 292 (doc. XIX, 1); translation in Chambers 1970a, 56–7.
58. Ibid., 67.
59. Sohm 1981, Appendix, 240–6.
60. P F Brown 1988, 293 (doc. XIX, 2a & 2b).
61. Dempsey; and see P F Brown 1988, 209.

Chapter 10: Piety and Patriotism

1. Paoletti 1893, I, 110 (doc. 89, 11 July 1438).
2. Goffen 1986a, 35–6.
3. Paoletti 1893, I, 48 (30 August 1448).
4. McAndrew, 22.
5. Paoletti 1893, I, 110 (doc. 89, 23 April 1495).

6. Howard 1980, 113.
7. *Templum inquam, tuum, quod te auctore mirifice constructum . . .*, see Paoletti 1893, I, 165 (September 1477); for other examples, see Puppi & Puppi (docs. I).
8. Puppi & Puppi, 258 (doc. III.a).
9. McAndrew, *passim*; see also Ackerman 1980.
10. The following discussion of the church is based on Lieberman 1972.
11. On the doctrine of the Immaculate Conception, see Goffen 1986a, 146-54; Goffen 1986b, 228-31; Mayberry.
12. Paoletti 1893, I, 144-5.
13. Ibid., 89 (doc. 5, 9 November & 8 December 1417); see also Goffen 1986, 179 n94.
14. Paoletti 1893, I, 110 (doc. 89, 21 June 1457).
15. Goffen 1989, 316 n87.
16. Ibid., 314 n73.
17. Goffen 1986, Ch. 2.
18. Goffen 1975, *passim*.
19. Janson, 151-61.
20. Seymour 1966, 176-8.
21. Goffen 1986a, 130-1.
22. Pincus, Appendix 2, 402-38; see also Goffen 1986, 87-91.
23. Goffen 1989, 154-5, 311 n52.
24. Howard 1980, 112.
25. C Gilbert 1980, 153-5.
26. On Andrea Vendramin's tomb, see Sheard.
27. F Gilbert 1979, 17-18.
28. Chambers 1970b, 26-8.
29. Onians 1988, 207-15.
30. Goffen 1986a, 64, 200 n113.
31. Paoletti 1893, I, 245 n1 (29 April 1501).
32. Fletcher 1983, 17.
33. Davies, 544-7.
34. Goffen 1986a, 228 n26.
35. Ibid., 116-17.
36. Howard 1980, 85-7.
37. Lane, 160.
38. Paoletti 1893, I, 20-8; Howard 1980, 92-4.
39. Paoletti 1893, I, 20 (18 January 1422 (1423)).
40. Ibid., I, 21 (1425).
41. Howard 1980, 94.
42. On the Ca' del Duca, see Beltrami; Spencer.
43. P F Brown 1988, 64-6 & Appendix, 241-2.
44. Onians 1988, 128.
45. Ibid., 127-8.
46. Davies, 330-4; Chambers 1970b, 27-8.
47. Meiss 1966a, *passim*.
48. Hope 1983, 35.
49. Hope 1983, *passim*.
50. Büttner, *passim*.
51. Howard 1985; Kaplan; but see Hope 1991 for the dangers of reading too much into the painting.
52. Kaplan, 405-7.

Chapter 11: The Italian Courts

1. Corvisieri, *passim*.
2. Tuohy, 29.
3. Ryder, 73-4.
4. Tuohy, 91-2.
5. Signorini, 242.
6. Hatfield 1970b, 237; Pius II, 103-4.
7. On music at the Italian courts, see Fenlon.

Chapter 12: Milan

1. Krautheimer 1983, Ch. 3.
2. On the power struggles in Milan and other city states, see Martines 1979.
3. Baron 1966, 25–42.
4. Mesquita, 136–8.
5. White, 510–12.
6. Welch 1989a, 353–4.
7. Ibid., 359.
8. Inventories published in Pellegrin; see also Krinsky, 45.
9. Parsons, 368–9 & 372.
10. Archival documents on Milan Cathedral published in Annali; on the early history of the building, see Ackerman 1949; White, 517–31.
11. Welch 1989a, 354–5.
12. Jenkins, 166–9.
13. Martines 1979, 190–201.
14. Ianziti 1987, 305.
15. Ibid., 304.
16. Welch 1989b, 371.
17. Mallett 1974, 91.
18. See, for examples, Ilardi 1989, 217–19; Mallett 1974, 124–5.
19. Bernstein, 193 n9; on Portinari, see Roover 1963, 262–3.
20. Roover 1963, 263.
21. Welch 1989a, 352–3.
22. Ianziti 1989, 82–4; see also Ianziti 1988.
23. Ianziti 1989, passim.
24. Ianziti 1987, 308.
25. Ibid., 303–11; see also Ianziti 1988.
26. Parsons, 370–8.
27. Welch 1990, 164–5.
28. Welch 1989a, 362.
29. On S. Sigismondo, see Giordano 1988, 118–19; on the Hieronymites, see Henderson, 235.
30. On S. Maria Incoronata, see Gatti Perer.
31. Giordano, 124–6.
32. Ilardi, 229.
33. Roover 1963, 266 (table 52); on business of Milan branch, see ibid., 264–72.
34. Ibid., 272–3.
35. Annali, II, 114 (11 April 1488), 140 (27 September 1450), 141 (17 January 1451), 142 (6 July 1451).
36. Ibid., II, 145 (24 June 1452), 146 (7 July 1452).
37. Ibid., II, 153 (5 July 1454), 155 (7 January 1455).
38. Ibid., II, 190 (8 March 1459).
39. Ibid., III, 1–2 (12 January 1481).
40. Giordano, 122.
41. On the Ca' del Duca, see Beltrami; Spencer.
42. On Portinari's chapel, see Bernstein.
43. For text and translation, see Filarete; see also Saalman 1959a; Lang; Onians 1988, Ch. 11.
44. Onians 1971, passim.
45. Onians 1988, 165–70.
46. Filarete, f47r.
47. Ibid., ff 7v–8r.
48. Hollingsworth 1984, 396–8.
49. Welch 1989a, 353.
50. Richter, I, 73–4; see also Fenlon.
51. Martines 1979, 311–12; Welch 1990, 168.
52. Welch 1990, 167.
53. Welch 1989a, 357.
54. Weiss, 200.
55. Welch 1989b, 383.
56. Ibid., 378–86.
57. The following discussion is based on Welch 1989a.

58. Welch 1990, *passim*.
59. Ibid., 167.
60. Ibid., 170–81.
61. Ibid., 170.
62. Ibid., 171–2.
63. Ibid., 178.
64. Signorini, 230–1; letters translated in C Gilbert 1980, 130–1.
65. Welch 1989a, 366–7.
66. Welch 1989b, 375–8.
67. Ibid., 380.
68. Mesquita, 143–5.
69. Martines 1979, 312.
70. Ianziti 1989, 81.
71. Ibid., 80.
72. Seymour 1966, 183–4.
73. Schofield 1986, 116–17.
74. Baxandall 1972, 25–7.
75. Richter, I, 383.
76. Davies, 261–81.
77. Lotz 1956, 9–11.
78. Schofield 1988, *passim*.
79. J Schulz, 41 n17.
80. Schofield 1989a, 213.
81. Seymour 1966, 195.
82. Onians 1984, 423–4.
83. Annali, III, 7 (27 June 1481), 14 (19 April 1482).
84. Ibid., III, 16–18 (16 May 1483).
85. Ibid., III, 33 (24 March 1487); see also Vatovec, 415.
86. Relevant documents in Annali, II, 38–44; see also Schofield 1989b, 71.
87. Vatovec, 60–3 (12 August 1487).
88. On genesis of *tiburio* design, see Schofield 1989b; text translated, ibid., 71–6.
89. Ibid., 89–94.
90. On Vigevano, see Schofield 1986; Lotz 1972.
91. Schofield 1986, 102–3.
92. Ibid., 94–7.
93. Ibid., 118–30; see also Lotz 1972.

Chapter 13: Naples

1. Nicolini, 157–75.
2. Ryder, 26.
3. Hersey 1973, 14–16.
4. Woods-Marsden 1990, 14.
5. For letter, see Filangieri 1938, 75–7 (doc. I); see also Filangieri 1937, 51 n2; Woods-Marsden 1990, 15.
6. Woods-Marsden 1990, 18–19.
7. Ryder, 57.
8. Ibid., 56.
9. Ibid., Ch. 3.
10. On humanism in Naples, see Bentley; Baxandall 1964.
11. Bentley, 47–62.
12. Ianziti 1987, 305; Ryder, 223.
13. Ryder, 27–8; Woods-Marsden 1990, 21.
14. Ryder, 70–2, 174.
15. Ibid., 179–80.
16. Filangieri 1938, 83 (doc. VII).
17. Ibid., 30.
18. Filangieri 1937, 10.
19. Ibid., 17.
20. On Pertello de Marino, see ibid., 11, 12 n7; on Sagrera, ibid., 40–1.

21. Ibid., 23–4.
22. Ibid., 12–16.
23. Ibid., 27.
24. Ibid., 24–38; see also Hersey 1973, 16–18.
25. Filangieri 1937, 18–19.
26. Ibid., 44–5.
27. On Arch, see ibid., 52–61; Hersey 1973, *passim*.
28. Filangieri 1937, 52–3.
29. Hersey 1973, 21–4.
30. See note 16 above.
31. For example Fazio & Panormita, excerpts quoted in Filangieri 1937, 6.
32. Woods-Marsden 1990, 13, 15–16.
33. Ibid., 21–5.
34. Filangieri 1937, 65.
35. Ryder, 188.
36. Filangieri 1938, 43.
37. Baxandall 1971, 108–9; see also Filangieri 1938, 43.
38. Baxandall 1971, 106.
39. Filangieri 1937, 11.
40. Ibid., 49–51.
41. Hersey 1973, Ch. 5.
42. On works commissioned by Ferrante I for Castel Nuovo, see Filangieri 1938, 4–9.
43. Ibid., 30–1.
44. Ibid., 7–9.
45. Filangieri 1937, 65–6.
46. Ibid., 56.
47. Hersey 1969, *passim*.
48. Ibid., 22.
49. On La Duchesca, see ibid., 70–5.
50. On Alfonso of Calabria and the arts, see ibid., *passim*.
51. Ibid., 7–11.
52. Ibid., 75–81.
53. Ibid., 72 n76.
54. Ibid., 118–24.
55. Ibid., 11–13, 72 n76; on Pontano, see also Bentley, 127–34.
56. Quoted in Hersey 1969, 23.
57. On Poggioreale, see ibid., 60–70.
58. Ibid., 59.
59. Ibid., 61.
60. Fabriczy 1897, 87–8 (doc. VII); see also Hersey 1969, 60.
61. Fabriczy 1897, 89 (doc. XVI); see also Hersey 1969, 60.
62. . . . *che già mi scrivesti che il Maiano avea tratto del vostro modello*, quoted in Martelli, 109; see also Hollingsworth 1984, 404.
63. . . . *che 'l Magnifico Lorenzo Medici . . . qual de modelli molto in essa era prontissimo, che a me fo noto per uno che con sue mani dispose al suo grandissimo domestico Giuliano da Magliano del degno palazzo detto Dogliuolo a la cità de Napoli* (Pacioli, 123); see also Hollingsworth 1984, 404.
64. On the Naples branch of the Medici bank, see Roover 1963, 257–61.
65. Hersey 1969, 65.
66. Ibid., 71.
67. See payments for salary and expenses in Weller, Appendix, 347–9 (docs. 22–34).
68. Fabriczy 1897, 111 (doc. VII).
69. Hersey 1969, 72.
70. Ibid., 65, 71.
71. Sagrera was paid 12 ducats a month (Filangieri 1937, 19), Fra Guillaume of Paris 400 ducats a year (ibid., 68).
72. Ibid., 68–9.
73. Ibid., 39.
74. Payments to Fra Giocondo in Fabriczy 1879, 103–5; see also Hersey 1969, 74–5.
75. On Francesco di Giorgio in Naples, see Weller; Millon; Dechert.

76. Betts, 4.
77. Weller, 382 (doc. 104).
78. Ibid., 385 (doc. 109).
79. Ibid., 389 (doc. 119).
80. Ibid., 390 (doc. 124); see also Hersey 1969, 91–2.

Chapter 14: Urbino

1. Thomson, 82.
2. For Federigo's military career, see Mallett 1974.
3. Clough 1973, 130.
4. On Federigo's income, see Dennistoun.
5. Clough 1967, 202.
6. Pius II, 142, 183–4.
7. Mallett, 104.
8. Clough 1973, 131.
9. Clough 1966, *passim*.
10. Inventories published in Guasti 1862–3 & Stornaiolo.
11. Seymour 1966, 171.
12. Meiss 1966b, 134.
13. On San Bernardino, see Burns 1970.
14. Vespasiano, 113; see also Meiss 1966b, 134.
15. Schofield 1989, 213.
16. Vespasiano, 113–4.
17. Rotondi, I, 109–10.
18. Vespasiano, 100.
19. Gaye, I, 274–7 (doc. CXVII); Vatovec, 239–40 (20 August 1481).
20. On the building history of the Palazzo Ducale, see Rotondi; Westfall 1978; Heydenreich & Lotz, 71–7.
21. Clough 1978b, 487–91 (document in Appendix 5, 503–4); Clough assumes the tapestries were for the palace in Gubbio but there is no evidence to support this and, moreover, tapestries were portable and often travelled with the court.
22. On the Studiolo, see Cheles 1986, *passim*.
23. Now Urbino, Galleria delle Marche; Clough 1978a, fig. 12a.
24. Now Hampton Court, Royal Collection; Clough 1973, fig. 27.
25. *de prospectiva pingendi* and *de corporibus regularibus*; see Stornaiuolo, xcvii; Guasti 1862–3, 55.
26. Clough 1978a, 11.
27. The altarpiece was there in 1703; see Meiss 1954, 110–5.
28. Ibid., 115–16, 121.
29. Patent published in Rotondi, I, 109–10.
30. Filangieri 1937, 39.
31. Cheles, 33–4.
32. On Francesco di Giorgio's career, see Weller; Millon; Adams 1984; Dechert.
33. Francesco di Giorgio, II, 339.
34. Burns 1981, 31.
35. Weller, 347 (docs. 20, 21), 350 (doc. 37).
36. Popham & Pouncey, 36–7.
37. See introduction to Francesco di Giorgio; Betts.

Chapter 15: Ferrara

1. Tuohy, 22; much of the material cited in this chapter will appear in the forthcoming book, Thomas Tuohy, *Herculean Ferrara: The Patronage of Ercole d'Este, 1471–1505* (1994).
2. Tuohy, 35–6; see also Zevi.
3. Tuohy, 73.
4. Baxandall 1963, 310; see also Weiss, 196.
5. Venturi, 13.

6. Onians 1988, 182.
7. On Decembrio, see Baxandall 1963, 305–9; part of text published ibid., 310–26.
8. Baxandall 1965, 196.
9. Baxandall 1963, 316–17.
10. Ibid., 314–15.
11. Baxandall 1965, 186–8.
12. Baxandall 1963, 324; Weiss, 167 n3.
13. On medals, see Woods-Marsden 1990, 11–12, 25 n2.
14. Tuohy, 87, 127–8.
15. On Borso's buildings, see ibid., 35–7.
16. Ibid., 98–9.
17. Ibid., 123–4; on exchange rates see ibid., Appendix A, 256: 1 ducat = 50 soldi (1450s); 57 soldi (1476); 63 soldi (1480s).
18. On the decoration of d'Este palaces, see ibid., 73–4.
19. Ibid., 59–75.
20. On the Sala dei Mesi, see Lippincott 1990, *passim*.
21. Contract published in Venturi, 13–14.
22. Venturi, 14–15; translated in C Gilbert 1980, 123.
23. Tuohy, 13–14.
24. Venturi, 16–20.
25. Tuohy, 64–5; translated in C Gilbert 1980, 9–10.
26. Tuohy, 64 n130, 124.
27. Ibid., 84.
28. Ibid., 108–9 (20,646 lire 8 soldi).
29. On Ercole's interest in theatre, see ibid., 219–34.
30. Gundersheimer 1972, *passim*.
31. For a general outline see Tuohy, 38–42.
32. Gundersheimer 1972, 62–5.
33. Tuohy, 61, 249.
34. Gundersheimer 1972, 50–79.
35. Tuohy, 43 n39 and Ch. 4.
36. Ibid., 43–4.
37. Zevi, 559–60.
38. Inventory in Bertoni 1903.
39. FW Kent 1977, 317.
40. Tuohy, 47–8.
41. Ibid., 48.
42. Ibid., 45.
43. Zevi, 600–1.
44. Tuohy, 257–63 (Appendix B).
45. Ibid., 240.
46. Ibid., 53–5.
47. Ibid., 71–3, 259.
48. Ibid., 72.
49. Ibid., 60, 68.

Chapter 16: Mantua

1. On Ludovico, see Woods-Marsden 1988, 48–50, 72–80.
2. Ibid., 50–1.
3. Signorini, 247–9.
4. BL Brown 1981, 63–4.
5. The cycle has been convincingly dated to Ludovico (Woods-Marsden 1985); see also Woods-Marsden 1988.
6. On the Tempio Malatestiano, see Heydenreich & Lotz, 30–2; Borsi; Hope 1992.
7. Chambers & Martineau, 109 (cat. 15).
8. Kristeller, 467–72 (docs. 3–9); see also Lightbown 1986, 76–8.
9. On the Camera degli Sposi, see Chambers & Martineau, 118–21 (cat. 29); Signorini; Lightbown, Ch. 6.
10. Signorini, 233–9.

11. Ibid., 246.
12. On Mantegna, see Kristeller; Lightbown 1986.
13. Gaye, I, 377–81 (doc. 183).
14. Elam 1981, 15; Lightbown 1986, 124–8.
15. See documents in Kristeller, 474 (doc. 20), 475 (doc. 22); see also Elam 1981, 16–17; Lightbown 1986, 125–8; C Gilbert 1980, 10–11.
16. Pius II, 109–10.
17. Vatovec, 86 (27 February 1460); see also Burns 1981, 37 n17.
18. Ibid., 119–20 (? October 1470).
19. Ibid., 102–3 (16 March 1473).
20. On S. Sebastiano, see Lamoureux; Chambers & Martineau, 125–6 (cat. 35).
21. On S. Andrea, see Johnson; Chambers & Martineau, 126–7 (cat. 36).
22. Alberti, VI, 2: *Beauty is that reasoned harmony of all the parts within a body, so that nothing may be added, taken away, or altered, but for the worse.*
23. The following account of Ludovico's struggle to acquire Sant'Andrea is based on Chambers 1977, *passim*.
24. Vatovec, 119–20 (? October 1470).
25. Hollingsworth 1993, *passim*.
26. Vatovec, 86 (27 February 1460).
27. Ibid., 97 (11 January 1465).
28. Alberti, prologue.
29. Hollingsworth 1984, 398–406.
30. See correspondence between Ludovico and Fancelli (Vatovec, *passim*).
31. . . . *poi, parlato che habiamo cum vui et dictovi la fantasia nostra et intesa anche la vostra, faremo quanto ve parerà sia meglio*, see Vatovec, 120 (22 October 1470).
32. On Fancelli, see Vatovec, *passim*; Burns 1981, 28–31.
33. Vatovec publishes numerous examples.
34. Ibid., 78, 91 (27 December 1463), 91–2 (26 January 1464).
35. Ibid., 127–8 (22 January 1473), 128–9 (20 February 1473), 129–31 (21 February 1473).
36. Ibid., 291–318 (2 October 1470–20 July 1471).
37. Ibid., 135 (2 August 1475, 2 letters); see also Burns 1981, 30.
38. Ibid., 287 n8.
39. Ibid., 233 (11 July 1480).
40. Ibid., 236–40 (8 May 1481, 29 May 1481, 11 July 1481, 20 August 1481 (2 letters)).
41. Burns 1981, 31.
42. Vatovec, 238–9 (6 August 1481).
43. Chambers & Martineau, 148–9 (cat. 78).
44. Ibid., 147 (cat. 75).
45. Burns 1981, 31–2.
46. Kristeller, 487–8 (doc. 55).
47. Ibid., 489 (doc. 58); see also J Schulz, 39–40.
48. Chambers & Martineau, 151–2 (cats. 85–7).
49. Ibid., 140–1 (cat. 62).
50. Lavin, *passim*.
51. See Chambers & Martineau, 153 (cat. 95).
52. Burns 1981, 32.
53. Kristeller, 490–1 (6 July 1496); translated in C Gilbert 1980, 135–6.
54. Chambers & Martineau, 103.
55. Ibid., 103–4 (cat. 2).
56. On the Triumphs of Caesar, see Martindale 1979; Lightbown, Ch. 6; Hope 1985.
57. Kristeller, 483 (doc. 46).
58. Martindale 1979, 58–74.
59. For a general outline of Isabella d'Este's patronage, see Fletcher 1981.
60. Chambers & Martineau, 152–3 (cat. 92).
61. Ibid., 178–9 (cat. 139).
62. CM Brown, 324.
63. On Isabella's collections, see Chambers & Martineau, 159–79 (cats. 108–40); CM Brown; Fletcher 1981.

64. Mallet, 39; Fletcher 1981, 52.
65. CM Brown, 332-3.
66. Radcliffe, 47; on the *Spinario*, see Haskell & Penny, 308-10.
67. Kristeller, 496 (doc. 76); Chambers & Martineau, 170 (cat. 122).
68. On Isabella's portraits, see Chambers & Martineau, 159-64 (cats. 108-13); Fletcher 1981, 56.
69. Chambers & Martineau, 160 (cat. 109).
70. Ibid., 164-5.
71. Ibid.; see also Fletcher 1981, 52-3.
72. Chambers & Martineau, 173-4 (cats. 127-30).
73. Ibid., 164, 165-6 (cat. 114); see also Lightbown 1986, 444; Fletcher 1981, 52.
74. Canuti, II, 209 (doc. 308), 210 (doc. 312); see also Fletcher 1981, 52.
75. Canuti, II, 210 (doc. 312).
76. Fletcher 1981, 52.
77. Ibid.; on the role of advisers, see Hope 1981; see also Hope 1990.
78. Gaye, II, 71-4 (doc. XXII); translated in Chambers 1970a, 131; see also Hope 1981, 309-10.
79. Canuti, II, 212-13 (doc. 316); translated in Chambers 1970a, 135-8 (doc. 76); see also Hope 1981, 293-4, 307-9.
80. Canuti, II, 224-7 (docs. 348-53).
81. Ibid., 228 (doc. 356).
82. Ibid., 228-32 (docs. 357-65).
83. Ibid., 236 (doc. 376).
84. Kristeller, 486-7 (doc. 52); see also Elam 1981, 15.
85. Ibid.

Chapter 18: The Return of the Papacy

1. Partner 1960, 259.
2. Magnuson 1958, 36-8; on Martin V's patronage, see Urban, Katalog, 263; Wohl 1982, 171-5.
3. Tomei, 34.
4. Davies, 352-61.
5. Vespasiano, 19.
6. The account books for 1436 show an income of 59,160 florins (Partner 1960, 259-60).
7. Ghiberti, 44; translated in C Gilbert 1980, 85.
8. On Eugenius IV's projects, see Urban, Katalog, 263; Wohl 1984, 240.
9. Tomei, 19.
10. On Filarete in Rome, see Seymour 1966, 115-19.
11. Westfall 1974, 74-7.
12. Leviticus 25, 8-17.
13. d'Amico, 121; Stinger 1982, 153-6.
14. Stinger 1982, 154.
15. Ibid.
16. G Manetti, 949-50; Westfall 1974, 33.
17. Westfall 1974, 93-7.
18. On Nicholas V's church projects, see Urban, Katalog, 264-7.
19. Krautheimer 1980, 78; Urban, Katalog, 267.
20. Burroughs 1982a & 1982b, *passim*.
21. Burroughs 1982a, 97-8.
22. Ibid., 96.
23. Westfall 1974, 38-43.
24. On Nicholas V's Borgo project, see Magnuson 1954; Westfall 1974; and Burroughs 1982a.
25. Burroughs 1982a, 95-6.
26. Alberti, IV, 5.
27. Ibid.
28. Westfall 1974, 31-4.
29. G Manetti, 926.
30. Westfall 1974, 151.
31. Stinger 1982, 160.

32. Ibid., 168 n53.
33. Mallett 1969, 80.
34. Ibid.

Chapter 19: A New Language

1. Hofmann, II, 110 (50); McManamon, 65; see also Martines 1963.
2. McManamon, 77.
3. On Alberti, see Mancini; Martines 1963.
4. Hofmann, II, 111 (68), 112 (76); see also d'Amico, 70-1.
5. Hofmann, II, 114 (98); see also d'Amico, 118-19.
6. d'Amico, Ch. 5.
7. McManamon, Ch. 4.
8. Krautheimer 1980, Chs. 7 & 8.
9. d'Amico, 119.
10. Onians 1988, Ch. 10.
11. Stinger 1981, 194-5; Chambers 1966, 290.
12. For biography, see Mack 1987, 27-9.
13. Hofmann, II, 112 (76).
14. Pius II, 28-31, 74-84, 194-201, 219-73.
15. Partner 1960, 260.
16. Ibid., 263.
17. Thomson, 90.
18. On Pius II's work on St Peter's and the piazza, see Frommel 1983; R Rubinstein 1967.
19. On the destruction of ancient Rome, see Weiss, 99-104.
20. R Rubinstein 1988, *passim*.
21. Ibid., 198.
22. Ibid., 199.
23. Frommel 1983, 127; see also R Rubinstein 1988, 202-3.
24. Frommel 1983, 115-16; R Rubinstein 1967, *passim*.
25. Pius II, 233-51.
26. Frommel 1983, 116; R Rubinstein 1967, 24.
27. Frommel 1983, 116-18, 141-3; R Rubinstein 1967, 24.
28. On Manfredino da Como, see Frommel 1983, 126.
29. Ibid., 126; Frommel 1984, 129-38.
30. Frommel 1983, 118-19, 126.
31. Ibid., 114-15.
32. See note 29 above.
33. R Rubinstein 1988, *passim*.
34. Mack 1987, 40.
35. On Pienza, see Mack 1987; Adams 1985.
36. Adams 1985, 103.
37. Mack 1987, 38.
38. Adams 1985, 102, 106-7 (docs. 9-12, 14); on Ammanati, see ibid., 102 n17.
39. Mack 1987, Ch. 3; Chambers 1966, 28-30; Adams 1985, 102.
40. Pius II, 281; see also Adams 1985, 102.
41. Adams 1985, 100.
42. Pius II, 277-80.
43. Onians 1988, 194.
44. Pius II, 274-7.
45. Adams 1985, 102; on Pius II's visit to Pienza, see Pius II, 274-83.
46. Adams 1985, 105.
47. Pius II, 280.
48. Biondo's text quoted and translated in Mack 1987, 166-9.
49. Ibid.
50. Onians 1988, 185-9, fig. 99.
51. Pastor, IV, 31-2.
52. Pastor, IV, 18.
53. Lee 1978, 112 n116.
54. Pastor, IV, 38.

55. Stinger 1982, 158.
56. Urban, Katalog, 268; on Marcus Aurelius, see Haskell & Penny, 252-5.
57. Inventory in Müntz 1882, II, 181-287; see also Weiss, 186-8.
58. Zippel, 254.
59. Weiss, 187-8.
60. Platina, 404 n3.
61. Frommel 1984, 120, 163.
62. Ibid., 128.
63. Urban, Katalog, 268.
64. Frommel 1983, 123.
65. On the building history, see Frommel 1984.
66. The Palazzetto was moved from its original position in 1911 during the clearing of the piazza Venezia and rebuilt on the other side of San Marco (Frommel 1984, 82).
67. Ibid., 126-7.
68. Ibid., 109, 120.
69. Ibid., 78; on Francesco del Borgo, see ibid., 129-38.
70. Ibid., 136.
71. Ibid., 111.
72. Frommel attributes the design to him (ibid., 129).
73. Müntz 1882, II, 55-77; see also Frommel 1984, 79-80.

Chapter 20: Morality and Extravagance

1. On Francesco della Rovere, see Lee 1978, 11-28; Moorman, 487-9.
2. Mallett 1969, 104.
3. Moorman, 487-500.
4. Pastor, IV, 418.
5. d'Amico, 216-17.
6. Pastor, IV, 394-5; Goffen 1986b, 220-7.
7. Goffen 1986b, 221.
8. Ibid., 229; Parks 1979, 293-4.
9. On Sixtus IV and the doctrine of the Immaculate Conception, see Goffen 1986b, 228-31; Mayberry.
10. d'Amico, Ch. 5; Lee 1978, 200-4.
11. Haskell & Penny, 8.
12. Lee 1978, 147.
13. Howe 1978, 381-2.
14. On Sixtus IV's urban project, see Lee 1978, Ch. 4.
15. d'Amico, 70.
16. Urban, Katalog, 269-79.
17. Müntz 1882, III, 152-3; on Sixtus IV and the revival of the culture of early Christian Rome, see Stinger 1985, 226-8.
18. Frommel 1984, 118.
19. Pastor, IV, 456.
20. Ettlinger 1953, 265-70.
21. Roover 1963, 199.
22. d'Amico, 27; Thomson, 86-7.
23. Lee 1978, Appendix, 230-1 (doc. 16).
24. Lee 1984, 132-42.
25. On Giovannino de' Dolci's career in Rome, see Squarzina, 199-212.
26. Lee 1978, 139-41.
27. Onians 1980, passim; Onians 1988, 195-200.
28. On the use of Doric in imperial and early Christian Rome, see ibid., 68.
29. On the decorative scheme, see Howe 1978.
30. Lee 1978, 141.
31. For an interpretation of the frescos, see Howe 1978.
32. Howe 1978, 186.
33. On Sixtus IV's library, see Müntz 1887; Pastor, IV, 433-5; Lee 1978, 110-22.
34. Pastor, IV, 435-6; on Platina, see Lee 1978, 111-14.
35. Lee 1978, 117.

36. Clark, *passim*.
37. On the decoration of the libary, see Lee 1978, 118-20.
38. The research on this building and its decoration is considerable: see Steinmann; Wilde 1958; Battisti 1957; Ettlinger 1965; Salvini; Goffen 1986b; Shearman 1986.
39. Shearman 1986, 27.
40. Vasari, II, 652.
41. Battisti 1957, *passim*; see also Salvini, 152-3.
42. Shearman 1986, 26; on its fortified aspect, see also Salvini, 153-4.
43. Ettlinger 1965, 12; Goffen 1986b, 231-2, 235; Shearman 1986, 34; see also note 17 above.
44. Goffen 1986b, 232-4.
45. Pastor, IV, 394; Goffen 1986b, 230-1.
46. Ettlinger 1965, Ch. 6; Salvini, 144-52; see also Goffen 1986b.
47. Howe 1982, *passim*.
48. Onians 1988, 200.
49. Hofmann, II, 100 (8).
50. Thomson, 90.
51. Urban, Katalog, 279-80.
52. Zahn, 177.
53. Urban, Katalog, 279; Frommel 1983, 132.
54. Pastor, V, 321; Frommel 1983, 125.
55. J Schulz, 36-44.
56. Vasari, III, 498; quoted in J Schulz, 36; on architectural framework, see ibid., 38-9.
57. J Schulz, 36-7 n6.
58. C Gilbert 1980, 12-13.
59. On Rodrigo Borgia, see Mallett 1969, Ch. 5.
60. On Alexander VI's pontificate, see ibid., Chs. 6-11.
61. Ibid., 206.
62. On the ceiling project, see Jacks; on the myth, see ibid., 65.
63. Urban, Katalog, 280-1; Jacks, 65 n3.
64. Jacks, 65 n3.
65. Frommel 1983, 123.
66. Pastor, VI, 170.
67. Pastor, VI, 168-70.
68. Pastor, VI, 178.
69. J Schulz, 47-8 n38.
70. Vasari, III, 499-500; see also J Schulz, 47-8 n38.
71. On the decoration of the Borgia apartments, see Parks, *passim*.
72. Ibid., 293-4.
73. Ibid., 296.
74. Ibid., 298.
75. On the impact of the discovery of the Golden House of Nero, see J Schulz, 46-50.
76. Ibid., 46-7.

Chapter 21: The Papal Court

1. Pius II, 255-61.
2. For a brief account of the cardinals in Rome, see Chambers 1966.
3. Details of all cardinals in Eubel.
4. On the Curia, see Partner 1990; Hofmann, II, 69-71, 87-8, 97-8.
5. This discussion of cardinals' income is based on Chambers 1966.
6. Antonovics, 101 (table 3).
7. Chambers 1977, 109-11.
8. Martines 1979, 310.
9. Chambers 1966, 300-3.
10. On importance of a palace and the problems in acquiring it, see Chambers 1976.
11. Weil-Garris & d'Amico, 99 n8, 100 n13; and see note 12 below.
12. Tomei, 36.
13. Onians 1988, 125-6.
14. On Branda Castiglione's career, see Pulin 1984; Bradshaw-Nishi.
15. Pulin 1982, 23-4.

16. On the chapel decorations, see Bradshaw-Nishi.
17. On Castiglione Olona, see Pulin 1984.
18. Text in Foffano; part translated in Pulin 1984, Appendix E, 377–90.
19. Onians 1988, 125–6.
20. On palace building in mid fifteenth-century Rome, see Magnuson 1958; Tomei; Chambers 1976; Weil-Garris & d'Amico 1980, 101 n21.
21. Pius II, 245–6.
22. Hofmann, II, 69–70 (4); on Borgia's career, see Mallett 1969, Ch. 5.
23. Documents quoted in Pastor, V, 537–8; on palace, see Tomei, 187–90.
24. Quoted in Magnuson 1958, 240 n56.
25. Letter translated in Hibbert, 204–5.
26. Onians 1988, 126.
27. Baron 1988, I, 244–6; Chambers 1966, 291.
28. Geiger 1981, 69.
29. Urban, Katalog, 264.
30. Lee 1978, 130 (and see Chapter 20 above).
31. Tomei, 190–3.
32. Frommel 1984, 104–8.
33. Urban, Katalog, 273.
34. Heideman, 3.
35. Tomei, 165–6.
36. Urban, Katalog, 271–2.
37. Ibid., 277–9.
38. Ibid., 266, 270–1.
39. Lee 1978, 26–7; Domenico and Cristoforo della Rovere belonged to the Piedmont branch of the della Rovere family and had close ties with the Savoy court. The other della Rovere and Riario cardinals, like Sixtus IV, came from Savona, and there is no real evidence of a close connection between the two families.
40. Ibid., 33.
41. Ibid.
42. Tomei, 194–9; Cannatà et al., 62–3.
43. Onians 1988, 128.
44. Weil-Garris & d'Amico, 101 n21.
45. N Clark, Pt. 2.
46. On Giuliano della Rovere, see Pastor, IV, 236–8.
47. Urban, Katalog, 274.
48. Onians 1988, 205.
49. Urban, Katalog, 269.
50. . . . Aedificatur praeterea sua impensa apud Apostolos . . . si quod Iulianus nepos mente concepit, etiam incohavit, tandem perficiet . . . (Platina, 418).
51. Urban, Katalog, 269.
52. See Chapter 20 n17 above.
53. Hofmann, II, 87 (5); on d'Estouteville, see Müntz 1882, III, 285–97.
54. Urban, Katalog, 273.
55. Müntz 1882, III, 39–42.
56. Jacks 1985, 72 n51.
57. Seymour 1966, 157–8.
58. Magnuson 1958, 218; see also Pulin 1982, 24 n5.
59. Lee 1978, 126.
60. Tomei, 123–8.
61. Tomei, 117–22; Cannatà et al., passim.
62. Hofmann, II, 101 (116).
63. Tomei, 118; Cannatà et al., 32–3.
64. Cannatà et al., 79.
65. Ibid., 75–6.
66. Ibid., 82 n1.
67. Ibid., 79–82.
68. On Michelangelo's Pietà, see Weil-Garris Brandt.
69. Müntz 1882, I, 285–9.
70. Müntz 1882, II, 43–9.

71. On Sixtus IV's tomb, see Ettlinger 1953.
72. On Innocent VIII's tomb, see Frank.
73. Contract published in Vasari, III, 519–22; translated in Chambers 1970a, 25–8.
74. See note 19 above.
75. On funeral orations, see McManamon.
76. See entries in Bober & Rubinstein, Appendix 2.
77. See Chapter 19 n73 above.
78. Haskell & Penny, 311–14 (80).
79. Bober & Rubinstein, Appendix 2; Weiss, 193–5.
80. d'Amico, 53; Bober & Rubinstein, 478 (Appendix 2).
81. Weiss, 192; Tolnay, I, 24–5, (cat. xvi); Bober & Rubinstein, 478.
82. D Brown, *passim*.
83. On Michelangelo's *Bacchus*, see Tolnay, I, 26–7 (cat. iv).
84. Hofmann, II, 87 (6).
85. d'Amico, 36.
86. Onians 1988, 203–4; on palace, see also Gnoli.
87. Gnoli, 179.
88. Onians 1988, 203–4.
89. On early sixteenth-century palace design, see Frommel 1973.
90. On Carafa, see Geiger 1986, 30–2; Chambers 1966, 309.
91. On Carafa's projects, see Geiger 1986, 33–9.
92. Ibid., Ch. 2; see also Geiger 1981.
93. Letter in Scharf, 88 (doc. 8); translated in Chambers 1970a, 23.
94. Friedman, 119–22.
95. Bruschi, Ch. 5.
96. Geiger 1986, 42 n63.
97. Bruschi, Ch. 8.
98. Onians 1988, 233–5.

Chapter 22: The Triumph of Rome

1. Pastor, VI, 213–14.
2. Sowards, *passim*.
3. Partner 1960, 268–9.
4. Ibid., 264–5.
5. Hofmann, II, 168–70 (table 1); see also Thomson, 90; d'Amico, 27–8.
6. Stinger 1981, 190–1.
7. Sowards, *passim*.
8. Suetonius (Loeb ed., I, xliv).
9. Pastor, VI, 455–606.
10. Bruschi, 168–73, 196.
11. Jones & Penny, 118, 158.
12. Pastor, VI, 496–7; on ceiling, see also J Schulz, 50.
13. Bruschi, 168–73.
14. Tolnay, I, cat. xxi.
15. Pastor, VII, 511–13; Stinger 1981, 191.
16. On Constantine's basilica, see Krautheimer 1975, 55–60; on Julius II and the new church, see Pastor, VI, 459–85; Bruschi, Ch. 9; Heydenreich & Lotz; Onians 1988, 241–6.
17. Pastor, VI, 469–72.
18. Bruschi, 154.
19. Stinger 1981, 191.
20. Partner 1976, 16.
21. Onians 1988, 241.
22. Shearman 1971, 370–4.
23. Ackerman 1951, plates 12a & 13; the open effect was ruined by Sixtus V's addition of an extension across the central piazza for his library.
24. Ibid., 83–5.
25. D Brown, *passim*; see also Haskell & Penny, 148–51 (cat. 8).
26. Haskell & Penny, 243–7 (cat. 52).
27. Ibid., 188–9 (cat. 25).

28. Ibid., 310–11 (cat. 79).
29. Ibid., 10.
30. Pastor, VI, 533–9; Tolnay, IV, *passim*.
31. Pastor, VI, 535; Tolnay, IV, 6.
32. Shearman 1986, 32.
33. Seymour 1972, 102 (doc. 1).
34. Ibid., 102–3 (doc. 2), 110–13 (letter December 1523).
35. Ibid., 109 (doc. 20).
36. Ibid., 110–13 (letter December 1523).
37. Robertson, *passim*.
38. Hope 1987, 201–2.
39. Seymour 1972, 90 n9; for an outline of the critical history, see ibid., 83–97, 155–233.
40. Ibid.
41. Ibid.
42. Ibid., 93–7.
43. Bull, *passim*.
44. Ibid., 604.
45. Wind, 320–1; this interpretation has been convincingly ruled out in Hope 1987.
46. Bull, 604–5.
47. Hope 1987, 202.
48. Ibid., 201.
49. Hope 1990, 538.
50. Jones & Penny, 157–9.
51. On the function of the rooms in Julius II's apartments, see Shearman 1971, 372–83.
52. Jones & Penny 1983, 66–8.
53. Shearman 1981, 384.
54. On the Stanza della Segnatura, see Jones & Penny 1983, Ch. 3.
55. Tolnay, II, 243 (July 1512).
56. Golzio, 22 (4 October 1509).
57. J Schulz, 47–8 n38.
58. See, for example, Albertini's descriptions of the Sistine Chapel (f Xiii ^{v}–Xiv ^{r}),
    S. Maria del Popolo (f Xiv ^{v}) and the Carafa chapel in S. Maria sopra Minerva (f Y ^{r}).
59. Frommel 1983, 127.
60. On Raphael at St Peter's, see Heydenreich & Lotz, 173–7.
61. Seymour 1972, 110–13 (letter December 1523).
62. Robertson, *passim*; letter quoted ibid., 96.
63. Frommel 1973, II, 80–7; Bruschi, 173–5.
64. Jones & Penny, 88–92.
65. Ibid., Ch. 7.
66. Ibid., 100–5.
67. Ibid., 105–11.
68. Frommel 1961, *passim*.
69. Jones & Penny, 93–7.
70. McManamon, 78–9.

Bibliography

Abbreviations

ASA	*Archivio Storico dell'Arte*
ASI	*Archivio Storico Italiano*
ASPN	*Archivio Storico per le Provincie Napoletane*
JMRS	*Journal of Medieval and Renaissance Studies*
JPK	*Jahrbuch der preussischen Kunstsammlungen*
JRSA	*Journal of the Royal Society of Arts*
JSAH	*Journal of the Society of Architectural Historians*
JWCI	*Journal of the Warburg and Courtauld Institutes*
MJBK	*Münchener Jahrbuch der Bildenden Kunst*
MKIF	*Mitteilungen des Kunsthistorischen Institutes in Florenz*
PBSR	*Papers of the British School in Rome*
RJK	*Römisches Jahrbuch für Kunstgeschichte*
RKW	*Repertorium für Kunstwissenschaft*
SMRH	*Studies in Medieval and Renaissance History*

Ackerman 1949
J. S. Ackerman, 'Ars Sine Scientia Nihil Est: Gothic Theory of Architecture at the Cathedral of Milan', *Art Bulletin*, **31** (1949), 84–111.

Ackerman 1951
—— 'The Belvedere as a Classical Villa', *JWCI*, **14** (1951), 70–91.

Ackerman 1954
—— *The Cortile del Belvedere*, Vatican City 1954.

Ackerman 1980
—— 'Observations on Renaissance Church Planning in Venice and Florence 1470–1570', in *Florence and Venice: Comparisons and Relations*, (Acts of Two Conferences at Villa I Tatti 1976–7), Florence 1980, vol. 2, 287–307.

Ackerman 1982
—— 'The Planning of Renaissance Rome', in Ramsey, 3–17.

Adams 1984
Nicholas Adams, 'Architecture for Fish: The Sienese Dam on the Bruna River – Structures and Design 1468–ca. 1530', *Technology and Culture*, **25** (1984), 768–97.

Adams 1985
—— 'The Acquisition of Pienza 1459–1464', *JSAH*, **44** (1985), 99–110.

Alberti
L. B. Alberti, *de re aedificatoria*; for text, see G. Orlandi (ed.) *L. B. Alberti, L'Architettura*, Milan 1966; for translation, see J. Rykwert, N. Leach & R. Tavernor (eds.), *Leon Battista Alberti, On the Art of Building in Ten Books*, Cambridge MA & London 1988.

Alberti *de pictura*
—— *de pictura*: for text see Cecil Grayson (ed.), *Leon Battista Alberti, On Painting and On Sculpture*, London 1972.

Albertini
Francesco degli Albertini, *Opusculum de mirabilibus novae et veteris urbis Romae*, reprinted in P. Murray (ed.), *Five Early*

Guides to Rome and Florence, Farnborough 1972.

Ames-Lewis 1979
Francis Ames-Lewis, 'Art History or Stilkritik: Donatello's bronze David Reconsidered', *Art History*, 2 (1979), 139–55.

Ames-Lewis 1987
—— 'Modelbook Drawings and the Florentine Quattrocento Artist', *Art History*, 10 (1987), 1–11.

Ames-Lewis 1989
—— 'Donatello's Bronze David and the Palazzo Medici Courtyard', *Renaissance Studies*, 3 (1989), 235–51.

d'Amico
John F. d'Amico, *Renaissance Humanism in Papal Rome*, Baltimore MD & London 1983.

Annali
Annali della Fabbrica del Duomo di Milano dall'origine fino al presente, (9 vols.), Milan 1877–85.

Antonovics
A.V. Antonovics, 'A Late Fifteenth-Century Division Register of the College of Cardinals', *PBSR*, 35 (1967), 87–101.

Baron 1966
Hans Baron, *The Crisis of the Early Italian Renaissance*, Princeton NJ 1966.

Baron 1988
—— *In Search of Florentine Civic Humanism: Essays on the Transition from Medieval to Modern Thought*, (2 vols.), Princeton NJ 1988.

Baroni
C. Baroni, *Documenti per la Storia dell'Architettura a Milano nel Rinascimento e nel Barocco*, (vol. I) Florence 1940, (vol. II) Rome 1968.

Battisti 1957
E. Battisti, 'Il Significato Simbolico della Cappella Sistina', *Commentari*, 8 (1957), 96–104.

Battisti 1981
—— *Brunelleschi*, London 1981.

Baxandall 1963
Michael Baxandall, 'A Dialogue on Art from the Court of Leonello d'Este', *JWCI*, 26 (1963), 304–26.

Baxandall 1964
—— 'Bartolomeo Facius on Painting', *JWCI*, 27 (1964), 90–107.

Baxandall 1965
—— 'Guarino, Pisanello & Chrysoloras', *JWCI*, 28 (1965), 183–204.

Baxandall 1971
—— *Giotto and the Orators*, Oxford 1971.

Baxandall 1972
—— *Painting and Experience in Fifteenth-Century Italy*, Oxford 1972.

Beck
James Beck, *Masaccio: The Documents* (I Tatti Studies 4), Locust Valley NY 1978.

Beltrami
L. Beltrami, *La Cà del Duca sul Canal Grande*, Milan 1900.

Bentley
Jerry H. Bentley, *Politics and Culture in Renaissance Naples*, Princeton NJ 1987.

Bernstein
Joanne Gitlin Bernstein, 'A Florentine Patron in Milan: Pigello and the Portinari Chapel', in *Florence and Milan: Comparisons and Relations*, (Acts of Two Conferences at Villa I Tatti 1982–4), Florence 1989, vol. I, 171–200.

Bertoni
G. Bertoni, *La Biblioteca Estense a Modena e la Cultura Ferrarese ai Tempi del Duca Ercole I 1471–1505*, Turin 1903.

Betts
Richard J. Betts, 'On the Chronology of Francesco di Giorgio's Treatises', *JSAH*, 36 (1977), 3–14.

Borgo & Sievers
Ludovico Borgo & Ann H. Sievers, 'The Medici Gardens at San Marco', *MKIF*, 33 (1989), 237–56.

Borsi
Franco Borsi, *Leon Battista Alberti*, London 1971.

Borsook
Eve Borsook, 'Cult and Imagery at Sant'Ambrogio in Florence', *MKIF*, 25 (1981), 147–202.

Bradshaw-Nishi
M.J. Bradshaw-Nishi, *Masolino's St Catherine Chapel, San Clemente, Rome: Style, Iconography, Patron and Date*, Ann Arbor MI & London 1988.

Braghirolli
W. Braghirolli, 'Documenti e Notizie intorno a Leon Battista Alberti a Mantova', *ASI*, 3rd series, 9 (1869), 3–31.

Braudel
F. Braudel, *The Mediterranean and the Mediterranean World in the Age of Philip II*, New York & London 1972.

Bridgeman   Jane Bridgeman, 'Filippino Lippi's Nerli Altarpiece – a New Date', *Burlington Magazine*, **130** (1988), 668–71.

A Brown   Alison Brown, 'Lorenzo, the Monte and the 17 Reformers', in Gian Carlo Garfagnini (ed.), *Lorenzo de' Medici Studi*, Florence 1992, 103–65.

BL Brown 1978   Beverley L. Brown, *The Tribuna of SS. Annunziata in Florence*, Ann Arbor MI & London 1980.

BL Brown 1981   —— 'The Patronage and Building History of the Tribuna of SS Annunziata', *MKIF*, **25** (1981), 59–146.

CM Brown   C. M. Brown, 'Lo Insaciabile Desiderio Nostro de Cose Antique: New Documents on Isabella d'Este's Collection of Antiquities', in C. H. Clough (ed.), *Cultural Aspects of the Italian Renaissance: Essays in Honour of Paul Oskar Kristeller*, Manchester & New York 1976, 324–53.

D Brown   Deborah Brown, 'The Apollo Belvedere and the Garden of Giuliano della Rovere at SS. Apostoli', *JWCI*, **49** (1986), 235–8.

PF Brown 1981   Patricia Fortini Brown, 'Laetentur Coeli: The Council of Florence and the Astronomical Fresco in the Old Sacristy', *JWCI*, **44** (1981), 176–80.

PF Brown 1984   —— 'Painting and History in Renaissance Venice', *Art History*, **7** (1984), 263–94.

PF Brown 1988   —— *Venetian Narrative Painting in the Age of Carpaccio*, New Haven CT & London 1988.

Brucker 1969   Gene Brucker, *Renaissance Florence*, New York 1969.

Brucker 1971   —— (ed.), *The Society of Renaissance Florence*, New York 1971.

Brucker 1990   —— 'Monasteries, Friaries and Nunneries in Quattrocento Florence', in Verdon & Henderson, 41–62.

Bruni   Leonardo Bruni, *Laudatio Florentinae Urbis*, in H. Baron, *From Petrarch to Leonardo Bruni*, Chicago & London 1968, 232–63.

Bruschi   Arnaldo Bruschi, *Bramante*, London 1977.

Bruschi et al.   —— et al. (eds.), *Scritti Rinascimentali di Architettura*, Milan 1978.

Bull   Malcolm Bull, 'The Iconography of the Sistine Chapel Ceiling', *Burlington Magazine*, **130** (1988), 597–605.

Bullard   Melissa Meriam Bullard, 'The Magnificent Lorenzo de' Medici: Between Myth and Mythology', in P. Mack & M. C. Jacob (eds.), *Politics and Culture in Early Modern Europe: Essays in Honour of H. G. Koenigsberger*, Cambridge 1987, 25–58.

Burke   Peter Burke, *The Italian Renaissance: Culture and Society in Italy*, Cambridge 1987.

Burns 1970   H. Burns, 'Progetti di Francesco di Giorgio per i conventi di San Bernardino e Sta Chiara di Urbino', in *Studi Bramanteschi: Atti del Congresso Internazionale Milano-Urbino-Roma 1970*, Rome 1974, 293–311.

Burns 1971   —— 'Quattrocento Architecture and the Antique – Some Problems', in R. R. Bolgar (ed.), *Classical Influences on European Culture AD 500–1500*, Cambridge 1971, 269–87.

Burns 1975   —— *Andrea Palladio 1508–1580: the Portico and the Farmyard*, (exhibition catalogue), London 1975.

Burns 1981   —— 'The Gonzaga and Renaissance Architecture', in Chambers & Martineau, 27–38.

Burroughs 1982a   Charles Burroughs, 'Below the Angel: An Urbanistic Project in the Rome of Pope Nicholas V', *JWCI*, **45** (1982), 94–124.

Burroughs 1982b   —— 'A Planned Myth and a Myth of Planning: Nicholas V and Rome', in Ramsey, 197–207.

Büttner   Frank Büttner, 'Die Geburt des Reichtums und der Neid der Götter: Neue Überlegungen zu Giorgione's *Tempesta*', *MJBK*, **37** (1986), 113–30.

Cannatà et al.   R. Cannatà, A. Cavallaro, C. Strinati & P. Cellini, *Umanesimo e primo Rinascimento in S. Maria del Popolo*, (exhibition catalogue), Rome 1981.

Canuti   F. Canuti, *Il Perugino*, 2 vols., Siena 1931.

Chambers 1966   D. S. Chambers, 'The Economic Predicament of Renaissance Cardinals', *SMRH*, **3** (1966), 287–313.

Chambers 1970a   —— *Patrons and Artists in the Italian Renaissance*, London 1970.

Chambers 1970b   —— *The Imperial Age of Venice 1380–1580*, London 1970.

Chambers 1976   —— 'The Housing Problems of Cardinal Francesco Gonzaga', *JWCI*, **39** (1976), 21–58.

Chambers 1977   —— 'Sant'Andrea at Mantua and Gonzaga Patronage 1460–1472', *JWCI*, **40** (1977), 99–127.

Chambers 1981   —— 'Mantua and the Gonzaga', in Chambers & Martineau, xvii–xxiii.

Chambers & Martineau   D. S. Chambers & Jane Martineau (eds.), *The Splendours of the Gonzaga*, (exhibition catalogue), London 1981.

Cheles   Luciano Cheles, *The Studiolo of Urbino: An Iconographic Investigation*, Wiesbaden 1986.

Christiansen   K. Christiansen, *Gentile da Fabriano*, Ithaca NY 1982.

Clark   J. W. Clark, 'On the Vatican Library of Sixtus IV', *Proceedings of the Cambridge Antiquarian Society*, **10** (1904), 11–62.

N Clark   Nicholas Clark, *Melozzo da Forlì*, London 1990.

Clough 1966   C. H. Clough, 'The Library of the Dukes of Urbino', *Librarium*, **9**, (1966), 101–4, (published in Clough 1981).

Clough 1967   —— 'The Relations between the English and Urbino Courts 1474–1508', *Studies in the Renaissance*, **14** (1967), 202–18 (published in Clough 1981).

Clough 1973   —— 'Federigo da Montefeltro's Patronage of the Arts 1468–1482', *JWCI*, **36** (1973), 129–44 (published in Clough 1981).

Clough 1978a   —— 'Federigo da Montefeltro's Artistic Patronage', *JRSA*, **126** (1978), 718–34 (published in Clough 1981).

Clough 1978b   —— 'Towards an Economic History of the State of Urbino at the Time of Federigo da Montefeltro and of his Son, Guidobaldo', in L. de Rosa (ed.), *Studi in Memoria di Federigo Melis*, Naples 1978, 469–504 (published in Clough 1981).

Clough 1981   —— *The Duchy of Urbino in the Renaissance*, London 1981.

Connell   S. M. Connell, *The Employment of Sculptors and Stonemasons in Venice in the Fifteenth Century*, unpublished PhD thesis, University of London (Warburg Institute) 1976.

Corvisieri   C. Corvisieri, 'Il trionfo romano di Eleonora d'Aragona nel Giugno del 1473', *Archivio della Società Romana per la Storia Patria*, **1** (1878), 475–91, and **10** (1887), 629–87.

Cracco   Giorgio Cracco, 'Patriziato e Oligarchia a Venezia nel Tre-Quattrocento', in *Florence and Venice: Comparisons and Relations*, (Acts of Two Conferences at Villa I Tatti 1976–7), Florence 1979, vol. I, 71–98.

Davies   Martin Davies, *National Gallery Catalogues: The Earlier Italian Schools*, London 1961.

Davisson   Darrell D. Davisson, 'The Iconology of the S. Trinità Sacristy 1418–1435: A Study of the Private and Public Functions of Religious Art in the Early Quattrocento', *Art Bulletin*, **57** (1975), 315–34.

Dechert   M. Dechert, 'The Military Architecture of Francesco di Giorgio in Southern Italy', *JSAH*, **49** (1990), 161–80.

Dempsey   Charles Dempsey, 'Renaissance Hieroglyphic Studies and

Gentile Bellini's "St Mark Preaching in Alexandria" ', in Ingrid Merkel & Allen Debus (eds.), *Hermeticism and the Renaissance: Intellectual History and the Occult in Early Modern Europe*, London & Toronto 1987.

Demus   Otto Demus, *The Church of San Marco in Venice*, Dumbarton Oaks Studies VI, Washington DC 1960.

Dennistoun   J. Dennistoun, *Memoirs of the Dukes of Urbino, 1440-1630*, 3 vols., London 1851.

Doren   Alfred Doren, 'Das Aktenbuch für Ghibertis Matthäusstatue an Or S Michele zu Florenz', *Italienishe Forschungen des Kunsthistorischen Institutes in Florenz*, 1 (1906) 1–58.

Elam 1978   Caroline Elam, 'Lorenzo de' Medici and the Urban Development of Renaissance Florence', *Art History*, 1 (1978), 43–66.

Elam 1981   —— 'Mantegna at Mantua', in Chambers & Martineau, 15–25.

Elam 1990   —— 'Il Palazzo nel Contesto della Città: Strategie Urbanistiche dei Medici nel Gonfalone del Leon d'Oro', in G. Cherubini & G. Fanelli (eds.), *Il Palazzo Medici-Riccardi in Firenze*, Florence 1990, 44–57.

Ettlinger 1953   L. D. Ettlinger, 'Pollaiuolo's Tomb of Pope Sixtus IV', *JWCI*, 16 (1953), 239–74.

Ettlinger 1965   —— *The Sistine Chapel before Michelangelo: Religious Imagery and Papal Primacy*, Oxford 1965.

Ettlinger 1978   —— *Antonio and Piero Pollaiuolo*, Oxford 1978.

Eubel   Konrad Eubel, *Hierarchia Catholica Medii Aevi*, Monasterii 1913–24; vol. 1 (1195–1431), vol. 2 (1431–1503) and vol. 3 (1503–92).

Fabriczy 1892   C. von Fabriczy, *Filippo Brunelleschi*, Stuttgart 1892.

Fabriczy 1897   —— 'Toscanische und oberitalienische Künstler in Diensten der Aragonesen zu Neapel', *RKW*, 20 (1897), 85–120.

Fabriczy 1902   —— 'Giuliano da Sangallo', *JPK*, 23 (1902) Beiheft, 1–42.

Fabriczy 1903   —— 'Giuliano da Maiano', *JPK*, 24 (1903) Beiheft, 137–76.

Fanelli   G. Fanelli, *Firenze*, Bari 1981.

Fenlon   Iain Fenlon (ed.), *Man and Music: The Renaissance*, London 1989.

Filangieri 1937   R. Filangieri, 'Rassegna Critica delle Fonti per la Storia di Castel Nuovo', (part 2), *ASPN*, 62 (1937), 5–71.

Filangieri 1938   —— 'Rassegna Critica delle Fonti per la Storia di Castel Nuovo', (part 3), *ASPN*, 63 (1938), 3–87.

Filarete   Filarete, *Trattato di Architettura*; see J. R. Spencer (ed.), *Filarete's Treatise on Architecture*, 2 vols., New Haven CT & London 1965.

Fiocco   G. Fiocco, 'La Biblioteca di Palla Strozzi', in *Studi di Bibiliografia e di Storia in Onore di Tammaro de Marinis*, Verona 1964, vol. 2, 289–310.

Fletcher 1981   J. M. Fletcher, 'Isabella d'Este, Patron and Collector', in Chambers & Martineau, 51–63.

Fletcher 1983   —— 'Patronage in Venice', in Martineau & Hope, 16–20.

Foffano   Tino Foffano, 'La costruzione di Castiglione Olona in un opuscolo inedito di Francesco Pizzolpazzo', *Italia Medioevale e Umanistica*, 3 (1960), 153–87.

Foster 1971   P. Foster, 'Alberti, Lorenzo de' Medici and S. Maria delle Carceri, Prato', *JSAH*, 30 (1971), 238–9.

Foster 1978   —— *A Study of Lorenzo de' Medici's Villa at Poggio a Caiano*, 2 vols., New York & London 1978.

Foster 1981   —— 'Lorenzo de' Medici and the Florence Cathedral façade', *Art Bulletin*, 63 (1981), 495–500.

Francesco di Giorgio	Francesco di Giorgio, *Trattati*, ed. C. Maltese, 2 vols., Milan 1967.
Frank	Eric Frank, 'Pollaiuolo's Tomb of Innocent VIII', in S. Bule, A.P. Darr & F. Superbi Gioffredi (eds.), *Verrocchio and Late Quattrocento Italian Sculpture*, Florence 1992, 321-42.
Frey	Karl Frey, 'Studien zu Michelagniolo Buonarroti und zur Kunst seiner Zeit', *JPK*, **30**, (1909), 103-80.
Friedman	David Friedman, 'The Burial Chapel of Filippo Strozzi in Santa Maria Novella in Florence', *L'Arte*, **9** (1970), 109-31.
Frommel 1961	C.L. Frommel, *Die Farnesina und Peruzzis Architektonisches Frühwerk*, Berlin 1961.
Frommel 1973	—— *Der Römische Palastbau der Hochrenaissance* (Römische Forschungen der Bibliotheca Herziana 21), 3 vols., Rome 1973.
Frommel 1983	—— 'Francesco del Borgo: Architekt Pius II und Pauls II', (part 1), *RJK*, **20** (1983), 107-53.
Frommel 1984	—— 'Francesco del Borgo: Architekt Pius II und Pauls II', (part 2), *RJK*, **21** (1984), 71-164.
Garin	Eugenio Garin, 'Gian Francesco Pico della Mirandola: Savonarolan Apologetics and the Critique of Ancient Thought', in Verdon & Henderson, 523-32.
Gaston	Robert Gaston, 'Liturgy and Patronage in San Lorenzo, Florence, 1350-1650', in Kent & Simons, 111-33.
Gatti Perrer	M.L. Gatti Perrer, 'Umanesimo a Milano: l'Osservanza Agostiniana all'Incoronata', *Arte Lombarda*, **53-4** (1980).
Gaye	Giovanni Gaye, *Carteggio Inedito d'Artisti dei Secoli 14-16*, 2 vols., Florence 1839-40.
Geiger 1981	Gail L. Geiger, 'Filippino Lippi's Carafa Annunciation: Theology, Artistic Conventions and Patronage', *Art Bulletin*, **63** (1981), 62-75.
Geiger 1986	—— *Filippino Lippi's Carafa Chapel*, Kirksville MO 1986.
Ghiberti	L. Ghiberti, *Commentari*, O. Morisani (ed)., Naples 1947.
C Gilbert 1980	Creighton Gilbert, *Italian Art 1400-1500: Sources and Documents*, Eaglewood Cliffs NJ 1980.
C Gilbert 1990	—— 'Some Special Images for Carmelites c.1330-1430', in Verdon & Henderson, 161-207.
F Gilbert 1957	Felix Gilbert, 'Florentine Political Assumptions in the Period of Savonarola and Soderini', *JWCI*, **20** (1957), 187-214.
F Gilbert 1979	—— 'Humanism in Venice', in *Florence and Venice: Comparisons and Relations*, (Acts of Two Conferences at Villa I Tatti 1976-7), Florence 1979, vol.1, 13-26.
F Gilbert 1980	—— *The Pope, his Banker and Venice*, Cambridge MA & London 1980.
Giordano	Luisa Giordano, 'Il trattato del Filarete e l'architettura Lombarda', in *Les Traités d'Architecture de la Renaissance*, (Actes du Colloque tenu à Tours June 1981), Paris 1988, 115-28.
Gnoli	D. Gnoli, 'La Cancelleria ed altri palazzi di Roma attribuiti a Bramante', *ASA*, **5** (1892), 176-84, 331-47.
Goffen 1975	Rona Goffen, 'Icon and Vision: Giovanni Bellini's Half-Length Madonnas', *Art Bulletin*, **57** (1975), 487-518.
Goffen 1986a	—— *Piety and Patronage in Renaissance Venice*, New Haven CT & London 1986.
Goffen 1986b	—— 'Friar Sixtus IV and the Sistine Chapel', *Renaissance Quarterly*, **39** (1986), 218-62.
Goffen 1989	—— *Giovanni Bellini*, New Haven CT & London 1989.
Goldthwaite 1968	Richard A. Goldthwaite, *Private Wealth in Renaissance Florence: a Study of Four Families*, Princeton NJ 1968.

Goldthwaite 1972 —— 'The Florentine Palace as Domestic Architecture', *American Historical Review*, 77 (1972), 977–1012.

Goldthwaite 1973 —— 'The Building of the Strozzi Palace: the Construction Industry in Renaissance Florence', *SMRH*, 10 (1973), 99–194.

Goldthwaite 1980 —— *The Building of Renaissance Florence*, Baltimore MD & London 1980.

Golzio V. Golzio, *Raffaello*, Vatican City 1936.

Golzio & Zander V. Golzio & G. Zander, *L'Arte in Roma nel secolo XV*, Bologna 1968.

Gombrich 1960 E. H. Gombrich, 'The Early Medici as Patrons of Art', in Jacob, 279–311.

Gombrich 1961 —— 'Renaissance and Golden Age', reprinted in *Norm and Form*, London 1971, 29–34.

Gombrich 1962 —— 'Alberto Avogadro's descriptions of the Badia of Fiesole and of the Villa of Careggi', *Italia Medioevale e Umanistica*, 5 (1962), 217–29.

Gombrich 1972 —— 'Botticelli's Mythologies: A Study in the Neo-Platonic Symbolism of his Circle', in *Symbolic Images*, Oxford 1972, 31–81.

Gregory 1981 Heather Gregory, 'A Further Note on the Greek Manuscripts of Palla Strozzi', *JWCI*, 44 (1981), 183–5.

Gregory 1987 —— 'Palla Strozzi's Patronage and pre-Medicean Florence', in Kent & Simons, 201–20.

Guasti 1857 C. Guasti, *La Cupola di Santa Maria del Fiore*, Florence 1857.

Guasti 1862–3 —— 'Inventario della libreria Urbinate', *Giornale Storico degli Archivi Toscano*, 6 (1862), 133–47, and 7 (1863), 46–55, 130–54.

Guasti 1887 —— *Santa Maria del Fiore*, Florence 1887.

Gundersheimer 1972 W. L. Gundersheimer, *Art and Life at the Court of Ercole I d'Este: the 'de triumphis religonis' of Giovanni Sabadino degli Arienti*, Geneva 1972.

Gundersheimer 1976 —— 'The Patronage of Ercole I d'Este', *JMRS*, 6 (1976), 1–19.

Haines Margaret Haines, 'Brunelleschi and Bureaucracy: The Tradition of Public Patronage at the Florentine Cathedral', *I Tatti Studies*, 3 (1989), 89–125.

Hale 1973 J. R. Hale (ed.), *Renaissance Venice*, London 1973.

Hale 1977 —— *Florence and the Medici: The Pattern of Control*, London 1977.

Hale 1981 —— (ed.), *A Concise Encyclopedia of the Italian Renaissance*, London 1981.

Hall Marcia B. Hall, 'Savonarola's Preaching and the Patronage of Art', in Verdon & Henderson, 493–522.

Hankins James Hankins, 'The Myth of the Platonic Academy of Florence', *Renaissance Quarterly*, 49 (1991), 429–75.

Harrison Martin Harrison, *A Temple for Byzantium: The Discovery and Excavation of Anicia Juliana's Palace Church in Istanbul*, Austin TX 1989.

Haskell & Penny Francis Haskell & Nicholas Penny, *Taste and the Antique*, New Haven CT & London 1981.

Hatfield 1970a Rab Hatfield, 'The Compagnia de' Magi', *JWCI*, 33 (1970), 107–61.

Hatfield 1970b —— 'Some Unknown Descriptions of the Medici Palace in 1459', *Art Bulletin*, 52 (1970), 232–49.

Hatfield 1976 —— *Botticelli's Uffizi 'Adoration': A Study in Pictorial Content*, Princeton NJ 1976.

Hay Denys Hay, *The Church in Italy in the Fifteenth Century*, Cambridge 1977.

Heideman	J. E. L. Heideman, *The Cinquecento Chapel Decorations in S. Maria in Aracoeli in Rome*, Amsterdam 1982.
Henderson	J. Henderson, 'Penitence and the Laity in Fifteenth-Century Florence', in Verdon & Henderson, 229–49.
Hersey 1969	George L. Hersey, *Alfonso II and the Artistic Renewal of Naples 1485-95*, New Haven & London 1969.
Hersey 1973	—— *The Aragonese Arch at Naples 1443-1475*, New Haven & London 1973.
Heydenreich	L. H. Heydenreich, 'Federigo da Montefeltro as a Building Patron', in *Studies in Renaissance and Baroque Art presented to Anthony Blunt on his 60th Birthday*, London & New York 1967, 1–6.
Heydenreich & Lotz	L. H. Heydenreich & W. Lotz, *Architecture in Italy 1400–1600*, Harmondsworth 1974.
Hibbert	C. Hibbert, *The Rise and Fall of the House of Medici*, Harmondsworth 1974.
Hofmann	W. von Hofmann, *Forschungen zur Geschichte der kurialen Behörden vom Schisma bis zur Reformation*, Rome 1914.
Hollingsworth 1982	Mary Hollingsworth, *Attitudes to Architecture around 1500 in Italy*, unpublished PhD thesis, University of East Anglia 1982.
Hollingsworth 1984	—— 'The Architect in Fifteenth-Century Florence', *Art History*, 7 (1984), 385–410.
Hollingsworth 1992	—— 'Lorenzo de' Medici: Politician, Patron and Designer', *Apollo*, 135 (1992), 376–9.
Hollingsworth 1993	—— 'Alberti: A Courtier and his Patrons', in C. Mozzarelli & R. Oresko (eds.), *The Court of the Gonzaga in the Age of Mantegna 1450-1550* (Acts of Conference, London 1992), 1993 (forthcoming).
Holmes	G. Holmes, 'How the Medici became the Pope's Bankers', in Nicolai Rubinstein (ed.), *Florentine Studies: Politics and Society in Renaissance Florence*, London 1968, 357–80.
Hood 1986	W. Hood, 'Saint Dominic's Manner of Praying: Gestures in Fra Angelico's Cell Frescoes at S. Marco', *Art Bulletin*, 68 (1986), 195–206.
Hood 1990	—— 'Fra Angelico at San Marco: Art and the Liturgy of Cloistered Life', in Verdon & Henderson, 108–31.
Hope 1981	Charles Hope, 'Artists, Patrons and Advisors in the Italian Renaissance', in G. F. Lytle & S. Orgel (eds.), *Patronage in the Renaissance*, Princeton NJ 1981, 293–343.
Hope 1983	—— 'Poesie and Painted Allegories', in Martineau & Hope, 35–7.
Hope 1985	—— 'The Chronology of Mantegna's Triumphs', in *Renaissance Studies in Honour of Craig Hugh Smyth*, Florence 1985, vol. 2, 297–316.
Hope 1987	—— 'The Medallions on the Sistine Ceiling', *JWCI*, 50 (1987), 200–4.
Hope 1990	—— 'Altarpieces and the Requirements of Patrons', in Verdon & Henderson, 535–71.
Hope 1991	—— 'Storm over the Storm: Salvatore Settis' Giorgione's Tempest: Interpreting the Hidden Subject, *New York Review of Books*, 38 (1991), no. 4, 25–7.
Hope 1992	—— 'The Early History of the Tempio Malatestiano', *JWCI*, 55 (1992).
Hoshino	Hidetoshi Hoshino, *L'Arte della Lana in Firenze nel Basso Medioevo*, Florence 1980.
Howard 1980	Deborah Howard, *The Architectural History of Venice*, London 1980.

Howard 1985   —— 'Giorgione's Tempesta and Titian's Assunta in the Context
                       of the Cambrai Wars', *Art History*, 8 (1985), 271–89.
Howe 1978   Eunice D. Howe, *The Hospital of S Spirito and Pope Sixtus IV*,
                       New York & London 1978.
Howe 1982   —— 'A Temple Facade Reconsidered: Botticelli's Temptation of
                       Christ', in Ramsey, 209–21.
Humfrey 1986   Peter Humfrey, 'Dürer's Feast of the Rose Garlands: A
                       Venetian Altarpiece', *Bulletin of the Society for Renaissance
                       Studies*, 4(1986), 29–39.
Humfrey 1988   —— 'Competitive Devotions: The Venetian "Scuole Piccole" as
                       Donors of Altarpieces in the Years around 1500', *Art Bulletin*,
                       70 (1988), 401–22.
Humfrey &   Peter Humfrey & Richard MacKenney, 'Venetian Trade Guilds
   MacKenney   as Patrons of Art in the Renaissance', *Burlington Magazine*,
                       128 (1986), 317–30.
Hyman 1975   Isabelle Hyman, 'Notes and Speculations on San Lorenzo,
                       Palazzo Medici and an Urban Project by Brunelleschi', *JSAH*,
                       34 (1975), 98–120.
Hyman 1977   —— *Fifteenth-Century Florentine Studies*, New York & London
                       1977.
Hyman 1979   —— 'The Venice Connection: Questions about Brunelleschi and
                       the East', in *Florence and Venice: Comparisons and Relations*,
                       (Acts of Two Conferences at Villa I Tatti 1976–7), Florence
                       1979, vol. I, 193–208.
Ianziti 1987   Gary Ianziti, 'Patronage and the Production of History: The
                       Case of Quattrocento Milan', in Kent & Simons, 299–311.
Ianziti 1988   —— *Humanistic Historiography under the Sforzas: Politics and
                       Propaganda in Fifteenth-Century Milan*, Oxford 1988.
Ianziti 1989   —— 'The Rise of Sforza Historiography', in *Florence and
                       Milan: Comparisons and Relations*, (Acts of Two Conferences
                       at Villa I Tatti 1982–4), Florence 1989, vol. I, 79–94.
Ilardi   Vincent Ilardi, 'The Banker-Statesman and the Condottiere-
                       Prince: Cosimo de' Medici and Francesco Sforza (1450–64)', in
                       Florence and Milan: Comparisons and Relations, (Acts of Two
                       Conferences at Villa I Tatti 1982–4), Florence 1989, vol. II,
                       217–39.
Jacks   Philip J. Jacks, 'Alexander VI's Ceiling for Santa Maria
                       Maggiore, Rome', *RJK*, 22 (1985), 63–82.
Jacob   E. F. Jacob (ed.), *Italian Renaissance Studies*, London 1960.
Janson   H. W. Janson, *The Sculpture of Donatello*, Princeton NJ 1962.
Jenkins   A. D. Fraser Jenkins, 'Cosimo de' Medici's Patronage of
                       Architecture and the Theory of Magnificence', *JWCI*, 33 (1970),
                       162–70.
Johnson   Eugene J. Johnson, *Sant'Andrea in Mantua: The Building
                       History*, University Park PA & London 1975.
Jones & Penny   Roger Jones & Nicholas Penny, *Raphael*, New Haven CT &
                       London 1983.
Kaplan   Paul H. D. Kaplan, 'The Storm of War: the Paduan Key to
                       Giorgione's Tempesta', *Art History*, 9 (1986), 405–27.
Kemp 1977   Martin Kemp, 'From Mimesis to Fantasia: The Quattrocento
                       Vocabulary of Creation, Inspiration and Genius in the Visual
                       Arts', *Viator*, 8 (1977), 347–98.
Kemp 1978   —— 'Science, Non-science and Nonsense: the Interpretation of
                       Brunelleschi's Perspective', *Art History*, 1 (1978), 134–61.
D Kent 1978   Dale Kent, *The Rise of the Medici*, Oxford 1978.
D & FW Kent   D. V. & F. W. Kent, 'Two Comments of March 1445 on the
   1979   Medici Palace', *Burlington Magazine*, 121 (1979), 795–6.

D & FW Kent 1982 —— *Neighbours and Neighbourhood in Renaissance Florence: The District of the Red Lion in the Fifteenth Century* (Villa I Tatti Studies 6), Locust Valley NY 1982.

FW Kent 1972 F.W. Kent, 'The Rucellai Family and its Loggia', *JWCI*, **35** (1972), 397–401.

FW Kent 1977 —— ' "Più superba de quella de Lorenzo": Courtly and Family Interest in the Building of Filippo Strozzi's Palace', *Renaissance Quarterly*, **30** (1977), 311–23.

FW Kent 1979 —— 'Lorenzo de' Medici's Acquisition of Poggio a Caiano in 1474 and an Early Reference to his Architectural Expertise', *JWCI*, **42** (1979), 250–7.

FW Kent 1981 —— 'The Making of a Renaissance Patron of the Arts', in *Giovanni Rucellai ed il suo Zibaldone*, (Studies of the Warburg Institute **24**), London 1981, vol. 2, 9–95.

FW Kent 1982 —— 'New Light on Lorenzo de' Medici's Convent at Porta San Gallo', *Burlington Magazine*, **124** (1982), 292–4.

FW Kent 1983 —— 'Lorenzo di Credi, his patron, Jacopo Bongianni and Savonarola', *Burlington Magazine*, **125** (1983), 539–41.

FW Kent 1987 —— 'Palaces, Politics and Society in Fifteenth-Century Florence', *I Tatti Studies*, **2** (1987), 41–70.

Kent & Simons F.W. Kent & Patricia Simons (eds.), *Patronage, Art and Society in Renaissance Italy*, Oxford 1987.

King Margaret L. King, *Venetian Humanism in an Age of Patrician Dominance*, Princeton NJ 1986.

Krautheimer 1975 Richard Krautheimer, *Early Christian and Byzantine Architecture*, Harmondsworth 1975.

Krautheimer 1980 —— *Rome: Profile of a City 312–1308*, Princeton NJ 1980.

Krautheimer 1982 —— *Lorenzo Ghiberti*, Princeton NJ 1982.

Krautheimer 1983 —— *Three Christian Capitals: Topography and Politics*, Berkeley & Los Angeles CA 1983.

Krinsky C.H. Krinsky, 'Seventy-Eight Vitruvian Manuscripts', *JWCI*, **30** (1967), 36–70.

Kristeller P.O. Kristeller, *Mantegna*, London 1901.

Lamoureux R.E. Lamoureux, *Alberti's Church of San Sebastiano in Mantua*, Ann Arbor MI 1979.

Landucci Luca Landucci, *Diario Fiorentino dal 1450 al 1516*, in Iodoco del Badia (ed.), Florence 1883.

Lane F. Lane, *Venice: a Maritime Republic*, Baltimore MD 1973.

Lang S. Lang, 'Sforzinda, Filarete and Filelfo', *JWCI*, **35** (1972), 391–7.

Laven Peter Laven, *Renaissance Italy 1464–1534*, London 1966.

Lavin Irving Lavin, 'On the Sources and Meaning of the Renaissance Portrait Bust', *Art Quarterly*, **33** (1970), 207–26.

Lee 1978 Egmont Lee, *Sixtus IV and Men of Letters*, Rome 1978.

Lee 1982 —— 'Workmen and Work in Quattrocento Rome', in Ramsey, 141–52.

Lee 1984 —— 'Humanists and the Studium Urbis 1473–84', in *Umanesimo a Roma nel Quattrocento* (Atti del Convegno New York, December 1981), Rome & New York 1984, 127–46.

Levine Saul Levine, 'The Location of Michelangelo's David: the Meeting of January 25, 1504', *Art Bulletin*, **56** (1974), 31–49.

Lieberman 1972 Ralph Lieberman, *The Church of Santa Maria dei Miracoli in Venice*, New York & London 1986.

Lieberman 1982 —— *Renaissance Architecture in Venice*, London 1982.

Lightbown 1986 Ronald Lightbown, *Mantegna*, Oxford 1986.

Lightbown 1989 —— *Botticelli*, London 1989.

Lillie 1977 Amanda Lillie, *Santuccio: One of Filippo Strozzi's Villas near Florence*, unpublished MA thesis, University of London (Courtauld Institute) 1977.

Lillie 1984 —— 'Francesco Sassetti and his Villa at La Pietra', in E. Chaney & N. Ritchie (eds.), *Writings in Honour of Sir Harold Acton*, London 1984, 83–93.

Lippincott 1989 Kristen Lippincott, 'The Neo-Latin Historical Epics of the North Italian Courts: an Examination of "Courtly Culture" in the Fifteenth Century', *Renaissance Studies*, 3 (1989), 415–28.

Lippincott 1990 —— 'The Iconography of the Salone dei Mesi and the Study of Latin Grammar in Fifteenth-Century Ferrara', in *La Corte di Ferrara e il suo Mecenatismo 1441–1598* (Atti del Convegno Internazionali, Copenhagen 1987), Copenhagen 1990, 93–109.

Logan Oliver Logan, *Culture and Society in Venice 1470–1790*, London 1972.

Lotz 1956 Wolfgang Lotz, 'The Rendering of the Interior in Architectural Drawings of the Renaissance', in Lotz 1977, 1–65.

Lotz 1972 —— 'The Piazza Ducale in Vigevano: A Princely Forum of the late Fifteenth Century', in Lotz 1977, 117–39.

Lotz 1977 —— *Studies in Italian Renaissance Architecture*, Boston MA 1977.

Luchs Alison Luchs, *A Cistercian Church of the Florentine Renaissance*, New York 1976.

McAndrew John McAndrew, 'Sant'Andrea della Certosa', *Art Bulletin*, 51 (1969), 15–28.

McManamon J. McManamon, *Funeral Oratory and the Cultural Ideals of Italian Humanism*, Chapel Hill & London 1989.

Mack 1974 Charles R. Mack, 'The Rucellai Palace: Some New Proposals', *Art Bulletin*, 56 (1974), 517–29.

Mack 1983 —— 'Building a Florentine Palace: The Palazzo Spinelli', *MKIF*, 27 (1983), 261–84.

Mack 1987 —— *Pienza: The Creation of a Renaissance City*, Ithaca NY & London 1987.

Magnuson 1954 T. Magnuson, 'The Project of Nicholas V for Rebuilding the Borgo Leonino in Rome', *Art Bulletin*, 36 (1954), 89–115.

Magnuson 1958 —— *Studies in Roman Quattrocento Architecture*, Rome 1958.

Mallet J. G. V. Mallet, 'The Gonzaga and Ceramics', in Chambers & Martineau, 39–43.

Mallett 1967 Michael Mallett, *The Florentine Galleys in the Fifteenth Century*, Oxford 1967.

Mallett 1969 —— *The Borgias: The Rise and Fall of a Renaissance Dynasty*, London 1969.

Mallett 1974 —— *Mercenaries and their Masters: Warfare in Renaissance Italy*, London 1974.

Mancini G. Mancini, *Vita di L. B. Alberti*, Florence 1911.

A Manetti Antonio di Tuccio Manetti, *The Life of Brunelleschi*, H. Saalman (ed.), University Park PA & London 1970.

G Manetti Giannozzo Manetti, *Vita Nicolai V*, in *Rerum Italicarum Scriptores*, 1734, vol. 3, pt. 2; (see also Magnuson 1954).

Marks L. F. Marks, 'The Financial Oligarchy in Florence under Lorenzo', in Jacob, 123–47.

Martelli Mario Martelli, 'I Pensieri architettonici del Magnifico', *Commentarii*, 17 (1966), 107–11.

Martindale 1972 Andrew Martindale, *The Rise of the Artist in the Middle Ages and the Early Renaissance*, London 1972.

Martindale 1979	—— *The Triumphs of Caesar*, London 1979.
Martineau & Hope	J. Martineau & C. Hope (eds.), *The Genius of Venice 1500-1600*, (exhibition catalogue), London 1983.
Martines 1963	Lauro Martines, *The Social World of the Florentine Humanists 1390-1460*, London 1963.
Martines 1979	—— *Power and Imagination: City States in Renaissance Italy*, London 1979.
Mayberry	Nancy Mayberry, 'The Controversy over the Immaculate Conception in Medieval and Renaissance Art, Literature and Society', *JMRS*, **21** (1991), 207-24.
Meiss 1954	Millard Meiss, 'Ovum Struthionis: Symbol and Allusion in Piero della Francesca's Montefeltro Altarpiece' in Meiss 1976, 105-29.
Meiss 1966a	—— 'Sleep in Venice: Ancient Myths and Renaissance Proclivities', in Meiss 1976, 212-39.
Meiss 1966b	—— 'Once Again Francesca's Montefeltro Altarpiece', in Meiss 1976, 130-41.
Meiss 1976	—— *The Painter's Choice: Problems in the Interpretation of Renaissance Art*, New York 1976.
Mesquita	D. M. D. de Mesquita, 'The Privy Council in the Government of the Dukes of Milan', in *Florence and Milan: Comparisons and Relations*, (Acts of Two Conferences at Villa I Tatti 1982-4), Florence 1989, vol. I, 135-56.
Middeldorf	Ulrich Middeldorf, 'Additions to Lorenzo Ghiberti's Work', *Burlington Magazine*, **113** (1971), 72-9.
Millon	H. Millon, 'The Architectural Theory of Francesco di Giorgio', *Art Bulletin*, **40** (1958), 257-61.
Molho 1971	Anthony Molho, *Florentine Public Finances in the Early Renaissance, 1400-1433*, Cambridge MA 1971.
Molho 1977	—— 'The Brancacci Chapel: Studies in its Iconography and History', *JWCI*, **40** (1977), 50-98.
Molho 1979	—— 'Cosimo de' Medici: Pater Patriae or Padrino', *Stanford Italian Review*, **1** (1979), 5-33.
Moorman	John Moorman, *A History of the Franciscan Order*, Oxford 1968.
Muir 1978	Edward Muir, 'The Doge as "primus inter pares": Interregnum Rites in early Sixteenth-Century Venice', in *Essays presented to Myron P. Gilmore*, Florence 1978, vol. 2, 145-60.
Muir 1979	—— 'Images of Power: Art and Pageantry in Renaissance Venice', *American Historical Review*, **84** (1979), 16-52.
Muir 1981	—— *Civic Ritual in Renaissance Venice*, Princeton NJ 1981.
Müntz 1882	Eugène Müntz, *Les Arts à la Cour des Papes pendant le XVe et le XVIe siècles*, 3 vols., Paris 1882.
Müntz 1887	—— *La Bibliothèque du Vatican au XVe siècle*, Paris 1887.
Müntz 1888	—— *Les Collections des Medicis au XVe siècle*, Paris 1888.
Muraro	M. Muraro, 'The Statutes of the Venetian Arti and the Mosaics of the Mascoli Chapel', *Art Bulletin*, **43** (1961), 263-74.
Nicolini	F. Nicolini, *L'Arte Napoletana del Rinascimento*, Naples 1925.
Norwich	J. J. Norwich (ed.), *Venice: A Traveller's Companion*, London 1990.
O'Malley 1979	John O'Malley, *Praise and Blame in Renaissance Rome: Rhetoric, Doctrine and Reform in the Sacred Oratory of the Papal Court c. 1450-1521*, Durham NC 1979.
O'Malley 1986	—— 'The Theology behind Michelangelo's Ceiling', in M. Giacometti (ed.), *The Sistine Chapel: Michelangelo Rediscovered*, New York 1986, 92-148.
Onians 1971	John Onians, 'Alberti and φιλαρετη', *JWCI*, **34** (1971), 96-114.
Onians 1980	—— 'The Last Judgement of Renaissance Architecture', *JRSA*, **128** (1980), 701-20.

Onians 1982   —— 'Brunelleschi: Humanist or Nationalist', *Art History*, 5 (1982),
                   259–72.
Onians 1984   —— 'On How to Listen to High Renaissance Art', *Art History*, 7
                   (1984), 411–37.
Onians 1988   —— *Bearers of Meaning*, Princeton NJ 1988.
Origo   Iris Origo, *The Merchant of Prato*, Harmondsworth 1963.
Pacioli   Luca Pacioli, *Tractato de l'architectura*, in Bruschi et al.,
                   23–144.
Paoletti 1893   P. Paoletti, *L'architettura e la scultura del Rinascimento in
                   Venezia*, 3 vols., Venice 1893.
Paoletti 1929   —— *La Scuola Grande di San Marco*, Venice 1929.
Parks   N. Randolph Parks, 'On the Meaning of Pinturicchio's Sala dei
                   Santi', *Art History*, 2 (1979), 291–317.
Parronchi   A. Parronchi, 'The Language of Architecture and the Language of
                   Sculpture,' *JWCI*, 27 (1964), 108–36.
Parsons   W. B. Parsons, *Engineers and Engineering in the Renaissance*,
                   Cambridge MA & London 1939 (repr. 1968).
Partner 1958   Peter Partner, *The Papal State under Martin V*, London 1958.
Partner 1960   —— 'The Budget of the Roman Church in the Renaissance Period',
                   in Jacob, 256–78.
Partner 1976   —— *Renaissance Rome 1500–1559*, Berkeley, Los Angeles CA &
                   London 1976.
Partner 1990   —— *The Pope's Men: The Papal Civil Service in the Renaissance*,
                   Oxford 1990.
Pastor   L. Pastor, *The History of the Popes from the Close of the Middle
                   Ages*, 29 vols., London 1894–1951.
Pellecchia   Linda Pellecchia, 'The Patron's Role in the Production of
                   Architecture: Bartolomeo Scala and the Scala Palace', *Renaissance
                   Quarterly*, **42** (1989), 258–91.
Pellegrin   E. Pellegrin, *La Bibliothèque des Visconti et des Sforza, Ducs de
                   Milan au XVe siècle*, Paris 1955.
Phillips   Mark Phillips, *The Memoir of Marco Parenti: A Life in Medici
                   Florence*, Princeton NJ 1987.
Pincus   D. Pincus, *The Arco Foscari: The Building of a Triumphal
                   Gateway in Fifteenth-Century Venice*, New York & London 1976.
Pius II   Aeneas Silvius Piccolomini, *Commentari*, see F. A. Gragg & L. C.
                   Gabel (eds.), *The Secret Memoirs of a Renaissance Pope*, (abridged
                   version), London 1988.
Platina   Bartolomeo Platina, *Liber de vita Christi ac omnium pontificum*,
                   in G. Gaida (ed.), *Rerum Italicarum Scriptores*, Città di Castello
                   1913–15 & Bologna 1917–33, vol. 3, pt. 1.
Poggi 1909a   Giovanni Poggi, *Il Duomo di Firenze: Documenti sulla
                   Decorazione della Chiesa e Campanile tratti dall'Archivio
                   dell'Opera*, 2 vols., Berlin 1909 (reprinted Florence 1988).
Poggi 1909b   —— 'Di un'opera di Andrea Sansovino nel Palazzo della Signoria',
                   Rivista d'Arte, 6 (1909), 144–6.
Pollitt   J. J. Pollitt, *The Art of Rome c. 753 BC–337 AD: Sources and
                   Documents*, Eaglewood Cliffs NJ 1966.
Popham &   A. E. Popham & Philip Pouncey, *Italian Drawings in the
  Pouncey   Department of Prints and Drawings in the British Museum*, 2
                   vols., London 1950.
Preyer 1981   Brenda Preyer, 'The Rucellai Palace', in *Giovanni Rucellai ed il suo
                   Zibaldone* (Studies of the Warburg Institute **24**), London 1981,
                   vol. 2, 155–255.
Preyer 1983   —— 'The "chasa overo palagio" of Alberto di Zanobi: A Florentine
                   Palace of about 1400 and its Later Remodelling', *Art Bulletin*, **65**
                   (1983), 387–401.

Preyer 1990 —— 'L'architettura del Palazzo Medici', in G. Cherubini & G. Fanelli (eds.), *Il Palazzo Medici-Riccardi in Firenze*, Florence 1990, 58–75.

Prodi Paolo Prodi, 'The Structure and Organisation of the Church in Renaissance Venice: Suggestions for Research', in Hale 1973, 409–30.

Pulin 1982 Carol Pulin, 'The Palaces of an Early Renaissance Humanist, Cardinal Branda Castiglione', *Arte Lombarda*, 61 (1982), 23–32.

Pulin 1984 —— *Early Renaissance Sculpture and Architecture at Castiglione Olona in Northern Italy and the Patronage of a Humanist, Cardinal Branda Castiglione*, Ann Arbor MI & London 1989.

Pullan 1971 Brian Pullan, *Rich and Poor in Renaissance Venice: the Social Institutions of a Catholic State to 1620*, Cambridge MA 1971.

Pullan 1990 —— 'The Scuole Grandi of Venice: Some Further Thoughts', in Verdon & Henderson, 272–301.

Puppi & Puppi L. Puppi & L. Puppi Olivato, *Mauro Codussi*, Milan 1977.

Radcliffe A. Radcliffe, 'Antico and the Mantuan bronze', in Chambers & Martineau, 46–9.

Ramsey P. A. Ramsey (ed.), *Rome in the Renaissance: The City and the Myth*, (Papers of the 13th Annual Conference of the Center for Medieval and Early Renaissance Studies), Binghamton NY 1982.

Richter J. P. Richter (ed.), *The Literary Works of Leonardo da Vinci*, 2 vols., (reprinted) London & New York 1970.

Robertson Charles Robertson, 'Bramante, Michelangelo and the Sistine Ceiling', *JWCI*, 49 (1986), 91–105.

Roover 1963 Raymond de Roover, *The Rise and Decline of the Medici Bank*, Cambridge MA 1963.

Roover 1967 —— *San Bernardino of Siena and Sant'Antonio of Florence: Two Great Economic Thinkers of the Middle Ages*, Cambridge MA 1967.

Rotondi P. Rotondi, *The Ducal Palace at Urbino*, 2 vols., London 1950.

N Rubinstein 1960 Nicolai Rubinstein, 'Politics and Constitution in Florence at the end of the Fifteenth Century', in Jacob, 148–83.

N Rubinstein 1966 —— *The Government of Florence under the Medici 1434–1494*, Oxford 1966.

N Rubinstein 1968 —— 'Florentine Constitutionalism and Medici Ascendancy in the Fifteenth Century', in N. Rubinstein (ed.), *Florentine Studies: Politics and Society in Renaissance Florence*, London 1968, 442–62.

N Rubinstein 1979 —— 'Oligarchy and Democracy in Fifteenth-Century Florence', in *Florence and Venice: Comparisons and Relations*, (Acts of Two Conferences at Villa I Tatti 1976–7), Florence 1979, vol.I, 99–112.

N Rubinstein 1980 —— 'Palazzi Pubblici e Palazzi Privati al Tempo del Brunelleschi', in *Filippo Brunelleschi: la sua opera e il suo tempo*, Florence 1980, vol. 2, 27–36.

N Rubinstein 1984 —— 'The Formation of the Posthumous Image of Lorenzo de' Medici', in E. Chaney & N. Ritchie (eds.), *Oxford, China and Italy: Writings in Honour of Sir Harold Acton on his Eightieth Birthday*, London 1984, 94–106.

N Rubinstein 1987 —— 'Classical Themes in the Decoration of the Palazzo Vecchio in Florence', *JWCI*, 50 (1987), 29–43.

N Rubinstein 1990 —— 'Lay Patronage and Observant Reform in Fifteenth-Century Florence', in Verdon & Henderson, 63–82.

R Rubinstein 1967 Ruth Rubinstein, 'Pius II's Piazza S. Pietro and St Andrew's Head', in D. Fraser et al. (eds.), *Essays Presented to Rudolf Wittkower on his Sixty-Fifth Birthday*, London 1967, 22–33.

R Rubinstein 1988 —— 'Pius II and Roman Ruins', *Renaissance Studies*, 2 (1988), 197–203.

Rucellai   Giovanni Rucellai, *Zibaldone*, in *Giovanni Rucellai ed il suo
                    Zibaldone* (Studies of the Warburg Institute 24), London 1981,
                    vol. I.
Ruda   Jeffrey Ruda, 'A 1434 Building Programme for San Lorenzo in
                    Florence', *Burlington Magazine*, 120 (1978), 358–9.
Ryder   Alan Ryder, *The Kingdom of Naples under Alfonso the
                    Magnanimous: The Making of a Modern State*, Oxford 1976.
Saalman 1959a   Howard Saalman, 'Early Renaissance Architectural Theory and
                    Practice in Antonio Filarete's Trattato di Architettura', *Art
                    Bulletin*, 41 (1959), 89–106.
Saalman 1959b   —— 'Giovanni di Gherardo da Prato's Designs Concerning the
                    Cupola of Santa Maria del Fiore in Florence', *JSAH*, 18 (1959),
                    11–20.
Saalman 1964   —— 'Santa Maria del Fiore 1294–1418', *Art Bulletin*, 46 (1964),
                    471–500.
Saalman 1966a   —— 'Michelozzo Studies', *Burlington Magazine*, 108 (1966),
                    242–50.
Saalman 1966b   —— 'Tommaso Spinelli, Michelozzo, Manetti and Rossellino',
                    JSAH, 25 (1966), 150–64.
Saalman 1978   —— 'San Lorenzo: the 1434 Chapel Project', *Burlington Magazine*,
                    120 (1978), 359–64.
Saalman 1980   —— *Filippo Brunelleschi: The Cupola of Santa Maria del Fiore*,
                    London 1980.
Saalman &   Howard Saalman & Philip Mattox, 'The First Medici Palace',
   Mattox   *JSAH*, 44 (1985), 329–45.
Sale   J. Russell Sale, 'Palla Strozzi and Lorenzo Ghiberti: New
                    Documents', *MKIF*, 22 (1978), 355–8.
Salvini   R. Salvini, 'The Sistine Chapel: Ideology and Architecture', *Art
                    History*, 3 (1980), 144–57.
Scharf   A. Scharf, *Filippino Lippi*, Vienna 1935.
Schofield 1986   Richard Schofield, 'Ludovico il Moro and Vigevano', *Arte
                    Lombarda*, 62 (1986), 93–140.
Schofield 1988   —— 'A Humanist Description of the Architecture for the Wedding
                    of Gian Galeazzo Sforza and Isabella d'Aragona (1489)', *PBSR*, 56
                    (1988), 213–40.
Schofield 1989a   —— 'Florentine and Roman Elements in Bramante's Milanese
                    Architecture', in *Florence and Milan: Comparisons and Relations*,
                    (Acts of Two Conferences at Villa I Tatti 1982–4), Florence 1989,
                    vol. I, 201–22.
Schofield 1989b   —— Amadeo, Bramante and Leonardo and the Tiburio of Milan
                    Cathedral', *Achademia Leonardi Vinci*, 2 (1989), 68–100.
Schofield 1991   —— 'Leonardo's Milanese Architecture: Career, Sources and
                    Graphic Techniques', *Achademia Leonardi Vinci*, 4 (1991), 111–56.
AM Schulz   Anne Markham Schulz, *Antonio Rizzo, Sculptor and Architect*,
                    Princeton NJ 1983.
J Schulz   J. Schulz, 'Pinturicchio and the Revival of Antiquity', *JWCI*, 25
                    (1962), 35–55.
Seymour 1966   Charles Seymour Jr, *Sculpture in Italy 1400–1500*, Harmondsworth
                    1966.
Seymour 1967   —— *Michelangelo's David: A Search for Identity*, Pittsburgh PA
                    1967.
Seymour 1972   —— *Michelangelo: The Sistine Chapel Ceiling*, New York &
                    London 1972.
Sheard   W. Sheard, *The Tomb of Doge Andrea Vendramin in Venice by
                    Tullio Lombardo*, 2 vols., Ann Arbor MI 1976.
Shearman 1971   John Shearman, 'The Vatican Stanze: Function and Decoration',
                    Proceedings of the British Academy, 57 (1971), 369–424.

Shearman 1986 —— 'The Chapel of Sixtus IV', in M. Giacometti (ed.), *The Sistine Chapel: Michelangelo Rediscovered*, New York 1986, 22–91.

Signorini Rodolfo Signorini, 'Federico III e Cristiano I nella Camera degli Sposi del Mantegna', *MKIF*, **18** (1974), 227–50.

Simons Patricia Simons, 'Patronage in the Tornaquinci Chapel, Santa Maria Novella, Florence', in Kent & Simons, 221–50.

Simpson W. A. Simpson, 'Cardinal Giordano Orsini as a Prince of the Church and a Patron of the Arts', *JWCI*, **29** (1966), 135–59.

Sinding-Larsen S. Sinding-Larsen, 'Some Functional and Iconographical Aspects of
1965 the Centralised Church in the Italian Renaissance', *Acta ad Archeologiam et Artium Historiam Pertinenta*, **2** (1965), 203–52.

Sinding-Larsen —— 'A Tale of Two Cities: Florentine and Roman Visual Context
1975 for Fifteenth-Century Palaces', *Acta ad Archeologiam et Artium Historiam Pertinenta*, **6** (1975), 162–212.

C Smith Christine Smith, 'Originality and Cultural Progress in the Quattrocento', *Rinascimento*, **28** (1988), 291–318.

W Smith Webster Smith, 'On the Original Location of the Primavera', *Art Bulletin*, **57** (1975), 31–40.

Sohm 1978 Philip Sohm, 'The Staircases of the Venetian Scuole Grandi and Mauro Codussi', *Architectura*, **8** (1978), 125–49.

Sohm 1981 —— *The Scuola Grande di San Marco 1437–1550: The Architecture of a Venetian Lay Confraternity*, Ann Arbor MI & London 1981.

Sowards J. K. Sowards, *The 'Julius Exclusus' of Erasmus*, Bloomington IN & London 1968.

Spencer J. Spencer, 'The Cà del Duca in Venice and Benedetto Ferrini', *JSAH*, **29** (1970), 3–8.

Sperling 1989 Christine M. Sperling, 'Leon Battista Alberti's Inscriptions on the Holy Sepulchre in the Cappella Rucellai, San Pancrazio, Florence', *JWCI*, **52** (1989), 221–8.

Sperling 1992 —— 'Donatello's Bronze David and the Demands of Medici Politics', *Burlington Magazine*, **134** (1992), 218–24.

Squarzina S. D. Squarzina (ed.), *Maestri Fiorentini nei Cantieri Romani del Quattrocento*, Rome 1989.

Steinberg Ronald M. Steinberg, *Fra Girolamo Savonarola, Florentine Art and Renaissance Historiography*, Athens OH 1977.

Steinmann E. Steinmann, *Die Sistinische Kapelle*, 2 vols., Munich 1901.

Stinger 1981 Charles L. Stinger, 'Roma triumphans', *Medievalia et Humanistica*, **10** (1981), 189–201.

Stinger 1982 —— 'Greek Patristics and Christian Antiquity in Renaissance Rome', in Ramsey, 153–69.

Stinger 1985 —— *The Renaissance in Rome*, Bloomington IN 1985.

Stornaiuolo C. Stornaiuolo, *Codices Urbinates Graeci Bibliothecae Vaticanae*, Rome 1895.

Teubner Hans Teubner, 'San Marco in Florenz: Umbauten vor 1500', *MKIF*, **23** (1979), 239–72.

Thomson John A. F. Thomson, *Popes and Princes 1417–1517*, London 1980.

Tolnay Charles de Tolnay, *Michelangelo*, 5 vols., Princeton NJ 1943.

Tomei P. Tomei, *L'Architettura a Roma nel Quattrocento*, Rome 1942.

Trachtenberg Marvin Trachtenberg, 'Archeology, Merriment and Murder: The First Cortile of the Palazzo Vecchio and its Transformations in the Late Florentine Republic', *Art Bulletin*, **71** (1989), 565–609.

Trexler R. Trexler, *Public Life in Renaissance Florence*, New York & London 1980.

Tuohy Thomas Tuohy, *Artistic Patronage and Princely Magnificence: Studies in Domestic Expenditure at the Court of Ferrara*

	1451–1505, unpublished PhD, University of London (Warburg Institute) 1982.
Ullman & Stadter	B. L. Ullman & P. A. Stadter, *The Public Library of Renaissance Florence: Niccolò Niccoli, Cosimo de' Medici and the Library of San Marco*, Padua 1972.
Urban	Gunter Urban, 'Die Kirchenbaukunst des Quattrocentos in Rom', *RJK*, 9–10 (1961–2), 72–287.
Vasari	G. Vasari, *Le Vite de' Più Eccellenti Pittori, Scultori ed Architettori Scritte da Giorgio Vasari Pittore Aretino*, G. Milanesi (ed.), 9 vols., Florence 1906 (repr. 1981).
Vatovec	C. Vasić Vatovec, *Luca Fancelli, Architetto: Epistolario Gonzaghesco*, Florence 1979.
Venturi	Adolfo Venturi, 'Cosma Tura genannt Cosmè 1432 bis 1495', *JPK*, 9 (1888), 3–33.
Verdon & Henderson	T. Verdon & J. Henderson (eds.), *Christianity and the Renaissance: Image and Religious Imagination in the Quattrocento*, Syracuse NY 1990.
Vespasiano	*The Vespasiano Memoirs: Lives of Illustrious Men of the XVth Century*, W. G. & E. Waters (eds.), London 1926.
Wackernagel	Martin Wackernagel, *The World of the Florentine Renaissance Artist* (tr. A. Luchs), Princeton NJ 1981.
Wazbinski	Zygmunt Wazbinski, 'L'Annunciazione della Vergine nella SS. Annunziata a Firenze: un contributo al moderno culto dei quadri', in *Renaissance Studies in Honor of Craig Hugh Smyth*, Florence 1985, vol. 2, 533–52.
Weil-Garris Brandt	K. Weil-Garris Brandt, 'Michelangelo's Pietà for the Cappella del Re di Francia', in *Il se rendit en Italie: Etudes offertes à André Chastel*, Paris 1987, 77–119.
Weil-Garris & d'Amico	K. Weil-Garris & J. d'Amico, 'The Renaissance Cardinal's Ideal Palace: A Chapter from Cortesi's "de cardinalitu" ', in H. Millon (ed.), *Studies in Italian Art and Architecture 15th through 18th Centuries* (Memoirs of the American Academy in Rome 35), Cambridge MA & London 1980, 45–123.
Weinstein 1968	Donald Weinstein, 'The Myth of Florence', in N. Rubinstein (ed.), *Florentine Studies: Politics and Society in Renaissance Florence*, London 1968, 15–44.
Weinstein 1970	—— *Savonarola and Florence: Prophecy and Patriotism in the Renaissance*, Princeton NJ 1970.
Weiss	R. Weiss, *The Renaissance Rediscovery of Classical Antiquity*, Oxford 1969.
Welch 1989a	Evelyn Samuels Welch, 'Galeazzo Maria Sforza and the Castello di Pavia 1469', *Art Bulletin*, 71 (1989), 352–75.
Welch 1989b	—— 'The Process of Sforza Patronage', *Renaissance Studies*, 3 (1989), 370–86.
Welch 1990	—— 'The Image of a Fifteenth-Century Court: Secular Frescoes for the Castello di Porta Giovia, Milan', *JWCI*, 53 (1990), 163–84.
Weller	A. S. Weller, *Francesco di Giorgio 1439–1501*, Chicago 1943.
Westfall 1974	C. W. Westfall, *In This Most Perfect Paradise*, University Park PA & London 1974.
Westfall 1978	—— 'Chivalric Declaration: The Palazzo Ducale in Urbino as a Political Statement', in H. Millon & L. Nochlin (eds.), *Art and Architecture in the Service of Politics*, Cambridge MA 1978, 20–45.
White	John White, *Art and Architecture in Italy 1250–1400*, Harmondsworth 1987.
Wilde 1944	J. Wilde, 'The Hall of the Great Council of Florence', *JWCI*, 7 (1944), 65–81.

Wilde 1958 —— 'The Decoration of the Sistine Chapel', *Proceedings of the British Academy*, **44** (1958), 61–81.

Wind E. Wind, 'Maccabean Histories in the Sistine Ceiling', in Jacob, 312–27.

Wohl 1982 Hellmut Wohl, 'Martin V and the Revival of the Arts in Rome', in Ramsey, 171–83.

Wohl 1984 —— 'Papal Patronage and the Language of Art: the Pontificates of Martin V, Eugene IV and Nicholas V', in *Umanesimo a Roma nel Quattrocento* (Atti del Convegno, New York, December 1981), Rome & New York 1984, 235–46.

Woods-Marsden 1985 Joanna Woods-Marsden, 'French Chivalric Myth and Mantuan Political Reality in the Sala del Pisanello', *Art History*, **8** (1985), 397–412.

Woods-Marsden 1988 —— *The Gonzaga of Mantua and Pisanello's Arthurian Frescoes*, Princeton NJ 1988.

Woods-Marsden 1990 —— 'Art and Political Identity in Fifteenth-Century Naples: Pisanello, Cristoforo di Geremia and King Alfonso's Imperial Fantasies', in Charles M. Rosenberg (ed.), *Art and Politics in Late Medieval and Early Renaissance Italy 1250–1500*, Notre-Dame & London 1990, 11–37.

Zahn Alberto de Zahn, 'Notizie artistiche tratte dall'Archivio Segreto Vaticano', *ASI*, **47** (1867), pt. 1, 166–94.

Zervas 1987 Diane Zervas, *The Parte Guelfa, Brunelleschi and Donatello* (I Tatti Studies 8), Locust Valley NY 1987.

Zervas 1988 —— ' "quos volent et eo modo quo volent": Piero de' Medici and the Operai of SS. Annunziata 1445–55', in P.Denley & C. Elam (eds.), *Florence and Italy: Renaissance Studies in Honour of Nicolai Rubinstein*, London 1988, 465–79.

Zevi Bruno Zevi, *Biagio Rossetti, Architetto Ferrarese*, Turin 1960.

Zippel G. Zippel, 'Paolo II e l'Arte', *L'Arte*, **13** (1910), 241–58.

Appendices

THE MEDICI

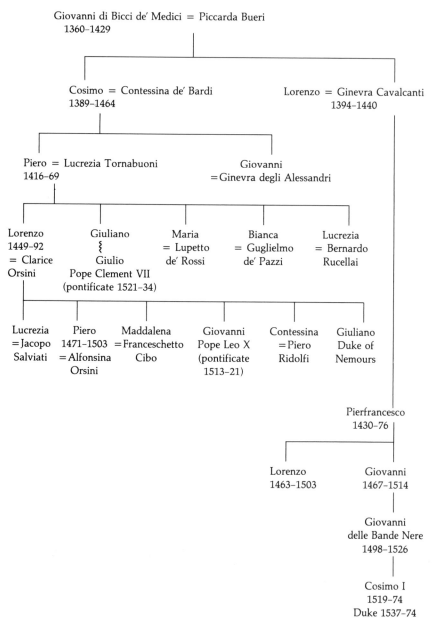

Giovanni di Bicci de' Medici = Piccarda Bueri
1360–1429

Cosimo = Contessina de' Bardi
1389–1464

Lorenzo = Ginevra Cavalcanti
1394–1440

Piero = Lucrezia Tornabuoni
1416–69

Giovanni
= Ginevra degli Alessandri

Lorenzo
1449–92
= Clarice
Orsini

Giuliano
{
Giulio
Pope Clement VII
(pontificate 1521–34)

Maria
= Lupetto
de' Rossi

Bianca
= Guglielmo
de' Pazzi

Lucrezia
= Bernardo
Rucellai

Lucrezia
= Jacopo
Salviati

Piero
1471–1503
= Alfonsina
Orsini

Maddalena
= Franceschetto
Cibo

Giovanni
Pope Leo X
(pontificate
1513–21)

Contessina
= Piero
Ridolfi

Giuliano
Duke of
Nemours

Pierfrancesco
1430–76

Lorenzo
1463–1503

Giovanni
1467–1514

Giovanni
delle Bande Nere
1498–1526

Cosimo I
1519–74
Duke 1537–74

VENETIAN DOGES

1382–1400	Antonio Venier
1400–13	Michele Steno
1413–23	Tomaso Mocenigo
1423–57	Francesco Foscari
1457–62	Pasquale Malipiero
1462–71	Cristoforo Moro
1471–3	Nicolò Tron
1473–4	Nicolò Marcello
1474–6	Pietro Mocenigo
1476–8	Andrea Vendramin
1478–85	Giovanni Mocenigo
1485–6	Marco Barbarigo
1486–1501	Agostino Barbarigo
1501–21	Leonardo Loredan

RULERS OF MILAN

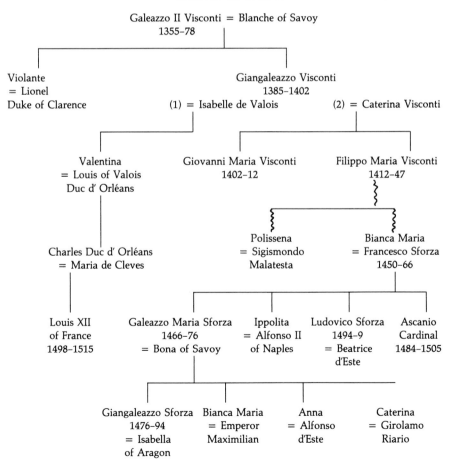

RULERS OF NAPLES

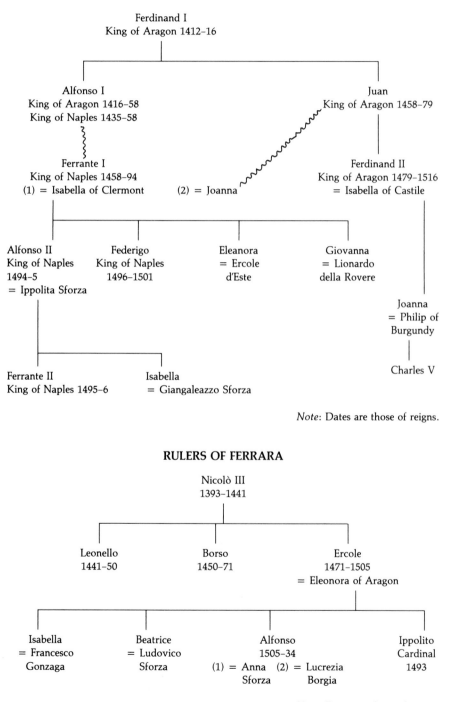

Ferdinand I
King of Aragon 1412–16

Alfonso I
King of Aragon 1416–58
King of Naples 1435–58

Ferrante I
King of Naples 1458–94
(1) = Isabella of Clermont   (2) = Joanna

Juan
King of Aragon 1458–79

Ferdinand II
King of Aragon 1479–1516
= Isabella of Castile

Alfonso II
King of Naples
1494–5
= Ippolita Sforza

Federigo
King of Naples
1496–1501

Eleanora
= Ercole
d'Este

Giovanna
= Lionardo
della Rovere

Joanna
= Philip of
Burgundy

Ferrante II
King of Naples 1495–6

Isabella
= Giangaleazzo Sforza

Charles V

Note: Dates are those of reigns.

RULERS OF FERRARA

Nicolò III
1393–1441

Leonello
1441–50

Borso
1450–71

Ercole
1471–1505
= Eleonora of Aragon

Isabella
= Francesco
Gonzaga

Beatrice
= Ludovico
Sforza

Alfonso
1505–34
(1) = Anna   (2) = Lucrezia
Sforza   Borgia

Ippolito
Cardinal
1493

Note: Dates are those of reigns.

RULERS OF MANTUA

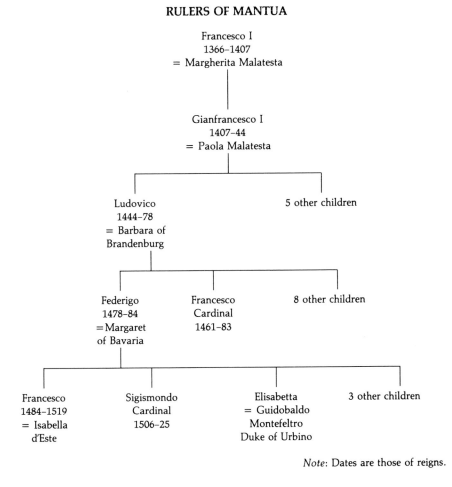

Francesco I
1366–1407
= Margherita Malatesta

Gianfrancesco I
1407–44
= Paola Malatesta

Ludovico
1444–78
= Barbara of
Brandenburg

5 other children

Federigo
1478–84
= Margaret
of Bavaria

Francesco
Cardinal
1461–83

8 other children

Francesco
1484–1519
= Isabella
d'Este

Sigismondo
Cardinal
1506–25

Elisabetta
= Guidobaldo
Montefeltro
Duke of Urbino

3 other children

Note: Dates are those of reigns.

THE POPES

1417–31	Martin V (Oddo Colonna)
1431–47	Eugenius IV (Gabriel Condulmer)
1447–55	Nicholas V (Tommaso Parentucelli)
1455–8	Calixtus III (Alfonso Borgia)
1458–64	Pius II (Aeneas Silvius Piccolomini)
1464–71	Paul II (Pietro Barbo)
1471–84	Sixtus IV (Francesco della Rovere)
1484–92	Innocent VIII (Giovanni Battista Cibo)
1492–1503	Alexander VI (Rodrigo Borgia)
1503	Pius III (Francesco Todeschini Piccolomini)
1503–13	Julius II (Giuliano della Rovere)

SIXTUS IV'S NEPHEWS

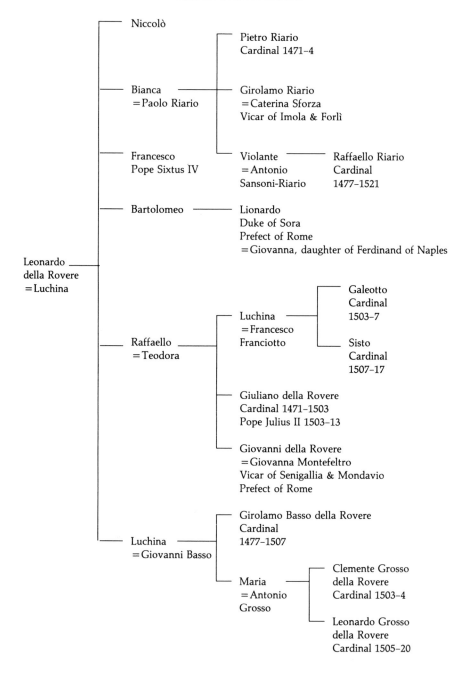

- Niccolò

- Bianca
  = Paolo Riario
  - Pietro Riario
    Cardinal 1471–4
  - Girolamo Riario
    = Caterina Sforza
    Vicar of Imola & Forlì
  - Violante
    = Antonio
    Sansoni-Riario
    - Raffaello Riario
      Cardinal
      1477–1521

- Francesco
  Pope Sixtus IV

- Bartolomeo
  - Lionardo
    Duke of Sora
    Prefect of Rome
    = Giovanna, daughter of Ferdinand of Naples

Leonardo
della Rovere
= Luchina

- Raffaello
  = Teodora
  - Luchina
    = Francesco
    Franciotto
    - Galeotto
      Cardinal
      1503–7
    - Sisto
      Cardinal
      1507–17
  - Giuliano della Rovere
    Cardinal 1471–1503
    Pope Julius II 1503–13
  - Giovanni della Rovere
    = Giovanna Montefeltro
    Vicar of Senigallia & Mondavio
    Prefect of Rome

- Luchina
  = Giovanni Basso
  - Girolamo Basso della Rovere
    Cardinal
    1477–1507
  - Maria
    = Antonio
    Grosso
    - Clemente Grosso
      della Rovere
      Cardinal 1503–4
    - Leonardo Grosso
      della Rovere
      Cardinal 1505–20

Index